KIDS LOVE The Carolinas

An Organized Family Travel Guide to Exploring Kid-Friendly North & South Carolina

800 Fun Stops &

Michele Darra

Dedicated to the Families of North & South Carolina

In a Hundred Years...It will not matter, The size of my bank account...The kind of house that I lived in, the kind of car that I drove...But what will matter is...That the world may be different Because I was important in the life of a child.

- author unknown

For the latest major updates corresponding to the pages in this book visit our website:

www.KidsLoveTravel.com

Although the authors have exhaustively researched all sources to ensure accuracy and completeness of the information contained in this book, we assume no responsibility for errors, inaccuracies, omissions or any other inconsistency herein. Any slights against any entries or organizations are unintentional.

- ***REMEMBER:*** *Museum exhibits change frequently. Check the site's website before you visit to note any changes. Also, HOURS and ADMISSIONS are subject to change at the owner's discretion. If you are tight on time or money, check the attraction's website or call before you visit.*

- ***INTERNET PRECAUTION:*** *All websites mentioned in KIDS LOVE THE CAROLINAS have been checked for appropriate content. However, due to the fast-changing nature of the Internet, we strongly urge parents to preview any recommended sites and to always supervise their children when on-line.*

- ***EDUCATORS:*** *There are suggestions for finding FREE lessons plans embedded in many listings as helpful notes for educators.*

TABLE OF CONTENTS

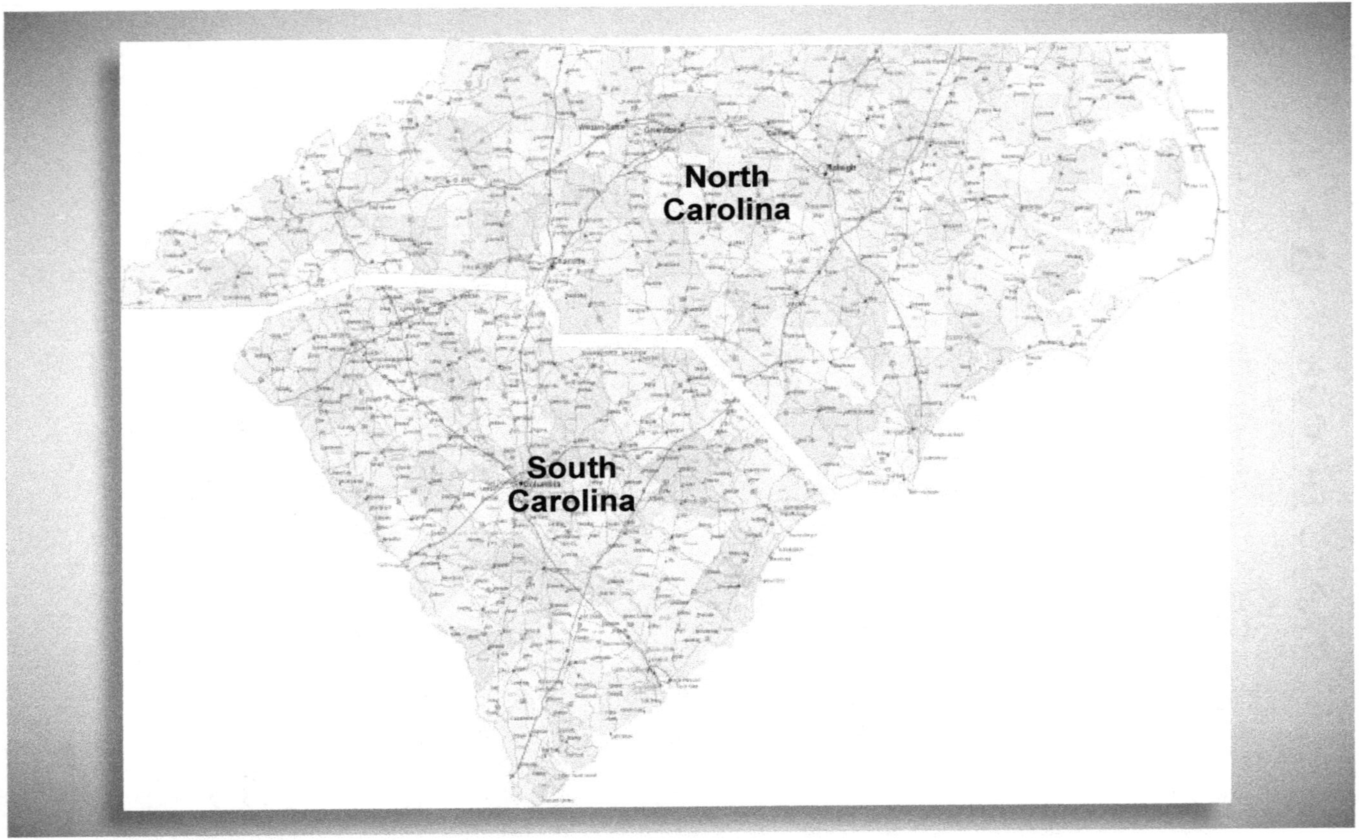

North Carolina

South Carolina

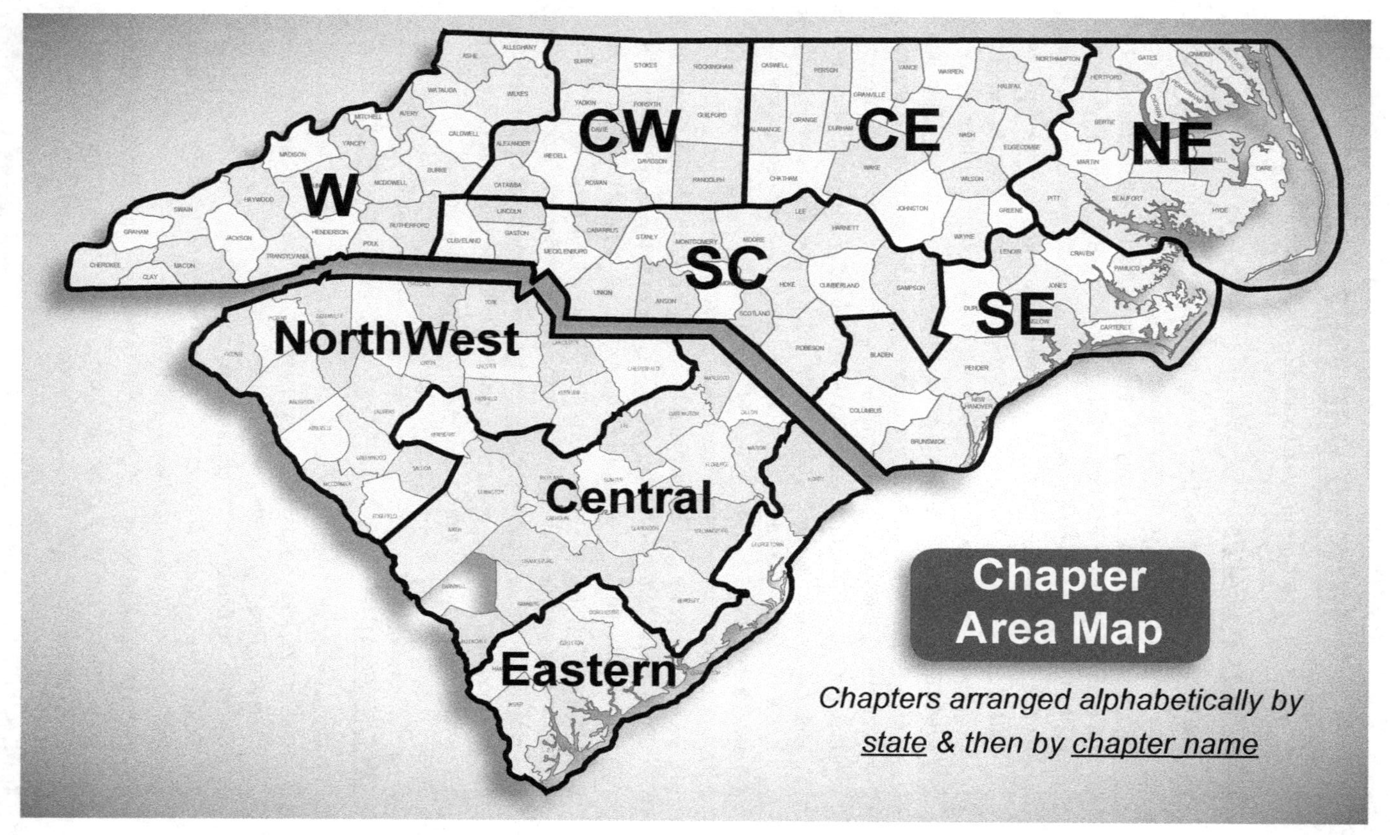
W
CW
CE
NE
SC
SE
NorthWest
Central
Eastern
Chapter
Area Map
Chapters arranged alphabetically by
state & then by chapter name

HOW TO USE THIS BOOK

(a few hints to make your adventures run smoothly:)

BEFORE YOU LEAVE:

- Each chapter represents a two hour radius area of the state or a Day Trip. The chapter begins with an introduction and Quick Tour of favorites within the chapter. The listings are by City and then alphabetical by name, numeric by zip code. Each listing has tons of important details (pricing, hours, website, etc.) and a review noting the most engaging aspects of the place. Our popular Activity Index in back is helpful if you want to focus on a particular type of attraction (i.e. History, Tours, Outdoor Exploring, Animals & Farms, etc.).
- Begin by assigning each family member a different colored highlighter (for example: Daniel gets blue, Jenny gets pink, Mom gets yellow and Dad gets green). At your leisure, begin to read each review and put a highlighter "check" mark next to the sites that most interest each family member or highlight the features you most want to see. Now, when you go to plan a quick trip - or a long van ride - you can easily choose different stops in one day to please everyone.
- Know directions and parking. Use a GPS system or print off directions from websites.
- Most attractions are closed major holidays unless noted.
- When children are in tow, it is better to make your lodging reservations ahead of time. Every time we've tried to "wing it", we've always ended up at a place that was overpriced, in a unsafe area, or not super clean. We've never been satisfied when we didn't make a reservation ahead of time.
- If you have a large family, or are traveling with extended family or friends, most places offer group discounts. Check out the company's website for details.
- For the latest critical updates corresponding to the pages in this book, visit our website: www.kidslovetravel.com. Click on *Updates*.

ON THE ROAD:

- Consider the child's age before you stop at an exit. Some attractions and restaurants, even hotels, are too formal for young ones or not enough adventure for teens. Read our trusted reviews first.
- Estimate the duration of the trip and how many stops you can afford to make. From our experience, it is best to stop every two hours to stretch your legs or eat/snack or maybe visit an inexpensive attraction.
- Bring along travel books and games for "quiet time" in the van. As an added bonus, these "enriching" games also stimulate conversation - you may get to know your family better and create memorable life lessons.

ON THE ROAD: *(cont.)*

- In between meals, we offer the family snacks like: pretzels, whole grain chips, carrots, pouches, water bottles, bite-size (dark) chocolates, grapes and apples. None of these are messy and all are healthy.
- Plan picnics along the way. Many Historical sites and State Parks are scattered along the highway. Allow time for a rest stop or a scenic byway to take advantage of these free picnic facilities.

WHEN YOU GET HOME:

- Make a family "treasure chest". Decorate a big box or use an old popcorn tin. Store memorabilia from a fun outing, journals, pictures, brochures and souvenirs. Once a year, look through the "treasure chest" and reminisce.

WAYS TO SAVE MONEY:

- Memberships - many children's museums, science centers, zoos and aquariums are members of associations that provide FREE or Discounted reciprocity to other such museums across the country. AAA Auto Club cards offer discounts to many of the activities and hotels in this book. If grandparents are along for the ride, they can use their AARP card and get discounts. Be sure to carry your member cards with you as proof to receive the discounts.
- Supermarket Customer Cards - national and local supermarkets often offer good discounted tickets to major attractions in the area.
- Internet Hotel Reservations - if you're traveling with kids, don't take the risk of being spontaneous with lodging. Make reservations ahead of time. We don't use non-refundable, deep discount hotel "scouting" websites (ex. Hotwire) unless we're traveling on business - just adults. You can't cancel your reservation, or change them, and you can't be guaranteed the type of room you want (ex. non-smoking, two beds). Instead, stick with a national hotel chain you trust and join their rewards program (ex. Choice Privileges) to accumulate points towards FREE night stays.
- State Travel Centers - as you enter a new state, their welcome centers offer many current promotions.
- Hotel Lobbies - often have a display of discount coupons to area shops and restaurants. When you check in, ask the clerk for discount pizza coupons they may have at the front desk.
- Attraction Online Coupons - check the websites listed with each review for possible printable coupons or discounted online tickets good towards the attraction.

Check out these businesses / services in your area for tour ideas:

AIRPORTS - All children love to visit the airport! Why not take a tour and understand all the jobs it takes to run an airport? Tour the terminal, baggage claim, gates and security / currency exchange. Maybe you'll even get to board a plane.

ANIMAL SHELTERS - Great for the would-be pet owner. Not only will you see many cats and dogs available for adoption, but a guide will show you the clinic and explain the needs of a pet. Be prepared to have the children "fall in love" with one of the animals while they are there!

BANKS - Take a "behind the scenes" look at automated teller machines, bank vaults and drive-thru window chutes. You may want to take this tour and then open a savings account for your child.

CITY HALLS - Halls of Fame, City Council Chambers & Meeting Room, Mayor's Office and famous statues.

ELECTRIC COMPANY / POWER PLANTS - Modern science has created many ways to generate electricity today, but what really goes on with the "flip of a switch". Because coal can be dirty, wear old, comfortable clothes. Coal furnaces heat water, which produces steam, that propels turbines, that drives generators, that make electricity.

FIRE STATIONS - Many Open Houses in October, Fire Prevention Month. Take a look into the life of the firefighters servicing your area and try on their gear. See where they hang out, sleep and eat. Hop aboard a real-life fire engine truck and learn fire safety too.

HOSPITALS - Some Children's Hospitals offer pre-surgery and general tours.

NEWSPAPERS - You'll be amazed at all the new technology. See monster printers and robotics. See samples in the layout department and maybe try to put together your own page. After seeing a newspaper made, most companies give you a free copy (dated that day) as your souvenir. National Newspaper Week is in October.

PETCO - Various stores. Contact each store manager to see if they participate. The Fur, Feathers & Fins™ program allows children to learn about the characteristics and habitats of fish, reptiles, birds, and small animals. At your local Petco, lessons in science, math and geography come to life through this hands-on field trip. As students develop a respect for animals, they will also develop a greater sense of responsibility.

PIZZA HUT & PAPA JOHN'S - Participating locations. Telephone the store manager. Best days are Monday, Tuesday and Wednesday mid-afternoon. Minimum of 10 people. Small charge per person. All children love pizza – especially when they can create their own! As the children tour the kitchen, they learn how to make a pizza, bake it, and then eat it. The admission charge generally includes lots of creatively made pizzas, beverage and coloring book.

KRISPY KREME DONUTS - Participating locations. Get an "inside look" and learn the techniques that make these donuts some of our favorites! Watch the dough being made in "giant" mixers, being formed into donuts and taking a "trip" through the fryer. Seeing them being iced and topped with colorful sprinkles is always a favorite with the kids. Contact your local store manager. They prefer Monday or Tuesday. Free.

SUPERMARKETS - Kids are fascinated to go behind the scenes of the same store where Mom and Dad shop. Usually you will see them grind meat, walk into large freezer rooms, watch cakes and bread bake and receive free samples along the way. Maybe you'll even get to pet a live lobster!

TV / RADIO STATIONS - Studios, newsrooms, Fox kids clubs. Why do weathermen never wear blue/green clothes on TV? What makes a "DJ's" voice sound so deep and smooth?

WATER TREATMENT PLANTS - A giant science experiment! You can watch seven stages of water treatment. The favorite is usually the wall of bright buttons flashing as workers monitor the different processes.

U.S. MAIN POST OFFICES - Did you know Ben Franklin was the first Postmaster General (over 200 years ago)? Most interesting is the high-speed automated mail processing equipment. Learn how to address envelopes so they will be sent quicker (there are secrets). To make your tour more interesting, have your children write a letter to themselves and address it with colorful markers. Mail it earlier that day and they will stay interested trying to locate their letter in all the high-speed machinery.

MISSION STATEMENT

At first glance, you may think that this is a book that just lists hundreds of places to travel. While it is true that we've invested thousands of hours of exhaustive research (*and drove over 5000 miles In The Carolinas*) to prepare this travel resource…just listing places to travel is not the mission statement of these projects.

As a child, I was able to travel extensively throughout the United States. I consider these family times some of the greatest memories I cherish today. Quite frankly, I felt most children had this opportunity to travel with their family. However, as I started my own family, I found this wasn't necessarily the case. We continually heard friends express several concerns when deciding how to spend "quality" and "quantity" family time. 1) What to do? 2) Where to do it? 3) How much will it cost? 4) How do I know that my kids will enjoy it?

Interestingly enough, as we compare experiences with other families, many of our fondest memories were not made at an expensive attraction, but rather when it was least expected.

It is our belief and mission statement that if you as a family will study and use the contained information to create family memories, these memories will grow a stronger, tighter family. Our ultimate mission is that your children will develop a love and a passion for quality family experiences they can pass to another generation of family travelers.

We thank you for purchasing this book, and we hope to see you on the road (*and hear your travel stories!*) God bless your journeys and Happy Exploring!

EXTRA SPECIAL THANKS TO:

So many places around The Carolinas remind us of family vacations years ago…

We want to express our thanks to the many Convention & Visitor Bureaus' staff for providing the attention to detail that helps to complete a project. We felt very welcome during our travels in The Carolinas and would be proud to call this area home!

My kids, Jenny and Daniel, were delightful and fun children during our trips across the state. What a joy it is to be their parent…we couldn't do it without them as our "kid-testers"!

Above all, we praise the Lord for His so many blessings through these travel years.

We think The Carolinas are wonderful, friendly areas of the country with more activities than you could imagine. Our sincere wish is that this book will help everyone "fall in love" with all of The Carolinas.

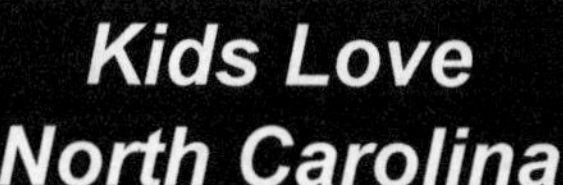

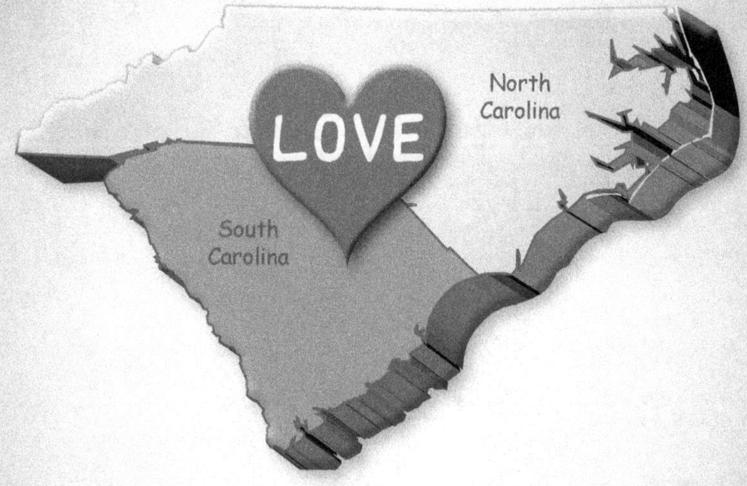

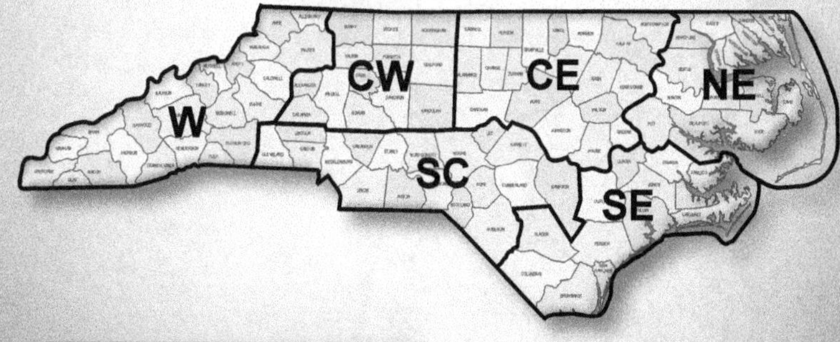

Chapter Area Map

Chapters arranged alphabetically
by Chapter Name

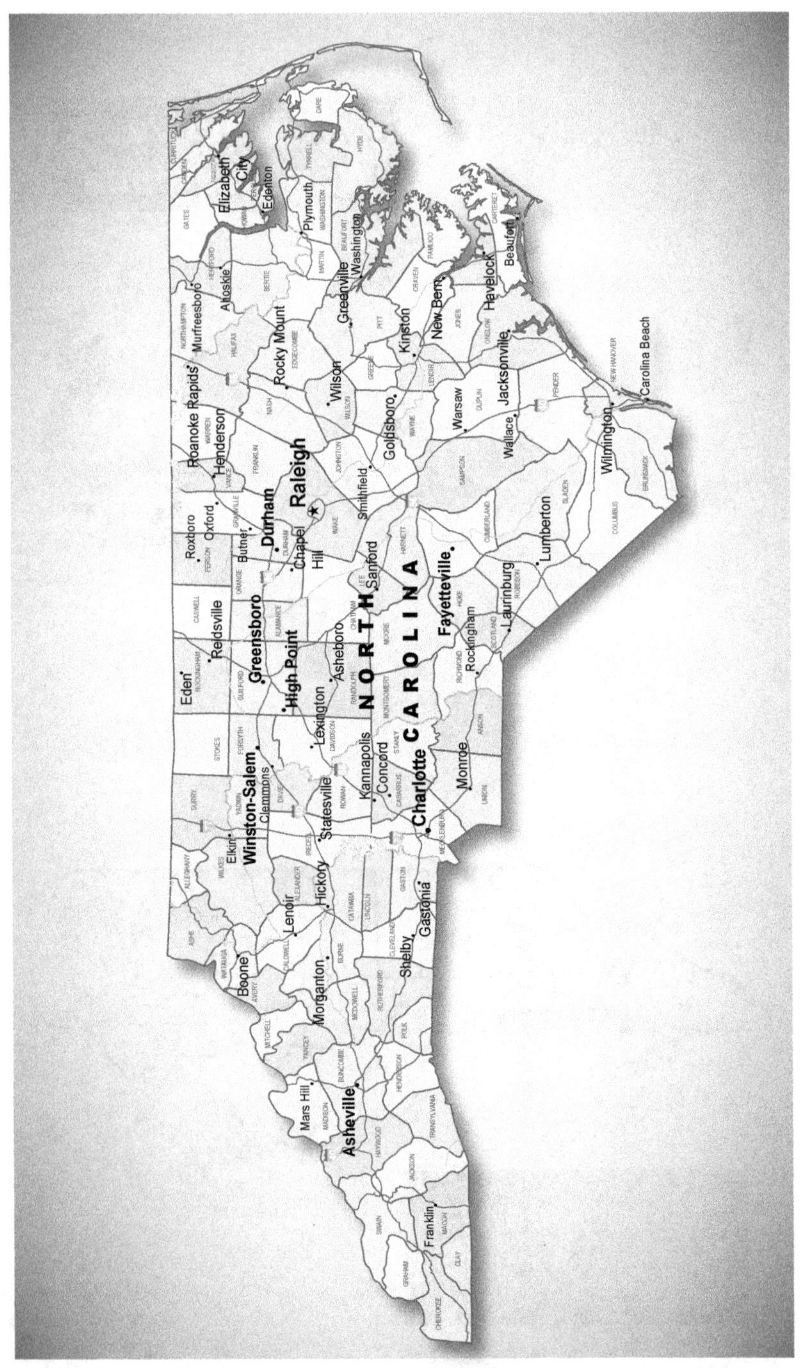
NORTH CAROLINA
Raleigh
Durham
Chapel Hill
Greensboro
High Point
Winston-Salem
Charlotte
Fayetteville
Asheville
Wilmington
Elizabeth City
Edenton
Plymouth
Washington
Greenville
Beaufort
Havelock
New Bern
Kinston
Jacksonville
Carolina Beach
Rocky Mount
Wilson
Goldsboro
Smithfield
Warsaw
Wallace
Lumberton
Laurinburg
Rockingham
Sanford
Asheboro
Lexington
Kannapolis
Concord
Monroe
Gastonia
Shelby
Statesville
Hickory
Lenoir
Morganton
Boone
Mars Hill
Franklin
Elkin
Clemmons
Eden
Reidsville
Roxboro
Oxford
Butner
Henderson
Roanoke Rapids
Murfreesboro
Ahoskie

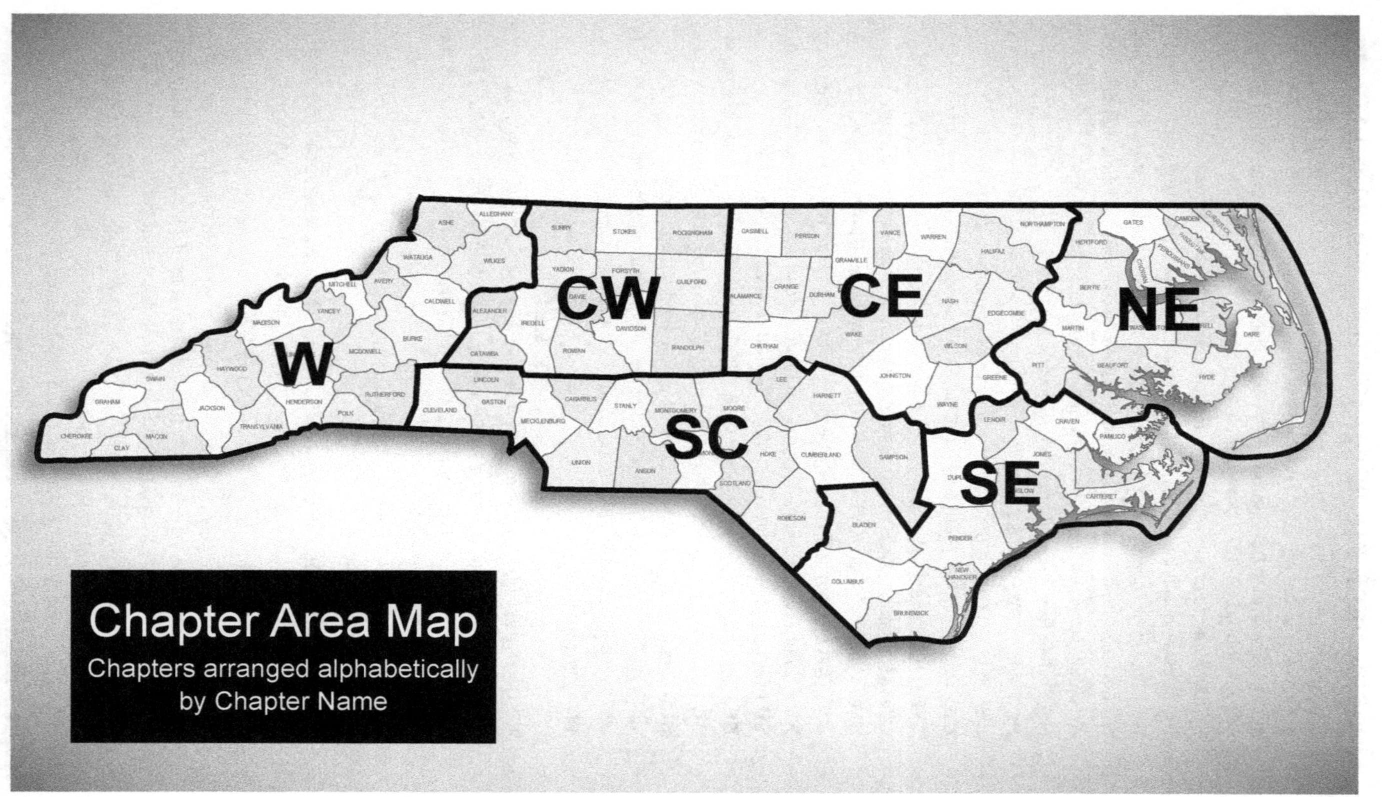
W
CW
CE
NE
SC
SE
Chapter Area Map
Chapters arranged alphabetically
by Chapter Name

General State Agency & Recreational Information

Call *(or visit websites)* for the services of interest. Request to be added to their mailing lists.

- NC Association of Agricultural Fairs. www.ncfairs.com.
- NC Department of Transportation Ferry Division. Morehead City. (252) 726-6446 or (800) 293-3779 or www.ncferry.org.
- NC Division of Forest Resources. Raleigh. www.dfr.state.nc.us.
- NC Division of Marine Fisheries. Morehead City. www.ncfisheries.net.
- NC Division of Tourism, Film & Sports Development. Raleigh. www.visitnc.com.
- NC Historic Sites. Raleigh. www.ah.dcr.state.nc.us/sections/hs/default.htm.
- NC Scenic Byways Program. www.ncdot.org/public/publications.
- NC Wildlife Resources Commission. www.ncwildlife.org.
- NC Assoc. of RV Parks & Campgrounds. Garner. www.campinginnorthcarolina.com
- **CE** - Durham CVB - (800) 446-8604 or www.durham-nc.com.
- **CE** - Raleigh CVB - (800) 849-8499 or www.visitraleigh.com.
- **CW** - High Point CVB - (800) 720-5255 or www.highpoint.org.
- **CW** - Greensboro CVB - (800) 344-2282 or www.visitgreensboro.com.
- **CW** - Winston-Salem CVB - (866) 728-4200 or www.visitwinstonsalem.com.
- **NE** - Craven County CVC/ New Bern - (800) 437-5767 or www.visitnewbern.com
- **NE** - Outer Banks Visitors Bureau - (877) OBX-4FUN or www.outerbanks.org
- **SE** - Crystal Coast Tourism - (252) 726-8148 or www.sunnync.com.
- **SE** - Wilmington/Cape Fear Coast CVB - (800) 222-4757 or www.cape-fear.nc.us
- **SC** - Cabarrus County CVB - (800) 848-3740 or www.cabarruscvb.com
- **SC** - Charlotte CVB - (800) 722-1994 or www.visitcharlotte.org.
- **W** - Asheville CVB - (800) 257-5583 or www.exploreasheville.com.
- **W** - Boone CVB - (800) 852-9506 or www.visitboonenc.com.
- **W** - Cherokee Tribal Travel And Promotion - www.cherokee-nc.com.

RECREATION

SKI RESORTS - skiing, snowboarding, some w/ outdoor ice skating. www.goskinc.com

- **W** - Cataloochee Ski Area - 1080 Ski Lodge Road, Maggie Valley. (800) 768-3588 or www.cataloochee.com. has its own specially-named tubing park: Tube World, featuring five runs.
- **W** - Appalachian Ski Mountain - Blowing Rock. (800) 322-2373 or www.appskimtn.com.
- **W** - Ski Beech - Beech Mountain. (800) 438-2093 or www.skibeech.com. Was the first resort in the South to open a tube run in the 1996-1997 season.
- **W** - Sugar Mountain - Banner Elk. (800) 784-2768 or www.skisugar.com
- **W** - Hawksnest Ski Resort - Banner Elk. www.hawksnest-resort.com or (800) 822-4295. Hawksnest Resort now also features a terrific snowtubing-only park. In fact, you'll find the longest tubing runs in the southeast here.
- **W** - Wolf Laurel Ski Resort - Mars Hill, (828) 689-4121 or (800) 541-1738 or www.skiwolflaurel.com. Summer activities include mountain biking, whitewater rafting, horseback riding and hiking. On site lodging.

PARKS & REC - North Carolina Division Of Parks & Recreation, Raleigh. (919) 733-4181 or www.ncparks.gov.

Chapter 1
Central East North Carolina

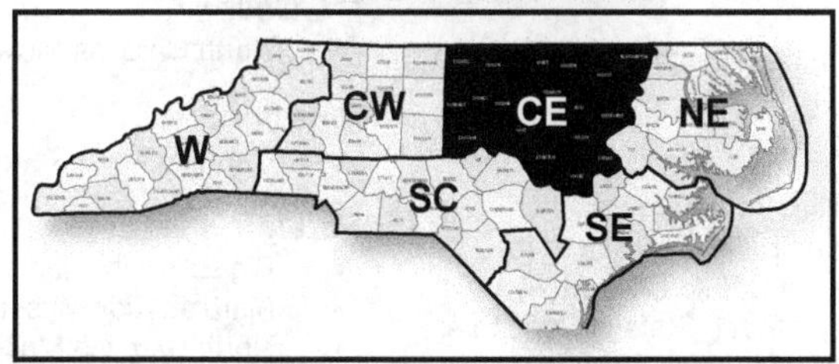

Apex
- Jordan Lake State Recreation Area

Bailey
- Country Doctor Museum

Benson
- Benson Mule Days

Burlington
- Alamance Battleground State Historic Site

Chapel Hill
- Jordan Lake Educational State Forest
- Kidzu Children's Museum
- UNC Tarheels Sports
- Morehead Planetarium And Science Center
- North Carolina Botanical Garden

Clayton
- Clemmons Educational State Forest

Durham
- Carolina Barnstormers
- Durham Bulls Baseball Club
- Museum Of Life & Science
- Bennett Place State Historic Site
- Duke Homestead State Historic Site
- Duke Lemur Center
- Elmo's Diner
- Eno River State Park
- Q Shack, The Original
- Rick's Diner
- Duke University
- Arrowhead Inn
- LaQuinta Inn & Suites Research Triangle Park
- Stagville, Historic
- Native American Powwow
- Pumpkin Country

Fremont
- Governor Charles B. Aycock State Historic Site

Goldsboro
- Waynesborough Historic Village

Goldsboro (Four Oaks)
- Bentonville Battlefield State Historic Site

Halifax
- Historic Halifax State Historic Site & Outdoor Drama

Henderson
- Kerr Lake State Recreation Area

Hillsborough
- Occoneechee Mountain State Natural Area
- Occaneechi - Saponi Spring Cultural Festival & Pow Wow

Hollister
- Medoc Mountain State Park

Littleton
- Lake Gaston

Mt. Olive
- North Carolina Pickle Festival

Pittsboro
- Carolina Tiger Rescue

Raleigh
- Big Ed's City Market
- Marbles Kids Museum
- North Carolina Museum Of History
- North Carolina Museum Of Natural Science
- North Carolina State Capitol
- North Carolina Symphony
- Pullen Park
- Raleigh City Museum
- Wake County Speedway
- Joel Lane Museum House
- Carolina Ballet
- Carolina Hurricanes
- North Carolina Museum Of Art
- Historic Oak View County Park
- Mordecai Historic Park / President Andrew Johnson's Birthplace
- Raleigh Symphony Orchestra
- Raleigh Trolley Tours

Raleigh (cont.)

- W. B. Umstead State Park
- Raleigh Little Theatre
- Solar House, NCSU
- North Carolina Renaissance Faire
- Capitol Easter Sunrise Service
- July 4th Celebration
- International Fest
- North Carolina State Fair
- A Christmas Carol

Raleigh (Bonsal/New Hill)

- New Hope Valley Railway & NC Railroad Museum

Roanoke Rapids

- Roanoke Canal Museum & Trail

Rocky Mount

- Children's Museum & Science Ctr

Selma

- American Music Jubilee Theatre

Seven Springs

- Cliffs Of The Neuse State Park

Wake Forest

- Falls Lake State Recreation Area

Wake Forest (Youngsville)

- Fall Harvest & Pumpkin Festival

Wilson

- Imagination Station

Wilson (Lucama)

- Whirligigs

CE

A Quick Tour of our Hand-Picked Favorites Around...

Central East North Carolina

Wanna visit the land of the FREE? Head to Raleigh, my friend. With 20 FREE attractions, including the North Carolina Museum of Art, North Carolina Museum of History and the North Carolina Museum of Natural Sciences, it's an affordable escape for parents and children alike!

The **North Carolina Museum of Natural Sciences** in Raleigh is a great free way to spend an afternoon indoors unearthing the natural mysteries of this diverse and beautiful state. "Meet" a giant whale, the Terror of the South, see a dino heart and then admire playful butterflies...all in one fabulous place.

Want a dose of contemporary science? Plan an old-fashioned picnic at **Pullen Park** and then head into the future at the **NC State Solar House** (both sites are on NC State campus in Raleigh). As you ring the doorbell and enter the house – you're now inside a giant science experiment using solar power to generate energy for the whole house. Is it the future?

Some other amazing museums can be found in Durham. Real, very talkative and different lemurs abound at the **Duke Lemur Center**. By appointment, you can walk into a controlled recreation of Madagascar and visit with their adorable leapers! Females rule here, but romeos work hard for your attention.

Rated among the top four family-friendly museums in Southeast, the **Museum of Life and Science** in Durham is a state-of-the-art, engaging indoor / outdoor science-technology center. The key is *Indoor And Outdoor.* Rainy days call for physical science experiments indoors. Any day it isn't raining – kids swarm outside along paths leading to so many outdoor exhibits – it's nearly a zoo. Butterflies, bears and lemurs, oh my!

Nearby, you can stand in the spot where the Civil War completely ended. **Bennett Place State Historic Site** is the simple farmhouse where two generals met in 1865, and signed surrender papers for the largest Southern armies to formally end the war. Spend the night in a real log cabin or historic **Arrowhead Inn** suite for a good nights rest before you go exploring.

Let's talk about some food joints around here. **Elmo's Diner** is a awesome pick by Rachel Ray's $40.00 a Day. We call this a gourmet diner – parents: try the spicy meatloaf or quiche or hummus – kids: try anything off the $3.00 kids menu. BBQ is all grown up at places like the **Q Shack**. Chili-rubbed sliced brisket, hand-pulled pork and ribs are must orders. Sides are Southern – everyone gets hush puppies. In Durham, you can get both the Eastern North Carolina style (with chopped pork and a clear sauce of vinegar, pepper, and salt) and the Western North Carolina style (with chopped or sliced pork with a red sauce that includes ketchup and sugar along with the other ingredients).

Sites and attractions are listed in order by City, Zip Code, and Name. Symbols indicated represent: ☐ Restaurants ☐ Lodging

JORDAN LAKE STATE RECREATION AREA

***Apex** - 280 State Park Road (21 miles southwest of Raleigh off US 64) 27539. Phone: (919) 362-0586. www.ncparks.gov/jordan-lake-state-recreation-area. Hours: Daily 8:00am- dusk. Admission: $6.00 per car - charged summer and some spring weekends. Educators: teaching resources about Predators and Prey (grades K-3): http://149.168.1.195/eeid/find_eele.php.*

A nearly 14,000 acre reservoir, Jordan Lake offers bald eagle watching, boating, camping, education and events, fishing, Heritage Day, hiking, picnicking, swimming. Visitor Center displays allow the visitors to explore the world of water environments and the species that those aquatic environments support. A major feature of the exhibit hall is the life-sized eagle's nest which allows visitors a bird's eye view of the interior of this massive nest. It is the largest summertime home of the bald eagle in the eastern United States (The observation deck is located five miles south of I-40 on NC 751, 6.5 miles north of US 64). The exhibit hall is open from 8:00am-5:00pm daily.

COUNTRY DOCTOR MUSEUM

Bailey - ***7089 Peele Road (from Hwy 264, take the Bailey exit south on SR 581. At the first light, turn right on Hwy 264 Alt. first left) 27807. Phone: (252) 235-4165. www.countrydoctormuseum.org. Hours: Tuesday-Saturday 10am-4pm. Tours on the hour until 3pm. Admission: $4.00-$8.00 per person (ages 3+). Educators: Print off the Scavenger Hunt sheet: www.countrydoctormuseum.org/PDF/Country%20 Doctor%20Museum%20scavenger%20hunt%20for%20student%20tours.pdf. to use as your trick to keep the kids attentive for "little" things.***

Honoring the "old family doctor", this museum consists of the restored offices of two country doctors who practiced from 1857 to 1887. The museum's collections include artifacts relevant to many aspects of health care including nursing, pharmacy, homeopathy, and dentistry. Along with surgical sets and microscopes, the collection now incorporates medicine kits, apothecary equipment, nursing uniforms, and tools that would scare a patient today. You'll read about a lot of home remedies your grandparents used. A medical herb garden located behind the Museum delights visitors throughout the year.

BENSON MULE DAYS

Benson - Created to celebrate the animal on which the livelihood of this small town once depended, Benson Mule Days has been a Southern tradition for over 50 years. Catch the kickoff concert on Thursday night and stay until the carnival ends on Sunday evening. In between enjoy rodeos, rides, games, barbecue, bluegrass and gospel music, a street dance, a mule pulling contest, arts and crafts, mule and horse rides, and, of course, a parade. And there's even camping allowed. www.bensonmuledays.com (fourth Saturday in September)

ALAMANCE BATTLEGROUND STATE HISTORIC SITE

Burlington - ***5803 South NC 62 (Interstate 40/85 in Burlington take NC 62 south, exit 143. Follow the directional signs) 27215. Phone: (336) 227-4785. www.nchistoricsites.org/alamance. Hours: Monday-Saturday 9am.-5pm. Adm: FREE.***

"A State Historic Site and a Primary Revolutionary War Site", this historic site is where Royal Governor William Tryon led the North Carolina militia in battle against the Regulators on May 16, 1771. A 1780 log house used by frontier people is also located on the grounds; the house contains its original furnishings. On the grounds is a three-quarter-mile Outdoor Exploring trail. Colored pennants mark the battle positions and Regulator campsite. An audiovisual presentation of the battle is offered in the visitor center. Best to visit during re-enactment weekend or Colonial Living Week in October.

ANNIVERSARY OF THE BATTLE OF ALAMANCE

Burlington - Alamance Battleground State Historic Site. Join in commemorative activities featuring a wreath-laying ceremony, picnic, and program. The weekend following is the Century Live-In & Militia Muster. Enjoy a recreation of colonial military and domestic life by costumed interpreters. (May 16th weekend)

JORDAN LAKE EDUCATION STATE FOREST

Chapel Hill - ***2832 Big Woods Road (I-40 exit 274, south on SR 751) 27514. Phone: (919) 542-1154. www.ncesf.org/JLESF/home.htm. Hours: Weekdays 9:00am-5:00pm (EST), Weekends 11:00am-5:00pm (EST) and 11:00am-8:00pm (DST). Season is mid-March to Mid-November. Admission: FREE.***

Located between the Piedmont and Coastal Plain, this forest showcases a wide variety of pines and hardwoods found in a wetland ecosystem (Wetlands Trails or Forest Trail). At the Forest, visitors can listen to the wind in the trees or they can listen to the trees tell a story (3/4 mile Talking Tree Trail). The Forest is home to a wide variety of wildlife including birds of prey, deer, songbirds, flying squirrels and beavers (Wildlife Trail). Picnic facilities are available, including a shelter to accommodate large groups.

KIDZU CHILDREN'S MUSEUM

Chapel Hill - ***105 E. Franklin Street (near intersection of S. Columbia and E. Franklin) 27514. Phone: (919) 933-1455. www.kidzuchildrensmuseum.org. Hours: Tuesday-Saturday 10:00am-5:00pm, Sunday 1:00-5:00pm. Admission: $8.50 person (age 1+). FREE admission on Sunday.***

Kidzu Children's Museum is a hands-on museum in the heart of downtown Chapel Hill where children 0-8 years old and the adults in their lives can safely discover, pretend, and play to their heart's content. The spaces are clean and full of inviting things to construct, count, shape or serve. Since opening in 2006, they have hosted a series of nationally recognized traveling exhibits, including "Mister Rogers' Neighborhood" and "Where the Wild Things Are." In addition, you'll find a changing Theatre and storytelling crafts each month.

UNC TARHEELS SPORTS

Chapel Hill - *Smith Center 27515. www.goheels.com*

The Tar Heel basketball team has produced famous players and garnered numerous championships and awards over the years while playing under the roofs of Carmichael Auditorium and the Dean E. Smith Center, completed in 1986. The structure is only one of 14 facilities that make up the Tar Heel athletics program, comprised of 26 separate sports.

MOREHEAD PLANETARIUM & SCIENCE CENTER

Chapel Hill - *250 E. Franklin Street (UNC Chapel Hill campus, follow signs) 27599. Phone: (919) 962-1236. www.moreheadplanetarium.org. Hours: Tuesday-Saturday 10:00am-3:30pm, Sunday 1:00-4:30pm. Open from 6:30-9:00 on Friday and Saturday nights for shows. Admission: $7.25-$8.25 per show. Combo discounts. Online coupons. NASA Digital Theater & Exhibits Admission is FREE.*

Visit the facility where American astronauts formerly trained. At Morehead Planetarium and Science Center you can experience dazzling 30-45-minute multimedia star shows (Magic Tree House Space Mission or Laser Show or Solar System Adventure), varied exhibits, and shopping at the Infinity Gift Shop. "Carolina Skies" is one of the oldest shows at the planetarium, but it's never the same twice. The show allows visitors to explore the heavens as they will appear each night above North Carolina. Other programs and events include "Destination: Space," examining the history and future of America's space program, and "Solar System Adventure," a character-driven tour through the cosmos. The Center's recent addition is a digital video theater that shows original science programming produced by world-class film studios.

NORTH CAROLINA BOTANICAL GARDEN

Chapel Hill - *100 Old Mason Farm Road (UNC campus, take Exit 273A, and turn right onto Highway 54 West) 27599. ncbg.unc.edu. Phone: (919) 962-0522. Hours: Tuesday-Saturday 9:00am-5:00pm, Sunday 1:00-5:00pm. Admission: FREE.*

The largest botanical garden in the southeast, established in 1966, consists of nearly 700 acres of preserved land with nature trails, carnivorous plant collections, aquatics and herb gardens, and revolving exhibits of artwork with a horticultural theme. It's like walking across the whole state in one place!

- PIEDMONT NATURE TRAILS - Provide over two miles of hiking trails through piedmont woodland. The easier Streamside Trail crosses Meeting-of-the-Waters Creek twice as it meanders through the lower sections. The more difficult Oak-Hickory Trail traverses hillier portions.
- COASTAL PLAIN AND SANDHILLS HABITATS - Reproduce the wide range of ecosystems present in the eastern part of the state, beginning with the rolling sandhills where you see the state tree of North Carolina, the longleaf pine. Soon the terrain becomes flatter, simulating the pocosin and wetland habitats common on the outer coastal plain. In this area grow myrtle and carnivorous plants, such as the Venus flytrap and pitcher plants.
-

- MOUNTAIN HABITAT GARDEN - Contains plants and trees that are characteristic of the mountainous areas of the southern Appalachians. Dense shade from canopy trees and abundant moisture create a cove-like environment for these species.
- HERB GARDEN - Interprets a series of gardens dealing with medicinal, culinary, economic, shade, poison, evergreen and Native American herbs. At the entrance of the Herb Garden, kids find a booklet that encourages them to take a closer look at the natural world of plants. Children can have fun while discovering the wonderful nature of herbs in the Zoo Garden (dig), a Fairy Find, a Weather Station, Game Boards, and even create their own nature art.

CLEMMONS EDUCATIONAL STATE FOREST

Clayton - ***2411 Old US 70 West (US 70 east of Raleigh) 27520. Phone: (919) 553-5651. www.ncesf.org/clemmons.html. Hours: Tuesday-Friday 9:00am-5:00pm, Saturday & Sunday 11:00am-5:00pm EST, 11:00am-8:00pm DST (mid-March to mid-November). Admission: FREE.***

Located between the Piedmont and the Coastal Plain, Clemmons' pine stands and hardwoods are set on rolling terrain highlighted by streams and rock formations. These features are accessible by a series of well-marked trails, accented by exhibits and displays depicting the ecology of the forest. Listen to the "talking" trees and rocks weave tales about the life there; hike the demo trail to see natural resource manager's duties; explore the new exhibit center; picnic, camp or join in on a ranger-conducted environmental education class.

CAROLINA BARNSTORMERS

Durham - ***4340 East Geer Street (Lake Ridge Aero) 27702. Phone: (919) 680-6642. www.facebook.com/carolinabarnstormers Admission: $125.00-$225.00 per ride, by reservation. Season: September thru the middle of June.***

Get a unique, aerial view of Durham during this "flight-seeing" tour aboard the open cockpit of a biplane and see sights such as Downtown Durham, the Research Triangle Park, the campuses of Duke and North Carolina Central universities, and Falls Lake. Twenty minute or one hour long tours are available. This is a memory, for sure.

DURHAM BULLS BASEBALL CLUB

Durham - ***409 Blackwell Street (home games at Durham Bulls Athletic Park) 27702. Phone: (919) 687-6500. www.durhambulls.com.***

Durham residents and visitors set national attendance records for this famous minor-league team. The Bulls are a triple-A farm team for the Tampa Bay Rays. Ball Park Corner has Bull's historic memorabilia and parents bring their kids for the entertaining and goofy seventh-inning stretch antics on the field. The ballpark's most distinctive feature is the Bull that stands tall above the Blue Monster. This Bull was modeled after the bull used in the 1987 film, Bull Durham. Wool E. Bull is the lovable mascot of the world famous Durham Bulls and his sidekick is Lucky the Wonder Dog. Special promo nights include $1.00 dogs, fireworks, or running the bases. Good, Americana fun.

MUSEUM OF LIFE & SCIENCE

Durham - ***433 Murray Avenue (I-85 exit 176B, Duke Univ. West campus) 27704. Phone: (919) 220-5429. www.lifeandscience.org. Hours: Tuesday-Sunday 10:00am-5:00pm. Members admitted at 9:00am. Open warm weather Mondays. Admission: $21 adult, $19 senior, $16 child (3-12). Educators: Free Field Kits will make your self-guided visit more meaningful. Kits are available at the Admissions Desk. These pre-designed, quick lessons enhance exhibits in Explore the Wild. Printable Wayfinders question sheets are available online, grade level specific. Note: Play to Learn area for kids 6 and under. Seasonal note: Some outdoor water exhibits close for the winter season to protect them from freezing. Gift shops. Stroller rentals. Grayson's Café. Train ride $5.00.***

The museum is an impressive, interactive, indoor/outdoor science-technology center that includes:

SCIENCE EXHIBITS – About weather and aerospace, and daily science shows. See giant rocket engines or a model of the Apollo 15. Make a giant tornado…taller than Dad!

INVESTIGATE HEALTH - Actual bones to touch, skulls to grind, work ants to watch.

MAGIC WINGS BUTTERFLY HOUSE - The largest museum butterfly house east of the Mississippi. The 3-story, tropical conservatory features rare species of butterflies from Asia, Africa, and Central and South America. So many different colors! And, they're all very friendly and may even hang on you a bit!

DINOSAUR TRAIL: The trail's first dino, the 18-foot long Parasaurolophus is friendly and patient, allowing children to climb its back, sit on its tail and pat its bumpy skin. But walk along the tree-laced path further and you'll meet some ready to pounce. Fossil digging area.

FARMYARD & LOBLOLLY PARK - Interactive outdoor exhibits include: a barnyard, water play and giant musical drums and bells.

EXPLORE THE WILD - A lush six-acre woodland habitat and thriving wetland site where you can walk in the steps of a wildlife biologist, using field cameras and remote sensing devices to study native black bears, red wolves, exotic lemurs, baby alligators and owls. Descend a 750-foot boardwalk to a preserved natural setting. You'll feel like a real safari scientist here.

CATCH THE WIND - You can captain a boat in a 5,000-square foot sailboat pond to learn about the invisible power of wind.

HIDEAWAY WOODS - treehouse canopy walk play area.

This is probably our favorite science museum for diversity of indoor/outdoor spaces and number of easy-to-understand hands-on activities!

BENNETT PLACE STATE HISTORIC SITE

Durham - ***4409 Bennett Memorial Road (Interstate 85 north, take exit 170 and follow U.S. 70 to Bennett Memorial Road) 27705. Phone: (919) 383-4345. www.bennettplacehistoricsite.com Hours: Tuesday-Saturday 9:00am-5:00pm. Closed major state holidays. Admission: FREE. Tours: Guided tours are scheduled on the half-hour. Note: Be sure to ask for the Activity Book. If they complete it, they get a prize. Reenactment weekends are held once per month, seasonally. Civil War Cinema movies are shown Saturday nights throughout the year.***

This simple farmhouse was situated between Confederate General Johnston'sheadquarters in Greensboro and Union General Sherman's headquarters in Raleigh, North Carolina. In 1865, the two generals met here, where they signed surrender papers for Southern armies in the Carolinas, Georgia, and Florida (largest troops of the War). This is where the war completely ended. Why did it take three separate days to compromise? How did President Lincoln's assassination affect their agreement? The surrender spared North Carolina the destruction experienced by her neighboring states. Equally important, the economy of the entire state and the development of Durham were boosted when troops in the area were introduced to "bright leaf" tobacco. The visitor center contains three rooms of exhibits on the Bennett family, the Civil War, and the surrender at the Bennett Place.

CE

There is also a model of the Bennett farm showing the arrival of Union and Confederate cavalry troops on April 17, 1865. The fifteen-minute audiovisual program titled "Dawn of Peace" is shown on the hour. Today James Bennett's reconstructed farmhouse, kitchen, and smokehouse give visitors a glimpse into the life-style of an ordinary Southern farmer during the Civil War years.

CIVIL WAR SURRENDER REENACTMENT

Durham - Bennett Place State Historic Site. This day reenacts the negotiations and surrender between Generals Sherman and Johnston that ended the Civil War. (last Saturday in April)

CHRISTMAS IN THE CAROLINAS DURING THE CIVIL WAR

Durham - Bennett Place State Historic Site. Visit Bennett Place during the holiday season and witness how Christmas was celebrated in the Piedmont Carolinas. The farm is decorated in a typical Christmas fashion. Music, caroling, and refreshments. (mid-December weekend)

DUKE HOMESTEAD STATE HISTORIC SITE

Durham - ***2828 Duke Homestead Road (Interstate 85 in Durham exit on Guess Road - Exit 175. Follow the signs north) 27705. www.nchistoricsites.org/duke/. Phone: (919) 489-3364. Hours: Tuesday-Saturday 9:00am-5:00pm. Admission: FREE.***

The patriarch of Duke Homestead was Washington Duke, an Orange County farmer whose chance discovery that Union troops were helping themselves to local Bright Leaf tobacco led him to the fortuitous decision to market this "golden weed." Retrace the beginnings of the modern-day tobacco industry at this National Historic Landmark where Washington Duke started his successful tobacco empire. The Duke family's home site includes authentic barns and original factories, as well as a museum filled with cigarette manufacturing and marketing memorabilia. Living history demonstrations of life on a typical yeoman farm in the 1800's are regularly performed. Keep in mind, this industry flourished and was heavily promoted before the dangers of tobacco use were so widely known.

AMERICAN TOBACCO TRAIL
www.triangletrails.org/ATT.HTM. Downtown to NC 54, eight miles of trails for bicycle, hiking, walking and running.

CHRISTMAS CANDLELIGHT TOURS

Durham - Duke Homestead State Historic Site. Celebrate an 1870 Christmas during evening tours of the Homestead. Period decorations, caroling, hot apple cider, and other goodies. Additional entertainment in visitor center. FREE. (first two Friday nights in December)

DUKE LEMUR CENTER

Durham - ***3705 Old Erwin Road at NC Hwy 751 (US 15/501 bypass south to NC 751 to Old Erwin Rd, left on Lemur Lane) 27705. www.lemur.duke.edu. Phone: (919) 489-3364. Admission: $14.00 adult, $12.00 child (3-12). Tours are appointment only. All visitors to the Center must schedule an appointment in advance of their arrival. It is not possible to "just stop by and see the animals." Tours typically last about an hour and include a tour of the Center's grounds and facilities. Monday-Saturday, best mornings. Behind the Scenes tour is new and guests (10 & older) go into animal areas for 1 hour tour. ($95 per person) Note: During the spring and summer months it is not unusual for all tours booked up to two weeks in advance so you should make your plans early! Educators: Coloring books, puzzles, species fact sheets, and mazes are found online.***

Encounter the largest population of lemurs outside of their native Madagascar at this research and study center, which is home to 250 prosimian primates. There is an outside walking tour and inside viewing of nocturnal prosimians (like the bizarre aye-aye). Dedicated to the study and understanding of these primates, this center houses many different primates including 233 lemurs encompassing 15 species, along with lorises from India and Southeast Asia and bushbabies from Africa. Some have crowns, some blue eyes and some look like a mouse. Lemurs are premonkeys, they are living fossils. Start your tour with an overview video. It explains that the center especially studies the lemurs' personality and use of their hands. What do all those barks, screams and calls mean? Do lemurs heal themselves using chemicals from plants? Girl lemurs may dominate but it's not hard to guess who Romeo is. He's big and handsome - and he knows it! Meet the actual "Zaboo" (or a relative) from PBS fame. If these guys grow on you during your wonderfully educational tour, adopt one (not to keep, of course).

Ruffed lemurs have an elaborate system of alarm calls that alert group members to danger from predators. As many as twelve different calls have been recorded at the Center.

CE

ELMO'S DINER

Durham - 27705. 776 Ninth St. Ninth Street District. 27705 www.elmosdiner.com or (919) 416-3823. Daily 6:30am-10:00pm. Food Network proclaims that the diner is an "awesome pick." Though breakfast is served all day, Elmo's whips up splendid lunch and dinner favorites. We call this a gourmet diner. Highly recommend the perfectly seasoned spicy Italian Meatloaf or the Hummus dip. There quiches are wonderfully creamy and fresh. Anything on the kids menu is great and ~$4.00. Breakfast specials run ~$5.00, lunches ~$8.00 and dinners slightly higher.

We feel Durham has some of the most eclectic, yet, family-budget-friendly eateries around! It's exciting to try these places - be sure to begin by trying one of their daily specials.

ENO RIVER STATE PARK

Durham - ***6101 Cole Mill Road (I-85, take exit 173 northwest onto Cole Mill Road, which ends at the park) 27705. www.ncparks.gov/eno-river-state-park. Phone: (919) 383-1686. Hours: Daily 8:00am-dusk. Admission: FREE. Educators: resource info for grades 6-8: http://149.168.1.195/eeid/find_eele.php.***

The Eno River begins in northwest Orange County, flowing eastward approximately 33 miles until, along with the Little and Flat rivers, it forms the Neuse and flows into Falls Lake. The Eno's waters roll through wilderness passing historic mill sites and river bluffs covered with flowering shrubs and fords used by early settlers. Upstream, rapids smash against rocks in the river's path. Further down, the Eno meanders quietly through serene surroundings. This makes for good spots for canoeing and rafting. Hike Cox Mountain Trail for a challenging climb through a scenic hardwood forest. Travel along Bobbitt's Hole Trail to one of the most scenic spots in the park, a place where water rushes around rocks and greenery overhangs stone-lined bluffs. The Eno River has approximately 21 miles of trails where you can enjoy nature at its best. All trails are blazed. See the park map for information on distance and difficulty. Camping and fishing are available at the park, too.

Q SHACK, THE ORIGINAL

Durham - 27707. 2510 University Drive, (919) 402-4227 or www.theqshackoriginal.com. Lunch and dinner, picnic style. Barbecue all grown up. Chili-rubbed sliced brisket (Texas style – excellent), hand-pulled pork and ribs are must-orders. Sides are Southern. When choosing your sides, don't forget to get a helping of Stanley's organic

collard greens, or their signature macaroni and cheese. Those two, along with a bowl of fried okra might just be the ticket for the hungry vegetarian in your crowd! Everyone (even kids size) gets hush puppies. Most BBQ's don't serve salads, but this one does. Try their giant salad greens topped with brisket and blue cheese dressing – yum! Kids Menu $5.95.

☐

HOPE VALLEY DINER

Durham - 27707. *3710 Shannon Road. www.ricksdiner.com or (919) 419-0907. They've consolidated two stores into one. Notice the historical photos from the Durham Herald Sun – fun to look at. Try their Blue Plate specials – salads, seafood and quiches are adult favorites. Secret recipe meatloaf, beef burgers or Carolina pork BBQ are their specialties. Everything on the kids menu is $4.25! Most specialty dishes here are Rick's recipes and some are from Uncle Ray and Mama. Daily Breakfast, Lunch, Dinner.*

☐

DUKE UNIVERSITY

Durham - *(southwest & west central campuses) 27708. www.duke.edu. or Phone: (919) 681-1704.*

Highlights of the Neo-Gothic campus are:

- **DUKE UNIVERSITY CHAPEL** - This chapel is one of the most popular features in North Carolina and represents one of the last great collegiate Gothic projects in the United States. Features of the chapel include a 5,200 pipe Flentrop Organ, stained glass windows, a 50 bell carillon, and a 210-foot tower. (Chapel Drive, West Campus)
- **DUKE SPORTS HALL OF FAME** - The Hall houses several decades of Duke University athletic history along the northwest side of the famed Cameron Indoor Stadium. The Hall of Fame includes video, audio, a theatre and exhibits that showcase some famous people in Duke sports. (8:00am-5:00pm, school weekdays, Towerview Road, Schwartz-Butters Athletic Center, West Campus)
- **DUKE BLUE DEVILS** - For schedules and ticket info, go to the Duke Blue website: www.goduke.com.
- **DUKE GARDENS** - Beautiful 55 acre garden that features three major areas including the original Terraces, the Blomquist Garden of Native Plants, and the Sulberson Asiatic Arboretum. Five miles of pathways and hiking trails dotted with waterfalls are located throughout the gardens. (418 Anderson Street, 919-684-3698)

- **NASHER / DUKE UNIVERSITY MUSEUM OF ART** - This museum houses beautiful works that include ancient, modern, Old Master, American, African American, and Russian Contemporary masterpieces. The museum also boasts Medieval & Renaissance Art and a pre-Columbian collection of Central & South America artwork. (North Buchanan Boulevard, Durham, NC 27701, Duke East Campus, 919-684-5135).

ARROWHEAD INN

LITTLE RIVER REGIONAL PARK & NATURAL AREA. www.tlc-nc.org Relics from tobacco farmland like barns, houses and sheds have been restored and now serve as picnic shelters and info centers. 15 miles of walking, hiking, mountain-biking, and horseback-riding trails.

Durham *- 106 Mason Road (north off Roxboro Road on the Indian Trading Path) 27712. Phone: (919) 477-8430 or (800) 528-2207 or www.arrowheadinn.com. Stay in a piece of history! This is a bed and breakfast property (4 star rating), but they are very family-friendly. The home was built in 1775, before the Revolutionary War. They are located on six acres and have swings, a hammock and a horseshoe throw. Owners Phil and Gloria Teber are so comfortable and have a servant's heart. Every morning, they serve a delicious multi-course breakfast. Try Phil's puff pancakes, moist scones, or killer brownies! Kids have a wide selection of coloring, toys and videos to choose from. Parents may want to explore all the history around the house and hear stories from the innkeepers (some history and mystery). For families, they have some large rooms, a log cabin w/ loft, and a cottage (best rates range from $129-$279). Rollaways and futons are readily available for kid's beds.* ______________________ ☐ ☐

LAQUINTA INN & SUITES SOUTHPOINT

Durham - 27713. *Spending the night? Try LaQuinta Suites at I-40 exit 278, 1910 WestPark Drive, (919) 484-1422 or www.lq.com. For $89-$130 per night you receive a spacious room with a nice outdoor pool and complimentary deluxe breakfast buffet. Fresh breads and pastries were abundant. Convenient location to base from, tons of eateries and unique shopping areas are nearby. One such find is PATTERSON'S MILL COUNTRY STORE. 5109 Farrington Rd between NC 54 & Old Chapel Hill Rd. (919) 493-8149. Open daily except Monday. This turn-of-the-century country store and doctor's office/pharmacy displays mercantile and pharmaceutical Americana. The best part - real Penny Candy! Enjoy a soda and sweet treat while browsing through gobs of crafted art and jewelry mixed with antiques. Something fills every square inch. Fall and Christmastime are good times to visit.*

____ ☐

STAGVILLE, HISTORIC

Durham - ***5825 Old Oxford Highway (I-85 North to exit 177, Roxboro Road North. Go approximately 1.4 miles north. Turn right onto Old Oxford Highway and proceed 7 miles) 27722. Phone: (919) 620-0120. www.stagville.org. Hours: Tuesday-Saturday 10:00am-5:00pm. Admission is FREE. Tours are given every other hour, with the first tour of the day at 11:00am. and the last at 3:00pm.***

One of the largest pre-Civil War plantations, this historic plantation offers visitors a glimpse into the past and especially the lives of the African American slaves who worked the plantation. By 1860, the family owned almost 30,000 acres and nearly 900 slaves. The American Girl figure, Addy, is loosely based on stories from this place. Two restored historic buildings (slave quarters) and an old barn are on site and self-guided tours of the extensive grounds are available. The slave cabins are unusual because they're off the ground (not dirt floors) and several stories high – once housing dozens of people. Historic buildings are only open during hourly guided tours.

JUNE 23 JUNETEENTH CELEBRATION

Durham - Stagville, Historic. Juneteenth is a celebration commemorating the end of slavery in the United States. This family-focused event has a jubilant atmosphere, with music, entertainment, period craft vendors and food. To commemorate the history of the site, costumed actors portray actual members of the enslaved community at Stagville. There is also a station with information about the enslaved community and the genealogy project at the site. Admission is free with a suggested donation of a few dollars. (third week of June)

JONKONNU

Durham - Stagville, Historic. Stagville's holiday celebration includes an 1815 Christmas celebration at the Bennehan House and an 1850's Christmas celebration at the Horton Grove quarter. This living history event focuses on the different ways that Christmas was celebrated on a Southern plantation. Enjoy costumed interpreters, games, crafts, cooking demonstrations and music. Admission is $5.00 (first Saturday in December)

PUMPKIN COUNTRY

Durham - Farmer Ganyard @ Upchurch Farm. (919) 596-8728 or www.pumpkincountry.com. Enjoy feeding farm animals in the barnyard, pumpkin patch (pick your own), hayrides, cotton field, corn field maze, mulch mountain, hay maze (great for young-uns), and general store. Pumpkin Activities: www.theteachersguide.com/PumpkinsLessonPlans.htm. Admission. (daily mid-September through October)

CE

GOVERNOR CHARLES B. AYCOCK STATE HISTORIC SITE

Fremont - ***264 Governor Aycock Road (I-95 S to Kenly/Fremont exit. Head southeast to south on Rte. 117) 27830. https://historicsites.nc.gov/all-sites/governor-charles-b-aycock-birthplace. Phone: (919) 242-5581. Hours: Tuesday-Saturday 9:00am-5:00pm. Admission: FREE. Educators: Teacher Packets. Call for dates of regular special events and living history demonstrations.***

The Site features the boyhood home of North Carolina's "Educational Governor". Aycock was elected governor in 1900. His ability to rouse people to support education at the local level stimulated the construction of approximately eleven hundred schools-one for every day he was in office. By the end of his term, citizens had seen enrollment increased, school districts consolidated, and teacher training improved. The farmstead home includes a mid-19th century farm, an 1893 one-room schoolhouse and a modern visitors center. The one-room schoolhouse was moved to the site to represent the grassroots educational revival that became statewide after Governor Aycock's election in 1900.

CHRISTMAS CANDLELIGHT TOURS

Fremont - Governor Charles B. Aycock State Historic Site. Celebrate the Holidays of the Past with Primative Baptist Singers, Shadow Play in the One room School House, Open-hearth cooking and more. (first week of December)

WAYNESBOROUGH HISTORIC VILLAGE

Goldsboro - ***801 S. US 117 Bypass 27530. www.oldwaynesborough.org Phone: (919) 731-1653. Hours: Tuesday-Saturday 9:00am-5:00pm, Sunday 1:00-5:00pm. Closed Easter, Thanksgiving, Christmas, and New Years Day. Admission: FREE.***

Founded in 1787 as the first seat of Wayne County, Waynesborough grew quickly into a bustling town. Its location along the Neuse River promoted plantation growth and successful river boat businesses. Stage coaches brought much activity and many passengers to the town. Visit a family home, a medical office, a one room school, a law office, and a Quaker Meeting House. Picnic near the General Store. Walk down to the Neuse River. Listen to the blacksmith beating upon his iron or smell the scents of herbs drying in the Tuscarora Indian Village. This is a nice place to picnic amongst the scents of history but best during special events when reenactors are present.

BENTONVILLE BATTLEFIELD STATE HISTORIC SITE

Goldsboro (Four Oaks) - ***5466 Harper House Road (I-40 exit onto U.S. 701 - Exit 343. Follow signs to State Road 1008) 27524. Phone: (910) 594-0789. https://historicsites.nc.gov/all-sites/bentonville-battlefield. Hours: Tuesday-Saturday 9:00am-5:00pm. Closed all major holidays. Admission: FREE. Tours: Guided tours of the Harper House and outbuildings are scheduled on the hour. Note: Summer Seasonal Living History Program and Artillery Demonstrations.***

The Battle of Bentonville, fought March 19-21, 1865, was the last full-scale action of the Civil War in which a Confederate army was able to mount a tactical offensive. Walk on the fields where 80,000 Union and Confederate soldiers fought. Tour the nearby Harper House (ca. 1855) furnished as a Civil War field hospital where wounded from both sides received medical treatment. The Harper children remained at home with their parents when the house was taken over by the Federal XIV Army Corps for use as a field hospital. Can you imagine what it was like? The site also includes a reconstructed kitchen and slave quarters. The visitor center features a 10-minute audiovisual program explaining the events leading up to the Battle of Bentonville. The center also exhibits artifacts from the battlefield and maps of troop movement during the three days of fighting. To engage in the site outside, try the Roadside Pull-Off Exhibits. Through interpretive text, photos, illustrations, and maps, visitors can step onto the battlefield and visualize the action as it unfolded around the pull-off sites.

BENTONVILLE BATTLEFIELD ANNIVERSARY

Goldsboro (Four Oaks) - Bentonville Battlefield State Historic Site. Costumed living historians evoke the lives of the average North Carolina Civil War soldier through infantry and artillery demos. Evening lantern tours. Reenactors portray both surgeons and wounded soldiers in the home. (third Saturday in March)

CHRISTMAS OPEN HOUSE

Goldsboro (Four Oaks) - Bentonville Battlefield State Historic Site. Costumed interpreters decorate the kitchen in festive themes, such as holly and magnolia branches, cotton stalks, various fruits and cranberry and popcorn strands, and serve cookies and hot cider. Also on hand, costumed military interpreters discuss how the common solider spent his time on furlough with friends and family. (first Saturday in December)

CE

HISTORIC HALIFAX STATE HISTORIC SITE & OUTDOOR DRAMA

Halifax - *St. David & Dobbs Streets (I-95 take exit 168. Follow the signs south on N.C. 903 to the town of Halifax) 27839. Phone: (252) 583-7191 or (800) 522-4282. https://historicsites.nc.gov/all-sites/historic-halifax. Hours: Tuesday-Saturday 9:00am-5:00pm. Admission: FREE. Donations accepted. Tours: Guided tours are offered on a rotating schedule. Tour lengths are Owens House, twenty-five minutes; Middle of Town, forty-five minutes; Sally-Billy House, thirty minutes. They ask that groups make reservations in advance. Note: Picnic sites and trails lead to the Roanoke River overlook. Every Saturday features costumed interpreters and craft demonstrations at the Visitor Center. Educators: Unit Study https://files.nc.gov/dncr-historicsites/halifax_printshop_worksheet.pdf.*

April 12, 1776, the date commemorated on the North Carolina flag, signifies the Fourth Provincial Congress' adoption of the "Halifax Resolves" during a meeting right here in Halifax. With that action, North Carolina became the first colony to take an official step toward declaring independence from England. The Historic Halifax Visitor's Center offers a thirteen-minute orientation program depicting the history of the first eighty years of Halifax and the surrounding area. A guided walking tour takes you into several authentically restored and furnished buildings. These include the 1760 home of a merchant, the house and law office of a nineteenth-century attorney, and the 1808 home of a wealthy landowner (exhibits and walkways over foundations exposed by the scholar's spade and trowel). The 1833 clerk's office, a jail, Eagle tavern, and a unique archaeological exhibit are also featured on the tour.

HALIFAX DAY

Halifax - Historic Halifax State Historic Site. Anniversary of the adoption of the Halifax Resolves. Living history activities, tours, and patriotic observance sponsored by the N.C. Society, Sons of the American Revolution. Halifax Day Parade. FREE. (April 12)

CHRISTMAS IN HALIFAX

Halifax - Historic Halifax State Historic Site. Join the historic site and town of Halifax as they celebrate the Christmas season. Historic buildings exteriors will be decorated with natural arrangements. Visit the local tavern for refreshments, learn about Christmas in colonial times, stroll the streets of Halifax and see the many historic homes and churches, see Christmas wreaths and decorations being created and feel the spirit of a small town Christmas.

KERR LAKE STATE RECREATION AREA

Henderson - *6254 Satterwhite Point Road (off I-85 exit 215) 27536. Phone: (252) 438-7791 or (252) 438-7582. www.ncparks.gov/Visit/parks/kela/main.php. Hours: Daily 8am-6pm, later in summer. Admission: $7/day per vehicle. Camping Fee.*

To say Kerr Lake is big is an understatement. Its 850 miles of shoreline stretches across Vance County and the North Carolina / Virginia state line, making it one of the largest lakes in the Southeast. It's also one of the most beautiful. Featuring wooded shores, secluded coves, and tranquil picnic areas. Explore Kerr Lake and enjoy the fishing, camping, boating, skiing, sailing, wind surfing, nature walking, and bird watching. Satterwhite Point has a visitor's center complete with an exhibit hall. An accessible nature trail with an overlook and an amphitheater are nearby. Enjoy yearly sailing regattas and fishing tournaments throughout the year.

OCCONEECHEE MOUNTAIN STATE NATURAL AREA

Hillsborough - *Virginia Cates Road (I-85, take exit 164) 27705. Phone: (919) 383-1686. www.ncparks.gov/Visit/parks/ocmo/main.php. Hours: Daily 8:00am-6:00pm, extended in warm weather seasons. Admission: FREE.*

Rising more than 350 feet from the Eno River, the Occoneechee Mountain summit is the highest point in Orange County. This 124-acre state natural area includes the eastern half of Occoneechee Mountain with an 867-foot-high summit, part of the Eno River. Hiking trails, scenic overlooks and two fishing ponds are popular. Some historic and nature programs are available.

OCCANEECHI - SAPONI SPRING CULTUREFEST/POWWOW

Hillsborough (Burlington) - 4902 Dailey Store Rd, On the banks of the Eno River. www.obsn.org. (336) 421-1317. Come out for two days of family fun filled American Indian dancing and singing. Native American vendors sell food, arts and crafts. Admission. (first or second weekend in June)

MEDOC MOUNTAIN STATE PARK

Hollister - *1541 Medoc State Park Road (21 miles southwest of Roanoke Rapids on State Road 1002) 27844. www.ncparks.gov/medoc-mountain-state-park. Phone: (252) 445-2280. Hours: Daily 8:00am-dusk. Educators: The Medoc Mountain program introduces students to basic geologic processes and relates them to the Medoc Mountain region. teacher's booklet and pdf: www.ncparks.gov/sites/default/files/ncparks/37/Medoc%20Mountain%20EELE.pdf*

The "mountain" is a granite outcropping with its highest point reaching 325 feet along with the remains of the core of an ancient mountain range. Most of the trails are easy or moderate in difficulty, and trail scenery includes an artesian well, granite outcroppings and miniature rapids. Winding along Little Fishing Creek, around the high ridge of Medoc Mountain and through the forests, the trails are the best way to appreciate the beauty and diversity of Medoc Mountain. Picnicking, canoeing, nature study, camping and fishing too.

LAKE GASTON

Littleton - *2475 Eaton Ferry Road (Eaton Ferry bridge by way of U.S. 158, N.C. 903) 27850. Phone: (252) 586-5711. www.lakegastonchamber.com. Admission: FREE.*

Straddling the North Carolina and Virginia border between I-85 and I-95, Lake Gaston has over 20,000 acres of "high quality" water, is 34 miles long, and approximately one and one half miles wide at the lower end of the lake. It has over 350 miles of shoreline offering a wide variety of watersports. Lake Gaston begins at Kerr Dam, a lake built in 1953 for flood control. Lake Gaston is well stocked with game fish which include striped bass or rock fish, large mouth bass, crappie, sunfish and several varieties of catfish. A valid adult license for either Virginia or North Carolina permits fishing from a boat in either state.

NORTH CAROLINA PICKLE FESTIVAL

Mt. Olive - Crafts, food, rides and concerts – most with pickles. Although the Mt. Olive Pickle Company isn't available for public tours, they welcome a visit and will show a brief video tour of the pickle operation. Corner of Cucumber and Vine. www.ncpicklefest.org. (last weekend in April)

CAROLINA TIGER RESCUE

Pittsboro - *1940 Hanks Chapel Road (Hwy 64 west, crossing Lake Jordan and Haw River. Take the first left at mile marker #387 on to Foxfire Trace, take a Left on Dee Ferrell Rd) 27312. Phone: (919) 542-4684. www.carolinatigerrescue.org. Tours: Weekends at 10:00am and 1:00pm (by reservation). Twilight Tours Available seasonally (April-October) on Saturday evenings at sunset. These special walks are during the most active part of our predators' days (age 13+, $28.00). Fee: $18.00 per adult on tour and $12.50 per child (4-12).*

The 60 acre reserve cares for a population of over 250 wildcats from 16 species. See threatened cats from around the world with a special focus on keystone species (species especially important to the ecosystem). Come join a guided tour where they will tell you all about the animals you are seeing, from scientific facts about the species, to the story of how different animals came to live with them. You will see up close and personal: Romeo, the 600 lb. Tiger; Jellybean, their white Bengal tiger; Disney, the friendliest binturong this side of South East Asia, and several more.

BIG ED'S CITY MARKET

__Raleigh__ - 220 Wolfe Street 27601. Fuel up with southern food (Breakfast, Lunch) at Big Ed's City Market just blocks walk away from the museums in downtown Raleigh. Big Ed (in red-checked shirt, denim overalls and a big smile) oversees the operations saying "I'm gonna fill your belly". Choose from 8 fresh meats and 12 fresh vegies for lunch. Ed uses ancestral recipes to create authentic traditional Southern staples like hot cakes (made from a pound cake recipe!), biscuits, collard greens and country cured ham. The restaurant itself provides a healthy dose of Americana, with Big Ed's own collection of antique farm implements, baskets, tin signs and other nostalgia items on display. Big, inexpensive breakfasts, too. Moderate pricing. Tuesday-Friday 7am-8pm, Saturday-Monday 7am-2pm. Phone: (919) 836-9909. www.bigedsnc.com. After lunch, stroll along cobblestone streets and browse the specialty shops and Artspace, where artists work in open studios. ______________________ ☐

MARBLES KIDS MUSEUM

Raleigh - ***201 East Hargett Street (corner of Blount Street and Hargett Street, directly opposite of City Market and Moore Square) 27601. Phone: (919) 834-4040. www.marbleskidsmuseum.org. Hours: Daily 9:00am-5:00pm. Admission: $7.00 (age one plus). IMAX tickets alone $7 - $12. Combo tickets to both, generally add $1.00. Note: Cafe. IMAX Theatre has several different shows daily. One show usually has a theme similar to a traveling exhibit on display. Educators: Dozens of age/theme appropriate lesson plans are found here: www.marbleskidsmuseum.org/educatorresources.***

This museum is geared toward families with children ages birth to twelve and features four indoor galleries, two outdoor escapes and an IMAX theater. Let's explore some of the "landscapes": What do you want to be when you grow up? Try out a few ideas in the Around Town Gallery. You can "pretend play" to be a farmer feeding and caring for animals in their stalls or a Broadway performer putting on shows with costumes and props for an audience. Other exhibits include an ambulance, a fishing boat, a delivery truck, a grocery store, a restaurant, a train, a tree house, a reading area and an underwater crawling area for babies under one. Water and paint activities are a big hit in the Splash Gallery. Two large towers supply a constant water supply to water tables below (full of toys). Step into a colorful world of money where kids play with smart ways to spend and save. Other galleries are geared towards the 8-12 set.

CE

NORTH CAROLINA MUSEUM OF HISTORY

Raleigh - ***5 East Edenton Street (downtown, between the Capitol and the Legislative Building) 27601. Phone: (919) 814-7000. http://ncmuseumofhistory.org. Hours: Monday-Saturday 9:00am-5:00pm, Sunday Noon-5:00pm. Admission: FREE. Parking in lots or meters nearby. Note: Gallery Backpacks at permanent exhibits and Times for Tots interactive days. Storytelling. FREEBIES: Kids Page of games & State Facts: http://ncmuseumofhistory.org/learning/kids***

The North Carolina Museum of History tells the stories of generations of North Carolinians and others who have shaped the state's history. It includes the largest historical flag collection in the United States, a Civil War exhibit, replica of the Wright Brothers' plane, and the North Carolina Sports Hall of Fame. The museum encourages visitors to discover the past, but not get bored with it - so, they change the exhibit spaces quite often. General Exhibits include:

NORTH CAROLINA AND WAR: Uniforms, weapons, flags, and other artifacts enhanced by historical settings, photographs, biographies, and computer interactives. Not only the soldier's life, but home life, too.

NORTH CAROLINA SPORTS HALL OF FAME: Audio, video, and interactive biographies, plus Richard Petty's stock car, Meadowlark Lemon's uniform, and other sports artifacts. Our favorite area, by the way.

DISCOVERY GALLERY: A whimsical "construction" site with dioramas of famous inventions. The area includes a Moving and Shaping activity guide for kids. How do you move a lighthouse? Who invented guns?

COMMUNITY & CULTURE: Famous Tar Heel racing or transportation; American Indian practices; Decorative arts from decoys to clothes; and notable music.

NORTH CAROLINA MUSEUM OF NATURAL SCIENCE

Raleigh - ***11 West Jones Street (on Bicentennial Plaza in downtown Raleigh between the Capitol and the Legislature Building, at the corner of Jones and Salisbury streets) 27601. www.naturalsciences.org. Phone: (919) 733-7450 or (877) 462-8724. Hours: Monday-Saturday 9:00am-5:00pm, Sunday Noon-5:00pm. Note: The Discovery Room, Naturalist Center, and Living Conservatory are closed Mondays. Admission: FREE. Note: Acro Café (with family-friendly offerings and***

pricing). Educators: Kids page with coloring pages, Nature Notebook sheets and web links. FREEBIES: Treasure Hunt: http://naturalsciences.org/files/documents/education/Treasure_Hunt.pdf.

A fossilized Dino Heart...

A science museum that houses four floors of exhibits. You're greeted by a giant shark's jaw. Take a relaxing stroll along a Carolina salt marsh and shoreline before passing cautiously under the 65-foot prehistoric blue whale fossil that welcomes you. The auditorium ahead is your introduction on a 17-minute journey through "Wilderness North Carolina." Hear the rushing waterfalls and mountain scenes as you enter the second floor. Now head to the third floor. Lightning flashes and thunder rumbles as the gaping dagger-toothed jaws of an Acrocanthosaurus (Acro-can-tho-saur-us) lunge for a sauropod dinner. You've just met the "Terror of the South!" Other features of the museum include a Fossil Lab (paleontologists work here), Willo - the dino with a heart (the first dinosaur discovered with a fossilized heart), and an Arthropod Zoo and Living Conservatory buzzing and crawling with giant creatures from butterflies to tarantulas. The Discovery Room is a special place where you can engage your senses by touching fossils, feeling bird wings, smelling tropical scents, watching the beehive, and more. Try on costumes, play with puppets, and find hidden animals in a dead tree critter hotel. A lot of things here are giant! Some items are small - a venus fly trap or baby sea turtles. "Oh, Look!" comments from kids throughout. We like that they focus more on habitats (dioramas) vs. specimens under glass. And, after exploring indoors, kids can take what they learned outside in the Prairie Ridge habitat hiking trails. Best Natural Science museum we've ever seen and it's free!

BUG FEST

Raleigh - North Carolina Museum Of Natural Science. Attracting more than 15,000 spectators, visitors may delve deeply into the insect world at this fun, wacky event. Enjoy food prepared at Café Insecta, cheer during the roach races and meet exotic insects from around the world. www.bugfest.org. FREE (mid-September Saturday)

NORTH CAROLINA STATE CAPITOL

Raleigh - ***1 East Edenton Street (Capitol Square) 27601. Phone: (919) 733-4994. https://historicsites.nc.gov/all-sites/n-c-state-capitol. Hours: Monday-Saturday 9am-5pm. Closed major state holidays. Admission: FREE. Tours: Guided tours available Saturday 11:00am & 2:00pm. Educators: quiz, lesson plans: https://historicsites.nc.gov/all-sites/state-capitol/educators/lesson-plan-capitol-and-civil-war-8th-grade/post-visit-activities.***

Originally housing the Governor's office, cabinet offices, legislative chambers, the state library, and state geologist's office, this building has been beautifully restored to its original appearance and is one of the best preserved examples of Greek Revival style architecture in a civic building. You'll be amazed by how worn the steps are from so many years of use. It's hard to believe that legislators used this building until 1963. The Governor and Lieutenant Governor currently maintain offices on the first floor. Peek in and say hello. Kids like the fancy "trimmings" on the doors and walls. Is a soldier still lurking the hallways? Did spies use "secret rooms" in the Capitol during the Civil War?

STATE CAPITOL HOLIDAY OPEN HOUSE & CIVIL WAR CHRISTMAS ENCAMPMENT

Raleigh - *North Carolina State Capitol. The Capitol is decorated for the holidays. Decorations feature the "North Carolina Tree," which is trimmed with ornaments from all 100 counties. Re-enactors demonstrate how to make period Christmas ornaments, dip candles, and train children to participate in Civil War drill routines. Local performing groups. FREE. (second week of December)*

NORTH CAROLINA SYMPHONY

Raleigh - ***2 East South Street (performances in Meymandi Concert Hall) 27601. Phone: (919) 733-2750. www.ncsymphony.org.***

Based in Raleigh, the North Carolina Symphony (a full-time, professional orchestra with 65 members) performs approximately 170 times each year... with international guest artists appearing frequently. Several times a year, pre-concert Instrument Zoos are held to engage kids to try an instrument on for size. Also, Music Education concerts for students.

PULLEN PARK

Raleigh - ***520 Ashe Avenue 27601. Phone: (919) 831-6468. https://raleighnc.gov/places/pullen-park. Hours: Monday-Thursday 10:30am-6:30pm, Friday-Saturday 10:30am-8:00pm, Sunday 1:00-8:00pm (summer). Hours vary at other times of the year. Admission: FREE. Small fee for amusement rides.***

One of the city's oldest and most loved parks, this beautiful park offers recreational opportunities for everyone and includes a 1911 Dentzel Carousel, a train ride, a community center, aquatic center, boat rentals, an arts center, ballfields, tennis courts, picnic shelters, a children's playground, and a concession stand. Home of the TV Land "Andy & Opie" statue!

CITY OF RALEIGH MUSEUM

Raleigh - ***220 Fayetteville Street (historic Briggs Bldg., downtown) 27601. Phone: (919) 832-3775. www.cityofraleighmuseum.org. Hours: Tuesday-Saturday 9:00am-4:00pm, Sunday 1:00-4:00pm. Admission: FREE, $5.00 donation box.***

Housed in an 1874 building that was the city's first "skyscraper", this museum aims at a better understanding of present day Raleigh through an exploration and understanding of its past history. Exhibits on display include the tracing of Raleigh's evolving architectural styles, a look at the businesses that built Raleigh, the history of North Carolina's State flag, and the history of the Civil Rights movement. Best if toured as an add-on to another special event. RCM Children's Hour- Fayetteville Street Walking Tour for Kids: occasional Saturdays afternoons, museum staff lead children and families on a historic walking tour w/ a detective notebook or holiday scavenger hunts.

WAKE COUNTY SPEEDWAY

Raleigh - ***2109 Simpkins Road 27601. www.wcspeedway.com.***

Wake County Speedway was built as a 1/4 mile clay oval in 1962 by members of the Simpkins family. Hosting stock car racing from April through early November, this speedway runs every Friday night with the 600 Racing Legends cars running several special events. ***(919) 779-2171***

JOEL LANE MUSEUM HOUSE

Raleigh - ***160 South St. Mary's Street (corner of Saint Mary's, near downtown) 27603. Phone: (919) 833-3431. www.joellane.org. Admission: $4.00-$8.00 (grade K thru adult). Tours: Wednesday-Friday 10:00am-2:00pm, Saturday 1:00-4:00pm (March - mid-December). Winter tours Saturday only.***

The home of Joel Lane was built on a knoll overlooking the future city of Raleigh. The little house was the center of many historic gatherings. Lane introduced the bill in the Legislature for the creation of Wake County in 1770 and sold 11,000 acres to the State in 1792 for the creation of the capital city of Raleigh; hence he is known as the "Father of Wake County." Costumed docents take you through the oldest home and dependencies in Raleigh.

CHRISTMAS TOUR AT JOEL LANE MUSEUM HOUSE

Raleigh - Joel Lane Museum House. Decorated in traditional colonial greenery and fruit, the Joel Lane Museum House, circa 1770, showcases ways in which our colonial ancestors celebrated the holiday season. Raleigh's oldest home is now fully restored to its appearance when it served as the residence of Joel Lane, a prominent statesman and patriot. FREE. (first weekend of December)

CAROLINA BALLET

Raleigh - *3401-131 Atlantic Avenue (Fletcher Opera Theater or Raleigh Memorial Auditorium) 27604. Phone: (919) 719-0900. www.carolinaballet.com. Admission: starts at $20.00.*

This company presents a full range of ballet from the finest classics to fresh, contemporary works, infused with new energy and excitement. The Triangle's pro ballet company features collaborations with the North Carolina Symphony to provide a variety of ballet performances from the classics to modern such as Romeo & Juliet or Cinderella.

NUTCRACKER BALLET

Raleigh - Carolina Ballet. A grand production of the holiday classic, performed by Carolina Ballet and the North Carolina Symphony. Magnificent costumes and sets plus dazzling special effects delight audiences of all ages in this production. Admission. (mid-November through December)

CAROLINA HURRICANES

Raleigh - *1400 Edwards Mill Road (home games played at RBC Center) 27604. Phone: (919) 467-7825 or (888) NHL-TIX1. www.carolinahurricanes.com. Admission: $15.00-$60.00.*

Enjoy hard-hitting, fun-filled hockey games by this National Hockey League team that plays from October to April.

NORTH CAROLINA MUSEUM OF ART

Raleigh - *2110 Blue Ridge Road (I-40 to exit 289 onto Wade Ave. to Blue Ridge Rd) 27607. Phone: (919) 839) 6262. www.ncartmuseum.org. Hours: Tuesday-Sunday 10:00am-5:00pm. Extended hours Friday nights. Admission: FREE. Tours: Daily guided tours at 1:30pm. Note: Puppet shows and Kids Summer Camps. The Museum Park Trail is a mile-long paved trail with works of environmental art, open to the public during daylight hours for bicycle and pedestrian use only (no motorized vehicles or skateboards). Museum restaurant.*

Peruse works by American artists as well as collections of African, Oceanic and New World art, Egyptian, Greek and Roman art, 20th-century art and more. 5,000 years of artistic heritage. Having trouble making the connection for kids? Good Company offers activities between art and other, more familiar images—pictures that resemble your own life or those found in popular culture. Bring the kids for other creative activities designed just for them, such as the Museum Cube. And be sure to pick up the simple take-along pocket guide to approaching art museums-Art Encounters.

HISTORIC OAK VIEW COUNTY PARK

Raleigh - ***4028 Carya Drive (I-440, Poole Road exit 15 east, 4 miles east of downtown) 27610. Phone: (919) 250-1013. www.wakegov.com/parks/oakview/Pages/default.aspx. Hours: Daily 8:30am-5:00pm. Closed major holidays. Admission: FREE. Tours: Main house by appointment only. Note: Occasional spring tea parties are a fun way to visit the past.***

The Greek Revival Farmhouse at Historic Oak View County Park was built by Benton S.D. Williams in 1855. This Antebellum farmstead features the 1855 Greek Revival house, a detached plank kitchen, a cotton gin museum, an herb garden, picnic facilities, a barn, and a large Farm History Center.

HISTORIC OAKVIEW CHRISTMAS & CANDLELIGHT TOUR

Raleigh - Historic Oak View County Park. This antebellum farmstead is lit with luminaries for the holiday open-house. Guests can tour the 1855 Greek Revival house and visit with Santa in the living room, devour freshly baked cookies in the plank kitchen, and explore the cotton gin house museum and a Farm History Center. Sleigh rides are given around the pecan grove, snow or shine. FREE. (Saturday in December)

MORDECAI HISTORIC PARK / PRESIDENT ANDREW JOHNSON'S BIRTHPLACE

Raleigh - ***1 Mimosa Street (corner of Mimosa St and Wake Forest Road) 27611. Phone: (919) 834-4844. https://raleighnc.gov/places/mordecai-historic-park Hours: Tuesday-Saturday 10:00am-4:00pm, Sunday 1:00-4:00pm. Admission: $3.00-$7.00 per person (slightly less for 1/2 tour). Tours: one-hour guided tour of the Mordecai House and outbuildings. Tours begin on the hour, last tour begins at 3:00pm. Admission charged for guided tours.***

Andrew Johnson was born in Raleigh, North Carolina in 1808, and like the previous North Carolina born presidents, Andrew Jackson and James K. Polk, he was elected to office from Tennessee. Although a native of the South, Johnson was a firm supporter of the Union. This beautiful historic park includes an Antebellum mansion that was home to a very influential Raleigh family.

Students will learn about the Mordecai Family and examine how families and life in North Carolina have changed over time. The surrounding plantation offers exhibits that detail plantation life plus features a small wooden house that was the birthplace of President Andrew Johnson (did you know he was born in a kitchen?). Slaves performed virtually all tasks on the plantation. Many continued traditional African farming practices, crafts, cooking and music. After the Civil War, some former slaves remained on the plantation, including Chaney, a cook, and Ananias, a gardener.

MORDECAI HISTORIC PARK HOLIDAY TOURS

Raleigh *- Mordecai Historic Park / President Johnson's Birthplace. Visitors experience the sights and sounds of Christmas past when they tour the historic Mordecai plantation house and grounds, all decked out for the holidays in period decorations. Admission. (tours will run in December, on dates to be determined)*

RALEIGH SYMPHONY ORCHESTRA

Raleigh *- **2 East South Street 27611. www.raleighsymphony.org. Phone: (919) 546-9755. Note: most concerts are at Holly Springs Cultural Center.***

With the belief that "music has the power to affect the lives of all people," this symphony orchestra regularly presents classical, family and pops concerts plus offers educational programs. The Family Series four productions (some interactive) are great for families.

RALEIGH TROLLEY TOURS

Raleigh *- **1 Mimosa Street (begin at Mordecai Historic Park or City Market) 27611. Phone: (919) 834-4844. www.raleighnc.gov/mordecai. Admission: $10.00 adult, $6.00 student (7-17). Tours: Every Saturday 11:00am-3:00pm. (March-December) Tour time is 45 minutes. Last tour begins at 3:00pm.***

See Raleigh's 200-year history from an old point of view on the Raleigh Trolley! Travel through the historic heart of the Capital City on this historic trolley that offers a narrated tour with six stops. Visit historic sites, art galleries, museums, shops and restaurants. Learn about the city's history, hear stories about Sir Walter Raleigh and other local personalities and notice some unique architecture. Start the tour looking at beautiful Victorian homes. Interesting stories at every stop. The Governor's Home was built (brick by brick, literally) by prisoners. Kids, look for the prisoners' signatures on the bricks.

W. B. UMSTEAD STATE PARK

Raleigh - *8801 Glenwood Ave. 27617. www.ncparks.gov/Visit/parks/wium/main.php. Phone: (919) 571-4170. Hours: Daily 8:00am-dusk. Visitor Center 9:00am-4:30pm. Admission: FREE. Canoe and cabin rental fees apply. Note: Campsite, rowboat and canoe rentals are available.*

Divided into two sections, Crabtree Creek and Reedy Creek, this 5,439-acre park is easily accessible from Interstate 40 and US 70. Visitor Center Exhibits include: "This Old Farmland Has Stories to Tell" which uses oral histories of past residents to describe daily life on what was once hardscrabble farmland. "Mills and the Community" depicts a replica of one of several gristmills found in the park. "The Kingdom Game" is a computer interactive exhibit that invites visitors to consider the effects of development and preservation.

Another series of exhibits describes the natural history of the land including stories of weather, soil and wildlife habitats. Twenty miles of hiking trails provide access to most of Umstead State Park. Visitors may choose between a short stroll along a nature trail or a more extensive hike into the woods. For people who prefer horseback, approximately 11 miles of bridle trails travel through some of the most scenic and secluded parts of the park. Signs mark the equestrian trails. The mountain-bike trails follow the same roads as the bridle trails and are entered at the same points.

RALEIGH LITTLE THEATRE

Raleigh - *301 Pogue Street 27650. www.raleighlittletheatre.org. Phone: (919) 821-4579. Admission: $10.00-$25.00.*

Named "Best Children's Theatre Program", the theatre showcases a mix of high stepping musicals, outrageous comedy, serious dramas and family favorites such as Cinderella or Miss Nelson is Missing. Opened in 1936, Raleigh Little Theatre is one of the oldest continuously operating community theatres in the country and no other theatre in North Carolina produces as many shows.

SOLAR HOUSE, NCSU

Raleigh - *North Carolina State Univ. campus, next to McKimmon Bldg. (corner of Western Blvd & Gorman Street, I-440 exit 2) 27695. Phone: (919) 515-3799. www.ncsc.ncsu.edu/solar_house.php. Hours: Monday-Friday 9:00am-5:00pm, Sunday 1:00-5:00pm (except holiday weekends). Admission: FREE. Tours: Group tours must be scheduled in advance. Best for 5th grade up. Educators: Ask for worksheets on solar projects.*

Constructed by the College of Engineering, this solar house serves as a demonstration and research facility and is open to the public. The roof of the garage powers their utility truck. Every major room is connected to the sunspace by an operable door or window. The basement/family room is full of experiments. Kids can actually make electricity from sunlight in a circuit. What if your hand blocks the light (ex. Clouds, trees)? - No power? How is energy stored when the sun doesn't shine? Ask about solar model car racing.

NORTH CAROLINA RENAISSANCE FAIRE

Raleigh - www.carolina.renfestinfo.com North Carolina State Fairgrounds. Have a jolly time in the court of Medieval England, from the time of King Arthur through Queen Elizabeth I. The celebration includes a feast of crafts, entertainment, jugglers, musicians, exotic food and drink, plus brave knights competing in full-contact jousts. Admission. (weekends in October thru late November)

CAPITOL EASTER SUNRISE SERVICE

Raleigh - NC State Capitol Square. (919) 733-4994. A non-denominational service with musical performances takes place on the east grounds. FREE. (6:30am Easter)

JULY 4TH CELEBRATION

Raleigh - Capitol Square. www.dcr.state.nc.us. Celebrate with a bang as you watch live bands, eat some good home-cooking and view craft demos. FREE.

INTERNATIONAL FEST

Raleigh - Downtown, Raleigh Convention Center. www.internationalfestival.org. A dazzling mosaic of world tastes, sights and sounds featuring international foods, cultural exhibits, a world bazaar, ethnic dancing, and music. Adm. (1st wkend in March)

NORTH CAROLINA STATE FAIR

Raleigh - NC State Fairgrounds, 1025 Blue Ridge Road. www.ncstatefair.org. (919) 733-2145. With over 700,000 people attending each year, the extravaganza features livestock, agriculture, arts and cultural exhibitions, an amusement midway and nightly nationally acclaimed musical performances. Adm. (begins mid-October for 10 days)

A CHRISTMAS CAROL

Raleigh - Raleigh's Theatre in the Park, Memorial Auditorium. www.theatreinthepark.com. (919) 831-6058, Production of the Charles Dickens classic, "A Christmas Carol." This wildly popular production, starring Ira David Wood III, is updated each year to include crowd-pleasing humor without losing the spirit of the original play. Tickets range from $12-$58. (one week in early to mid-December)

NEW HOPE VALLEY RAILWAY & NC RAILROAD MUSEUM

Raleigh (Bonsal/New Hill) - ***3900 Bonsal Road (Take US 1 south to Exit #89 at New Hill to Bonsal Road) 27562. Phone: (919) 362-5416. www.nhvry.org. Admission: FREE to walk around and peek in museum. Rides run: $10.00 adult, $7.00 child (2-12). Regular Trains leave 4 times per ride day. Rides last about 40 to 70 minutes. Order online. Unsold tickets available at the rail yard.***

This line connected with the Seaboard Airline Railroad at Bonsal and was used to haul, among other things, tobacco to Durham for processing and finished cigarettes to market. A collection of antique trains including classic steam and diesel locomotives, as well as other train cars, are on display. This museum is open for self-guided tours on weekends. On ride days (May-December), visitors may take an eight-mile, round-trip train ride in open or enclosed cars and cabooses. Nice forest scenery along the way. At the New Hill Yard Limit, the engine is decoupled and switched to a siding. It then passes the cars to travel to another switch, gets back on the main track, and is recoupled with the cars to haul you back to Bonsal. This is the highlight of the trip. Santa Train first two weekends in December. Extra Pumpkin Trains in October.

ROANOKE CANAL MUSEUM & TRAIL

Roanoke Rapids - ***1640 Julian Allsbrook Highway, Hwy 158 27870. Phone: (252) 537-2769. http://roanokecanal.com/. Museum Hours: Tuesday-Saturday 10:00am-4:00pm. $4.00 per person (age 9+)***

ROANOKE RIVER FALLS PARK - This safe still water harbor offers easy access to the Roanoke River and the overlook offers an excellent view of the river's picturesque rapids. Canoeing and fishing are among the most popular activities along the river banks. The park has a picnic area with grills and is an entry point to the Roanoke Canal Trail. Located just off Hwy 301 in Weldon.

ROANOKE CANAL TRAIL - This trail contains some of the most impressive and best preserved early nineteenth century canal construction in the nation. It was designed to connect the Blue Ridge Mountains of Virginia with Norfolk, over a distance of 400 miles. Today you can experience the 7-mile trail along the old Canal in Roanoke Rapids.

ROANOKE RIVER MUSEUM - The museum storyline weaves together the navigational history of the Roanoke River, the beginning of the railroad, transportation during the Civil War, and the coming of hydro-electric power with the river and the canal as common threads.

CHILDREN'S MUSEUM & SCIENCE CENTER

Rocky Mount - *270 Gay Street (Imperial Centre for the Arts and Sciences) 27804. Phone: (252) 972-1167. www.imperialcentre.org. Hours: Tuesday-Saturday 10:00am-5:00pm, Sunday 1:00-5:00pm. Closed Thanksgiving and Christmas Day. Admission: $6.00 per person (age 2+). Planetarium $3.50. Sundays - FREE for local residents! Note: In town (Sunset Avenue on River Drive) is Sunset Park - mini-train, historic carousel, sport courts, and swimming pool (252-972-1151).*

The Children's Museum and Science Center is housed in the oldest of the factory buildings which also includes permanent and rotating exhibits, a puppet theater, live animal habitats and a NC coastal "living marsh" where kids get to touch creatures. The SciDome planetarium features live and recorded sky tours, laser light concert shows and exhibits. In Microbes, through high-tech video games, visitors can combat bacteria with antibiotics, use virtual reality, help microbes gobble up oil spills and participate in a microbes "quiz show."

The NEW Children's Museum includes 35 interactive learning stations designed to engage "budding scientists" ages 6 months to 6 years. From experimenting with sounds, opening doors to reveal hidden surprises, matching characters to their shadows and exploring their stimulating and colorful surroundings.

AMERICAN MUSIC JUBILEE THEATRE

Selma - *300 N. Raiford Street (Rudy Theatre) 27576. Phone: (919) 202-9927 or (877) 843-7839. www.amjubilee.com.*

A little bit of Branson, a little bit of Myrtle Beach entertainment style. Their student matinee show includes comedy and songs about self-discipline, responsibility, patriotism, loyalty, respect and much more. Please check the Schedule for start times. Regular shows around $13.50-$19.50 each. All teachers and school employees admitted Free of Charge (Character shows).

CLIFFS OF THE NEUSE STATE PARK

Seven Springs - *345A Park Entrance Road (I-40 east, take US 70 east through Goldsboro. Turn right onto NC 111) 28578. www.ncparks.gov/Visit/parks/clne/main.php. Phone: (919) 778-6234. Hours: Daily 8:00am to sunset. Admission: FREE. Fee for camping, swimming and rowboat rental.*

At the turn of the century visitors flocked to the area. They drank mineral water from local springs to cure their ills and they took riverboat excursions to the cliffs. Things have changed since then. Witness the effects of erosion that carved cliffs in the south bank of the Neuse River. The cliffs extend 600 yards and rise 90 feet above the water. The cliff's face is multi-colored, adding to the beauty. A path bordered by a rail fence leads along the riverbank. The park offers three 1/2 mile hiking trails, seasonal swimming lake, and canoeing on the river. Creative dioramas and audio-visuals in the museum depict the unique geology and natural history of the area (the museum is open seasonally).

FALLS LAKE STATE RECREATION AREA

Wake Forest - ***13304 Creedmoor Road (US 1 north to NC 98 west to NC 50. Turn right on NC 50 and travel north one mile) 27587. www.ncparks.gov/Visit/parks/fala/main.php. Phone: (919) 676-1027. Hours: Daily 8:00am-dusk. Admission: $7.00 per vehicle. Educators: Rangers hold regularly scheduled educational and interpretive programs about Falls Lake and its aquatic environment/food chain: www.ncparks.gov/sites/default/files/ncparks/37/Falls%20Lake%20EELE.pdf***

A total of 13 miles of trails through a variety of terrain are open for single-track mountain biking. Located in the Beaverdam area, the park offers three loop trails totaling a distance of 6.5 miles of easy / intermediate riding. For hikers, Falls Lake Trail will eventually travel the entire south shore of the lake. A portion of the Mountains-to-Sea Trail, the trail will connect two recreational areas and provide camping for backpackers. Sandling Beach, Rolling View and Beaverdam provide sandy swim beaches with nearby restrooms and changing facilities. Holly Point offers swimming for campers only. US 1 north to NC 98 at the town of Wake Forest.

FALL HARVEST & PUMPKIN FESTIVAL

Wake Forest (Youngsville) - Hill Ridge Farms, 703 Tarboro Road. (800) 358-4170. www.hillridgefarms.com. Fall hayrides where you choose a pumpkin from the patch out in the fields. Pony rides, train rides, gem stone panning, live music, food, a petting barn, fish feeding dock and a kids' playland. Adm. (mid-Sept thru Oct weekends)

IMAGINATION STATION

Wilson - ***224 East Nash Street (Hwy 264 East to Wilson. Take Exit 36B onto Alternate 264 East) 27893. Phone: (252) 291-5113. scienceandhistory.org. Hours: Tuesday-Saturday 9:00am-5:00pm, Sunday 1-4pm. Admission: $5.00 (age 4+).***

Located in the historic Wilson Federal Courthouse that was built in 1928, this hands-on science and technology center features over 200 exhibits that are related to the environment, space, and health. They want you to push, pull and handle everything. Exotic animals from around the state are a favorite but the best part is the up-close science experiments and demonstrations. Can you: Generate your own electricity? Look in a mirror and see yourself floating in air? Or, race against a bat, bear and a cheetah?

WHIRLIGIGS

Wilson (Lucama) - ***Wiggins Mill Road (I-95 exit 107 north to town. Turn left at light at Clints Korner, go to Wiggins Mill Road. Turn left approx. 4 miles) 27542. www.facebook.com/pages/V.SWhirligigPark/. Phone: (800) 497-7398. Hours: Who knows?? Best to stop by the Wilson County Visitors Center just off the freeway for daily schedules. Daylight hours preferred. This is someone's home so respect his privacy and follow any instructions. Admission: FREE.***

Vollis Simpson's Windmill Farm is a remarkable collection of elaborate "whirligigs" produced by local folk artist Vollis Simpson. The works incorporate complex movement and sound as an integral part of the more than 30 GIANT works erected on Simpson's property. Simpson's welded and painted constructions are large in scale and have been exhibited at noted art museums and are featured in downtown Raleigh. Vollis can often be seen at the front of his shop, working non-stop.

He's happy to talk to you, but he doesn't ever interrupt his work. Inside, the shop is filled with over a hundred smaller whirlygigs, all completely finished and painted.

Chapter 2
Central West
North Carolina

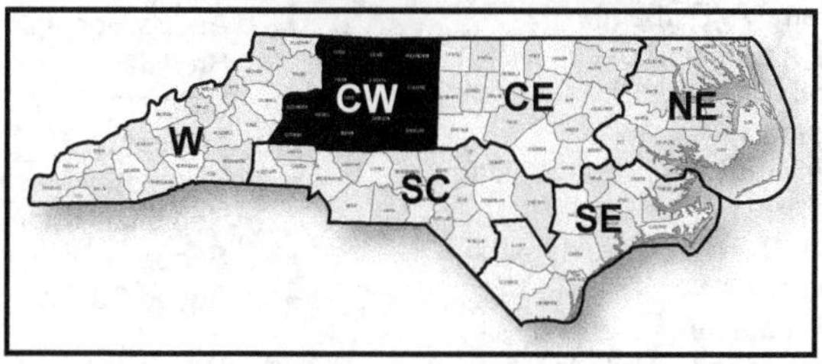

CW

Asheboro
- North Carolina Aviation Museum
- North Carolina Zoo

Asheboro (Seagrove)
- North Carolina Pottery Center

Danbury
- Hanging Rock State Park

Gold Hill
- Village Of Gold Hill

Greensboro
- Artquest!
- Greensboro Ballet
- Greensboro Children's Museum
- Greensboro Historical Museum
- International Civil Rights Center & Museum
- Stamey's Barbeque
- Barn Dinner Theatre
- Bog Garden & Bicentennial Garden
- Guilford Courthouse National Military Park
- Wet N' Wild Emerald Pointe Water Park
- Wingate Inn
- Tannenbaum Historic Park
- Natural Science Center Of Greensboro

Greensboro (Browns Summit)
- Triad Highland Games

Greensboro (Sedalia)
- Charlotte Hawkins Brown Memorial State Historic Site

Hickory
- Catawba Valley Arts & Science Center

Hickory (Catawba)
- Murray's Mill Historic Complex

High Point
- Millis Regional Health Education Center
- Piedmont Environmental Center
- World's Largest Chest Of Drawers
- High Point Museum & Historical Park
- Kersey Valley Zip Line

Jamestown
- Castle McCulloch Gold Mill
- Mendenhall Plantation

Mooresville
- Dale Earnhardt Inc.
- Lazy 5 Ranch
- Queen's Landing
- North Carolina Auto Racing Hall Of Fame

Mount Airy
- Andy's Homeplace Bed & Breakfast
- Mayberry & Andy Griffith Museum
- Mount Airy Museum Of Regional History
- Snappy Lunch
- Squad Car Tours

Mount Airy (Pinnacle)
- Horne Creek Living Historical Farm
- Pilot Mountain State Park

Randleman
- Richard Petty Museum

Salisbury
- Dan Nicholas Park

Salisbury (Mount Ulla)
- Patterson Farm Market & Tours

Spencer
- North Carolina Transportation Museum

Statesville
- Carolina Balloonfest
- Harvest Day At The Cabins
- Crossroads Pumpkin Fest

Statesville (Troutman)
- Lake Norman State Park

Welcome
- RCR (Richard Childress) Museum

Winston Salem
- Winston Cup Museum
- Kaleideum Children's Museum Of Winston-Salem
- Embassy Suites
- Old Salem
- Historic Bethabara Park
- Bowman Gray Racing Stadium
- Museum Of Anthropology, Wake Forest University

Winston-Salem (Clemmons)
- Mrs. Hanes Handmade Moravian Cookies Tour
- Festival Of Lights

Winston-Salem (Kernersville)
- Korners Folly

A Quick Tour of our Hand-Picked Favorites Around...

CW

Central West North Carolina

If you take I-40 east of Winston-Salem just a bit, your kids won't want to miss the "strangest house in the world" at **Korner's Folly** in Kernersville. Kids are surprised by all the many hidden nooks and crannies. This home is quirky but so full of whimsy!

Still in the mood for some strange stuff? Wake Forest University **Museum of Anthropology**'s permanent exhibits consist of cultural objects from the Americas, Africa, Asia and the Pacific. The kimonos and masks are big hits with the kids. Learn how to make a Kimono (w/paper). Play a painted gourd or sleep on a wooden head rest. What's that? Find out when you visit.

Deeply rooted in a pre-Revolutionary War history, folks in the Piedmont region needed to clear wilderness to begin a colony. The town of Winston-Salem has built a reputation for a connection to the arts that ties back to the pioneering Protestant group of Moravians that founded the original settlement called "Salem." Head to **Old Salem** and take your time to enjoy the historic museums here. In addition to a collection of antique toys and the playful **Children's Museum** (dress up), you can walk through this restored community dating back to 1766. Families seem to gravitate to the church and the old schools. The wafting smell of ginger from the bakery draws them in by the dozens to this cozy little space to purchase a bag of goodies to snack on.

Now that you're hooked on that bakery smell, **Mrs. Hanes Moravian Cookies Tour** is a must on your itinerary after lunch. Guess what, you get to be taste-testers! A sample of one of the 6 different flavors is given at each "station" along the tour. They make around 10 million Moravian cookies, each cut out one by one using a cookie cutter!

With your cookies as your "trail" snack, let's head east to Greensboro to visit favorite museums. Diversity is the best way to describe the **Natural Science Center** - so many different things - no signs of boredom here... inside and outside. Look up, look down, look all around. We notice they only have a handful of exhibits in each theme room, but they have the things kids really love.

Children can learn as they explore the PROCESS of art at **ArtQuest**. Travel on an art expedition where you can dig in the clay garden or construct a house of fabric. Then, weave on a giant 7-foot loom or crawl into Pablo's Place of puppets. Make a story quilt or create a mosaic postcard. The best part - you get to take most everything home!

The **World's Largest Chest of Drawers** is a building shaped like a chest of drawers built in 1926 to call attention to High Point as the "Home Furnishings Capital of the World." The **World's Largest Chair** is a similar oddity in Thomasville. It's one of those odd side trips you just have to say you've seen. Explore the history of High Point and many of its inhabitants as you tour the **High Point Museum & Historical Park**. You will be introduced to the Native Americans who first settled the land; to the development of the town from a small Quaker village; and then through the establishment of the furniture and textile industries. The awesome exhibits of the Furniture Discovery Center should be on display in the future.

For a big dose of the outdoors, try two zoos – one you WALK through, the other you DRIVE through. What a treat to have a drive-thru safari right in the middle of North Carolina! The **Lazy 5 Ranch** in Mooresville is now home to over 750 animals from 6 continents, this place is anything but lazy. Still haven't got your fill of animals? The **North Carolina Zoo** (Asheboro) was America's first zoo designed around the natural habitat philosophy and contains over 1,100 animals.

Step back to a simpler time when you visit Mount Airy. Actor Andy Griffith grew up here, and it's no coincidence that a stroll down Mount Airy's Main Street reminds people of the town of **Mayberry** from The Andy Griffith Show. Fans of the show can visit Floyd's City Barber Shop, Opie's Candy Store, Wally's Service Station, Mayberry Soda Fountain, Mayberry Courthouse, the Old City Jail, Snappy Lunch, and take a ride in a Squad Car Tour. You may even want to stay overnight in his childhood home (**Andy Griffith's Home & Town**). On a clear day you can see **Pilot Mountain** (Mount Pilot in the series). Take an adventure hike towards the top!

Sites and attractions are listed in order by City, Zip Code, and Name. Symbols indicated represent: ☐ Restaurants ☐ Lodging

CW

NORTH CAROLINA AVIATION MUSEUM

Asheboro - ***2109 Pilots View Road (Hwy 49 south, go two miles and turn left on Tot Hill Farm Road) 27205. Phone: (336) 625-0170. www.ncamhof.com Hours: Thursday-Sunday 11am-5pm. Admission: $10 adult, $5 student (over age 6).***

In this Museum you will see many examples of America's greatest warplanes from WWII through Vietnam, all flyable, except for one. First, you'll enter "Hangar 1" and come face-to-face with the "Flitfire" flown by Orville Wright! Surrounding the aircraft, you will find collections of authentic military uniforms and memorabilia. You might read a newspaper headline and then look up and see the same aircraft that made those headlines. Kids like the fun names of War Birds. New planes are often from recent commands - even a Homeland Security Condor.

NORTH CAROLINA ZOO

Asheboro - ***4401 Zoo Parkway (US 220 south) 27205. Phone: (800) 488-0444. www.nczoo.org. Hours: Daily 9:00am-4:00pm. Open until 5:00pm (April - October). Only closed Christmas Day. Admission: $15.00 adult, $13.00 senior (62+), $11.00 child (2-12). 4-D adventure Theater, carousel and giraffe deck extra fee. Note: Free parking. Picnic sites, restaurants and gift shop. KidZone is open many afternoons for animal encounters. Educators & Scouts: Kids scavenger games and teacher lesson plans: www.nczoo.org/education/EducatorResources/educatorresources.html.***

> If you walk the whole zoo - it's 5 miles! This place is so large and spread out, you may want to ride the tram around so you don't "tucker out".

This was America's first zoo designed around the natural habitat philosophy. In the African Pavilion, watch colobus monkeys and meerkats or herds of antelope leaping and running across the African Plains. At Forest Edge, climb up the Giraffe Deck, eye-to-eye with the long-legged giants. The North America exhibit has everything from arid deserts, to grassland prairies, to dense swamps to cold northern coasts. See alligators bask in the sun while polar bears wade in the cold water. In the indoor desert, look for cactus, roadrunners and rattlesnakes. Another indoor exhibit is the Forest Aviary. Scores of birds swoop and call noisily from their overhead roosts. But, to what are kids looking the most forward? - the western lowland gorilla. This chest-thumping primate routinely scares the willies right out of you with his noisy charges at the glass enclosure. Newer features include an Air Hike Ropes Course ($12 additional fee). Obstacles include swinging logs, plank walk, tight rope, Burma bridge, spider web, post hop and balance beam to name a few.

NORTH CAROLINA POTTERY CENTER

Asheboro (Seagrove) - ***250 East Avenue 27341. www.ncpotterycenter.org. Phone: (336) 873-8430. Hours: Tuesday-Saturday 10:00am-4:00pm. Closed Good Friday, the 4th of July, thanksgiving, and Christmas through New Years. Admission: $1.00-$2.00 (9th grade and up). Note: Most Saturday afternoons they have live demos.***

See exhibits of North Carolina pottery and related activities from prehistoric Native American times to the present at this pottery center. The museum is a great introduction to Seagrove - the oldest and largest community of working potters in the U.S. Found your favorite styles? Now, go out and meet the potters at their studios nearby. Visitors to Seagrove are often confounded by the notion that tucked in amongst the farms and fields are some of the best-known pottery families in the country.

HANGING ROCK STATE PARK

Danbury - ***1790 Hanging Rock Road (I-40, take US 52 north. Take the Germanton/ NC 8 exit, and turn left, following NC 8 for 25 miles through town. Follow signs) 27016. www.ncparks.gov/hanging-rock-state-park. Phone: (336) 593-8480. Hours: 8:00am-dusk. Admission: FREE. Boat rentals, swimming (small), camping and cabin fees apply. Educators: a grade 5 geology study: www.ncparks.gov/sites/default/files/ncparks/37/Hanging%20Rock%20EELE.pdf***

For the adventuresome, there's Hanging Rock State Park, located just north of Winston-Salem near Danbury. The area is composed of sheer cliffs and peaks of bare rock, quiet forests and cascading waterfalls, and views of the piedmont plateau that stretch for miles.

A hall in the visitor's center offers a variety of interactive exhibits. Open panels of a dead tree to see what's inside. Or, watch a video about the people who formed the park. Learn about geology, bend a rock, or try to build a wall out of stone. Enjoy dioramas of the plants and animals that live on rocky cliffs and near creeks. Hike one of the eleven trails of Hanging Rock State Park. An easy adventure for smaller children is Upper Cascade Falls. Older children will find their efforts rewarded with two beautiful waterfalls, Window Falls and Hidden Falls, within a short distance of each other. Rent a vacation cabin or camp. Nestled in the hills is the cool Sauratown Mountains with a lake that beckons to swimmers, canoers and fishermen.

CW

VILLAGE OF GOLD HILL

Gold Hill - ***770 St. Stephen's Church Road (tours start at EH Montgomery General Store) 28071. Phone: (704) 209-3280. www.historicgoldhill.com. Hours: Thursday-Sunday 11:00am-5:00pm. Extended holiday hours. Admission: FREE. Note: Mama Ts restaurant, the Gold Hill Bakery & many old-fashioned gift stores.***

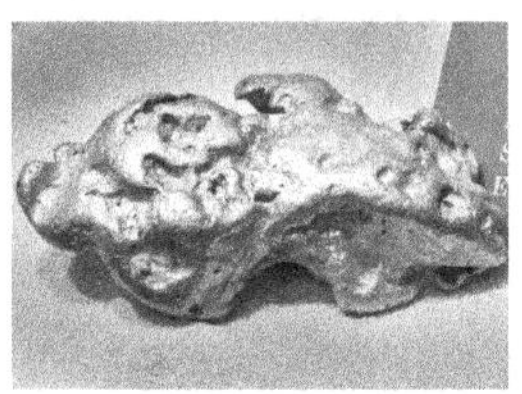

"The richest mining property east of the Mississippi." This was the message sent to England in the mid-1800s after gold was discovered here in 1824. Once a thriving, rough and rowdy mining town, the village is coming to life again with the restoration of area homes and stores. Visit the Rock Jail, Mauney's 1840 Store and Museum, and the E.H. Montgomery General Store. Gold Hill Mines Historic Park has a walking trail extending from the barn to the amphitheater. It crosses the bridge and joins the Gold Hill Rail Trail. Picnic and playground area in the park.

ARTQUEST!

Greensboro - ***200 North Davie Street (corner of Friendly & Davie) 27401. Phone: (336) 333-7460. www.greenhillnc.org. Hours: Tuesday-Saturday 12:00-5:00pm. Closed holidays. Admission: $7.00 per person (age 2+).***

This upscale visual arts center and gallery features changing exhibitions by North Carolina artists and offers a variety of educational programs for children and adults. You may want to first take a look at the FREE galleries including original works in glass, fiber and wood, as well as pottery, jewelry and paintings. Now, apply those visual mediums to the hands-on children's gallery of creative fun in ArtQuest. Travel on an art expedition where you can dig in the clay garden (using North Carolina clay) at Claytown; construct a house of fabric in the Architecture Corner; weave on a giant 8-foot loom; or crawl into Pablo's Place of puppets. Make a story quilt or create a mosaic postcard. The best part - you get to take most everything home! No trouble engaging here!

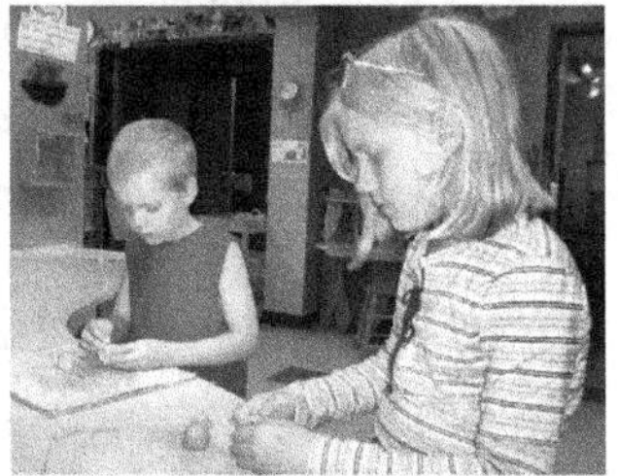

Clay Sculpting Fun

GREENSBORO BALLET

Greensboro - ***200 North Davie Street, Box 12 (Greensboro Cultural Center) 27401. Phone: (336) 333-7480. www.greensboroballet.org. Admission: $15.00-$25.00.***

Performances given by this professional ballet company include fairy tale classics, contemporary works, comedic ballets, and the holiday favorite, "The Nutcracker." The Ballet for a Buck program is an introduction to the art of classical ballet where the audience will enjoy a fun and informative demonstration and even some audience participation.

GREENSBORO CHILDREN'S MUSEUM

Greensboro - ***220 North Church Street (downtown Greensboro) 27401. Phone: (336) 574-2898. www.gcmuseum.com. Hours: Tuesday-Saturday 9:00am-5:00pm, Fridays until 8:00pm, Sunday 1:00-5:00pm. Admission: $10.00 general, $9.00 senior, Family Friday Fun (evenings) $5.00. Note: Tot Spot Early Childhood Area. Outdoor Play Plaza. Creation Station arts & crafts area. Sign up for classes in the Edible School - modern food and nutrition. Good museum for age 10 and under.***

This museum is designed around an "Our Town" theme. Since adults go to work in a town, children can learn their roles in the community in their version inside the museum. Children can shop, scan and buy pretend groceries, use a real ATM to get "kid cash", hop into a real US Postal jeep or climb the steps to a real DC-9 jet cockpit, slither through the window of a real Petty NASCAR Pontiac, scramble into the driver's seat of a real Greensboro Fire Department tanker, hit the lights and siren inside a real patrol car, and stand inside a hug bubble. They even make music or direct a symphony or play in a huge pretend campground. Nice layout.

GREENSBORO HISTORICAL MUSEUM

Greensboro - ***130 Summit Avenue (downtown, near the Children's Museum) 27401. Phone: (336) 373-2043. www.greensborohistory.org. Hours: Tuesday-Saturday 10:00am-5:00pm, Sunday 2:00-5:00pm. Closed City holidays except Fourth of July. Admission: FREE.***

Discover the history of the area and the Piedmont people at this museum that features twelve exhibit spaces and two American History restored homes. Among the 10,000 artifacts housed in the museum, have the kids see who can first find: the churns and sewing machines; a dagger found on the battlefield at Guilford Courthouse; a letter from the great short-story writer O. Henry to his sweetheart; Dolley Madison's, wife of the fourth president of the United States, snuff box; and phonograph records from the 1920s. Visit in an old-fashioned general store, doctor's office or schoolhouse. Be sure to save time to view the elegant miniature rooms.

INTERNATIONAL CIVIL RIGHTS CENTER & MUSEUM

Greensboro - ***134 South Elm Street 27401. www.sitinmovement.org. Phone: (336) 274-9199. Hours: Monday-Saturday 10:00am-6:00pm. Self-guided tours are from 2pm-6pm. Admission: $15.00 adult, $12.00 senior (65+) & students, $10.00 child (6-12).***

Franklin McCain, Joseph McNeil, Ezell Blair Jr. and David Richmond were refused service February 1, 1960, but they sat their ground. Located in the 1929 F.W. Woolworth building where the sit-ins were launched, the museum boasts a section of the actual lunch counter where the Greensboro Four sat. The counter and stools have never been moved from their original footprints. The sit-in was only the beginning of the Greensboro Four's work. After the store closed for the day, the students returned to campus and recruited others, the only prerequisite being that fellow demonstrators refrain from violence. By February 4, more than 300 students, including whites, were involved. The sit-ins, eventually more than 70 of them, spread across the South, making the Greensboro Four an important catalyst in the nation's budding civil rights movement.

Other highlights of the Museum's exhibits include: A filmed reenactment of the discussion between the Greensboro Four on the night of Jan. 31, 1960, when the freshmen quartet decided to take action. A bus seat, circa 1950, signed by Rosa Parks. An authentic wooden slave auction sign. Green Book, a circa 1950 travel directive to identify "safe houses" and establishments that would service African Americans. A medical bag used by Dr. George Evans, the first African-American physician allowed to practice medicine in what had been an all-white Greensboro hospital. And a travel typewriter used by anti-segregationalist Ralph McGill, a Pulitzer Prize winning author and publisher of the Atlanta Journal-Constitution.

The building has been restored to look like the original "Woolworth" store. A good way to teach Civil Rights to youth ages 10 plus.

STAMEY'S BARBEQUE

Greensboro - 2206 W Gate City Blvd. Greensboro Coliseum & Battleground 27403. www.stameys.com On your way back towards the interstate, drive-thru Stamey's Barbeque for Carolina pork and slaw. (I-40 exit 217, across from Coliseum). Inexpensive and with regional flavor (tangy). Kids Meals run around $3.99. Monday-Saturday 11am-9pm.

BARN DINNER THEATRE

Greensboro - ***120 Stage Coach Trail (I-40 to Guilford College Rd/Jamestown Exit 213) 27405. Phone: (336) 292-2211 or 800-668-1764. www.barndinner.com. Shows: Evening performances at 8:00pm. Dinner served 6:00pm-7:30pm. Matinee buffet seating begins at 1:00pm. Dinner/Lunch Theatre: $40.00-$45.00 adult, about half-price child (12 & under). Children under 5 not recommended for dinner theatre.***

The oldest dinner theatre in continuous operation in the United States, this entertaining theatre allows visitors to enjoy a popular Broadway style play, such as musicals, comedies, and mysteries, after sampling a wonderful traditional buffet. Playtime Theatre shows are shorter and don't include a meal. Special, spectacular Christmas shows.

BOG GARDEN & BICENTENNIAL GARDEN

Greensboro - ***1101 Hobbs Road (just north of Friendly Avenue, corner of Hobbs Road & Starmount Drive) 27405. Phone: (336) 373-2199. http://greensborobeautiful.org/gardens/bog_garden.php. Hours: Daily, sunrise to sunset. Admission: FREE. Note: Drive over to the nearby Greensboro Arboretum.***

The 17-acre arboretum includes nine areas that change with the seasons. Special displays and features include a hosta and wildflower trail, vine covered overlook and arbor, a butterfly garden and a lighted fountain. The Garden of Fragrance is very popular because of its unique scents and the bronze sculpture, "The Student," commemorating the David Caldwell Log College. Stroll across the street and visit the Bog Garden, a "swamp-like" park featuring a half-mile elevated wood walkway that provides easy and safe access through the bog. You'll have a rare chance to see unusual trees, wildflowers and ferns. We especially liked the boardwalk trail, the bamboo garden, and the many beautiful ducks and geese. Neat nature!

GUILFORD COURTHOUSE NATIONAL MILITARY PARK

Greensboro - ***2332 New Garden Road (US 220, Battleground Avenue) 27405. Phone: (336) 288-1776. www.nps.gov/guco. Hours: Daily 8:30am-5:00pm. Closed New Year's Day, Thanksgiving and Christmas Day. Admission: FREE. Educators: http://www.nps.gov/history/nr/twhp/wwwlps/lessons/32guilford/32guilford.htm.***

March 15, 1781 was the battle of Guilford Courthouse - one of the last battles of the Revolutionary War. Cornwallis held the field after an intense, two-hour fight, but he lost 1/4 of his army...leading to the eventual defeat at Yorktown months later.

Today, the park's wooded grounds can be seen by taking a 2 1/2 mile auto or bicycle tour, or by walking along three miles of trails. Along the way, visitors can see 28 monuments commemorating heroes of the battle. The Visitor's center offers a 30-minute film (shown on the hour); an animated battle map; and exhibits featuring original Revolutionary War Weaponry and artifacts. Exhibits include: sample firing of muskets, scavenger hunts with stamping stations, and silhouettes of soldiers on the field. Be sure to allow time to see the mini-movie - they take the perspective of soldiers - it personalizes it.

WET N' WILD EMERALD POINTE WATERPARK

Greensboro - ***3910 S. Holden Road (I-85 exit 121) 27405. Phone: (336) 852-9721 or (800) 555-5900. www.emeraldpointe.com. Hours: Call for seasonal hours of operation (May-September). Admission: Day Tickets ~$45.00 regular, junior (under 48") rates are normally $10.00 less, FREE (age 2 and under). Save with presale Good Any Day Price tickets. Discounts after 4:00pm. Snack bar food extra.***

The largest waterpark in the Carolinas offers more than 35 rides and attractions. Thunder Bay, one of only four tsunami (giant wave) pools in the country, makes massive, perfect waves. Enclosed slides, drop slides, tube rides and cable glides provide thrills for all ages and sizes. Try the Dragon's Den in the dark - if you dare. Two great children's areas and a drifting lazee river.

WINGATE INN

Greensboro - 6007 Landmark Center Blvd 27407. www.wingategso.com. I-40 exit 214, Wendover Avenue (336) 854-8610. At about $109/night, this is a value. The larger than average guest rooms have separate work and sleep areas plus FREE internet and expanded continental breakfast (even fresh tropical fruit). Outdoor pool and a micro/frig in every room. Celebration Station amusement center is 2 miles away. From $92.00.

TANNENBAUM HISTORIC PARK

Greensboro - ***2200 New Garden Road 27410. www.exploresouthernhistory.com/tannenbaum.html Phone: (336) 545-5315. Hours: Tuesday-Saturday 9:00am-5:00pm. In winter, park closes one-half hour early. Admission: FREE. Tours: Guided tours are offered Tuesday-Thursday. Call ahead for daily schedule. Reservations for groups. Note: Picnic area. Museum store.***

Operated by the local Parks & Recreation Department, this park was the 18th-century farmstead of Joseph Hoskins (the town sheriff). During the Battle of

Guilford Courthouse, Hoskins' land served as a staging area for British troops. The Colonial Heritage Center offers exhibits depicting life in colonial Guilford County. Best to visit for Living History Weekends.

BATTLE OF GUILFORD COURTHOUSE REENACTMENT

Greensboro - Tannenbaum Historic Park. On the anniversary date of the March, 1781 battle, hundreds of re-enactors portray British and American soldiers who fought in the American Revolution. www.nps.gov/guco. (weekend closest to March 15)

GREENSBORO SCIENCE CENTER

Greensboro - *4301 Lawndale Drive (I-40 exit Wendover Ave. East. Take Benjamin Pkwy. N exit, adjacent to Country Park) 27455. www.natsci.org. Phone: (336) 288-3769. Hours: Daily 9:00am-5:00pm. Admission: $14.50 adult, $13.50 senior (65+) or child (3-13). OmniSphere shows run $3.00-$5.00 per show. Note: Adjacent to Country Park, the site also offers outdoor picnic facilities, a modern playground, two small lakes and nature trails. Kids Alley for young ones. Educators: Activity Booklet: www.natsci.org/activity%20booklet.html.*

This hands-on museum features a zoo, an aquarium, a planetarium, educational programs and a gift shop.

Visitors can roam through a Dinosaur Gallery (hands-on rubbings to take home), learn about gems and minerals (how about the giant geode and the emeralds and gold found in North Carolina!), see snakes and amphibians in the Herpetarium, and enjoy a petting zoo. Visit with lemurs and enjoy touch labs. The new Animal Discovery zoological park features tigers, gibbons, wallabies, alligators and many other unique animals. Omnisphere Immersion Theater has regular and 3-D shows. Be sure to plan on seeing one of these shows each visit. Diversity is the name of this place - so many different things - no signs of boredom here...inside and outside. Look up, look down, look all around. We noticed that they only have a handful of exhibits in each theme room, but they have the things kids really love.

TRIAD HIGHLAND GAMES

Greensboro (Browns Summit) - Come celebrate Scottish culture and heritage at the Triad Annual Highland Games. This wonderful family event features traditional Scottish heavy athletics, music, dancing, food, border collie demonstrations, bagpipes, entertainment, children's events, music jam tent, sword fighting, tea tent, fly casting competition, shortbread competition, and much more! http://nctriadhighlandgames.org/. Admission. (first weekend in May)

CW

CHARLOTTE HAWKINS BROWN MEMORIAL STATE HISTORIC SITE

Greensboro (Sedalia) - ***6136 Burlington Road.Hwy 70 (I-40 exit 135, 10 miles east of town) 27342. https://historicsites.nc.gov/all-sites/charlotte-hawkins-brown-museum Phone: (336) 449-4846. Hours: Monday-Saturday 9:00am-5:00pm. Admission: FREE.***

The museum is a historic site at the former Palmer Memorial Institute, a preparatory school established in 1902 by Charlotte Hawkins Brown, a noted African American educator and national civic leader. This is the first state historic site honoring the contributions of African Americans and a woman. The visitor's center has exhibits and a video is shown. Here's a quote that best sums up her passion: "I must sing my song. There may be other songs more beautiful than mine, but I must sing the song God gave me to sing, and I must sing it until death." —C. H. Brown

CATAWBA VALLEY ARTS & SCIENCE CTR

Hickory - ***243 Third Avenue Northeast 28602. www.catawbascience.org. Phone: (828) 322-8169. Hours: Tuesday-Friday 10:00am-5:00pm, Saturday 10:00am-4:00pm, Sunday 1:00-4:00pm. Admission: $8.00-$10.00 (age 3+).***

Discover the fun of science while experiencing the trembling of an earthquake, meeting live animals, making a cloud, being a puppeteer, and much more at this hands-on science center. Discover science North Carolina style - Try climbing the mountain wall, check out the Piedmont tree house and experiment with sound. Touch live Nurse Sharks, Cownose and Southern Stingrays in a truly hands-on, aquatic habitat. Explore the surface of Mars or launch rockets. Look for colorful poison dart frogs in the Amazon Basin. You can even search for fossils at the end of the brook or walk into a butterfly cage. Modest, not over-stimulating, facility.

MURRAY'S MILL HISTORIC COMPLEX

Hickory (Catawba) - ***1489 Murray's Mill Road (near Hickory, N.C. and is easily accessible from interstates 40 & 77 and state highways 10) 28609. Phone: (828) 241-4299. www.catawbahistory.org/murrays-mill. Hours: Saturday 9:00am-4:00pm, Sunday 1:30-4:30pm (March-December 21). Closed Easter & Thanksgiving holidays. Admission: $7.00 per person. Tours: Guided tours are $10.00/person. Note: Annual Harvest Folk Festival the last weekend of September.***

Nestled in the rolling hills along Balls Creek in rural Catawba County, this site is a historic complex, with four restored buildings open for tours. During your visit you will learn how grain was transported between buildings and the four levels of the mill. The large gears will turn and the original millstones often grind local corn. The Murray & Minges General Store, which dates back to 1890, has provided merchandise for barter/sale for several generations. Today it is restored and open for business, selling anything from old-time candy and yo-yos to pickles and pottery. Refreshments include delicious ice cream. John Murray's millwright home is fully restored and provides groups an opportunity to see how earlier generations lived.

MILLIS REGIONAL HEALTH EDUCATION CENTER

High Point - ***600 North Elm Street (Route 311 towards High Point. Follow 311 for approximately 10 miles and take 311 Business/Main Street exit. See website for more details) 27260. Phone: (336) 878-6713. www.millishealth.com. Hours: Monday-Friday 8:30am-5:00pm. By reservation. Admission: $5.00 per person. Tours: Program reservations are required and you must be part of a tour. Just your family? Ask to be part of another group.***

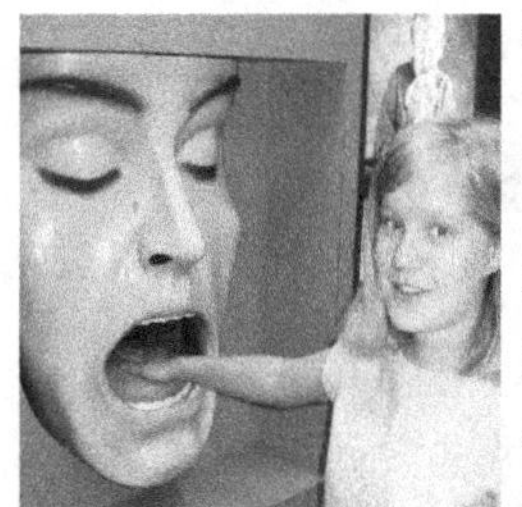

A very unique interactive health education center where you can ride a bike with Mr. Bones, the bicycling skeleton, or measure your height against a life-size Michael Jordan. You can also get health tips from TAM, a talking, transparent mannequin. We absolutely love their programs here. Initially, begin with a classroom orientation. Start with models of brains (works at 200 mph); then, on to the heart (60-100 beats/minute); lungs; and finally, the digestive system (food to waste and everything in between). The demos are fantastic. Individuals learn about the human body and how to eat right and keep themselves healthy. Touch-screen computers and two specialized learning theaters round out this space...best designed for group academic program visits.

PIEDMONT ENVIRONMENTAL CENTER

High Point - ***1220 Penny Road (off I85 Business) 27260. Phone: (336) 883-8531. www.highpointnc.gov/Facilities/Facility/Details/Piedmont-Environmental-Center-18. Hours: Monday-Friday 9:00am-5:00pm. Weekends for events. Trails open sunrise to sunset. Admission: FREE, donations accepted.***

Take a part of a unique, interactive ecotourism experience at this environment center on 376 acres including hiking trails, a visitor's center, nature preserve, nature store, small animal exhibits, and access to the six mile Greenway Trail.

Eleven miles of relaxing hiking trails wind along creek beds and lake shore, through hardwood and pine forests and in a fragrant wildflower meadow on the Center's North and South Preserves. The most unique part of the site: The walk-on map of North Carolina geography. Six different vertical scales are used to render the highly variable topography of each region. It's pretty cool to "walk across" the state.

WORLD'S LARGEST CHEST OF DRAWERS

High Point - *508 North Hamilton Street (corner of Hamilton & Westwood, downtown. Ask Visitor Info for directions) 27260. Phone: (336) 884-5255 or (800) 720-5255. www.roadsideamerica.com/attract/NCHIGbureau.html*

The "Home Furnishings Capital of the World" is crowded with furniture manufacturing operations and bargain hunters. There is a 32 feet tall Chest of Drawers containing the headquarters of the High Point Jaycees...offering a unique photo opportunity. Built in 1925, it stood as the "Bureau Of Information". It has been restored as an 18th century dresser, now twice as tall, with a new façade. A human can only reach as high as the top of the chest's legs. Furnitureland South, way out near the interstate, threw up their own chest of drawers -- over 80 feet tall.

HIGH POINT MUSEUM & HISTORICAL PARK

High Point - *1859 East Lexington Avenue (I-85 to Hwy 311 north to College Drive. Right onto College Drive. Go approximately 4 miles. Right on Lexington Avenue) 27261. Phone: (336) 885-1859. www.facebook.com/HighPointMuseum Hours: Tuesday-Saturday 10:00am-4:30pm. Admission: FREE.*

Explore the history of High Point and many of its inhabitants as you tour the museum. You will be introduced to the Native Americans who first settled the land; to the development of the town from a small Quaker village; through the establishment of the furniture and textile industries. Did you know that many of the yellow school buses used around the country are made here?

Weekends you can also step back in time with costumed guides to tour the historical 1754 Hoggatt House (demonstrates colonial chores) and the 1786 Haley House (lifestyles of wealthy Quaker household).

Using items from the old Discovery Center, their latest exhibit is High Point's Furniture Heritage. How is furniture designed? How is furniture assembled? What goes into making a sofa? The interactive center simulates a modern furniture factory.

KERSEY VALLEY ZIP LINE

High Point - ***1615 Kersey Valley Road (I-85 exit 113, Hwy 62, head west) 27263. Phone: (336) 802-1962. www.kerseyvalleyzipline.com. Tours: Daily, by appointment. $69.00-$79.00 zipline tour. High Ropes Course $32.00.***

Kersey Valley Zip Line! Take flight on over 1.5 miles of zip line that takes you across 14 sky towers above the corn maze and through the woods. Fly at day and see the maze or at night through the laser lights.

MAIZE ADVENTURE CORN MAZE

High Point (Archdale) - 1615 Kersey Valley Road. 27263 www.maizeadventure.com. This ten acre cornfield maze is filled with miles of twisting, turning pathways. Picnic areas are on site and catered lunches are available. Admission (age 5+). (September-October Friday evening and weekends)

MENDENHALL PLANTATION

Jamestown - ***603 West Main Street 27282. www.mendenhallhomeplace.com. Phone: (336) 454-3819. Hours: Tuesday-Friday 11:00am-3:00pm, Saturday 1:00-4:00pm. Friday and Saturday only in January & February. Admission: $2.00-$5.00. Note: City Lake Park is right across the street.***

A beautiful early 19th century Quaker plantation includes a school house, medicine school, as well as a museum and one of two existing false-bottom wagons used to transport runaway slaves during the time of the Underground Railroad. Enter "The Other South" of 19th century dissenters, see how they lived, and learn of their anti-slavery and pacifist views, their respect for education, honesty, plain living, and self-reliance. Notice the half door (master bedroom) used to bring in furniture hoisted up on the outside since furniture could not be brought up the winding staircase. Touch and feel cotton, flax, wool and silk. Notice the use of the word "Thy" (why?) and the tremendous simplicity.

CW

DALE EARNHARDT INC.

Mooresville - *1675 Coddle Creek Highway (I-77 north to Hwy 150, exit 36. Turn right on Iredell that turns into Earnhardt Hwy 3) 28115. Phone: (877) DEI-ZONE. www.daleearnhardtinc.com. Hours: Monday-Friday 9:00am-5:00pm, Saturday 10:00am-4:00pm. Admission: FREE.*

You may be greeted by Dale's relatives, if you're lucky! This racing facility was created by Earnhardt and today houses three top Winston Cup race teams. The public showroom honors the incredible career of the late Dale Earnhardt with mementos from his public and private life. Other displays focus on Junior and other racing heroes. Most fans can't resist shopping in the gift shop.

LAZY 5 RANCH

Mooresville - *15100 Highway 150E (I-77 exit 36 on NC 150 for 10 miles east) 28115. Phone: (704) 663-5100. www.lazy5ranch.com. Hours: Monday-Saturday 9:00am until one hour before sunset. Sunday 1:00pm until one hour before sunset. Admission: $11.00 adult (plus $5.00 for wagon ride), $8.00 senior (60+) and child (2-11) (plus $3.00 for wagon ride). Cash Only! Note: Petting areas, a blacksmith shop, gift store, horse barn, playground and picnic areas. Please bring any allergy medication or inhalers with you on your wagon ride. No pets!*

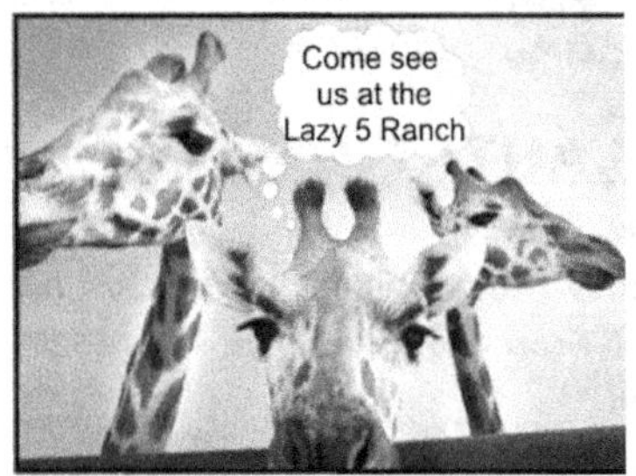
Come see
us at the
Lazy 5 Ranch

What a treat to have a drive-thru safari right in the middle of North Carolina! Now home to over 750 animals from 6 continents, the animals can be viewed everyday of the year from a horse drawn wagon or from your vehicle while traveling along a 3.5 mile safari ride. Its purpose is to educate while entertaining; and to provide a suitable habitat for safety and reproduction of species of several endangered animals. The Grevy Zebra, Scimitar Horned Oryz, and Ring-Tailed Lemur are just three threatened species making their home on the Lazy 5. The best part is petting and feeding the big and small animals - even giraffe. So you get animal slobber all over your car and some of your bucket of feed... everything will wash up later. Spring and Summer is Baby Time. How cute!

QUEEN'S LANDING

Mooresville - *1459 River Hwy 704 (Lake Norman) 28115. Phone: (704) 663-2628. www.queenslanding.com. Hours: Daily 10:00am-dark. Tours: Sightseeing & Luncheon Cruises: $17.99-$19.99 adult, $7.00-$14.99 child. Add $9.00 for box lunches. Tours leave at 11:00am and 1:00pm daily (May-September).*

This place offers everything from miniature golf and bumper boats to lunch and sightseeing cruises on the Catawba Queen or Lady of the Lake paddlewheelers. The show boats glide over Lake Norman. Several restaurants and snack cafes line the docks for a meal with a view.

NC AUTO RACING HALL OF FAME

Mooresville - ***119 Knob Hill Road (I-77 exit 36 to Lakeside Park) 28117. Phone: (704) 663-5331. www.ncarhof.com. Hours: Monday-Friday 10:00am-5:00pm, Saturday 10:00am-3:00pm. Admission: $4.00-$6.00 per person (age 6+).***

The museum, dedicated to all types of racing, features over 35+ race cars on display. Relive racing's greatest moments in the Goodyear Mini-Theater now featuring "NASCAR's Greatest Drivers". You can simply stroll the hallways and floor car exhibits at your leisure. Some old cars are neat to see especially since they look so different from current models.

ANDY'S HOMEPLACE BED & BREAKFAST

Mount Airy - *27030. 711 East Haymore Street (US 52 E bypass into town. Hampton Inn (check in) is a right on Rockford, the house is left on Rockford, right on Haymore). Phone: (336) 789-5999 (Hampton Inn reservations, http://mountairy.hamptoninn.com). www.facebook.com/pages/Andy-Griffiths-Home-Place/109338309106747*

Enjoy Mayberry while staying in Andy Griffith's childhood home. This house was home to Andy until the time he left to attend the UNC at Chapel Hill. This lovely home is filled with period style furnishings and offers two double beds, a private bath, and a full-size kitchen with a coffee maker, stove, microwave, and refrigerator. Host your own Andy Griffith rerun marathon with the videos/VCR provided. Test your knowledge of the show by playing the trivia game. Before turning in, "sit a spell" on the porch swing. Bring your guitar and gather everyone together for a family sing-along. From dated curtains to printed cupboards or the skinny closet doors to the dips in the floors - this is a special treat! It even smells like grandma's house. $150.00-$175.00 per night, including access to the facilities at the Hampton Inn nearby (includes complimentary continental breakfast, pool). Reservations please. ______________________________ ☐

Andy's kitchen...we kept looking for Aunt Bea...it looks like she just left!

MAYBERRY & ANDY GRIFFITH MUSEUM

Mount Airy - *218 Rockford Street, downtown (US 52, follow the signs for Andy Griffith Playhouse) 27030. Phone: (336) 786-7998. www.surryarts.org/agmuseum/index.html Hours: Monday-Friday 9:00am-5:00pm, Saturday 11:00am-4:00pm, Sunday 1:30-4:30pm. Town open Monday-Saturday during business hours. Admission: Minimum donation of $6.00 per person. Tours: There's a visitors center downtown where you can get maps to all these attractions. Note: One of a few remaining drive-in movie theatres is in town. The Bright Leaf Drive-In is open year round.*

Located in a beautiful, historic home that was built in 1910, this museum and visitors center contains the largest collection of Andy Griffith memorabilia in the country including everything from a Matlock suit to a chair he was rocked in as a baby.

MAYBERRY AROUND TOWN: Now venture over to the OLD CITY JAIL (215 City Hall Street) and peek at a recreation of the "Courthouse" seen in so many episodes of the "Andy Griffith Show". Come on inside and see what it feels like to sit behind Andy's desk. Or maybe you'd like to go see Otis' favorite cell. This building was Mt. Airy's real jail for many years and features a vintage 1962 Ford Galaxie squad car sitting out front. The new TVLand Opie & Andy statue sits on the lawn out front of the ANDY GRIFFITH PLAYHOUSE. Stop by FLOYD'S BARBER SHOP for a pic and a cut. What kid can resist OPIE'S CANDY SHOP or MAYBERRY SODA SHOP. A tour of this town is to step back in time!

MAYBERRY DAYS

Mount Airy - Each year, the three-day festival includes a golf tournament, bowling tournament, horseshoe tournament, apple peel-off, concerts, the Mayberry Days Parade (Saturday morning) and "Colonel Tim's Talent Time" (Saturday night). Other events are a Mayberry trivia contest, a pie-eating contest, free walking tours, children's games with the Ernest T. Bass rock throwing contest (Mount Airy granite – of course!), a pickle toss, and live Bluegrass music - Darling-style, of course. Mayberry Days look-alikes can be found throughout the festival. Every year, an actual star from the hit show is the special guest. www.mayberrydays.org. (last weekend in September)

MOUNT AIRY MUSEUM OF HISTORY

Mount Airy - ***301 North Main Street 27030. www.northcarolinamuseum.org. Phone: (336) 786-4478. Hours: Tuesday-Saturday 10:00am-5:00pm. Admission: $4.00-$6.00 per person (age 6+).***

Mount Airy or "The Granite City" is home to the largest open-face granite quarry in the world.

The desire for independence was the driving force of those who came to the back country and settled in "The Hollows" at the foot of the Blue Ridge Mountains. This area is referred to as "The Hollows" because the entire Mount Airy region rests in a saucer-like depression circled by mountains. The panoramic view from the museum's observation tower captures the beauty of this mountainous circle. Look for dioramas of native animals and native Saura Indians around their Bark House and dugout canoe. Visit the General Store to hear the latest news or view a miniature of early Eastern Wagon Roads. See the Hill Log Cabin and a display of tools used in early farming. Later, see life during the Victorian era and the "Age of Innocence". This area is also famous for Andy Griffith, Siamese Twins, a famous fiddler named Tommy, and granite quarries.

SNAPPY LUNCH

Mount Airy *- 125 N Main Street. (early breakfast thru early lunch Monday-Saturday), home of the famous Pork Chop Sandwich (ask for everything on it - sloppy, but fun!), or if you prefer, a big breakfast. Walk off a few calories checking out "Mayberry" stores and museums. www.thesnappylunch.com* ______________________________ ☐

SQUAD CAR TOURS

Mount Airy - ***625 S. Main Street (tours leave from Wally's Service Station) 27030. Phone: (336) 789-OPIE. www.tourmayberry.com. Admission: $40.00 a carload.***

Where else can you ride in Barney's car except Mayberry? Start off at the famous Wally's Service Station, then take a ride down main street and check out all the sites and then swing by Andy's original homeplace (also a B&B, see separate listing) and finally the rock quarry. Cruise in Mayberry style down Main Street past Floyd's Barber Shop and Snappy Lunch. You'll cruise by other Mayberry attractions like The Andy Griffith Playhouse and Museum), The Old Jail and the Visitors Center. You will also view the world's largest open faced granite quarry and the statue of Andy and Opie going to the fishin' hole. While at Wally's Fillin' Station, don't miss the best photo opportunity of the day - your photo in front of the Squad Car-or Gomer and Goober's tow truck.

CW

HORNE CREEK LIVING HISTORICAL FARM

Mount Airy (Pinnacle) - ***308 Horne Creek Farm Road (From Interstate 74/U.S. 52, take the Pinnacle exit (129) 27043. Phone: (336) 325-2298. https://historicsites.nc.gov/all-sites/horne-creek-farm. Hours: Tuesday-Saturday 9:00am-5:00pm. Admission: Varies with event. General visit is by donation. Tours: Hands-on activities are available spring, summer, and fall for scheduled groups. Guided tours are available upon request. Note: Horne Creek Walking-Nature Trail (moderate, approximately one-quarter mile) starts at the temporary visitor center and runs through the historic area past the family cemetery, along Horne Creek, and through a beautiful wooded ridge, returning to the visitor center parking lot.***

Nestled among the gently rolling hills of Surry County in the northwestern Piedmont of North Carolina stands Horne Creek Living Historical Farm. Costumed guides interpret everyday life as it was during the early Twentieth Century, when Thomas and Charlotte Hauser raised their 12 children at the Pinnacle community farm. Visitors may encounter farm animals of all but vanished breeds once kept on the Farm or savor old-fashioned apple varieties grown in Horne Creek's heritage apple orchard. You can try your hand at cutting grass with a scythe or listen to a talk on how to cook on a wood stove. You can almost see the Hauser family caught up in their annual cycle of everyday chores, farm labor, and festive celebrations.

PILOT MOUNTAIN STATE PARK

Mount Airy (Pinnacle) - ***1792 Pilot Knob Park Road (From US 52, take the Pilot Mountain State Park exit and travel west) 27043. Phone: (336) 325-2355. www.ncparks.gov/Visit/parks/pimo/main.php. Hours: Daily 8:00am-dusk. Admission: FREE. Fee for camping.***

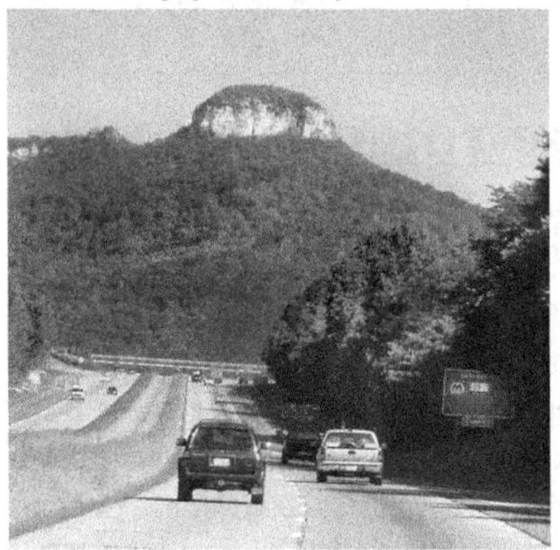

Does the title of this park sound familiar? Pilot Mountain or "Mount Pilot" is nearby Mount Airy. The Indians called it "Jomeokee," meaning "Great Guide" or "Pilot." Early white settlers called it Mount Ararat for the mountain where Noah's Ark came to rest after the Flood. Andy Griffith referred to it as "Mount Pilot" in numerous episodes of The Andy Griffith Show. A switch on words, but near Andy's home town and worth a stop on your way south of Mayberry (Mount Airy). Approach from any direction and see Pilot Mountain rising more than 1,400 feet above the rolling countryside of the upper Piedmont plateau. This solitary peak is the centerpiece of Pilot Mountain State Park. The park is divided into two sections with 1,000 acres located on the Yadkin River. Little Pinnacle Overlook offers hikers a close-up view of Big Pinnacle and distant views of the valley below. Try to meet up with a ranger lead hike as they tell you "secrets" of nature and folklore along the path. Treat yourself to a horseback ride through the woods or challenge the river from raft or canoe. They have hiking trails, scenic overlooks, picnicking, and family and group camping.

RICHARD PETTY MUSEUM

Randleman - ***309 Branson Mill Rd 27317. www.rpmuseum.com. Phone: (336) 495-11143. Hours: Monday-Saturday 9:00am-4:00pm. Admission: $12.00 adult, 10.00 senior (60+), $7.00 student (4-12). Note: Gift shop.***

Honoring the seven-time Winston Cup Series champion, this unique museum highlights Petty's 35-year career and includes awards, photos, more than 800 dolls, belt buckles, a movie, race cards and a Winston #1 showcar display and NASCAR history from the "dirt days" to recent competition.

DAN NICHOLAS PARK

Salisbury - ***6800 Bringle Ferry Road (I-85 exit 76A or 79, follow signs) 28145. Phone: (704) 636-2089. www.dannicholas.net. Hours: 8:00am until sunset. Some activities only have business hours. Admission: FREE. Small fee for gemstone mining, petting zoo, mini-train or carousel. Note: If there's enough time before nightfall, you might want to take a hike at the Eagle's Nest Nature Preserve. Continue past Dan Nicholas Park and across High Rock Lake (about 3 miles). Currently a little over two miles of trails including a self interpretive tree and plant identification loop, a *high water canoe access to High Rock Lake, and an additional trail leading to isolated coves are open to the hiker and nature lover.***

Begin the day by packing a picnic lunch and heading to Dan Nicholas Park which is situated in the scenic countryside. Spend the morning playing a round of putt-putt, riding the little train and Haden's carousel, feeding the ducks, paddling the paddleboats around the lake, and panning for beautiful gems at the gem mine. "Nicks Playground" is the park's latest addition, a specially designed and equipped playground for all children of every skill level. The Water Plaze is spurts of splashing (seasonal). The Nature Center and Petting Zoo are free and open to the public and boast a collection of slithering snakes, fun fish and native wildlife from bears to owls, many up close. For a small donation, you are able to get face-to-face with a calf, pig or goat. Every month has a themed event: example: Easter Egg Hunt, Fishing Tournament, Teddy Bear Picnic.

CW

PATTERSON FARM MARKET & TOURS

Salisbury (Mount Ulla) - ***10390 Caldwell Rd. 28125. Phone: (704) 857-5242. www.pattersonfarminc.com. Tours: Group farm tours are offered during strawberry, tomato and pumpkin seasons. Please call for an appointment. $3-8.00 per person. Themes for tours: Strawberry, Pizza, NC history and Dirt on Dirt.***

Patterson Farm Inc. is a 4th generation working farm. They grow 350 acres of tomatoes, 25 acres of strawberries, 40 acres of pumpkins, and poinsettias. From April until Christmas, enjoy fresh-from-the-field seasonal produce, plants and much more. Strawberries, tomatoes, pumpkins and poinsettias are grown in abundance on a seasonal basis and may be picked on-your-own or picked from the bountiful selection at the Market. During strawberry (late April - May) and pumpkin (mid September; mid November) seasons, festival weekends are filled with activities for all ages. Enjoy the petting farm, local music and dancing, hayrides in the fall or pack a picnic. Hours vary with the season, so please call ahead to verify that the farm and market are open.

NORTH CAROLINA TRANSPORTATION MUSEUM

Spencer - ***1 Samuel Spencer Dr (I-85 exit 79, follow signs for 2 miles) 28159. Phone: (704) 636-2889. http://nctrans.org. Hours: Tuesday-Saturday 9:00am-5:00pm, Sunday Noon-5:00pm (April-Labor Day). Admission: $4.00-$6.00. Diesel Cab Rides (ride with the engineer) are $15.00 per person. Tours: $12 adult, $10 senior/military, $8 child (3-12). Train runs daily during peak season several times per day. Weekends only fall, winter. Special events fees. FREEBIES: Download & print activity sheets (before you ride) to complete on the train (For Kids icon).***

Get your tickets at Barber Junction for train rides around the site and pick up information about tours and exhibits. The exhibit "Wagons, Wheels, and Wings" touches on transportation from a dugout canoe to a 1922 fire engine. There are videos and interactive exhibits along with shop areas at which locomotives are still worked on today. One of the largest roundhouses remaining in the country houses more than 25 restored locomotives and rail cars! The 25-minute train rides offer a narrated tour of the 57-acre site, pulled by an antique diesel engine. Visitors who are here after the last train ride of the day can see the engine run onto the turntable and into the Roundhouse, where it remains for the night on cool evenings. $1.00 turntable rides.

DAY OUT WITH THOMAS™

Spencer - *North Carolina Transportation Museum. Take a 25-minute train ride with Thomas the Tank Engine™, a real steam locomotive. "Bob the Builder" will perform* *live on stage. Meet Sir Topham Hatt™, see a magician show, play in bounce castles, get a temporary tattoo, and much more. Model train layouts, live railroad music and a Caboose Train are part of the fun. (fee, tickets required) (last weekend of September and first weekend in October)*

POLAR EXPRESS

Spencer - *North Carolina Transportation Museum. Santa rides the 25-minute train, passing out oranges and candy canes, a Southern Railway tradition. Storytelling of classic Christmas tales and an ornament-making activity are also part of the fun. Jingle Bell: Children hear readings of Christmas stories while riding the museum's 25-minute on-site train during this event for school and other children's groups. Cookies & Cocoa with Santa: Take a 25-minute evening train ride to the Roundhouse and enjoy a treat with Santa, and hear Christmas stories read by one of Santa's helpers. Limited space available; advance reservations required. Special fees apply. (weekends in December)*

CAROLINA BALLOONFEST

Statesville - *Statesville Regional Airport. www.carolinaballoonfest.com. One of the oldest and biggest balloon rallies on the East Coast. 50 or more balloons, kids fun zone, crafts, balloon rides. Admission. (late October weekend)*

HARVEST DAY AT THE CABINS

Statesville - *Heritage Farmstead Log Cabins, 1335 Museum Road, I-40 exit 150, near the 1899 Water Pump Station. (704) 873-4734. www.iredellmuseums.org. Step back in time as you walk through the cabin site, witness demonstrations from the blacksmith and learn how to make Apple Butter in a copper kettle. Listen to the sounds of the dulcimer, smell the wood fires and taste the food cooked on the open hearth. (second Saturday in October)*

STATESVILLE PUMPKIN FEST

Statesville - *(704) 873-2892. www.statesvillepumpkinfest.com Pummel pumpkins at the smashorama, pig out on pumpkin pie, try pumpkin bowling, watch a pumpkin catapult contest and make a scarecrow. Activity fees. (first Saturday in November)*

LAKE NORMAN STATE PARK

Statesville (Troutman) - ***159 Inland Sea Lane (I-77 by taking exit 42 onto US 21 north. Travel north on US 21 to Troutman. In Troutman, turn left on Wagner St.) 28166. Phone: (704) 528-6350. www.ncparks.gov/Visit/parks/lano/main.php. Hours: Daily 8:00am-dusk. Admission: FREE. Fee for camping and rentals. Educators: water quality and conservation grades 4-7: www.ncparks.gov/sites/default/files/ncparks/37/Lake%20Norman%20EELE.pdf.***

It's the largest manmade lake in the state - thus its nickname, the "Inland Sea." Thirteen miles of shoreline are in the state park, which provides boating access and fishing. Alder Trail: Begin this easy .8-mile loop at the parking lot near the swim beach. The trail crosses the picnic area, circles the peninsula between Norwood and Hicks creeks, and then skirts the edge of the lake. Take a short side path to the dam and view the spillway and gates that control the lake's water level before returning to the trailhead. Itusi Trail: this 4.2-mile mountain bicycle trail winds through mature hardwood forests and offers a unique mountain bicycling experience. Campgrounds.

RCR (RICHARD CHILDRESS) MUSEUM

Welcome - ***299 Austin Lane (NC 8 halfway between Winston-Salem and Lexington) 27374. Phone: (336) 731-3389 or (800) 476-3389. www.rcrracing.com. Hours: Monday-Friday 10:00am-4:00pm, Saturday 10:00am-2:00pm. Admission: $10.00 adult, $8.00 senior (55+), $5.00 student (7-18).***

The site allows fans to see many of RCR's greatest race cars along with famous machines from Indy car races and NHRA. See the winning car that Dale Earnhardt drove to victory in the 1998 Daytona 500. Inside, there are 47 race vehicles (46 cars and one NASCAR Truck) and a tractor-trailer transporter rig. Get to see what the inside of the high-tech trailer looks like. There are 16 video screens in the facility, showcasing key victories in RCR history. This is one of the most comprehensive displays of #3 Dale Earnhardt race cars (different paint schemes) in the country and it's a self-guided, video directed tour so take your time, fans.

WINSTON CUP MUSEUM

Winston Salem - ***1355 Martin Luther King, Jr. Drive 27101. Phone: (336) 724-4557. www.winstoncupmuseum.com. Hours: Thursday-Saturday 10:00am-5:00pm. Hours vary race weeks. Admission: $4.00-$8.00 (ages 5+).***

The Winston Cup Museum is now open! Located in the former Bob Neill Pontiac dealership building that has been renovated. The museum highlights the NASCAR Winston Cup Series. It houses over 30 authentic Winston Cup racecars and Winston #1 Show Cars along with one-of-a-kind racing artifacts. Dale Earnhardt and Jr.; Jeff Gordon, and even the first showcar used in the pre-race parade are here along with uniforms and helmets. Because the cars on display rotate to highlight different stories from the Winston Cup era, the museum is different every time.

KALEIDEUM CHILDREN'S MUSEUM

Winston-Salem - ***390 South Liberty Street (I40 Business to exit 5 C or D. Follow to corner of Brookstown and Liberty) 27101. https://downtown.kaleideum.org/. Phone: (336) 723-9111. Hours: Tuesday-Friday 9am-4pm, Saturday 10am-5pm, Sunday 1:00-5pm. Open Mondays during Summer and school holidays. Admission: $10 general (age 1+). Note: Gift shop. Outdoor Garden, Kaleidoscape.***

The museum is designed around the themes of storytelling and children's books, and is targeted to an audience of birth through fifth grade. Children can climb into Jack's Beanstalk and scale the overlapping, carpeted leaves to the second floor. Once there, they are invited to scamper around the Animal Alphabet to identify all 26 letters in the giant playroom. Nearby, doughnuts tumble down the conveyer belt as children race back and forth in the Doughnut Factory working to fill their boxes and then empty them again. Children can also play with giant foam logs and differently shaped blocks made of wood, plastic and foam in the Prop Shop. Additional exhibits include the Supermarket.

EMBASSY SUITES

Winston-Salem - 400 North Cherry Street 27101. www.twincityquarter.com. Phone: (336) 724-2300. You can walk a block or two to many restaurants or bring some entrees and reheat them in the mini-kitchen suite. Speaking of food, our favorite part of Embassy Suites is the hot, full breakfast. You can order an omelet from one of the friendly chefs. Or, just wander through each station and grab some fresh scrambled eggs, meat, French toast, maybe grits and muffins, cereal, juice and fresh cut fruit. And, for lunch or dinner, their soups and salad or appetizers were really quite good (sides $5.00, lunch avg. $8.00, dinner $16.00). Kids Menu runs around $6.00. In-house amusement starts with the central glass elevators, ending with the pool. Oh, and there's a Starbucks in the lobby right by the elevators. Current rack rate is $179, but weekend rates are $129.

OLD SALEM

Winston-Salem - ***900 Old Salem Road (southwest of the intersection of Business 40 and U.S. Hwy. 52, look for brown signs) 27101. Phone: (336) 721-7300 or (888) 348-5420. www.oldsalem.org. Hours: Old Salem Interpretive Buildings: Tuesday- Saturday 9:30am-4:30pm, Sunday 1:00 - 4:30pm (except Thanksgiving, December 24, Christmas Day and Easter Sunday). Admission: $35.00 adult, $16.00 child (6-16). Includes admission to the self-guided historic tour buildings plus museums. About half the shops and the visitors center are FREE to roam around, browse and shop (we recommend young ones just hang out-don't pay admission). Short on time? Pay a reduced admission to just choose 2 buildings to visit. Note: Deli, Tavern and Soda Shop open for light lunch fare most of the village hours. The Winkler bakery is especially good. Saturdays often include arts and crafts for kids.***

CW

Founded in 1766 to house professional Moravian craftsmen, Salem was a haven for entrepreneurs. This living historical museum is in an outdoor town setting in which costumed guides recreate common Salem household activities and trades of the 18th and 19th century Colonial life. Begin with a short video presentation at the Visitors Center. Your tour will help you take a look at the ways in which these pioneers worked, taught, played, worshipped, performed - and how their lives changed as the community and the country grew. In the village, visit with a Tavern wait staff or crafters such as a Tinsmith. Watch him make spoons from scratch. Learn things about their customs. Did you know Moravian girls studied and went to college just like the boys? Churches: Why did the races worship together, then apart? During special events and most weekends, the village comes alive even more with crafters around every corner. Hands-on spaces allow kids to: roll marbles, learn proper manners, watercolor paint, paper-cutting, write with a quill pen, or build with "bricks." They even have puppet shows for kids that are so cute.

FOURTH OF JULY

Winston-Salem *- Old Salem. Interpretations of the Fourth starting in 1783 through the 1860s, plus dinner foods and a medicine show. Admission.*

HOLIDAY SEASON AT OLD SALEM

Winston-Salem *- Old Salem. Take time to enjoy a traditional holiday celebration including a visit by St. Nicholas, candlelight evening tours (CandleTea), etc. Admission. (day after Thanksgiving thru day after New Years)*

HISTORIC BETHABARA PARK

Winston-Salem ***- 2147 Bethabara Road (Business I-40, off University Pkwy/ Cherry Street) 27106. Phone: (336) 924-8191. www.bethabarapark.org. Admission: $1.00-$4.00. Guided Tours: Tuesday-Friday 10:30am-4:30pm, Weekends 1:30-4:30pm (April-early December, except Thanksgiving Day).***

This 175-acre historic park is dedicated to presenting the history of the religious sect that settled this village in 1753. It was a frontier trade center from 1753 to 1772 in an 18th-century wilderness, full of bears, wolves, Indians and outlaws. The Moravians, a German speaking Protestant sect, migrated to North Carolina from Pennsylvania and constructed this village which features a reconstructed church, a French and Indian War fort, colonial and medical gardens, Moravian-costumed guides, and a visitors center with an introductory video. Outside, explore the trails to the mill site, stroll the boardwalk over the beaver pond and spot otters, mink, foxes, deer and woodchucks or picnic overlooking the village. The fort and boardwalk trails are what the kids gravitate to as this historic attraction is in more of a park setting and a more casual (and less expensive) approach to observing Salem history.

CELTIC FESTIVAL

Winston-Salem - Historic Bethabara Park. Salute the Celtic contribution to colonial Bethabara with music, food, step dancing, border collie demonstrations, Highland athletics, the annual Parade of Tartans, children's activities and pipe and drum bands. Bethabara Park. (second Saturday in May)

BOWMAN GRAY RACING STADIUM

Winston-Salem - ***1250 S Martin Luther King Jr. Dr [I-40 to 52 north (exit 193-B), exit Stadium Drive (exit 108-C) then follow signs] 27107. Phone: (336) 723-1819. www.bowmangrayracing.com.***

NASCAR racing was established in 1949 at this stadium that features a flat, quarter mile oval racetrack. From 1958 to 1971, this asphalt track hosted 28 events in NASCAR's premier series. The Dodge Weekly Series, a NASCAR-sanctioned event, remains the featured division Saturday nights from May to August. Admission ($10.00 general, Kids $2.00).

MUSEUM OF ANTHROPOLOGY, WAKE FOREST UNIVERSITY

Winston-Salem - ***1834 Wake Forest Road (US 52 at the University Pkwy South exit, behind the Kentner Stadium) 27109. www.wfu.edu/MOA/. Phone: (336) 758-5282. Hours: Tuesday-Saturday 10:00am-4:30pm. Closed university holidays and breaks. Admission: FREE. FREEBIES: Scavenger hunts - www.wfu.edu/moa/education/for-parents/.***

The only museum in the Southeast that is dedicated to the study of world cultures, this museum explores the cultures and people of the Americas, Asia, Africa, and Oceania including household and ceremonial items, textiles, hunting and fishing gear, and objects of personal adornment. Materials collected by Moravian missionaries can be found here, as well as prehistoric artifacts from North Carolina's Yadkin River Valley (from archeological digs). "How Do They

Know...? The Science of Archeology in the Yadkin River Valley" really brings out the treasure seeker in you. The kimonos and masks are also big hits with the kids. As the visitor explores each themed room, a printed gallery scavenger hunt sheet allows the kids to search and find. Learn how to make a Kimono (w/paper). Play a painted gourd or sleep on a wooden head rest. They offer lots of inexpensive culture toys in their gift shop. Small but wonderful.

CW

MRS. HANES HANDMADE MORAVIAN COOKIES TOUR

Winston-Salem (Clemmons) - *4643 Friedberg Church Road (Hwy 150 west (Peters Creek Parkway), turn right on Central Road. Go to Friedberg Church Road, turn left.) 27012. Phone: (336) 764-1402. www.hanescookies.com. Tours are given Monday-Friday 10:00am-2:00pm (January-October), by reservation only. $5.00 per person. Note: Nearby,* **Tanglewood Park**, *a 1,100-acre county park in Clemmons, features an arboretum and rose garden, plus a championship golf course, horseback riding, an outdoor play aquatic center, tennis and canoe/ paddleboat rentals.*

If you don't have time to arrange a group tour, you can see cookie crisp bakers at work hand cutting and rolling cookies through a specially placed window in the lobby.

Their cookies are made from an old family recipe that has been handed down over seven generations. Each cookie is rolled and cut by hand, the same way it was made a century ago. Then flavor is literally rolled into the cookies...in six delicious flavors: Ginger, Sugar, Lemon, Chocolate, Butterscotch, and Black Walnut. Guess what, you get to be taste-testers! A sample of one of the 6 different flavors is given at each "station". They make around 10 million Moravian cookies, each cut out one by one using a cookie cutter! Each year they use approximately: 65,000 lbs. of flour, 40,000 lbs. of Molasses, 35,000 lbs. of Sugar, and 450 lbs. of Ginger. Only the family is involved in the dough making process (secret family recipe, ya know). How do they keep the cookies from breaking? Believe us, this will be one of the most amusing (and yummy) tours you will ever take. Parents: Kids even learn about weights, measurements and estimating...and, working hard has benefits.

FESTIVAL OF LIGHTS

Winston-Salem (Clemmons) *- Tanglewood Park. www.tanglewoodpark.org. (336) 778-6300. Southeast's biggest display. Viewers drive along an almost 4-mile route past more than 1,000,000 colorful lights in 180 themed displays (many animated). Hayrides and* *carriage rides are also available. Admission. (mid-November thru December nights)*

KORNERS FOLLY

A Strange and Fun House !

Winston-Salem (Kernersville) - ***413 South Main Street (I-40 Business to Kernersville Main Street exit, south one mile) 27284. www.kornersfolly.org. Phone: (336) 996-7922. Admission: $10.00 adult, $6.00 youth (6-18). Tours: Wednesday, Thursday, Friday & Saturday 10:00am-4:00pm. Sunday 1:00-4:00pm. Note: The little theatre upstairs hosts shows a few times/year. Click on events tab. There's a gift shop there, too.***

Touted the "strangest house in the world," this oddity was built by Jule Körner and rises to 100 feet in height, creating a structure that includes 22 rooms on three floors and seven levels with ceilings ranging from six to 25 feet, and no two doors or windows in a room that are alike. Körner's Folly was always open to the children's (Gilmer and Doré) playmates for games and activities. The house includes a theatre that was used by the Körner children, 20 unique fireplaces of differing designs, decorative murals, and elaborate tile and woodwork. How do the trap doors, tunnels and fake windows actually air condition the house? Körner's Folly is a home chock-full of contrasts and comparisons (that's what makes it fun to tour, every room is its own surprise). Kid's favorites may be the many hidden nooks and crannies. This home is quirky but so full of whimsy! Children are very welcome. They even offer a scavenger hunt for children.

Chapter 3
North East
North Carolina

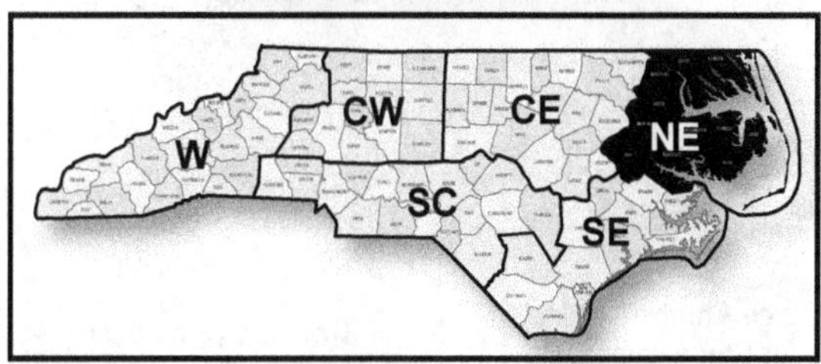

Bath

- Bath State Historic Site

Columbia

- Pocosin Lakes National Wildlife Refuge & Center For The Sounds

Corolla

- Currituck Beach Lighthouse
- Outer Banks Center For Wildlife Education

Creswell

- Pettigrew State Park
- Somerset Place State Historic Site

Edenton

- Edenton National Fish Hatchery
- Edenton Trolley Tours

Elizabeth City

- Museum Of The Albemarle

Gatesville

- Merchants Millpond State Park

Greenville

- Science And Nature Center, Walter Stasavich
- Pitt County Fair

Hamilton

- Battle Of Fort Branch Reenactment

Hatteras Island

- Cape Hatteras Lighthouse
- Day At The Docks - A Celebration Of Hatteras Island Watermen

Hatteras Island (Frisco)

- Frisco Native American Museum & Natural History Center

Hatteras Island (Rodanthe)

- Chicamacomico Lifesaving Station

Hatteras Island (Village)

- Graveyard Of The Atlantic Museum

Hertford

- Newbold-White House: A Colonial Quaker Homestead

Kill Devil Hills

- Comfort Inn On The Ocean
- Wright Brothers National Memorial

Manteo

- Cape Hatteras National Seashore
- Fort Raleigh National Historic Site
- Guided Water Tours - Outer Banks
- Lost Colony Outdoor Drama
- North Carolina Aquarium On Roanoke Island
- Pea Island National Wildlife Refuge
- Roanoke Island Festival Park

Manteo (East Lake)

- Alligator River National Wildlife Refuge

Manteo (Roanoke Island)

- Island Farm

Nags Head

- Jockey's Ridge State Park
- Kitty Hawk Kites Easter Eggstravaganza
- Outer Banks Pirate Festival

Ocracoke

- Ocracoke Island / Lighthouse
- Ocracoke/ North Carolina Ferries
- Portmouth Island ATV Tours

Plymouth

- Battle Of Plymouth Living History Weekend

South Mills

- Dismal Swamp Canal Visitor

Center & State Natural Area

Swan Quarter

- Mattamuskeet Wildlife Refuge

Washington

- Goose Creek State Park
- North Carolina Estuarium

Windsor

- Cashie Wetlands Walk & Mini Zoo
- Hope Plantation
- Roanoke River National Wildlife Refuge

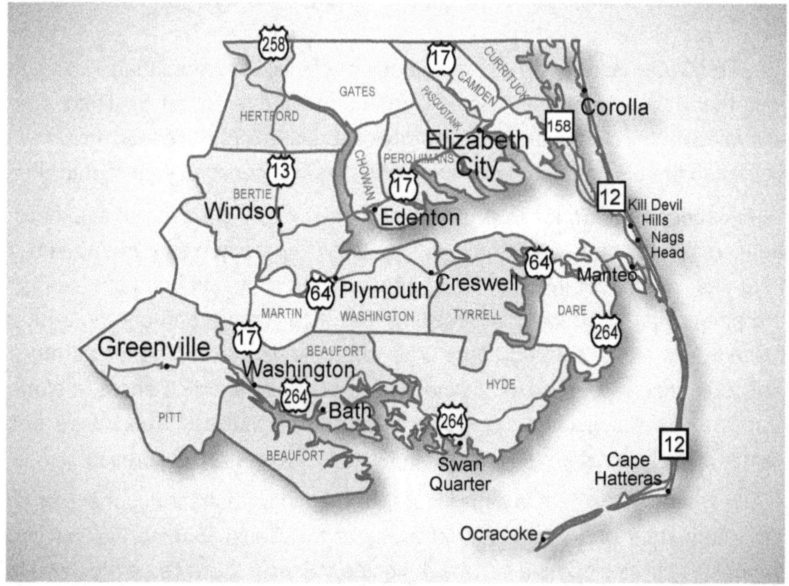

Travel Journal & Notes:

A Quick Tour of our Hand-Picked Favorites Around...

North East North Carolina

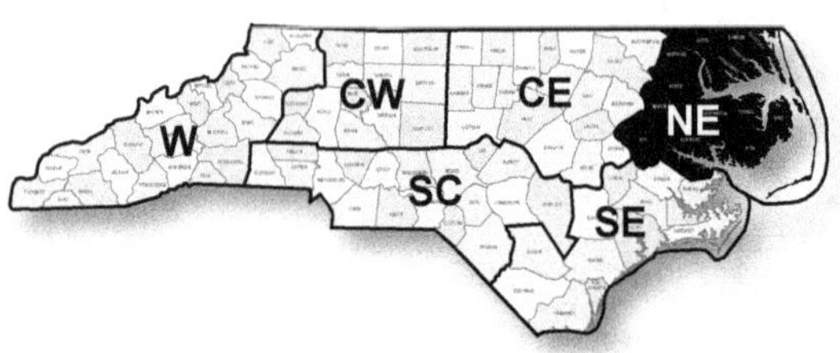

The **Outer Banks** is a string of sandy barrier islands more than 130 miles long that bow out into the Atlantic Ocean and cup the shoreline. There's no escaping it. With beautiful sunshiny days and just a hint of seasonal change, you'll find there's much to do on the North Carolina coast all year round.

A sunrise walk on a North Carolina beach offers a wealth of seashells, treasures from the sea for those willing to get up early. You can find shells here year-round, but in early spring after a storm or during hurricane season are particularly good times for shelling. One hour before and one hour after low tide are prime shelling times. This coast is also the home for as many as 1,000 species of mollusks. Where's the best place to find shells in North Carolina? Shell collectors say **Cape Hatteras National Seashore** and **Ocracoke Island** are all excellent places to find these treasures.

Any time of the year is a great for hiking, biking, watersports, or exploring the many state parks and natural areas of the Coast. Birding, fishing and canoeing activities abound and the region near **Swan Quarter** is the place to go to see thousands of tundra swans that make the area their winter home.

If you're looking for adventure, try hang gliding, body surfing or dune climbing near **Jockey's Ridge State Park**. The park encompasses the highest living sand dune on the Atlantic Coast and gives visitors a feeling of a windy desert. If that's too much adventure, you can relive the original flight at Kitty Hawk made by Wilbur and Orville at the **Wright Brothers National Memorial.** Retrace those 12 seconds that changed the world, and get a bird's eye view of the past. Spend the next day in the 16th Century at the **Roanoke Island Festival Park**. The park offers a living history of the first English colonists in America with special events scheduled throughout the year. Make sure you purchase tickets for the lavish production, the **Lost Colony**, based on early colonists who vanished into thin air. It is one of the best outdoor dramas we've ever seen.

Near the southernmost tip of this region, the 208-foot **Cape Hatteras Lighthouse** is the tallest lighthouse in America. Its signature black/white tower stands over dangerous Diamond Shoals, warning travelers away from the area known as the "**Graveyard of the Atlantic**."

There are many wonderful ways to travel when visiting the spectacular sites of the North Carolina Coast. But, perhaps the most scenic, serene and peaceful route is that of the **Ocracoke Ferry**. Stretching along the eastern portion of the state, the ferry system transports more than 2 million visitors each year. Extending among the Outer Banks, it is a very necessary form of transportation that efficiently takes you from island to island. In fact, if your schedule allows, we suggest a trip to the coast to go ferry hopping (with snacks and games in tow)!

Sites and attractions are listed in order by City, Zip Code, and Name. Symbols indicated represent: ☐ Restaurants ☐ Lodging

BATH STATE HISTORIC SITE

***Bath** - 207 Carteret Street (US 264 east to south on NC 92 to downtown) 27808. Phone: (252) 923-3971. https://historicsites.nc.gov/all-sites/historic-bath. Hours: Tuesday-Saturday 9:00am-5:00pm. Closed winter holidays. Admission: $1-$2.00. Includes tours of the Palmer-Marsh and Bonner Houses. Note: Several geocaching sites are within 10 miles of historic Bath. Children's History Programs.*

Guided tours originate at the visitor center. The video, "Bath: The First Town" is shown every fifteen minutes. Learn about the early nineteenth century, the Marsh and Bonner families and how folks like Jacob Van Der Veer added to the vitality of the town as merchants, shippers, and active citizens. Van Der Veer manufactured rope outside of town and was a partner with Joseph Bonner in an early steam sawmill. Bonner also operated a turpentine distillery. Bath was also the haunt of Edward Teach, better known as the pirate "Blackbeard." An expedition of the British Navy killed him in a naval battle near Ocracoke in 1718. Now, take the guided tour of some of the buildings filled with historical artifacts. Restoration efforts in Bath have saved the St. Thomas Church, the Palmer-Marsh House, 1790 Van Der Veer House, and the 1830 Bonner House.

CHRISTMAS OPEN HOUSE

***Bath** - Bath State Historic Site. Tour the Palmer-Marsh House, the Bonner House, the Van Der Veer House and the St. Thomas Episcopal Church, decorated in period holiday fashion. Enjoy music, apple cider and fresh-baked gingerbread. (second Saturday)*

POCOSIN LAKES NATIONAL WILDLIFE REFUGE & CENTER FOR THE SOUNDS

Columbia - *205 S. Ludington (on the south side of Highway 64 on the Scuppernong River) 27925. Phone: (252) 796-3004. www.facebook.com/PocosinLakes/. Admission: FREE.*

Pocosin is an Indian word meaning "swamp on a hill." These refuge lands were once the southern extremity of the Great Dismal Swamp. You'll find concentrations of ducks, geese tundra swans, raptors and black bears. The visitor center hosts exhibits and a film about the area. The Scuppernong River runs through the property and the Interpretive Trail is a 3/4 mile loop and boardwalk actually through the bottomland swamp. Interpretive signs explain the workings of the blackwater swamp ecosystem and encourage visitors to look, listen, and learn while they stroll along the path during daylight hours.

NE

CURRITUCK BEACH LIGHTHOUSE

Corolla - ***1101 Corolla Village Road (Route 12 heading north towards Duck and Corolla) 27927. Phone: (252) 453-8152. www.currituckbeachlight.com. Hours: Daily 9:00am-5:00pm (Eastertime - Thanksgiving time). Open later in the summer. Admission: There is a $10 fee to climb the tower for everyone 8 years of age and older. Tours of the Sound: Corolla Outback Adventures. One of their trademarks is an ATV (all-terrain vehicle) tour that takes you and the family on the Wild Horse Safari – a 2 hour eco-tour during the course of which you'll see local wildlife like red foxes, dolphin, white-tail deer and of course the area's famous wild ponies. You'll also hear some fascinating local legends. For reservations, call (252) 453-0877 or visit www.corollaoutback.com. $50 adult, $25 child (12 and under).***

This lighthouse illuminates the northernmost island on the Outer Banks. At 158 feet, the unpainted red brick structure's light can be seen for 18 miles at sea. Built in 1875, it was the last brick lighthouse built on the Outer Banks. Visitors can climb the 124 steps to the top observation deck. The lighthouse was constructed to fill the dark gap between Bodie Island and Cape Henry where many cargoes and lives had been lost in years past.

OUTER BANKS CENTER FOR WILDLIFE EDUCATION

Corolla - ***1160 Village Lane (located in Currituck Heritage Park on Highway 12 - near the historic Whalehead Club) 27927. Phone: (252) 453-0221. www.ncwildlife.org/Learning/Education-Centers/Outer-Banks. Hours: Daily 9:00am-5:00pm. Closed Sundays and winter Saturdays. Closed state holidays in winter. Admission is FREE - please call to sign up for programs.***

Exhibits include an 8,000-gallon aquarium stocked with native fish of Currituck Sound, a special decoy gallery with more than 250 antique waterfowl decoys, and a life-size diorama of a duck blind in a salt marsh. A 20-minute feature presentation, "Life by Water's Rhythms," screens daily in the auditorium. Because the center is located on the Currituck Sound, it offers visitors a chance to experience a barrier island first-hand. Kids can participate in the animal tracking, birdwatching, and marshwalk activities. They may also fish and kayak in the sound for FREE through the center. The wildlife guides provide all supplies for the activities, as well as act as instructors and nature guides. They also have herp hunt, duck calling and decoy making programs.

JULY 4TH FESTIVAL AND FIREWORKS

Corolla - Corolla Currituck Heritage Park - food, fun and entertainment from 6:00- 11:00pm. Parade earlier in nearby Duck. No alcohol and no on-street parking. $1.00 donation per person. (July 4th)

PETTIGREW STATE PARK

Creswell - ***2252 Lake Shore Road (seven miles south of Creswell off US 64, 20 miles west of Nags Head) 27928. www.ncparks.gov/Visit/parks/pett/main.php. Phone: (252) 797-4475. Hours: 8:00am-dusk. Admission: FREE.***

This park is home to Lake Phelps, a 16,600 acre natural lake and a virgin forest. Recreational facilities include a family campground, trails, boating, and fishing. A cloud of mystery shrouds the park's Lake Phelps. Scientists have debated the lake's beginning for centuries. Fed only by rainfall, the lake has an average depth of 4.5 feet and a beautiful, clear appearance – quite a contrast to many other lakes in this region. The lake is ideal for shallow draft sailboats, canoeing and windsurfing. Today, a carriage road makes up a portion of the Bee Tree Trail. Beginning at the park office, a one-mile section winds past the campground and Somerset Place. After wandering through a sweet gum forest, the trail leads to Bee Tree Overlook, a wooden platform offering a view of the lake and a place to observe wintering waterfowl.

VISITORS CENTER: In the exhibit hall, view displays of prehistoric Indian culture or head outdoors, near the lake, to dugout canoes. Among many of the artifacts uncovered, perhaps the most amazing is a series of 30 dugout canoes, which sank in the lake; the oldest is estimated to be 4,400 years old. It is believed that the Algonquian Indians placed the canoes in shallow water for seasonal hunting and they somehow sank over time. Two of the canoes, the nation's longest and second oldest, are displayed at the center. Rent a canoe to explore the area just as the early Native American explorers did.

SOMERSET PLACE STATE HISTORIC SITE

Creswell - ***2572 Lake Shore Road (U.S. 64 in Creswell follow the brown signs south through downtown, past Pettigrew State Park) 27928. Phone: (252) 797-4560. https://historicsites.nc.gov/all-sites/somerset-place. Hours: Tuesday - Saturday 9:00am-5:00pm. Admission: FREE. Educators: A Hands-On Educational Program is offered. Note: Nature trails link Somerset Place with Pettigrew State Park. Picnic facilities and gift shop.***

NE

Originally, this atypical plantation encompassed more than 100,000 densely wooded, predominantly swampy acres bordering Lake Phelps. During its 80-year tenure as an active plantation (1785-1865), hundreds of acres were converted into high yielding fields of rice, corn, oats, wheat, beans, peas, and flax; and sophisticated sawmills turned out thousands of feet of lumber. Somerset Place offers a view of the diverse lifestyles of the plantation's residents, from the perspective of owners and slaves, employed whites and free blacks. After the Civil War, nearly all of the emancipated black families left the plantation. The mansion and buildings are preserved from that time.

CHRISTMAS OPEN HOUSE

Creswell *- Somerset Place State Historic Site. Enjoy historic decorations, homemade desserts, a free meal of black-eyed peas cooked over the open flame and cornbread cooked the old-fashioned way in the fireplace hearth. (first Sunday in December)*

EDENTON NATIONAL FISH HATCHERY

Edenton - ***1104 West Queen Street (US 17 S) 27932. www.fws.gov/edenton/. Phone: (252) 482-4118. Hours: Weekdays 7:00am-3:30pm. The hatchery is also open weekends & holidays July thru mid-December (no staff on wkends). Admission: FREE. Tours: Groups are given tours with advance arrangements.***

Edenton National Fish Hatchery is a warm water hatchery which means they raise fish that do best in water temperature above 65 degrees. The hatchery has a public aquarium, a raised boardwalk through a wetland area, and classroom facilities. All facilities are open to the public for self-guided tours. The Hatchery is featured on the Charles Kuralt Trail. Edenton produces 2-4 million striped bass yearly for stocking local rivers. The nearby Chowan River, Albemarle Sound and county creeks offer abundant fishing opportunities for large-mouth bass, crappie, striped bass, bluegill and white perch.

EDENTON TROLLEY TOURS

Edenton - ***108 North Broad Street (departs from the Visitors Center) 27932. Phone: (252) 482-2637. www.visitedenton.com/trolley.php. Admission: $12.50***

per adult, small rate for kids. Tours: several times daily. Closed major winter holidays and during poor weather conditions. Note: The Visitors Center provides a 14-minute audiovisual program and some exhibits to browse before or after your tour.

Have kids? We've found the best way to historically tour is by trolley (vs. walking tours). On this 45 minute tour, you'll see the 1758 Cupola House; the restored 1767 Courthouse and the St. Paul's Church, the second oldest in the state. All students of history are familiar with the Boston Tea Party. But how many have ever heard of the Edenton Tea Party? Hear about the beautiful teapot that commemorates the 1774 Edenton Tea Party, colonial America's first political action by women. Learn that, on a per capita basis, Edenton is one of the state's largest boat-building towns, as well as a farming and lumbering community.

MUSEUM OF THE ALBEMARLE

Elizabeth City - ***501 South Water Street 27909. www.museumofthealbemarle.com. Phone: (252) 335-1453. Hours: Monday-Saturday 9:00am-5:00pm. Closed major state holidays.***

The Museum of the Albemarle is the northeastern regional branch of the North Carolina Museum of History. Serving thirteen counties in northeastern North Carolina, the Museum allows visitors to explore the history of the oldest section of North Carolina, many times considered the birthplace of English America. The Discovery Room features many "hands-on" history displays and interactives for families ("play" with 19th century fabrics and pretend school). The exhibit space titled "Our Story" is where all the real artifacts are. The Jackson House and the Proctor Smokehouse remain as anchors to the gallery.

CIVIL WAR LIVING HISTORY DAY

Elizabeth City - Museum Of The Albemarle. Visitors from across the Albemarle Area commemorate the Battle of Elizabeth City, fought February 10, 1862 with a living history reenactments, demonstrations, displays, exhibit tours, lectures and more. (Saturday closest to Feb. 10)

MERCHANTS MILLPOND STATE PARK

Gatesville - ***176 Millpond Road (From I-95, take US 158 east) 27938. Phone: (252) 357-1191. www.ncparks.gov/Visit/parks/memi/main.php. Hours: Daily 8:00am-dusk. Admission: FREE. Fee for camping and canoe rentals. Educators: The Merchants Millpond program introduces students to basic animal characteristics, focusing on the beaver. Majors concepts covered include adaptation, habitat, beaver-human similarities, animal signs and stewardship. Online resources.***

An "enchanted forest," primitive species of fish relatively unchanged over thousands of years, towering bald cypress trees with massive trunks, luxuriant growths of Spanish moss near dark swamp waters - this is Merchants Millpond State Park. Paddle through the pond and creek where you might encounter beavers, owls, otters and fish. Cypress Point Trail, 1/3 mile in length, is wheelchair accessible. A total of nine miles of trails traverse the park however they are heavily infested with ticks during warm weather months. The park also offers an accessible campsite and picnic tables.

SCIENCE & NATURE CENTER, RIVER PARK

Greenville - ***1000 Mumford Road (River Park North) 27834. Phone: (252) 329-4562. www.greenvillenc.gov/government/recreation-parks/river-park-north. Hours: Tuesday-Saturday 9:30am-5:00pm, Sunday 1:00-5:00pm. Adm: $1-$2.00.***

The Center houses a 70-seat theater and exhibits including a turtle touch tank, waterfowl of the Atlantic Flyway, a 10,000 gallon freshwater aquarium, live snakes, and the North American Diorama. River Park North is a 324 acre park and has 3 miles of hiking trails. Stop in at the Adventures in Health hands-on exhibits on anatomy and physiology. Take a stress test or learn safety tips.

PITT COUNTY FAIR

Greenville - *Pitt County Fairgrounds / Hwy 264 Extension. (800) 537-5564. www.pittfair.org. Besides your regular county fair exhibits, competitions and food, the East Carolina Village of Yesteryear is open for touring. Depicting Eastern North Carolina from 1840 to 1940, the village maintains a country store, a traditional school house, a log church, farm machinery, and other artifacts from the period. (late week in September)*

BATTLE OF FORT BRANCH REENACTMENT

Hamilton - *Fort Branch. www.fortbranchcivilwarsite.com. Re-enactors perform drills, encampments, cannon firings and battles. Museum is open also. Site is normally open weekend afternoons. FREE. (first weekend in November)*

CAPE HATTERAS LIGHTHOUSE

Hatteras Island - ***46375 Lighthouse Road (north end of city, look for brown signs) 27920. Phone: (252) 995-4474. www.nps.gov/caha/planyourvisit/. Hours: Lighthouse/Visitor Center: Daily 9:00am-5:00pm (except Christmas). Open until 6:00pm summer. Lighthouse open late April - Columbus Day only. Admission: Museum: FREE. Lighthouse: $8.00 adult, $4.00 senior (62+) and child (12 and under). Tours: Self-guided tours begin at 9:00am and run every 20 minutes until 5:00pm, with a limit of 60 people per tour. Tickets are available only for the day of purchase and are expected to sellout by noon each day, so visitors are advised***

to arrive early. Children must be with adults and over 38 inches tall to climb. They must climb themselves. Bring a water bottle per person. The climb is considered strenuous because it is equivalent to 12 stories. There is a handrail on only one side of the stairs, and there is two-way traffic on the stairs. Note: Ranger-led historical and environmental tours are offered from mid-June through mid-August. Talks are held many times daily in the summer.

The nation's tallest brick beacon (made from 1.25 million bricks), standing a proud 208 feet high, can be seen from 20 miles out to sea. Visitors are welcome to climb the 268 steps for a spectacular view of the seashore. For more than 100 years, it has warned sailors of the treacherous Diamond Shoals, the shallow sandbars that extend into the ocean.

It is said that the engineer got the plans mixed up and the diamond-shaped figures, suitable for warning traffic away from Diamond Shoals, went to Cape Lookout and this lighthouse instead became **"The Big Barber Pole."**

So many ships and lives were lost here in the 1500s, that the area was named the "Graveyard of the Atlantic." Adjacent to the lighthouse site are framed buildings that originally served as quarters to the keepers of the light and now serve as a visitor center and maritime museum. It's a beauty and a fun climb!

DAY AT THE DOCKS CELEBRATION OF WATERMEN

__Hatteras Island__ - Hatteras Village. The commercial and charter fishing fleets display their boats, skills, products and gear in a variety of competitions and demonstrations. There are a number of maritime-inspired games for children and fresh, local seafood is featured in a chowder cook-off and cooking demos. Traditional wooden boats, including a shad boat, NC's State Boat, a beach dory and a mullet skiff are on site. Musical entertainment. Blessing of the Fleet begins at 5:30pm. www.dayatthedocks.org. (third weekend in September)

FRISCO NATIVE AMERICAN MUSEUM & NATURAL HISTORY CENTER

Hatteras Island (Frisco) - ***(NC Hwy 12) 27936. www.nativeamericanmuseum.org. Phone: (252) 995-4440. Hours: Tuesday-Sunday 10:30am-5:00pm. Weekends only each winter. Admission: $5.00 per person, $3.00 senior, $15.00 per household.***

The Museum takes visitors back in time to follow the development and achievements of the island's earliest Native inhabitants. Artifacts from these inhabitants as well as from Native Americans across the US are displayed in galleries. Local finds include a dug-out canoe discovered on museum property as well as items recovered from the site of ECU's archaeological dig at Buxton Village. Visitors can also enjoy nature trails, which wind through several acres of beautiful maritime forest, and feature labeled specimens and exhibits, open space with benches for resting, and roped walkways through wooded areas.

NE

INTER-TRIBAL POWWOW, JOURNEY HOME

Hatteras Island (Frisco) *- Frisco Native American Museum & Natural History Center. Traditional Powwow set in a beautiful maritime forest with activities for the entire family. Drumming, singing, dancing, native crafts, exhibits, displays, story telling, native food and more! Open to the public. Admission. (last weekend in April)*

CHICAMACOMICO LIFESAVING STATION

Hatteras Island (Rodanthe) - ***23645 NC Hwy 12, milepost 39.5 (near Rodanthe, south of Manteo) 27968. Phone: (252) 987-1552. www.chicamacomico.net. Hours: Monday-Friday 10:00am-5:00pm (April thru August). Saturdays also each summer. Admission: $8.00 adult, $7.00 senior (65+) and students. $6.00 youth (4-17). Tours: Visitors are able to tour the site and buildings at their own pace through the aid of a self-guided tour pamphlet. Staff members and volunteers are present to answer questions.***

Established in 1873 for crews to patrol the beaches looking for ships in distress along the coastal "Graveyard of the Atlantic", the stations were built at seven-mile intervals. Each station was patrolled by a crew of five to ten men on foot or horseback. Chicamacomico became the most famous of the stations, given its crews' many daring rescues. The buildings on the site today survive as one of the most complete US Lifesaving Service/Coast Guard Station complexes on the Atlantic. Exhibits display pieces of the hundreds of vessels shipwrecked off the coast of North Carolina during a 400-year time span.

GRAVEYARD OF THE ATLANTIC MUSEUM

Hatteras Island (Village) - ***59200 Museum Dr. (adjacent to the ferry docks, you can't miss its outstanding structure) 27943. www.graveyardoftheatlantic.com. Phone: (252) 986-2995. Hours: Monday-Saturday 10:00am-4:00pm. Adm: FREE.***

Learn how this coastline earned the nickname "Graveyard of the Atlantic". Witness the conservation of prized artifacts: German U-boat, the first enemy sub destroyed off the coast in WWII; a ship's bell; a captain's desk from the Deering, the "Ghost Ship of Diamond Shoals"; the wheel from the John Duke; assorted beach finds and salvaged cargo; and the Huron shipwreck that started the Lifesaving Service reorganized to Coast Guard.

VISIBLE SHIPWRECKS along the Outer Banks: Schooner Francis Waters on display at the Nags Head Town Hall (sank Oct 1889); Schooner Laura Barnes (sank June 1921) on display at Coquina Beach in Cape Hatteras National Shoreline; Trawler Lois Joyce (sank Dec 1981) is visible in the surf at Oregon Inlet; Federal Transport Oriental (sank May 1862) - her boiler stack is visible from the second beach access after the Oregon Inlet Bridge; Schooner Kohler (sank Aug1933) is visible on the beach at Ramp 27, just north of Avon; and Schooner Altoona (sank 1878) is visible north of the pond at Cape Point.

NEWBOLD-WHITE HOUSE: A COLONIAL QUAKER HOMESTEAD

Hertford - ***151 Newbold White Road (midway between Edenton and Elizabeth City, off of Highway 17 on Harvey Point Road) 27944. https://perquimansrestoration.org/ Phone: (252) 426-7567. Admission: $3.00-$5.00 (age 6+). Tours: 45-minute guided tours of the 1730 House and grounds offered Thursday-Saturday 10:00am-4:00pm (March-Thanksgiving). Each tour begins with a 10-minute orientation video. Note: The Periauger Project is a replica of an 18th century workboat docked at this site. It is 30 ft overall, with 7 ft beam and was originally designed to carry many barrels and/or sacks of corn, wheat & rice, bricks, rum, etc., or to be fitted out for military duty. Visitors can also watch a video on the Periauger.***

From the shores of the Perquimans River, the site tells a story about Abraham and Judith Sanders, a Colonial Quaker family from the early 1700s. Sanders' riverside plantation was a diverse agricultural operation that included raising corn, cotton, wheat, flax, indigo, tobacco and rice. He also produced wood products such as barrels and shingles for roofs. The house is authentically restored and features period furnishings, enormous fireplaces, pine woodwork and a winding corner stair. The historic house is undergoing restoration and provides visitors with a unique and close-up look at the restoration process.

COLONIAL CHRISTMAS OPEN HOUSE

Hertford - Newbold-White House: Gather around the Yule Log and enjoy musical performances by a children's choir, a harpist and a barbershop quartet. Cookies, hot mulled cider, cakes, and much more available. See the Newbold-White House decorated for Christmas in the eighteenth century style and then cap off the evening with the Lord Mayor in a fireside ceremony to bless the New Year. Admission is free although donations are welcomed. (second or third Friday in December)

COMFORT INN ON THE OCEAN

NE

Kill Devil Hills - 27948. 1601 S. Virginia Dare Trail. www.choicehotels.com/north-carolina/kill-devil-hills/comfort-inn-hotels/nc416 (252) 441-7779. The hotel is located in the beautiful and historic Outer Banks. Watch the sun rise over the Atlantic Ocean and set over the Roanoke Sound. This full-service hotel has the family amenities we look for: spacious rooms, frig and microwave, warm outdoor pool with hot tub, and easy ocean access and showers plus small patio snack bar. The hotel offers its guests a free breakfast with hot waffles. The restaurant serves dinner too. Peak rates start ~$139/ night. ☐

WRIGHT BROTHERS NATIONAL MEMORIAL

Kill Devil Hills - ***1000 North Croatan Hwy (milepost 8 on the US 158 Bypass) 27948. Phone: (252) 441-7430. www.nps.gov/wrbr. Hours: Daily 9:00am-5:00pm. Closed Christmas. Admission: $10.00 adult (16+), FREE child. Educators: First Flight online simulations & Lesson plans: www.nps.gov/history/nr/twhp/wwwlps/lessons/109wrightnc/109wrightnc.htm.***

Stand on the same spots where the Wrights their first flights!

The Outer Banks became known as "Home of the First Flight" following the monumental aviation event that took place over 100 years ago on December 17, 1903. Bicycle shop owners Orville and Wilbur Wright spent years developing the 40-foot glider that would become a history-making aircraft. As their glider lifted off the ground at 10:35 that morning, the Wright Brothers achieved the first successful powered flight along the beaches of Kitty Hawk. Though the glider flew for only 12 seconds and 120 feet, it was an accomplishment that forever changed transportation.Numbered markers indicate the distance of each of the four flights made that historic day.

The site also hosts a visitors center with exhibits that include a full-scale replica of the Wright Brothers' original plane, the "Wright Flyer", and reproductions of the camp buildings used by the brothers - one as a hanger and the other as a workshop and living quarters. Be sure to sit through a ranger talk given in the visitors center - it's very well done and easy to follow. The Centennial Pavilion has exhibits that depict various aspects of aviation and space travel as well as the Outer Banks at the turn of the century, including walking through a camp tent or watching video of making a reproduction bi-plane.

Outside, climb Big Kill Devil Hill for a breath taking view of the area from sound to sea. Atop the Hill, stands the 60ft. Pylon - the site the Wilbur and Orville used for their glider experiments.

WILBUR WRIGHT'S BIRTHDAY

***Kill Devil Hills** - Wright Brothers National Memorial. This festive celebration will be a full day of family fun, play, picnic, and learning just as the Wright Brothers had at their own birthday celebrations more than 100 years ago. (mid-April Sunday)*

WRIGHT KITE FESTIVAL

***Kill Devil Hills** - Wright Brothers National Memorial. This kite festival celebrates 100+ years of flight with professional kite fliers from all over the world. Spectators can see a large kite including a 75ft. octopus and 40ft. Manta Ray's, fly in the air at the base of the Wright Brothers Monument. Stunt kite demos, games, kid's kite making, etc. will all be highlights of this event. 877-FLY-THIS or www.kittyhawk.com. (second wkendin July)*

NATIONAL AVIATION DAY

***Kill Devil Hills** - Wright Brothers National Memorial. In 1939, President Franklin D. Roosevelt established August 19th, Orville Wright's birthday, as National Aviation Day to honor the Wright Brothers and all flying pioneers and heroes. Special aviation related activities. (August 19)*

OUTER BANKS STUNT KITE COMPETITION

***Kill Devil Hills** - Wright Brothers National Memorial. This Eastern League event brings the best kite fliers on the circuit to The Wright Brothers National Memorial for stunt kite competition. Come see kite flying ballets, team competition, etc. Kid's games and lesson from professionals will be available as well. For more information visit www. kittyhawk.com or call (877) FLY-THIS. (first weekend in October)*

WRIGHT BROTHERS' "FIRST FLIGHT" CEREMONY

***Kill Devil Hills** - Wright Brothers National Memorial. www.firstflight.org. Celebrate the anniversary of the first powered flight. (December 17th)*

NE

CAPE HATTERAS NATIONAL SEASHORE

Manteo - ***1401 National Park Drive (NC Highway 12) 27954. Phone: (252) 473-2111. www.nps.gov/caha. Hours: Visitor Centers open Daily 9:00am-5:00pm. Open until 6:00pm (summer). Closed Christmas. Admission: FREE. Educators: A Lifesaving Station Lesson Plan is online.***

The Seashore stretches 70 miles north to south across three barrier islands. The islands are linked by a narrow, paved road and the Hatteras Inlet Ferry. Recreational opportunities include fishing, sunning, swimming, beach combing, boating, canoeing, kayaking, sailing and surfing. Among the sand dunes, marshes and woodlands, many like to auto tour, bike, bird watch, camp and hike. Bicycle paths are prevalent in Sanderling, Duck, Southern Shores, Kitty Hawk, Kill Devil Hills, Nags Head and Roanoke Island. These are paved separate routes that wind along parallel to the highway or through wooded areas. The islands are a wintering area for migrating waterfowl. In Ocracoke Village, view wild ponies that have roamed the salt marshes for more than 200 years. Visitors can view the ponies from a wooden platform overlooking the fenced pasture. Picnic tables are on site. The Seashore offers three visitor centers, each one is located in a famous lighthouse station - Bodie Island, Cape Hatteras & Ocracoke lighthouses.

FORT RALEIGH NATIONAL HISTORIC SITE

Manteo - ***(north end of Roanoke Island, 3 miles from Manteo) 27954. Phone: (252) 473-5772. www.nps.gov/fora. Hours: Daily 9:00am-5:00pm, except Christmas. Visitor center open until 6:00pm when the Lost Colony outdoor drama is presented. Admission: FREE. Educators: Roanoke Trading Cards: www.nps.gov/fora/learn/kidsyouth/cards.htm***

The park commemorates the first English attempts to colonize the New World from 1585-1587...before the colony vanished without a trace. The park is home to a visitors center, museum, Elizabethan Gardens (www.elizabethangardens.org), "The Lost Colony" outdoor drama, historic earthen fort works, a gift shop and picnic area. The Nature Trail offers a 20-minute pocket wilderness experience of the island's natural setting. Wayside signs on the trail relate what English explorers observed of the natural resources and the commodities that could be made from them.

Roanoke Island is the birthplace of Virginia Dare, the first English-speaking child born in the New World.

The other trail, the Freedom Trail leads 1.25 miles from the Elizabethan Gardens to the western edge, offering a similar view that the native Algonquians enjoyed. Other trail signs discuss the Civil War Battle of Roanoke Island and the freedom found on the island by escaped slaves. Be sure to view the 17-minute film "Roanoke" at the center to learn the background of the Roanoke voyages and Sir Walter Raleigh's efforts to colonize the area.

GUIDED WATER TOURS - OUTER BANKS

Manteo - If paddling one's own boat isn't appealing, there are 14 area operators who provide guided water tours of the area. They offer a range of site-seeing cruises, from daytime harbor tours during which visitors can look for schools of dolphin and indigenous species of birds to moonlit sailings.

- OUTER BANKS CRUISES. A SHRIMPING-CRABBING CRUISE. (252) 473-1475 or www.outerbankscruises.com. Pulls a small commercial-type shrimp net behind its boat so passengers can sort the catch and examine the fish, shrimp, crabs and other marine life that's harvested.
- NAGS HEAD DOLPHIN WATCH. (252) 449-8999, www.nagsheaddolphinwatch.com. Operates a 40-foot covered pontoon boat that spends the summer in Roanoke Sound to introduce cruisers to some of the dolphins there. Reservations a must.
- DOWNEAST ROVER. (252) 473-4866 or www.downeastrover.com. A 55-foot topsail schooner takes passengers on a two-hour sunset cruise from Roanoke Island.

LOST COLONY OUTDOOR DRAMA

Manteo - ***Waterside Theatre (Fort Raleigh National Historic Site) 27954. Phone: (252) 473-6000. www.thelostcolony.org. Hours: Nightly at 7:30pm, except Sundays (late May-late August). Admission: $30.00 adult, $27.00 senior & teens (13-18) half price child (6-12). Backstage Tours: $10.00TICKETS ARE NON-REFUNDABLE UNLESS CANCELLED DUE TO RAIN. Note: Concessions and gift shop.***

In order to colonize the New World, Sir Walter Raleigh sent an expedition of three ships led by John White to the Outer Banks. The expedition, which included women and children for the first time, arrived at Roanoke Island in 1587. Colonists used the abandoned quarters of former British explorers as their settlement. John White left the 117 colonists on the Outer Banks to return to England for food, supplies, and more colonists. When he returned, three years later, the colony had disappeared and the settlement was deserted. White's family and other English colonists had vanished, leaving no trace except for two cryptic carvings. "Croatoan" was etched into one tree near the fort (an important clue). "The Lost Colony" is America's longest running outdoor symphonic drama (over 60 years). Best of all, it keeps the kids' interest! As the story unfolds, can you solve the mystery? (and the costumes are gorgeous)

VIRGINIA DARE FAIRE

Manteo - Lost Colony Outdoor Drama. Celebrate Virginia Dare's birthday. Attend a day of free activities with music, games and fun for the family. Reserve your seats early for the evening performance of The Lost Colony that cameos infant actors as baby Virginia. (August 18)

LOST COLONY BACKSTAGE TOURS

Manteo - Lost Colony Outdoor Drama. Experience behind-the-scenes at the Waterside Theatre. Tours include the theatre, costume shop, props and history of the drama. Tea with the Queen at Elizabethan Gardens features high tea followed by a behind-the-scenes tour of theatre. Reservations & Adm required. (tours are nightly @5:30pm during season, $10.00 per person, tea once/month)

NORTH CAROLINA AQUARIUM ON ROANOKE ISLAND

Manteo - ***374 Airport Road, off Business 64 (northern end of Roanoke Island, overlooking Croatan Sound) 27954. www.ncaquariums.com/roanoke-island. Phone: (252) 473-3494. Hours: Daily 9:00am-5:00pm, except Christmas Day. Admission: $12.95 adult, $11.95 senior (62+) & military, $10.95 child (3-12). Tour: "Behind the Scenes Tour" (extra fee + reservation required). Learn how and what the animals are fed, get an up close look at how aquarists do their jobs.***

The huge building houses seven major exhibits and 18 tanks from 300 - 285,000 gallons. The biggest tank is 17 feet deep and roughly the size and shape of a baseball infield (with a replica warship sunk inside). It features 450 fish and a number of sharks; and a live webcam monitors the tank's activity for internet visitors. In "Storms", you'll hear commentary from actual hurricane victims. Kids can touch a stingray or marvel at river otters swimming freely in their pond. They can see alligators (the way the tank is designed, it's the closest you'll probably ever get to one!), sea turtles, moray eels, snakes and other marine life. The "Sea Turtle Maze" is an interactive exhibit for all ages. As you make your way through the maze, you are taught to think like a sea turtle. Wrong answers to certain questions will leave you at a dead end. When you leave the maze, you will know more about the thoughts of the sea turtle than you ever imagined. There are daily dive shows, animal feedings, a webcam birds-eye view of a real osprey's nest...live, and a variety of educational videos. Outside is a nature trail, shoreline boardwalk with observation decks and mounted telescopes, and an excavation area where visitors can dig for fossilized shark's teeth.

PEA ISLAND NATIONAL WILDLIFE REFUGE

Manteo - *Hwy 12, Sound side (northernmost section of Hatteras Island, between Oregon Inlet and Rodanthe) 27954. Phone: (252) 473-1131. www.fws.gov/refuge/pea_island. Hours: Refuge open year round during daylight hours. Visitor Center: Daily 9:00am-4:00pm (March-November), Thursday-Sunday only during winter months. Admission: FREE, small charge for guided canoe tours.*

The refuge is comprised of beautiful, barrier island beach, sand dunes, upland, fresh and brackish water ponds, salt flats and salt marsh. More than 400 species of wintering waterfowl regularly visit the refuge, including snow geese, egrets, herons and a large variety of wading, shore and song birds. Several shorebird nesting areas and wading bird rookeries are located on the refuge, too. It's "Birder's Paradise". The refuge is also home to 25 species of mammals, 24 species of reptiles and five species of amphibians. Endangered species include: peregrine falcons, American bald eagles, loggerhead sea turtles and piping plover. The refuge itself features a visitor center, two wildlife trails, observation platforms and towers with spotting scopes, guided canoe tours and children's programs in the summer months.

WINGS OVER WATER

Manteo - *Pea Island National Wildlife Refuge. The premier birding & nature festival on the Outer Banks, offering over 100 birding, paddling & natural history tours throughout eastern North Carolina. www.wingsoverwater.org. (six days late October)*

ROANOKE ISLAND FESTIVAL PARK

Manteo - *One Festival Park (over the bridge from Manteo) 27954. Phone: (252) 475-1500. www.roanokeisland.com. Hours: Monday-Saturday 9:00am-5:00pm, Sunday Noon-5pm (March-December). Closed Christmastime & Thanksgiving. Admission: $11.00 adult, $8.00 student (age 3-17). No charge to visit the picnic areas, boardwalks, fossil site, museum store, and parking is free. Admission stickers are honored for two consecutive days. Discount coupon online. Note: Children's Performance Series, Picnic areas, fossil pit and boardwalks. Many summer daytime performances are free with museum admission tickets. Educators: Online activity sheets: http://roanokeisland.ncdcr.gov/files/articles/TeachersPacket.pdf.*

The Park presents the evolution of Roanoke Island and the Outer Banks from the late 16th century to the early 20th century.

Begin your journey on the island by viewing "The Legend of Two Path" film that gives the Native American reaction to the arrival of the English settlers and the permanent changes it brought the Algonquians (45 minutes long). Kids can then go outside and climb aboard Elizabeth II, a sailing ship representative of those sent by Sir Walter Raleigh to the New World in the 16th century. Interpreters dressed as Elizabethan sailors tell seafaring tales to bring the story to life. Visitors can also explore the Settlement Site, a recreated military camp manned by costumed soldiers who are constantly on the lookout for Spaniards and Algonquin Indians. Visitors learn by doing as they explore the camp, tent and equipment. For entertainment, try playing board games or 9-pin bowling. Finally, back inside, tour the Roanoke Adventure Museum, where interactive exhibits explore 400 years of Outer Banks history. Don a cloak (you too, Mom and Dad) as you venture through history. Answer these questions: Did the English abandon the Colonists? What became of the Lost Colony? The museum chronicles boat-building, shipwrecks, pirates, lighthouse keepers, the Lost Colony, the Freedom Colony, the Civil War, and Lifesaving Services up to the 1950s. Very colorful and interactive with lots of hands-on history fun!

FOURTH OF JULY CELEBRATION

***Manteo** - Roanoke Island Festival Park. Waterfront Pavilion, www.NCSASummerFest.org. NCSA's Woodwind Quintet, Jazz Ensemble and jazz singers perform an evening of patriotic music to precede and accompany fireworks by the Town of Manteo. Don't miss this July 4th tradition on the Outer Banks! FREE! (July 4th)*

ELIZABETHAN CHRISTMAS

***Manteo** - Roanoke Island Festival Park. Roanoke Island Festival Park celebrates the third day of Christmas. Visitors to the Park get a taste of 16th century holiday traditions as they make decorations, learn dances, sing songs, discover food and drink of the season, etc. Many activities take place indoors. In the Settlement Site visitors join with the interpreters as they "recreate" their celebration in the American wilderness, with simple decorations and a roast over the open fire. Admission. (a few days after Christmas in December)*

ALLIGATOR RIVER NATL WILDLIFE REFUGE

Manteo (East Lake) - ***(west of Manteo on US 64/264) 27954. Phone: (252) 473-1131. www.fws.gov/refuge/alligator_river Hours: Daily during daylight hours. Admission: FREE. Nominal fee for guided canoe tours.***

The refuge is home to at least 200 species of birds, including owls, ducks and warblers. Endangered and threatened species that can be found on the refuge include the American alligator and the red-cockaded woodpecker. One of the largest remaining concentrations of black bears along the mid-Atlantic coast also has found a home at the refuge. During the winter months you might even hear the howl of a red wolf. There are hiking trails, wildlife trails and canoe and kayak trails, as well as a fishing dock. A half-mile paved trail leads to a 50 foot boardwalk with an observation platform that overlooks Creef Moist Soil Unit and a 250 foot boardwalk over a freshwater marsh. At the beginning of the trail, behind the interpretive kiosk, is a handicapped accessible fishing dock. Perhaps the best way to see the refuge, though, is by water.

ISLAND FARM

Manteo (Roanoke Island) - ***US Highway 64 27954. Phone: (252) 473-6500. www.theislandfarm.com. Hours: Tuesday-Friday 10:00am-4:00pm (April-November). Admission: $8.00 (age 6+).***

A living history site, Island Farm interprets daily life on Roanoke Island in the mid-1800s. The centerpiece of the site is the Etheridge farmstead. Visitors can explore nearly a dozen buildings. Stroll along the pasture fences and visit with the farm animals, listen to the ringing of the blacksmith's hammer, help a farmer hoe his corn or carry water to the garden. In the cookhouse, hear the sizzle of salted ham in the skillet or help the cook make corn cakes. Often, kids can play 19th-century games in the yard or go on a horse-drawn wagon ride. Exhibits in the Visitor Center help put daily life on the farm into historical context, with information on island culture, fishing, farming, boatbuilding, windmills, slavery, and the Freedmen's Colony.

JOCKEY'S RIDGE STATE PARK

Nags Head - ***300 W Carolista Dr (US 158 Bypass at milepost 12.5) 27959. Phone: (252) 441-7132. www.ncparks.gov/Visit/parks/jori/main.php. Hours: Park open daylight hours. Exhibit Hall open 9:00am-5:00pm daily. Admission: FREE. Tours: Rangers are on hand to conduct interpretive, casual tours. Note: Sand is typically 30 degrees hotter than air. Wear durable sandals or shoes. Educators: grades 4-6 learn animal adaptation & behavior in dunes: www.ncparks.gov/sites/default/files/ncparks/37/Jockeys%20Ridge%20EELE.pdf***

The State Park gives visitors a chance to experience the world of the desert. Shifting sands, high winds, extreme temperatures and a lack of water make the park resemble barren environments such as the Sahara Desert. Visitors can climb the 90-foot dune or park staff can drive people needing assistance to the top. Besides the adventure of climbing a dune (aerobic) and the view of panoramic vistas of the Ocean and Roanoke Sound, families can also hike one of the park's two self-guided nature trails, kite-fly, sand-board or picnic. Soft sand and easy runs down the dune are the best part. Most people also tour the exhibit hall. They discover what dunes are made of, how they are created and how they are shaped. Kids can play several matching games in which they match tracks to the animals that created them and dune names to their locations across the country. Next, study the history of storms and their effect on the dunes. Ever seen petrified lightning? You will here! Wonder where the names "Kill Devil Hills" and "Nags Head" came from? Visit the exhibit hall to find out more about these legends, including Blackbeard's treasure.

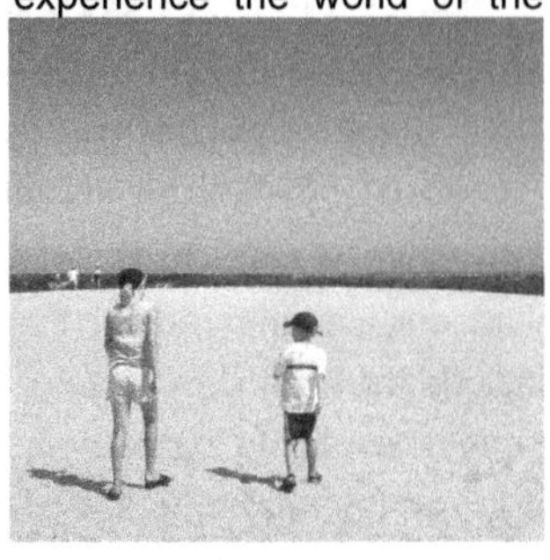

HANG GLIDING SPECTACULAR

***Nags Head** - Jockey's Ridge State Park. Come see the best sport hang gliders from around the world compete on the dunes. During this competition there are also activities for the whole family taking place across the street from Jockey's Ridge State Park at Kitty Hawk Kites. Activities include: climbing wall, face painting, kite making, etc. For more information: www.kittyhawk.com. (second or third weekend in May)*

ROGALLO KITE FESTIVAL

***Nags Head** - Jockey's Ridge State Park. Honoring Francis Rogallo, inventor of the flexible wing and resident of the Outer Banks. The festival takes place atop Jockey's Ridge State Park. Across the street at the Kitty Hawk Kites store there are kids activities including face painting, kite making, etc. www.kittyhawk.com. (mid-June weekend)*

KITES WITH LIGHTS

***Nags Head** - Jockey's Ridge State Park. Kids can get their picture taken with Santa* *each day at Kitty Hawk Kites. On Saturday, come see the kites with lights display on top of Jockey's Ridge State Park at sunset. Christmas carols, hot apple cider and cookies served. www.kittyhawk.com. (Saturday after Thanksgiving)*

KITTY HAWK KITES EASTER EGGSTRAVAGANZA

***Nags Head** - www.kittyhawkkites.com. Kite making games, chalk coloring contests, and surprise visits from Wil-Bear and friends. 2,000 toy-filled plastic eggs are waiting to be found. Easter Bunny visit. (Saturday before Easter)*

OUTER BANKS PIRATE FESTIVAL

***Nags Head** - MP 12.5, Kitty Hawk Kites, Nags Head. Appearances by pirates. The main event is on Saturday with an entire day of pirate appearances, games and stories. For more information and schedule of events visit www.outerbankspiratefestival.com FREE, some activities have fee. (few days mid-Aug)*

OCRACOKE ISLAND / LIGHTHOUSE

Ocracoke - *27960. www.ocracoke-nc.com.*

Ocracoke is a small fishing village lined with small hotels, down-home restaurants and quiet residents. Several public beaches dot the area. One may also catch a glimpse of the wild ponies that call the island home. Ocracoke Island was known to be a hideout of the infamous pirate, Blackbeard, who lost his head on the island in the 1700s. Local legend says that he still roams the island in search of it. Built in 1823, the OCRACOKE LIGHTHOUSE is the oldest North Carolina lighthouse and the second oldest lighthouse in the United States. The 76-foot high structure is also the shortest among the North Carolina beacons. Visitors are invited to tour the grounds surrounding the lighthouse; however, the structure itself is not open to the public. Ocracoke Island can only be reached by ferry.

OCRACOKE/ NORTH CAROLINA FERRIES

Ocracoke - *27960. Phone: (800) BY-FERRY. www.ncferry.org. Hours: See or call about schedule. Varies on season and weather. Make reservations. Admission: FREE for link to Hatteras. Nominal charge for Cedar Island to Ocracoke. Generally 15.00 per vehicle-one way. Reservations required for the ferries from Ocracoke. Note: There are vending machines (soda, coffee and snacks) on the fee ferry. Restrooms on board. The long rides also have arcade games. Restroom facilities are available at all ferry terminals and on all ferry vessels. Pets are permitted on the ferries as long as they are either in the vehicle or on a leash.*

We suggest bringing along some travel games to play.

North Carolina boasts approximately 10 one-way ferry passages. Once on the ferry, guests can either relax in the comfort of their own vehicle or walk aroundthe deck of the ship. This provides an amazing chance to take photos as well as meet other passengers along the way. Gaggles of seagulls dance and dive along the wake of the traveling ship. Dolphins often follow playfully, hoping for a handout or even more attention from their adoring fans.

Starting in the most northern part of the state, the first ferry is a transport from Knotts Island to Currituck. Locals use it as others would the subway. The ferries even transport school buses with students to and from school each day. The next step along the ferry journey is from Hatteras to Ocracoke Island. Although only a 45-minute journey, the route is reminiscent of sailors' journeys long ago when they ventured into seas undiscovered. Leaving Ocracoke, the longest ferry ride along the NC Coast, guests may go atop the boat to be greeted with coffee, video games and vending machines. The two-hour-plus ride leaves you no choice but to relax and enjoy the sound of the waves. We set up chairs and played travel games on top of our large cooler - only interrupted by an occasional seagull looking for a snack.

PORTMOUTH ISLAND ATV TOURS

Ocracoke - ***Jolly Roger Marina & Restaurant (Hwy 12) 27960. Phone: (252) 928-4484. https://portsmouthislandatv.com/. Admission: $90.00 per person, max. 6/ tour. Ages 4+. Tours: Either 8:00am-Noon or 1:00-5:00pm (April-November).***

"Discover an Island Frozen in Time" with this tour company and visit some secret spots. Tours begin with a 20-minute boat ride from Silver Lake Harbor to Portsmouth Island where you will discover the historical settlement that was once a thriving port town with over 685 residents in 1860. On the beach you can discover excellent shorebird and dolphin watching, sea turtle tracks and other fascinating seashore creatures. Wear your bathing suits for a dip in the ocean and they'll supply the shell bags for the best shelling on the Outer Banks.

BATTLE OF PLYMOUTH LIVING HISTORY WEEKEND

Plymouth - Port-O-Plymouth Museum, 302 E. Water Street. (252) 793-1377 or http://portoplymouthmuseum.org/events-3/living-history-weekend/ This weekend highlights the Civil War Battle of Plymouth in 1864 and was not only the state's largest battle but also the last major Southern victory of the war. In the museum, view bullet shells and artifacts collected, as well as a 3/8 scale, 63-foot replica of the CSS Albemarle. Outside, they'll have artillery drills, boat rides and a battle reenactment on Sunday. Adult Admission, FREE for children. (last weekend in April)

DISMAL SWAMP CANAL VISITOR CENTER & STATE NATURAL AREA

South Mills - ***2356 Highway 17 North (3 miles south of the VA/NC border) 27976. Phone: (252) 771-8333. http://dismalswampwelcomecenter.com/ Hours: Monday-Saturday 9:00am-5:00pm, Sunday 1-5pm. Admission: FREE. Note: Gift Shop. Nature walks are available at the Great Dismal Swamp National Wildlife Refuge, approximately 40 miles from the Visitor Center.***

The historic Swamp Canal Visitors Center is the only such center that can be accessed by either car or boat. It connects the Chesapeake Bay in Virginia and the Albemarle Sound in North Carolina. The Swamp supports a variety of mammals, including otter, bats, raccoon, mink, gray and red foxes, and gray squirrel. White-tailed deer are common, and black bear and bobcat also inhabit the area. Three species of poisonous snakes are found here - cottonmouth, canebrake rattler, and the more common copperhead - along with 18 non-poisonous species. Yellow-bellied and spotted turtles are commonly seen, and an additional 56 species of turtles, lizards, salamanders, frogs, and toads have been observed on the Refuge. It may sound creepy to spend the day in a swamp, but oh, how much wildlife your kids will get to see - firsthand.

MATTAMUSKEET WILDLIFE REFUGE

Swan Quarter - ***38 Mattamuskeet Road/ US 94 & US 264 (on Hwy 94) 27885. Phone: (252) 926-4021. www.fws.gov/refuge/Mattamuskeet/ Hours: Daylight hours only. Admission: FREE.***

Established primarily as a resting and breeding area for migratory birds, the area consists of over 66,000 acres of water, salt marsh land and forested wetlands. Mattamuskeet and Swan Quarter NWR lie in the middle of the Atlantic Flyway and provide a valuable wintering area for the waterfowl using this migration route which extends from Canada southward.

Thousands of tundra swans make the area their winter home.

Thousands of Canada geese, snow geese, tundra swan and 22 species of ducks winter on the refuge annually. The Refuges also provides habitat for endangered species such as the bald eagle and peregrine falcon. Deer, bobcats, otters, black bear, 240 species of birds and other wildlife species are common to the area. The refuge areas are open to the public for wildlife viewing, canoeing, hunting and fishing. The endangered bald eagle may be observed during the fall, winter and early spring.

GOOSE CREEK STATE PARK

Washington - ***2190 Camp Leach Road 27889. www.ncparks.gov/Visit/parks/gocr/main.php. Phone: (252) 923-2191. Hours: Daily 8:00am to sunset. Admission: FREE. Fee charged for camping. Educators: hands-on wetland wonders:www.ncparks.gov/sites/default/files/ncparks/37/Goose%20Creek%20EELE.pdf***

Nature beckons you to the marsh and swamp along the borders on the Pamlico River and Goose Creek. Visitors can canoe the unhurried creeks, fish on the River shores or learn about these wetlands at the Environmental Education visitor Center. In the Discovery Room, aquariums are set up to simulate a hardwood swamp and brackish marsh. Mounts, replicas and animal signs, both on tabletops and in pullout drawers, allow close-up study and encourage hands-on learning. The Discovery Room also has a bird observation station with an excellent view of the bird feeder outside. Sit down and wait to see which birds stop by. In addition, a five-minute film is available to introduce visitors to the park and its creatures. Birders and hikers are welcome to explore the eight miles of well-marked hiking trails.

NORTH CAROLINA ESTUARIUM

Washington - ***223 Water Street (on the Pamlico River, downtown) 27889. Phone: (252) 948-0000. www.facebook.com/ncestuarium Hours: Tuesday-Saturday 10:00am-4:00pm. Admission: $2.00-$4.00 (age 6+). Tours: River Roving, a FREE pontoon boat tour of the Pamlico-Tar River waterways (Ages 6 & up. Reservations required.) Educators: Ask for Scavenger Hunts. The Estuarium will supply clip boards and pencils for use during the visit.***

An estuary is formed where fresh water and salt water mix together. Situated on the waterfront, this estuarium tells the story of the state's sounds and coastal rivers, using the Pamlico/Tar River Esuary, the second largest in the nation behind Chesapeake Bay, as an example. Begin by watching the introductory film about the Pamlico region. Art and science exhibits feature living aquariums, historic artifacts, antique boats, hands-on displays, a film, plus a river tour. Program topics include Black Bears, Birds, Blue Crabs,

Reptiles and Amphibians, or Wetlands. The buttons, gadgets, colors and sounds make the estuarium a fun and educational spot for children. Watch tubes drip water in different concentrations of salt to represent the amounts of salt in the ocean, brackish water, estuaries vs. fresh water. Why is the wind so important in estuaries? Like chemistry? Try experiments and read gauges from samples of water collected just beyond the docks.

CASHIE WETLANDS WALK & MINI ZOO

Windsor - ***101 York Street 27983. www.windsorbertiechamber.com/16.html. Phone: (919) 794-5553. Hours: Monday-Friday 8:00am-8:00pm, Weekends 9:00am-8:00pm. Winter Hours: Daily 8:00am-5:00pm. Admission: FREE.***

The Zoo features over 30 different species of foreign and domestic animals including llamas, donkeys, goats, rheas, a bird house with all types of birds including turkeys, pea fowl, peacocks and Polish hens. Across the street from the Zoo is the Cashie Wetlands Walk. The Walk has an 1800 foot handicapped accessible walkway to the Cashie River and features a fishing pier at its end. The walk takes visitors to the edge of the Cashie River, which is 20 miles long and as deep as 80 feet. The observation deck allows views of several different species of endangered waterfowl and other swampland animals in their natural habitats. Canoes available, too.

HOPE PLANTATION

Windsor - ***132 Hope House Road (four miles northwest of town on NC 308) 27983. Phone: (252) 794-3140. www.hopeplantation.org Tours: 11am-4:30pm daily (mid-March thru late December). $12.00 adult, $11.00 senior (65+), $8.00 students. Educators: Lesson units for Fourth and Eighth grade curriculums available upon request. Heritage Day and Living History Days.***

Tour the authentically furnished c. 1803 Hope Plantation, home of Governor David Stone, the 1763 King-Bazemore House, and the Samuel Cox House. The Hope was the centerpiece of a completely self-sustaining plantation. At Hope they operated a water powered grist mill, a still, a saw mill, a blacksmith shop, a cooper's shop and houses for spinning and weaving. His farm lands produced wheat, corn, oats, rye, flax, and cotton, for which he had a cotton machine. On his pastures he raised cattle, sheep and horses, in his woods he raised hogs, while his forests produced timber for the sawmill.

Walk the plantation grounds and the Hope Forest nature trails. The modern Heritage Center features regional exhibits and annual celebrations of Native American and African-American heritage. No fee to roam.

A CHRISTMAS TRADITION....AT HISTORIC HOPE

Windsor - Hope Plantation. The Mansion and the King Bazemore House are decorated for the season & open to everyone by donation. Holiday punch & cookies in the Heritage Center. There will be special musical treats, so be sure to stay on... (first Sunday in December)

ROANOKE RIVER NATIONAL WILDLIFE REFUGE

Windsor - ***27983. Phone: (252) 794-5326. www.fws.gov/roanokeriver/index.html. Hours: Daily during daylight hours. Admission: FREE. Fee for camping.***

The refuge is home to animals such as deer, otter, beaver, muskrat and black bear. There are more than 191 species of migrating birds that find seasonal homes here. The largest inland heron rookery in North Carolina is on refuge. The informal trail tracts are open to the public for hiking and birdwatching - although, some of the trails are only accessible by boat.

Travel Journal & Notes:

Chapter 4
South Central
North Carolina

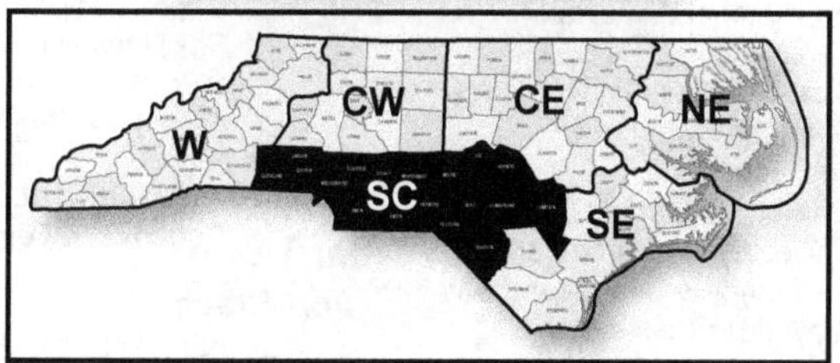

Lillington
- Raven Rock State Park

Lumberton
- Exploration Station
- Robeson Planetarium & Science Center

Lumberton (Pembroke)
- Museum Of The Native American Resource Center

Midland
- Reed Gold Mine State Historic Site

Mount Gilead
- Town Creek Indian Mound State Historic Site

Waxhaw
- Museum Of The Waxhaw

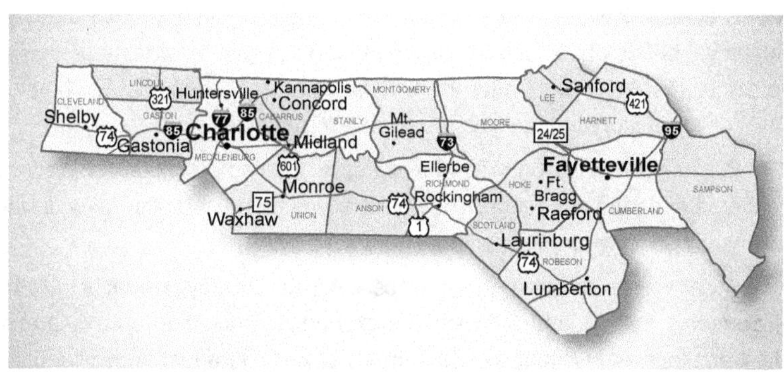

Travel Journal & Notes:

A Quick Tour of our Hand-Picked Favorites Around...

South Central North Carolina

In Charlotte, you'll find rides that go in circles at **Carowinds**, or you can slow the pace with some indoor time at the **Levine Museum of the New South** in downtown Charlotte. What is the "New South?" Visitors enjoy an interactive, hands-on experience as they tour 6 different "environments" within the exhibit that begin right after the Civil War up to present day. Each space tells a different story but the kids must "unlock" the clues.

Need to refuel? Try lunch at a **Fuel Pizza**, located in old 50s gas stations, the theme and food are so fun! They have a kids menu and offer "play dough" while you wait for your food or Pizza Tour.

When you're finished there, race over to nearby **Lowe's Motor Speedway** for a complete NASCAR experience, including an exhilarating race track tour and visits to neighboring race team garages. Wait 'til you see what's inside those transport trailers!

What's your wing-span? Check it out at the **Carolina Raptor Center.** Meet one turkey vulture who likes to untie shoe laces. Another turkey vulture at the center, is a movie star. Did you know Bald Eagles nests can be as large as a small car?

Head a litte further east on SR 24/25 to Midland. The Old North State led the nation in gold production until 1848, when the great rush to California began. The gold business fizzled out here. But you can experience some of the excitement of days gone by at **Reed Gold Mine**. Learn how to pan for gold and explore a real gold mine!

Spend an afternoon in Fayetteville at the **Airborne & Special Operations Museum**, which honors the shared history of airborne and special operations soldiers at Fort Bragg. Parachutes dropping out of the sky, soldiers in bunkers, motion theatre and simulators make the drama of military action very real.

Sites and attractions are listed in order by City, Zip Code, and Name. Symbols indicated represent: ☐ Restaurants ☐ Lodging

MALCOLM BLUE FESTIVAL

***Aberdeen** - Malcolm Blue Farm. School Children's Day to learn what daily life and work was like in the 19th century. Some of the crafts and skills demonstrated are pottery, basket making, woodworking, blacksmithing, spinning, weaving, soap and candle making and fringe tying. Farm animals fill the stable; pony and wagon rides are available. Folk and country musicians and dancers entertain during the three-day event. In the meadow, Civil War reenactment troops are encamped and steam engines are demonstrated. www.facebook.com/MalcolmBlueFarmNC (last weekend of September)*

OLD FASHIONED CHRISTMAS

***Aberdeen** - Malcolm Blue Farm. Open House with musicians, carolers, traditional food, 19th century children's games, quilters, cornhusk angels, garlands of popcorn and cranberries. (second Saturday in December)*

SC

MORROW MOUNTAIN STATE PARK

Albemarle ***- 49104 Morrow Mountain Road (NC 24 east and veer right on NC 740. After about six miles, turn right on Morrow Mountain Road) 28001. Phone: (704) 982-4402. www.ncparks.gov/Visit/parks/momo/main.php. Hours: Daily 8:00am - dusk. Exhibit Hall open 10:00am-5:00pm. Admission: FREE. Fee for boat rentals, cabins, camping and swimming.***

These steep, rugged hills - unusual topography for the area - form a stark contrast with the rolling countryside of the piedmont plateau. The park offers an exhibit hall and a historical site. The hall includes exhibits about Native Americans, plant and animal communities, early explorers, and rocks and minerals. Visit the homestead of a 19th-century doctor, Dr. Francis Kron, the first physician in the area. His home, doctor's office and infirmary, and greenhouse were reconstructed and appear today much as they did in 1870. Recreation is plentiful in and around the waters of Lake Tillery and the Pee Dee River. Fishing, boating and swimming are popular pastimes. Nature lovers can pick from miles of trails to travel on foot or horseback. And for those who want to stay and take it all in, cabins and camping are available.

BUGGY FESTIVAL

***Carthage** - (910) 947-2331. www.thebuggyfestival.com. For more than half a century, this town had the largest buggy factory in the nation during a time when carriages were essential to life in rural areas. The town celebrates with an all buggy parade, food, live entertainment and fun. (first or second weekend in May)*

CHARLOTTE SPORTS

CHARLOTTE HORNETS - Time Warner Cable Arena. Their offense is fast paced, exciting, and they are willing to scrap for every point. The arena has colorful exhibits and displays plus a kid's interactive center. www.nba.com/hornets. Tickets start at $15.00.

CHARLOTTE HURRICANES - Charlotte is known as the birthplace of pro hockey in the South. Many family-oriented events occur monthly. www.nhl.com/hurricanes/. PNC Arena.

CHARLOTTE KNIGHTS - www.charlotteknights.com. The AAA affiliate of the Chicago White Sox plays games in Knight Stadium, just over the border in South Carolina (off I-77). Meet their mascot, Homer the Dragon. Inexpensive general seats, a playground, post-game fireworks, and even a miniature golf course round out the fun for kids. BB&T Ballpark.

FUEL PIZZA

***Charlotte** - Need to refuel? Try lunch at Fuel Pizza. www.fuelpizza.com. Located in old 50s gas stations, the theme and food are so fun! They have a kids menu and offer play dough (real pizza dough), crayons and fun sheets. Try an Extreme Fuel, Whole Engine or Lasagna Pizza with a side of wings and garlic knots. They give Pizza Tours at some of their eight locations (mornings by appointment).*

CAROLINA PANTHERS

Charlotte - ***800 S. Mint Street (Bank of America Stadium) 28202. Phone: (704) 358-7800 tickets. www.panthers.com.***

Begin your game day experience on The Catwalk. Located outside the North Gate, all fans can enjoy free games, music, entertainment, and appearances by the TopCats, Sir Purr and former Panthers players. Activities begin 2 1/2 hours prior to kickoff and conclude at kickoff. The Carolina Panthers mascot, Sir Purr has been a beloved fixture of football in the Carolinas since the team's first season in 1995. Armed with nimble feet, a great smile and one big shaking belly, this cat is best known for his silly antics and creative skits that can be seen on game day.

CAROLINA PANTHERS STADIUM TOURS

Charlotte - ***Bank of America Stadium (meet at the Ticket Office, between East and South gates on Mint Street) 28202. www.panthers.com/stadium/tours.html. Phone: (704) 358-7538. Admission: $6.00 adult, $5.00 senior (55+), $4.00 child (5-17). Tours: Wednesdays at 10:00am. Fridays at 10:00am and Noon. Public tours do not require a reservation but are limited to the first 25 people that arrive.***

Tours of the Bank of America Stadium for the general public are offered each Wednesday, beginning at 10:00am. See the Panthers' Locker Room, Weight Room, Training Room, Luxury Suites, the Stadium Bowl, Practice Fields and even the Press Box. Behind-the-scenes stadium tours are the insider way to learn more about your favorite teams and their "workplace."

DISCOVERY PLACE

Charlotte - ***301 North Tryon Street (I-77 north exit 11, Brookshire Freeway. Bear right to Church St/Tryon St exit. Follow signs) 28202. Phone: (704) 372-6261. www.discoveryplace.org. Hours: Monday-Friday 9:00am-4:00pm, Saturday 9:00am-5:00pm, Sunday Noon-5:00pm. Closed Thanksgiving Day, Christmas Eve, Christmas Day and Easter Sunday. Admission: $15.00-$19.00 (age 2+). IMAX extra $9.00-$10.00. Combo tickets offer discounts.***

One of the top hands-on science facilities in the nation, this unique center provides ever-changing and entertaining facilities such as an IMAX, a 3D Theatre, planetarium, Life Lab, Think it Up, Machine Shop (with giant levers), a wonderful aquarium w/ touch pools and a Rain Forest. In Science Theatre check out the show "Sparks Anyone?" or unravel the double helix or meet microbes in THEM. Reach out and touch a simulated tornado, check out the weather or view a gem collection while exploring video presentations and hands-on exhibits. Get a scoop of liquid nitrogen ice cream made in minutes right before your eyes. Explore the heart exhibit, with its giant walk-through heart or check out the giant eyeball. Build and apply high tech skills at other spaces. Kidscience is the younger version of the big kids experiments (ages 0-7). We promise stimulation abounds here!

LEVINE MUSEUM OF THE NEW SOUTH

Charlotte - ***200 East 7th Street (I-277 North - exit 9B - to the College Street exit. Take College St. to 7th Street. or I-77 exit 10B) 28202. Phone: (704) 333-1887. www.museumofthenewsouth.org. Hours: Monday-Saturday 10:00am-5:00pm, Sunday Noon-5:00pm. Closed Thanksgiving, Christmas and New Years. Admission: $10.00 adult, $8.00 senior (62+) and $6.00 student (6-18). Half off Admission Sundays. Note: Free 2 hour parking is available in the Seventh Street Station.***

So what is the New South? Travel through the exhibit "Cotton Fields to Skyscrapers" to discover how the New South was reinvented from field to factory to finance. Visitors tour 6 different "environments" within the exhibit: Step inside a one-room tenant farmer's house; Run a hand through a pile of seed cotton, then card, spin and weave cotton thread; Listen to the churning of the cotton mill; Play checkers on the front porch of a mill house; Sit in Good Samaritans Hospital Chapel, one of the first African-American hospitals in the South; Walk down main street and try on a hat in an early Belk department store; or, Sit at a lunch counter and hear personal accounts from local sit-in leaders. You can't really learn here unless you engage - we liked the fact that the kids had to touch things in order to understand what they were.

MINT MUSEUMS OF ART, CRAFT & DESIGN

Charlotte - ***2730 Randolph Road/ 500 South Tryon Street (I- 77 Northbound: Take the Trade Street/Fifth Street exit 10. Turn right on Trade Street, head east toward downtown. Follow signs) 28202. Phone: (704) 337-2000. www.mintmuseum.org. Hours: Tuesday-Saturday 11:00am-6:00pm, Sunday 1:00-5:00pm. Closed major holidays. Admission: $15.00 adult, $10.00 senior (65+) and college student, $6.00 youth (5-17). Certain weekdays offer FREE admission times.***

- MINT MUSEUM OF ART: North Carolina's first art museum features many famous American and European paintings. The major focus traces American art including the art of Native Americans and other cultures that influenced the shaping of American culture from pre-Colombian times through Colonial times to the present.
- MINT MUSEUM OF CRAFT + DESIGN: This museum takes a look at the evolution of crafts and how the changing style of the artifacts produced by artisans reflects the various ages in which these objects were created. Unique objects include the traditional craft mediums of ceramic, fiber, glass, metal, and wood. Adult-child workshops introduce parents and young children to an exhibition, and finish with an art activity. Family Days include scavenger hunts.

CHARLOTTE TROLLEY

Charlotte - ***1507 Camden Road (I-77 S to West Blvd. Exit 9A. Depot at Atherton Mill, Historic South End) 28203. Phone: (704) 375-0850. https://charlottenc.***

gov/cats/rail/cityLYNX/Pages/Riding-Streetcar.aspx. Hours: Tuesday-Saturday 1:00-5:00pm. Carolina Panthers Game Days: 10:00am until one hour after game ends. The Car Barn, Museum & Gift Shop are open during the same hours, and admission is free. Tours: A roundtrip trolley ride through Historic South End takes about 20 minutes. Riders may board the trolley at any of the stops along the route, but most visitors join from the starting point at Atherton Mill. Trolleys leave the Barn on the hour and the half-hour. Parking at Atherton Mill is free.

Ring, Ring, Ring Goes the Trolley. A trip along the trolley route will take you past some of the most important and interesting sites of Charlotte's history, from the 19th Century right into the 21st. Drive by an original cotton mill or the factory that coined the phrase "air-conditioning". The trolley runs over the Westin Hotel's parking lot and through the Charlotte Convention Center via a 250-foot long tunnel that allows streetcars to rumble by without disrupting hotel guests. Volunteer docents, riding the cars during peak tourist hours, explain the role of the electric streetcar system and offer a guided tour of the personalities and landmarks associated with the trolley corridor. Get the lowdown on some of the funny, little-known stories about Charlotte's past.

CHARLOTTE NATURE MUSEUM

Charlotte - ***1638 Sterling Road (I-77 exit 6A. Bear right on Woodlawn, heading east. Left on Park Rd. Right on Princeton. Left on Sterling. Adjacent to Freedom Park) 28209. Phone: (704) 372-6261. https://nature.discoveryplace.org/ Hours: Tuesday-Friday 9:00am-4:00pm, Saturday 9:00am-5:00pm, Sunday Noon-5:00pm. Admission: $8.00 (age 2+).***

The Charlotte Nature Museum is an urban science center that exhibits the animals and plants of the Piedmont including an ever-changing Butterfly Garden. The child-oriented museum features numerous hands-on exhibits that relate to natural history, as well as a live animal room, a puppet theatre, and a scenic outdoor nature trail. Our Big Backyard allows visitors to splash through a stream, dig through dirt, climb through secret tunnels and discover the world underground. The Nature Dome takes on the ambiance of a night in the forest around a campfire as Grandpa Tree tells about the nocturnal creatures. Insect Alley has games, videos and interactives and serves as a great primer for the Butterfly Garden. Make sure you meet the guard over the butterflies – Lovey Dovey or Queen Charlotte, the groundhog. Their Grandpa Tree room is the best show of its kind we've ever seen!

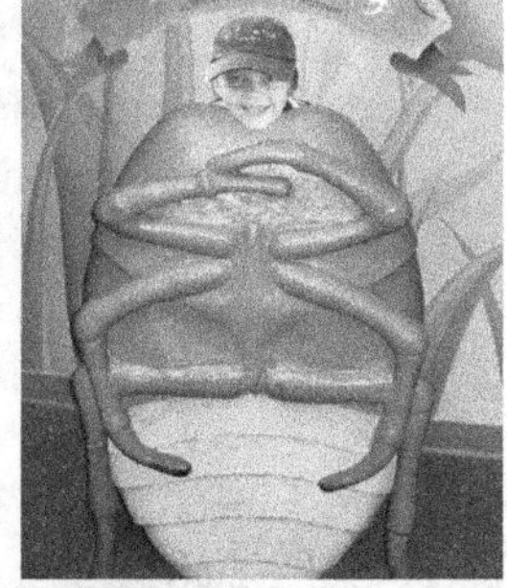

US NATIONAL WHITEWATER CENTER

Charlotte - *820 Hawfield Road (I-85 south to exit 29 (Sam Wilson Rd) 28214. Phone: (704) 391-3900. www.usnwc.org. Hours: Open daylight hours. Courses closed to public for competitions (spectators allowed). Trails not open during poor weather conditions. See website for current status. Admission: Trails are FREE. AllSport Pass runs $59.00 adult (age 10+), $49.00 child (9 & under). Additional fees for gear or mountain bike rentals. Note: Rivers Edge grill w/ panoramic view of rapids and wide selection of entrees and light fare.*

Eco Caching here gives explorers an opportunity to get into the woods. Use GPS-receivers with programmed treasure hunting destinations to log each find in your own "passport."

Come see future Olympians from around the world compete - or, try some Class III/IV rapids yourself (ages 12 and up)! Cross the Catawba River and explore the world's largest manmade recirculating river with multiple channels. It's a sight to see - rapids in the middle of lowland Piedmont. Your tweens and teens will love the challenge of the rough rapids, while the younger set may opt for whitewater kayaking/flatwater courses for ages eight and up. They have one of the largest outdoor climbing facilities in the US and a unique ropes course and zip line, too. Not into the extreme sports? Try their seasonal bike or hike trails surrounding the facility.

SC

CHARLOTTE MUSEUM OF HISTORY

Charlotte - *3500 Shamrock Drive (I-85 N to exit 41. Turn Right onto Sugar Creek Rd. Bear Right onto Eastway Dr. Turn Left onto Shamrock. Follow Sugar Creek for approx. 3 miles). 28215. Phone: (704) 374-1565. www.charlottemuseum.org. Hours: Tuesday-Saturday 11:00am-5:00pm. Closed major holidays. Admission: $10.00 adult, $7.00 senior/student (6-17). Tours: Docents dressed in historic 18th century costume guide tours are offered daily Tuesday -Saturday every hour beginning at noon. Educators: The Hands-on-History Room provides activities based on current exhibits and colonial life.*

Located on the homestead site of Hezekiah Alexander, this museum displays artifacts and dioramas that relate to American and local history. The 18th century gallery takes you back to a time when this region was still rugged frontier. Long before the first European settlers came to the Piedmont, a group of Native American tribes inhabited the region. A visit to the 19th century gallery begins with the discovery of gold in the region, represented by a model gold mine. The cotton industry grew substantially during this time and Mecklenburg became the third largest cotton-producing county in the State. The role of slave labor and local participation in the Civil War is here, too. In addition to the House, the grounds offer elements of 18th Century life in the kitchen, herb garden, and springhouse.

CHARLOTTE SYMPHONY ORCHESTRA

Charlotte - ***201 South College Street, Suite 110 (concerts held in Belk Theater) 28244. Phone: (704) 972-2000. www.charlottesymphony.org. Sept thru July.***

The largest and most active professional performing arts organization in the area, this symphony orchestra features over 100 professional musicians performing beautiful music from September through July. Lollipops concerts - Sometimes just music, but sometimes add in a movie or theatrical act. Shorter, funnier performances for youth with a lollypop treat at the end.

MARRIOTT COURTYARD CHARLOTTE - UNIVERSITY

Charlotte - 28262. 333 West Harris Blvd. (I-85 exit 45A), (704) 549-4888. Rooms feature seasonal outdoor comfortable pool area, indoor jacuzzi, and moderate-sized rooms. They are close to the speedway and racing shops. www.marriott.com/hotels/travel/cltun-courtyard-charlotte-university-research-park/. Nightly rates from $99.00. ☐

SC

CAROWINDS & CAROLINA HARBOR

Charlotte - ***14523 Carowinds Blvd. (I-77 to SC exit 90, at the NC/SC border. Park is 15 minutes south of Uptown Charlotte & 15 north of Rock Hill, SC) 28273. Phone: (704) 588-2600. www.carowinds.com. Hours: Weekends (mid-March to mid-October). Daily (late May to Mid-August). Park generally opens at 10:00am, closes from 6:00-10:00pm. Waterpark is open on public operating days from Mid-May through Labor Day, hours vary. Admission: ~$60.00 (over 48") and ~$45.00 (senior - 62+ and child - ages 3-6 or under 48"). Save $10.00-$20.00 per person at twilight or online bundles. Note: Campground near premises is a budget-friendly option for many families traveling to the area. Snoopy's Starlight Nighttime spectacular light sound and motion shows.***

The premiere 105 acre water and theme park in the Carolinas, this park features over 100 state-of-the-art rides, shows, and movie-themed experiences for all ages, as well as a Zoom Zone children's area, and Carolina Harbor water park. PEANUTS™ includes two rapids or waterfall rides, Boo Blasters, and a junior inverted roller coaster. Snoopy vs. Red Baron - all ages can steer their course swooping up and down, weaving side to side, gliding thru the air; and the PEANUTS™ Pirates – all ages can navigate rotating mini-pirate ships pivoting, twisting and turning a full 180 degrees while sloping up and down along the terrain. Several rides are for the preschool set, other mini-coasters for the preteens.

Throughout the park, notice one thing: the name of the ride pretty much tells the story. Example: Hurler (stomach leaves the body); Cyclone (loopy); Richochet (jerky side-to-side motion). The waterpark area was nice and compact but beware of pre-summer weekends when the water feels cool for awhile. Bondi Beach is the park's Wave Pool.

CANDLEWOOD SUITES CHARLOTTE-ARROWOOD

Charlotte - 28273. 7924 Forest Pine Dr. (704) 527-8889. www.staybridge.com. We'd recommend staying overnight at the Arrowood exit off I-77. Just a few miles from Carowinds park. All suites have kitchens (equipped) and free high speed internet.

The property offers guests a convenience store, sport court, heated outdoor pool, BBQ pavilion, DVD rentals and a library. Oh, and the (hot/cold) items on the deluxe breakfast bar were good. Rates from $105.00 ☐

SC

MCDOWELL NATURE CENTER & PRESERVE

Charlotte - *15222 York Road (I-77 Exit 90 onto Carowinds Blvd. Go west approx. 3 miles to Hwy 49 (York Road). Turn left on Hwy 49 and travel 4 miles) 28278. Phone: (704) 588-5224. www.mecknc.gov/ParkandRec/StewardshipServices/NatureCenters/Pages/McDowell.aspx Hours: Nature Center: Monday-Saturday 9:00am-5:00pm, Sunday 1:00-5:00pm. Preserve: Daily 7:00am-sunset. Admission: FREE. Note: Mountain bikes are permitted only on paved roads within the preserve.*

Serving as the gateway to the 1,108 acre McDowell Outdoor Exploring Preserve, this Outdoor Exploring center and preserve has numerous features including live native animals, an outdoor amphitheater, an exhibit hall, educational programs, a habitat garden with butterfly gardens, numerous picnic decks and tables, seven miles of hiking trails, fishing, canoeing (rentals), and a 58 site primitive and RV family campground. The Backyard Habitat Garden includes bird feeding stations, butterfly gardens, garden pond, and a demonstration compost area. The Four Seasons Trail, a 1-mile loop located near the nature center, is paved and handicap accessible.

600 FESTIVAL

Charlotte - Uptown. www.600festival.com. (704) 455-6814. Race week is under way when thousands of fans pack the streets for the Parade, a colorful collection of NASCAR drivers, show cars, marching bands, clowns, floats and local celebrities. The streets of town showcase motorsports with non-stop entertainment on three stages, appearances by top NEXTEL Cup drivers, a large assembly of NASCAR show cars and simulators. (week before Memorial Day)

BATTLE AT BOST GRIST MILL

Charlotte (Concord) - *Bost Grist Mill. www.bostgristmill.com. Surrounding the mill, re-enactors and visitors set up and walk around a Civil War camp. Real horses, tents and cannons are used to recreate an encampment scene. Vendors on site serving Breakfast, lunch, and various foods all day long. Admission. (weekend after Labor Day)*

A TOUCH OF YESTERDAY

Charlotte (Concord) - *Bost Grist Mill. www.bostgristmill.com Come and take a guided tour of Bost Grist Mill and see the 1700lb stone grind corn into cornmeal and grits. Learn the history of the mill and see articles dating back to the 1800 located around the grounds. They grind periodically throughout both days during the show. Door Prizes, Kiddy Tractor Pull, Gold Panning, Games, Lots of Tractors and equipment, live music, food, handmade crafts and much, much more. (first weekend in October)*

BACKING UP CLASSICS CAR MUSEUM

Charlotte (Concord) - ***4545 Concord Parkway S (just one mile north of Lowe's Motor Speedway entrance) 28027. www.backingupclassics.com. Phone: (704) 788-9500. Hours: Open daily during gift shop business hours. Monday, Tuesday, Thursday, Friday and Saturday.***

Camaros, Cadillacs and Corvettes (plus many more)…are displayed as you stroll down a memory lane of fine motorcars. A fascinating collection of antique, classic and race cars. Just 1 minute from racing mecca, they, too, have loads of NASCAR and auto-related gift items.

GREAT WOLF LODGE WATERPARK RESORT

Charlotte (Concord) - ***10175 Weddington Road Exn NW (near Lowes Speedway, 20 miles north of Charlotte). 28027. Phone: (704) 549-8206. www.greatwolf.com.***

Plunge, splash or float at their gigantic indoor waterpark, reserved exclusively for guests. Unwind in any spacious suite, designed to capture the atmosphere of the Northwoods. Thrill-seekers flock to the water raft rides or the wave pool. Mellow guests go with the flow in the endless lazy river. And, zero-depth entry pools and kiddie slides provide a safe, dedicated space for the little ones still getting their sea legs. The waterpark is staffed by 100 certified lifeguards. Be sure to get the full Great Wolf experience during your stay: Visit the Elements Spa for a massage, play in Northern Lights Arcade, or hang out in the teens-oriented Gr8 gaming area. Two restaurants are on the property. The resort offers 10 different styles of suites, starting at $179/night. Basic suites accommodate up to six people and feature refrigerators and microwaves for light meal preps (save $$!). ☐ ☐ ______________________________

CHARLOTTE MOTOR SPEEDWAY TOURS

Charlotte (Concord) - ***5555 Concord Parkway South (US 29 North) 28027. Phone: (800) 455-FANS (tickets). www.lowesmotorspeedway.com. Tours: Tours are available daily (on non-event days) from 9:30am-3:30pm (beginning at 1:30pm on Sunday). Tours run one hour later in the summer. (children who weigh 40 lbs. or less must be in a car seat). Tickets of $10.00-$12.00 per person are available at the Speedway Gift Shop (704) 455-3223. Go to the back of the gift shop to purchase them and sign waivers. (If a child needs a car seat, please provide your own) Note: Several go-kart speed racing tracks are nearby including NASCAR Speedpark (www.nascarspeedpark.com). Carolina Christmas drive thru light park each holiday season. Kids can join the Little Luggies club.***

Located 12 miles northeast of Uptown Charlotte (the heart of stock car racing), Lowe's Motor Speedway is truly the "Mecca of Motorsports". The speedway annually hosts NASCAR Sprint Cup series, Nationwide and Truck Series races; gigantic AutoFairs, a 10-week Legends Car Summer Shootout Series, stock car driving schools and a variety of annual events at The Dirt Track.

FEEL THE THRILL TOUR: Your grand tour of LMS includes a close-up look at areas that are usually off-limits during a race. Go behind the scenes to the Garage, travel down pit road where every second counts, and take a picture in the same Victory Circle that has hosted the greatest drivers in NASCAR history. Learn about the new Speedway lights built from an idea learned from the "Field of Dreams" movie (mirrored lighting in the corn fields). View Redneck Hill and Spotters Railing. The highlight of the tour is a fast (60-70 mph!) van ride around Charlotte's 1.5-mile oval where you will experience the full-tilt action of 24-degree banks! A thrilling tour for any race or speed enthusiasts!

ROUSH FENWAY RACING MUSEUM

Charlotte (Concord) - ***4600 Roush Place (I-85 exit 49, 10 minutes from Speedway) 28027. Phone: (704) 720-4600. www.roushfenway.com. Hours: Monday-Friday 8:30am-5:00pm. Closed at lunchtime and early on Fridays. Special extended hours during May and October race weeks. Admission: FREE.***

The team headquarters and team shops offer self-guided tour of historical photos, trophies and race vehicles from memorable events in racing history. Each of the shops has a viewing window. Sights and sounds can be seen and heard from inside the 60-seat theatre.

SEALIFE AQUARIUM

Charlotte (Concord) - ***8111 Concord Mills Parkway (I-85 exit 49 28027. Phone: (704) 720-4600. www.visitsealife.com. Hours: Monday-Friday 10:00am-6:00pm, Saturday 10:00am-8:00pm, Sunday Noon-6:00pm. Admission: $21.95 adult, $16.95 child (3-12). Online discounts.***

Ten themed zones and 250 species including sharks, rays, seahorses, sea stars, seahorses, jellyfish & more. Meet the giant Pacific Octopus, one of the ocean's cleverest creatures or the new Turtle Talks zone. Daily educational talks & feeding demonstrations. The 180 degree Ocean Tunnel and interactive Touchpool Experience are favorite areas.

HENDRICK MOTORSPORTS

Charlotte (Harrisburg) - ***4400 Papa Joe Hendrick Blvd. (I-85 exit 49 to Hwy 29 south. Right on Morehead, right on Stowe) 28075. Phone: (704) 455-3400 or (877) 467-4890. www.hendrickmotorsports.com. Hours: Monday - Friday 10:00am - 5:00pm. Saturday 10:00am-3:00pm. Periodically, the complex will close for holidays and vacations so we advise visitors to call ahead. Admission: FREE. Note: Garages are closed on Saturday. Only the store & museum is open.***

The Thrill of Victory...

This sophisticated complex provides Hendrick Motorsports with facilities to design, test and make cars and engines for all of their race teams. Visitors are also welcome to view the 15,000-square-foot Hendrick Museum and Speed Shop which showcases almost two decades of HMS racing. Special one-of-a-kind items include Rick Hendrick's very first car - a 1931 Chevrolet. At age 14, he bought this 1931 Chevrolet in a "totally stock" condition, then rebuilt it for drag racing. Items also on display include the very first production ZR1 Chevrolet Corvette; the powerful, 1,000 horsepower "Spirit of Charlotte" GTP Corvette; one of the Chevrolet Lumina racecars used in the Days of Thunder feature film staring Tom Cruise; and many other collectibles. Watch a dissected Impala SS "Car of Tomorrow" being pieced together. Even see a surviving crash vehicle and actual working shop floors. On a good day, you may be able to watch the pit crews practice in a back lot or observe the team loading up the truck for a race!

RURAL HILL CENTER OF SCOTTISH HERITAGE

***Charlotte (Huntersville)** - 4431 Neck Road (I-77 South to Exit #25) 28078. Phone: (704) 875-3113. www.ruralhill.net. Hours: Monday-Saturday 9:00am-4:00pm. Closed: Week of Thanksgiving November 18 - 24, December 23 - 31. Admission: $4.00-$6.00 (age 6+). Please note SPECIAL EVENTS have different dates, times, and admission prices from regular daily hours and admission prices. Educators: Teacher's Guides online under Teachers. Picnics and pets are allowed.*

Rural Hill Plantation is a haven for area Scots. The homestead was built by Major John and Violet Davidson, who raised ten children here and became a prosperous plantation. A reproduction home can be toured, as well as the original smoke house, ash house, well, barn, chicken coop and granary. Two old schoolhouses are on the property also. Most educational tours last 2 hours so take note of that with antsy young ones. Want to enjoy more outside? Travel down the historic Mill Lane (dating back to the 1700's) or walk through the woods on our walking trails which extend 3-4 miles around the perimeter of present day Rural Hill.

LOCH NORMAN HIGHLAND GAMES

***Charlotte (Huntersville)** - Center Of Scottish Heritage Rural Hill. World Class athletes come to compete in various competitions which include Heavy Athletics both professionally and amateurs, bag-piping, fiddle and harp, and Scottish Dance. More than 90 Scottish and Scots-Irish Clans and organizations bring their banners to demonstrate support and share family genealogy and heritage exhibits with visitors. Enjoy world renowned Celtic and Scottish bands while getting a taste of Scottish cuisine (Scotch Eggs and Meat Pies) along with other local delicacies like Carolina BBQ or Smoked Turkey Legs. Admission. (long weekend in mid-April)*

AMAZING MAIZE MAZE

***Charlotte (Huntersville)** - Center Of Scottish Heritage Rural Hill. A historical or related theme to Rural Hill is carefully chosen for each maze. This is a great opportunity for families to work together in exploring and solving the clues to make it through the maze. Admission. (Thursday-Sunday in September/October)*

SHEEP DOG TRIALS

***Charlotte (Huntersville)** - Center Of Scottish Heritage Rural Hill. More than 75 Border Collies compete. The trials are a competition in performance not conformation. The competition is based on daily tasks that the dog is asked to do on the farm. Flying Disc dog activities, tractor show, unusual livestock expo and hayride tours will be provided. Admission. (first full long weekend in November)*

ENERGY EXPLORIUM - DUKE ENERGY

Charlotte (Huntersville) - ***13339 Hagers Ferry Road (McGuire Nuclear Station) 28078. www.duke-energy.com/visitor-centers/energyexplorium.asp. Phone: (704) 875-5600. Hours: Tuesday-Friday 9:00am-5:00pm, by appt. Admission: FREE. Educators: Exhibit worksheets, lesson plans (grade appropriate) and educational backpacks are available for group visits. www.duke-energy.com/visitor-centers/ee-information-for-teachers.asp. This is a harder subject to teach so these materials may be great curriculum.***

The explorium is the facility where you can take a virtual tour of a real Nuclear Station. Here you can pretend to throw the switch, convert your own energy into enough electricity to power a TV, play computer games, or figure out how much energy you get for one dollar. Maybe watch a movie about Lake Norman or nuclear energy. Now, take some of that pent up energy outside to the mile-long nature trail along the shore of Lake Norman.

LATTA PLANTATION, HISTORIC

Charlotte (Huntersville) - ***5225 Sample Road, 28078. Phone: (704) 875-2312. www.lattaplantation.org. Hours: Grounds open: Tuesday-Saturday 10:00am-5:00pm, Sunday 1:00-5:00pm. Admission: $9.00 adult, $8.00 senior (62+) and students. Tours: Includes a 15-minute introductory video and access to the house, outbuildings, cabin, log barns, gardens, and livestock. Tours are self-guided and are supported through walking tour maps and costumed interpreters when available. House tours several times daily. Note: Historic Latta Plantation is within Latta Plantation Park, on Mountain Island Lake. The park offers hiking and horseback riding trails, canoe rentals, and fishing. Educators: Teacher Resources including vocabulary and pre- and post-test questions are available upon request. FREEBIES: old-fashioned toys and games to create are online.***

Historic Latta Plantation is a circa 1800 cotton plantation and living history farm. At the end of a country road, you see the Lattas' white two-story frame house. Enjoy wandering the grounds. See the barnyard animals (especially lambs and sheep). Visit the outbuildings, replica log house, and garden. Participate in a pre-arranged group tour led by a costumed docent and learn interesting, little-known facts about the Early Republic. Best to visit as a group or during special events. From Colonial to Revolutionary to Civil War periods - demonstrations of period cooking techniques, music, blacksmithing, basketmaking, weaving in the house and cabin, and outside war camp settings abound during event weekends...held nearly every month.

EASTER EGG HUNT

Charlotte (Huntersville) - *Latta Plantation. Children ages 1 to 10 years old can hunt for thousands of Easter eggs across the beautiful plantation grounds. (Easter Saturday or Saturday before)*

LATTA PLANTATION CHRISTMAS

Charlotte (Huntersville) - *Latta Plantation. The plantation home decorated for a 19th century Christmas and open throughout December. Candlelight Christmas: a candlelit evening filled with the sites, sounds, and smells of a Christmas from the past! Lantern led walks around the plantation include the carriage barn, kitchen, plantation home, slave cabin. Admission. (starts last wknd in Nov. Candlelight is first full wknd in Dec)*

CAROLINA RAPTOR CENTER

Raptors are a type of bird that preys on other animals. Hawks, eagles, falcons, and owls are examples of raptors you'll see.

Charlotte (Huntersville, Lake Norman) - *6000 Sample Road (I-77 N to exit 16B, Sunset Rd. Right on Beatties Ford Road, go 5 miles. Left on Sample Road and head straight into Latta Plantation Nature Preserve) 28031. Phone: (704) 875-6521. www.carolinaraptorcenter.org. Hours: Monday-Saturday 10:00am - 5:00pm, Sunday Noon - 5:00pm. Closed major winter holidays. Closed Mondays & Tuesdays (November-Feb). Admission: $12.00 adult, $10.00 senior, $8.00 student. Tours: Carolina Raptor Center often conducts special behind the scenes tours where you get a sneak peak from patients' initial exam to strengthening their wings in outdoor flight cages. Educators: Raptor Fact Sheets, games and vocabulary are online: www.carolinaraptorcenter.org/qa.php. Note: Carolina Raptor Center is an outdoor facility. Visitors are encouraged to prepare for weather. Most of the outdoor center is shaded. Gift shop on premises.*

Birds of prey, also known as raptors, often are the victims of harmful collisions with other species, including humans. Luckily, Carolina Raptor Center is there to nurse them back to health and often place them back in the wild. Stroll along the nature trail for a self-guided tour as you observe raptors in their aviaries. Along the way, watch a presentation of live raptors, chat with the Wild Wings Educators about your favorite bird of prey, or read personal stories about resident birds and how they came to live at the Center. Meet one turkey vulture who likes to untie shoe laces. Another turkey vulture at the center is a movie star. The bird with the prickly personality appeared in The Chase. In another aviary is a sweet albino hawk and an adorable small owl. Before a healed bird can be released, it must be able to pass the "capture a rodent" test! A favorite area is the eagles' cages. Did you know Bald Eagles nests can be as large as a small car? Another fact: Barn owls can locate prey by sound alone - in the pitch dark. Before you leave, be sure to "Measure your Wing Span" against an eagle's span. They have Vulture feedings every Saturday at 12:30pm and live bird presentations most every weekend. Nice combo of nature trail and bird "zoo"- worth the admission.

How big is a raptor's wingspan?

PRESIDENT JAMES K. POLK STATE HISTORIC SITE

Charlotte (Pineville) - ***308 S. Polk Street (I-77 south to I-485 east to Pineville exit US 521 south) 28134. Phone: (704) 889-7145. www.jameskpolk.net. Hours: Tuesday-Saturday 9:00am-5:00pm. Closed Sunday, Monday, and most major state holidays. Admission: FREE. Tours: Guided tours of the main house and kitchen are provided throughout the day. Educators: great bio and activities on the Teacher Packet page.***

SC

This site is located on land once owned by the parents of James K. Polk, the 11th U.S. president. Determined and stubborn, Polk entered the presidency with a clear-cut program. He set forth five goals, all of which he carried out successfully during his single term in office. The memorial commemorates significant events in the Polk administration: the Mexican War, settlement of the Oregon boundary dispute, and the annexation of California. Reconstructions of typical homestead buildings - a log house, separate kitchen, and barn - are authentically furnished. The Visitor Center features a 23-minute film on Polk's life and civic contributions.

POLK BIRTHDAY CELEBRATION

Charlotte (Pineville) *- President James K. Polk State Historic Site. This living history program brings back to life the Polk family of Mecklenburg County in November 1795, when James K. Polk was born into the family. Activities include a historic cooking demonstration, children's games and other hands on activities. (first Saturday in Nov)*

CHRISTMAS PROGRAM

Charlotte (Pineville) *- President James K. Polk State Historic Site. Come and participate in a day of Christmas festivities. Visitors see a living history vignette in the main house. Each building is decorated in the 19th century style! Come and learn about food and customs from Christmas in 1802! (second Saturday in December)*

RANKIN MUSEUM OF AMERICAN HERITAGE

Ellerbe - *131 West Church Street 28338. www.rankinmuseum.com. Phone: (910) 652-6378. Hours: Monday-Saturday 9:00am-5:00pm, Sunday 2:00- 5:00pm. Closed Wednesdays. Admission: $4.00 adult, $1.00 students.*

Rare and unique artifacts and specimens constitute the museum's display of archaeology, paleontology, natural history and early Americana. Look for large fossils, giant shark teeth, beaded apparel and especially the masks and dishes from Southeast to Plains to Artic Indians. How was each culture different?

The Natural History displays showcase full-size mounted animals such as polar bears, buffalo and mountain lions. All animals important to early natives. Each room chronologically links the stages of civilization and how they tie together - a welcome feature as parents try to sneak in a natural history lesson.

AIRBORNE & SPECIAL OPERATIONS MUSEUM

Fayetteville - ***100 Bragg Boulevard (I-95 exit 52B to NC 24, left on Bragg) 28301. Phone: (910) 483-3003. www.asomf.org. Hours: Tuesday-Saturday 10:00am-5:00pm, Sunday Noon-5:00pm. Closed major winter holidays. Open some holiday Mondays. Admission: FREE. Fee for Simulator (age 8+) - $8.50 each. FREEBIES: Print off scavenger hunts, word searches and crossword puzzles to do on the road. Educators: Curriculum guides (grade appropriate): www.asomf.org/pages/education_curriculum_guides.php.***

Have you ever wondered what it was like for that first person to make the decision to jump from a moving airplane in order to serve his country? Well, now you may be able to learn the answer along with some other historically significant facts. The site chronicles the growth of Ft. Bragg and the surrounding area from the inception of Camp Bragg in 1918 to modern day construction, with particular attention to the spectacular build-up to World War II. The lobby features two fully deployed parachutes, a WWII era T-5 round chute and a modern MC-4 square chute. They look very real. Filmed in Vistascope, the movie is designed to put the viewer into the exciting military action and to show military operations in a vivid way. Similar to the movie, the Pitch, Roll, and Yaw Vista-Dome Motion Simulator adds another dimension by physically moving a specially designed seating area up to 18 degrees in concert with the film. The 24-seat simulator provides visitors with an extreme taste of what the Army's finest are trained to do. The whole museum uses curiosity and visual lighting (or darkness) to get the kids engaged.

CAPE FEAR BOTANICAL GARDEN

Fayetteville - ***536 North Eastern Blvd. (I-95, take Exit 52 (Hwy 24 West). Go approximately 5 miles. Turn right onto Hwy 301N (Eastern Blvd.) Go 1/8 mile. CFBG is on the right) 28301. Phone: (910) 486-0221. www.capefearbg.org. Hours: Daily 9:00am-5:00pm. Reduced winter hours. Admission: $10.00 adult, $9.00 military, $5.00 child (6-12). Note: Treasure Hunt: each month, a new treasure hunt clue worksheet is introduced.***

Nestled on 85 acres that overlook Cross Creek and the Cape Fear River, this botanical garden includes numerous species of native plants, wild flowers, and majestic oaks. An authentic 1800s farmhouse and outbuildings are also on site, as well as nature trails, a Heritage Garden, and a demonstration garden. In the Children's Garden: The Lilliput Labyrinth - based on the tale of Gulliver's Travels. The items Gulliver left behind are giant-sized, which sets the garden's theme of contrasting the immense with the miniature. Must see sculptures are a 15' swing, a 5' pair of eyeglasses, and a 17' chair. The Friendship Garden is formed in the shape of a heart, the garden has seven beds, each representing plantings from each continent of the world.

HERITAGE FESTIVAL

Fayetteville *- Cape Fear Botanical Garden - Celebrate old-time farm life! Shell corn, scrub clothes, learn quilting and spinning, and have a healthy good time with refreshments and live bluegrass music! Hayrides, old-fashioned games, pony rides, and food. (first Sunday in October)*

FASCINATE-U CHILDREN'S MUSEUM

Fayetteville - ***116 Green Street (next to the Markethouse, downtown) 28302. Phone: (910) 433-1573. www.fascinate-u.com. Hours: Tuesday-Friday 9:00am-5:00pm, Saturday 10:00am-5:00pm, Sunday Noon-5:00pm. Open Wednesday evenings until 7:00pm. Admission: $4.00 child, $3.00 adult.***

Fascinate-U began as the brainchild of two young mothers building educational opportunities for the area's children. Housed inside historic City Hall, this museum features a host of innovative role-playing and interactive exhibits that allow children to discover occupations such as banking, grocery, media, government, theater, medicine, and law. Come on in. You can touch and play with everything. In the mini-city everything is kid-sized. Children can go shopping at the Gro-Rite Grocery & Deli, put on a judge's robe and pass their sentence-gavel in hand, respond to calls at the 911 Emergency Dispatch Center, and give the weather forecast at the WNUZ center. Let TAM show you how the body works.

CAPE FEAR REGIONAL THEATRE

Fayetteville - *1209 Hay Street 28305. Phone: (910) 323-4233. www.cfrt.org.*

This award-winning theater has been performing musicals, classic dramas, off-Broadway productions, comedies, and children's shows/camps (Huck Finn) for over 40 years. Well known stars of the stage and screen are often seen performing here. Single ticket prices range from $15 to $30.

BEST CHRISTMAS PAGEANT EVER

Fayetteville - Cape Fear Regional Theatre. Annual production of this modern holiday classic. This is the story of how the awful Herdman children learn the true meaning of Christmas and will delight children and adults alike. There are both daytime school performances and weekend public performances. (runs two weeks mid-December)

COTTON BLUE FESTIVAL

Fayetteville (Laurinburg) - 13040 X-Way Road. www.facebook.com/johnbluecottonfestival/. Teams of mules hitched to a turnstile that powers a working pre-civil war cotton gin. The Cotton Blossom Railroad provides rides behind a real steam powered miniature locomotive. A mill cuts wooden shingles and fresh ground corn meal pours from an operating grist mill. Tour the historic John Blue House Museum. Live bands, food, hayrides, old-time games, petting farm, crafts, displays of early engines and tractors and demonstrations. Even an old style Sunday church service on the grounds on Sunday. FREE, fees for some activities. (second wkend in Oct)

82ND AIRBORNE DIVISION WAR MEMORIAL MUSEUM

Fort Bragg - ***Ardennes Street 28307. Phone: (910) 432-3443 or (910) 432-5307. http://82ndairbornedivisionmuseum.com/. Hours: Tuesday-Saturday 10:00am-4:30pm. Admission: FREE.***

Dedicated to the glory and memory of all Airborne and Special Operations soldiers from 1940 to the present, the museum houses photographic exhibits and artifacts but mostly real airplane displays outdoors. See the Curtis Commando - The first aircraft with jump doors on both sides of the fuselage. Skytrain - The C-47 was the workhorse of the Army Air Corps transport units. The C-47 carried 82d Airborne troops into battle at Sicily, Salerno, Normandy and Holland. The C-7 was used to provide logistic support (particularly in Vietnam) and support airborne training through the 1970s. It was even used by the U.S. Parachute Demonstration Team, The Golden Knights. See weapons displayed including: The Vulcan - a six barrel, 20mm-air defense weapon system which saw service with the 82nd from 1970-1994. This weapon fired on enemy aircraft during the Persian Gulf War. Also for viewing are Reconnaissance Tanks, Airborne Assault Vehicles, and many more.

PARACLETE XP SKYVENTURE

Fort Bragg (Raeford) - *190 Paraclete Drive (off US 401 W, 21 miles off I-95) 28376. Phone: (888) 4SKYFUN. www.paracletexp.com. Hours: Daily opens at 9:00am. Sunday-Thursday closes at 7:00pm. Friday-Saturday closes at 9:00pm. Admission: Basic (2 flights, flight training, gear and flight certificate) starts at: $64.00. Specials include a flight t-shirt and DVD for $10-$20.00 more. Note: Entire experience takes about one hour. Reservations are suggested.*

Have you ever wished you could fly? Well you can! A new wind tunnel in North Carolina, called Paraclete XP, is the world's largest wind tunnel. While observers can watch from an observation level window, skydivers are taken to the training room to get suited up and learn the basic techniques of indoor vertical wind tunnel flight. Each person takes individual turns in the tunnel - with an instructor present to coach you. Remember to relax and enjoy this amazing experience. Kids are naturals and even parents learn easily, no matter how flexible you are. To commemorate this event, you'll receive a flight certificate and we highly recommend you order the flight DVD and t-shirt, too. What a rush!

WEYMOUTH WOODS SANDHILLS NATURE PRESERVE

Fort Bragg (Southern Pines) - *1024 North Ft. Bragg Road 28387. Phone: (910) 692-2167. www.ncparks.gov/Visit/parks/wewo/main.php. Hours: Daily 8:00am-dusk. Museum: 9:00am-5:00pm.*

Home of the endangered red-cockaded woodpecker, a permanent resident of the Sandhills, this nature preserve features 898 acres of wildflowers, streams, and ponds, as well as over four miles of hiking trails, a beaver pond, and a museum with participation exhibits. Inside the popular Interpretive Center: A 10-foot-high "wall of fire," a lighted photomural that introduces the role of prescribed burning in restoring the fabled longleaf pine forests of central North Carolina; An underground diorama where visitors can crawl beneath the forest to view wildlife that seek shelter there; and a large mural by illustrator Brooks Pearce that depicts flora and fauna in the park. Pushbuttons allow visitors to hear their calls; Another exhibit allows visitors to stir an old-time bucket of resin; and the nighttime diorama allows visitors to experience "Darkness in the Pines," "Ghosts of the Sandhills Swamps and Seeps" and "Things That Go Bump in the Night."

SCHIELE MUSEUM OF NATURAL HISTORY

Gastonia - *1500 East Garrison Blvd. (I-85 south to exit 20, New Hope. Follow signs to right on Garrison Blvd.) 28054. www.schielemuseum.org. Phone: (704) 866-6900. Hours: Monday-Saturday 9:00am-5:00pm, Sunday 1:00-5:00pm. Admission: $6.00-$7.00 (age 6+). Gastonia residents discounts.*

Educators: Print off online scavenger hunt ("Kids") before visit. Teachers can order Explorer Packs from the Schiele Museum Store. Explorer Packs range in price. Note: Planetarium (extra fee) shows. Half-mile Nature Trail (villages along the way). Gastonia is home to the WORLD'S LARGEST FLYING AMERICAN FLAG (visible for 30 miles from 4025 West Franklin Blvd.)

SC

The largest collection of land mammal specimens in the Southeast is on display at this natural history museum. It includes six geographic areas of the state depicted at different seasons of the year: the Coastal Plain in the early summer, the Sandhills in early autumn, the Piedmont in mid-autumn, a cave in early winter, and the mountains in mid-winter. The Hall of Earth and Man encompasses the history of the Earth. Models, graphics, fossils, artifacts, and interpretive texts complement each exhibit and provide the visitor a glimpse of the Earth's past. Marine Touch Tanks, too. The 18th-century Backcountry Farm (located along the Nature Trail close to the main museum parking lot) contains a log cabin and kitchen, barn, blacksmith shop, woodworking shop, and several other outbuildings. The Catawba Indian Village contains a replicated prehistoric bark-covered house, a large council house, and two log cabins. We'd suggest coming for a group tour or Kids Club program. These are more engaging vs. exhibits behind glass.

GASTON COUNTY MUSEUM

Gastonia (Dallas) - *131 West Main Street 28034. www.gastoncountymuseum.org. Phone: (704) 922-7681. Hours: Tuesday-Friday 10:00am-5:00pm, Saturday 10:00am-3:00pm. Admission: FREE. Note: Terrific Toddler Tuesdays art or history stories, craft, song and tour.*

Housed in an 1852 Greek Revival style old hotel, this museum features authentically furnished period rooms, a "hands-on" parlor, and changing art and history exhibits. The largest public collection of horse-drawn carriages and sleighs in North Carolina is also housed here. In the Carolinas Textile main exhibit, discover how cotton textile manufacturing transformed the Carolinas. Sights and sounds of the past combine with original objects, such as the world's longest running, original Edison generator (1884), the Loray Mill whistle, a ball gown and a baseball uniform. Most historical sites are old homes, not hotels, so this museum has more intrigue...wondering what famous Victorian folks stayed here and what they might have said if the walls could talk.

CROWDERS MOUNTAIN STATE PARK

Gastonia (Kings Mountain) - ***522 Park Office Lane (southbound I-85, take exit 13 to Edgewood Road) 28086. www.ncparks.gov/Visit/parks/crmo/main.php. Phone: (704) 853-5375. Hours: Daily 8:00am-dusk. Admission: FREE. Fee for camping and canoe rental. Educators: The Crowders Mountain program introduces students to basic geologic concepts, including the rock cycle, rock and mineral identification, weathering and erosion, and resource use: www.ncparks.gov/sites/default/files/ncparks/37/Crowders%20Mountain%20EELE.pdf***

Climb rugged peaks rising 800 feet above the surrounding countryside and watch raptors soar in the wind currents. The park includes two giant mountains: Crowders Mountain and Kings Pinnacle. The beauty and diversity of Crowders Mountain State Park is best appreciated on its miles of hiking trails. Hiking trails lined with wildflowers and mountain laurel lead along the ridges and to the summits of Crowders Mountain and Kings Pinnacle. Other trails are easier. Circle the lake on a gravel path or view aquatic plants and animals along a narrow creek. There is also a 9-acre lake, canoe rentals, hiking and nature trails and primitive camping.

RAVEN ROCK STATE PARK

Lillington - ***3009 Raven Rock Road (take US 421 east. Turn left onto Raven Rock Road, and follow it for three miles to the park) 27546. Phone: (910) 893-4888. www.ncparks.gov/Visit/parks/raro/main.php. Hours: Daily 8:00am-dusk. Admission: FREE. Fee for permit camping.***

Educators: The Raven Rock program introduces students to the geologic processes along the fall zone: www.ncparks.gov/sites/default/files/ncparks/37/Raven%20Rock%20EELE.pdf

Raven Rock offers a variety of trails. Travel them on foot or on horseback (separate, undeveloped paths). A number of trails in the park traverse a variety of terrains. Raven Rock Loop Trail travels through a hardwood forest on its one-mile trip to the park's centerpiece, Raven Rock. Wooden stairs down the face of the river bluff lead to the base of Raven Rock where the river bank provides a place to examine the area beneath the overhang. A stone balcony along the way overlooks the river and the flood plains beyond. Other trails offer access to fishing holes and idyllic scenery. There are areas for picnicking and primitive backpack camping, too.

EXPLORATION STATION

Lumberton - *104 North Chestnut Street (I-95 exit 22 into town) 28358. Phone: (910) 738-1114. www.robesonpartnership.org Hours: Wednesday-Saturday 10:00am-5:00pm, Sunday 1-5:00pm. Open until 7:00pm on Thursday & Friday. Admission: $5.00 per child, $3.00 per adult.*

The Children's Museum contains eleven interactive spaces where kids can play educational make-believe. Dress up and play doctor in the hospital, milk a cow, teach a class in school, shop at the general store or watch ducks cascade down a waterfall. There's a separate play area for infants.

ROBESON PLANETARIUM & SCIENCE CENTER

Lumberton - *420 Caton Avenue (I-95 S to exit 17, Hwy 72 northwest past Board of Education Bldg.) 28358. Phone: (910) 671-6015. www.robeson.k12.nc.us. Shows: Weekend public shows are generally held at 11:00am and 1:00pm or evenings. Admission: Varies depending on group. Small fee for monthly shows.*

The science center is located in a one room schoolhouse and offers many hands-on exhibits and activities. The planetarium is located adjacent to the center and uses light, sound, and color to recreate the images of the universe. Some available programs of interest: Tonight's Sky (part of all programs); Space Station (NASA's exploration vision); Skytellers; and Apollo Magnus (pieces of the moon).

MUSEUM OF THE SOUTHEAST AMERICAN INDIAN

Lumberton (Pembroke) - *Old Main Building, Univ. of NC at Pembroke (ten miles west of the intersection of U.S. 74 and I- 95) 28372. www.uncp.edu. Phone: (910) 521-2433. Hours: Monday-Friday 9:00am-5:00pm. Admission: FREE.*

A very unique museum and resource center that contains 19th century artifacts, as well as arts and crafts from Lumbee Indian tribes. Favorite family displays include an authentic log canoe and log cabin, Indian dress and music or video presentations. Particular focus is placed on the largest North Carolina tribe, the Lumbee. Today, the Lumbee number over 50,000, with the majority residing in Robeson and adjoining counties. According to local legends, the Indians of Robeson County are descendants of several tribal groups (three languages families - Eastern Siouan, Iroquoian and Algonkian) and John White's Lost Colony.

REED GOLD MINE STATE HISTORIC SITE

Midland - ***9621 Reed Mine Road (U.S. 74 - Independence Blvd - east to N.C. 24/27 - Albemarle Rd. Follow N.C. 24/27 to Reed Mine Rd or US 601 to NC200) 28107. Phone: (704) 721-GOLD (4653). https://historicsites.nc.gov/all-sites/reed-gold-mine Hours: Tuesday-Saturday 9:00am-5:00pm. Admission: No fee is charged for admission or tours of the mine. Gold panning is $3.00 per pan (April - October). Tours: Tours of the underground tunnels are offered each hour, and stamp mill tours are available several times each day. Note: Picnic area and easy walking trails wind past old digging holes left behind. The Lower Hill Trail features "Talking Rocks" that describe the mining activities. Educators: Online links cover History, Science, Math & Language Arts.***

Many industrious men made fortunes in North Carolina during the nation's first gold rush. But...it was a boy who started it all.

Reed Gold Mine is the site of the first documented gold find in the United States. Mr. Reed's son found a large yellow rock out in the creek one day and the family initially used it as a doorstop. When a jeweler valued it as gold (a 17 lb. chunk), Reed and his fellow farmers began panning for gold during the off-season farming. Creek gold mining led to underground mining when it was learned in 1825 that the metal also existed in veins of white quartz rock. Portions of the underground tunnels at the Reed mine have been restored for guided tours. The underground tour is so interesting! Pretty much everything you hear about in the movies, you'll see for real on the tour. A visitor center contains exhibits of gold and historical mining equipment. An orientation film highlights the first gold discovery and techniques of removal of gold from the earth. At the panning station, they will instruct you on the stages of removal of dirt and rock to get to the gold. Why are the ridges in the mining pan so important?

....workin' in a Gold Mine...

SC

TOWN CREEK INDIAN MOUND STATE

Mount Gilead - ***509 Town Creek Mound Road (Signs point the way south from N.C. 731 and north from N.C. 73) 27306. Phone: (910) 439-6802. https://historicsites.nc.gov/all-sites/town-creek-indian-mound. Hours: Tuesday-Saturday 9:00am-5:00pm, Sunday 1:00-5:00pm. Admission: FREE.***

Around A.D. 1200, a new cultural tradition arrived in the Pee Dee River Valley. That new culture, called "Pee Dee" by archaeologists, was part of a widespread tradition known as "South Appalachian Mississippian." Throughout Georgia, South Carolina, eastern Tennessee, western North Carolina, and the southern North Carolina Piedmont, the new culture gave rise to complex societies. These inhabitants built earthen mounds for their spiritual and political leaders, engaged in widespread trade, supported craft specialists, and celebrated a new kind of religion. The reconstructed ceremonial center includes the major temple on an earthen mound, minor temple, mortuary, game pole and stockade surrounding the ceremonial area. The burial hut contains an exhibit depicting a burial scene with an accompanying audio program. The modern visitors center shows a slide presentation and features exhibits of artifacts found in the area. A self-guided nature trail leads out to and past the reconstructed area.

SC

TOWN CREEK HERITAGE FESTIVAL

Mount Gilead - *Town Creek Indian Mound State Historic Site. Celebrating the Native American heritage of the region, features an authentic pow-wow with singing, dancing and drum. Admission. (last weekend in September)*

MUSEUM OF THE WAXHAW

Waxhaw - ***8215 Waxhaw Highway (NC 16 & NC 75) 28173. Phone: (704) 843-1832. www.museumofthewaxhaws.org. Hours: Museum: Saturday 10:00am-5:00pm. Admission: Museum: $2.00-$5.00 (age 6+). Note: Nearby at the Museum of the Alphabet: 1,000s of tourists per year go to Museum of the Alphabet to learn about writing systems and unique languages.***

This museum collection contains historic artifacts that document the development of the region from the time of the Waxhaw Indians, for whom the region is named, until 1900. As part of the permanent exhibit, the museum shows a 12-minute introductory film that outlines the general history and important events of the region. Subjects include the first European explorers, early settlers, and the boyhood days of Andrew Jackson. Also the culture of the Scotch-Irish settlers who courageously forged a new civilization in the Carolina back county called "the Waxhaws" is remembered in this memorial.

Chapter 5
South East North Carolina

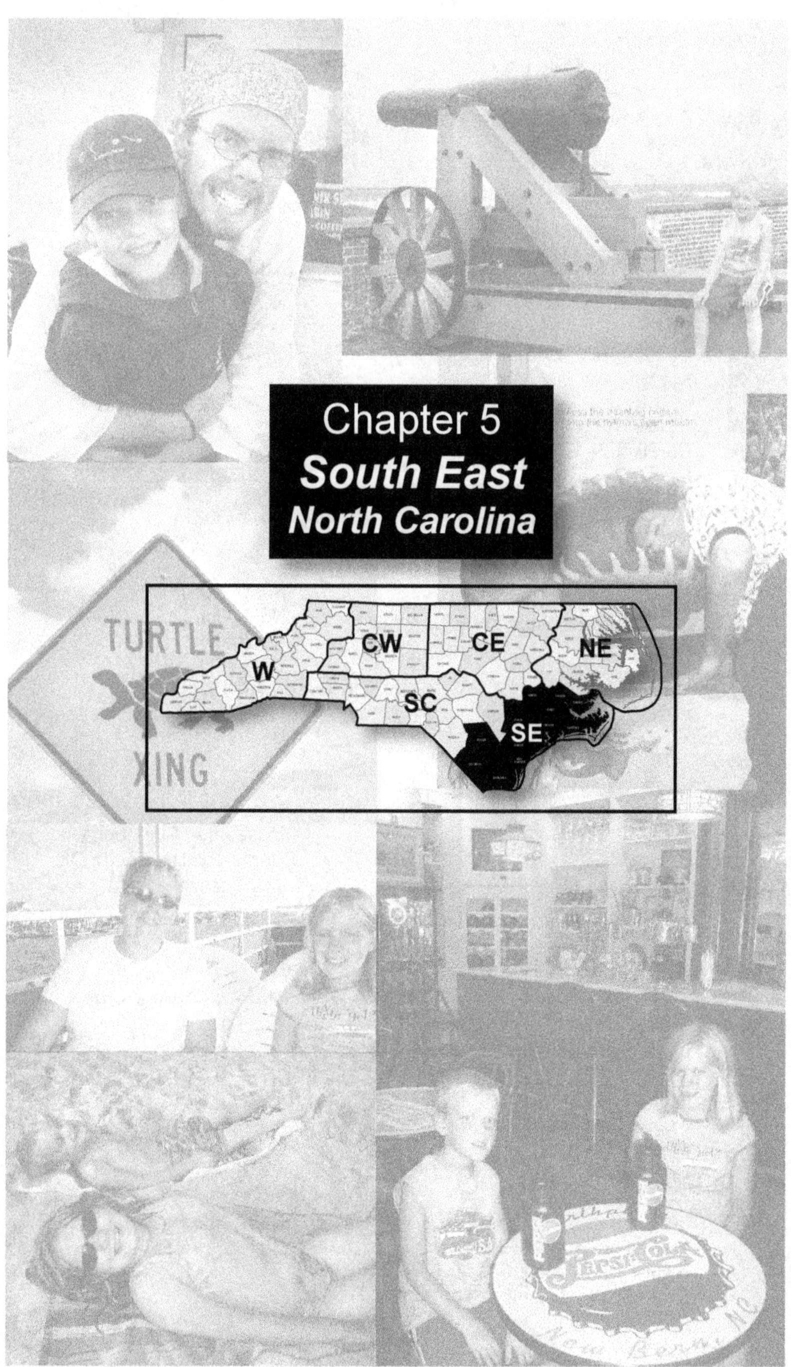

Atlantic Beach
- Fort Macon State Park
- North Carolina Aquarium At Pine Knoll Shores

Aurora
- Aurora Fossil Museum

Bald Head Island (Southport)
- Bald Head Island Tours

Beaufort
- Beaufort Boat Tours
- Beaufort Historic Site Tours
- NC Maritime Museum

Carolina Beach
- Carolina Beach State Park
- Michael's Seafood Restaurant
- Island Of Lights Parade & Flotilla

Chadbourn
- North Carolina Strawberry Festival

Cherry Point
- MCAS Cherry Point Air Show

Currie
- Moore's Creek National Battlefield

Elizabethtown
- Jones Lake State Park

Harkers Island
- Cape Lookout National Seashore

Jacksonville
- Lynnwood Park Zoo

Kinston
- Neuseway Nature And Science Center
- CSS Neuse

Kure Beach
- Fort Fisher State Historic Site & Civil War Museum
- North Carolina Aquarium At Fort Fisher

Kure Beach (cont.)
- Island Of Lights New Years Eve Countdown

Morehead City
- Carolina Chocolate Festival

Morehead City & Crystal Coast
- July 4th Celebration

Morehead City (Waterfront)
- NC Seafood Festival

New Bern
- Birthplace Of Pepsi
- New Bern Trolley Tours
- Tryon Palace Historic Site
- Fireman's Museum
- New Bern Civic Theatre

Oak Island
- Oak Island Nature Center

Ocean Isle Beach
- North Carolina Oyster Festival

Pine Knoll Shores
- Hampton Inn & Suites Atlantic Beach

Southport
- North Carolina Maritime Museum At Southport
- North Carolina Fourth Of July Festival

Sunset Beach
- Ingram Planetarium

Sunset Beach (Ocean Isle Beach)
- Museum Of Coastal Carolina

Swansboro
- Hammock's Beach State Park

Topsail Island
- Sea Turtle Rescue & Rehab Ctr, Karen Beasley

Whiteville
- Lake Waccamaw State Park

Wilmington

- Battleship North Carolina
- Cape Fear Museum
- Children's Museum Of Wilmington
- Hollywood Location Walk Of Old Wilmington
- Wilmington Railroad Museum
- Cape Fear Riverboats
- Thalian Association Children's Theatre
- Wilmington Trolley Company
- Airlie Gardens
- Jungle Rapids Family Fun Park
- Tregembo Animal Park
- Screen Gems Studios / EUE Tours
- Poplar Grove Plantation
- North Carolina Azalea Festival
- July 4th Celebration
- Wooden Boat Show
- Riverfest
- Colonial Christmas At Burgwin-Wright House

Wrightsville Beach

- Blockade Runner Beach Resort
- Wrightsville Beach Scenic Cruises & Water Taxi
- Cape Fear Kite Festival
- North Carolina Holiday Flotilla

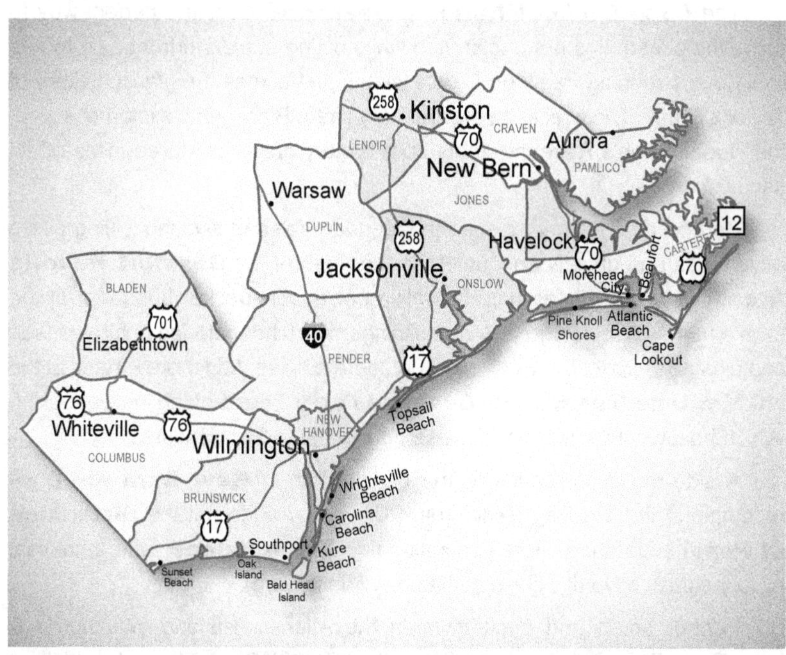

A Quick Tour of our Hand-Picked Favorites Around...

South East North Carolina

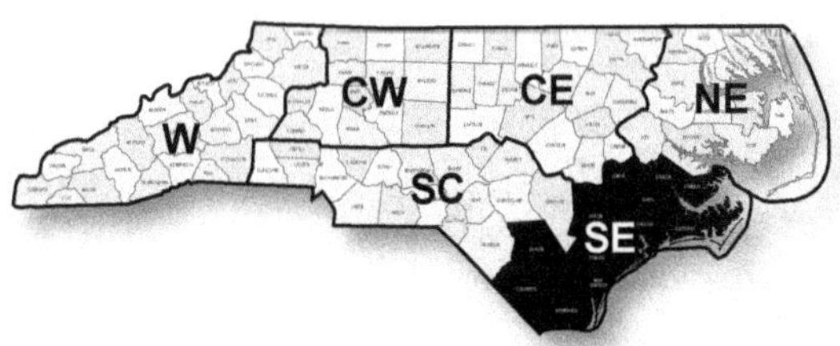

Along North Carolina's Crystal Coast, beaches, nature and history all wait to be explored. From the sands of Atlantic Beach and Emerald Isle to the history of Beaufort, this unspoiled stretch of the Southern Outer Banks coast is rich with beauty, heritage and activities in, on and around the water. The barrier islands take a curious southward curve, blessing the Crystal Coast with beaches that course east and west. It's possible to admire the dazzlingly bright sun rise to greet the day and then slip into the shimmering translucent blue waters in the evening during a spectacular sunset.

The **Cape Lookout National Seashore** offers the perfect way to enjoy the ocean. It is not uncommon while dining at a waterfront café to see wild horses running freely on Carrot Island, just across the glassy waters of Taylor's Creek. The wreckage of legendary pirate Blackbeard's infamous ship, the Queen Anne's Revenge, rests in its watery grave just three miles off its sandy shores.

An eccentric history steeped in legendary tales of swashbuckling pirate adventures and ghostly encounters is the "feel" of the **Beaufort Historic Area**. Costumed guides narrate walking or double-decker bus tours of the town's narrow streets and historic buildings. You'll hear stories of pirates, sea captains, star-crossed lovers, and Confederate spies. Add more Pirates at the **NC Maritime Museum** and **Beaufort Ferry Tours** along the waterfront. Which boat would you choose to use on a quest to find treasure?

A side trip inland leads to the quaint town of **New Bern** where we recommend the **Trolley Tour** first, followed by a stop at the **Birthplace of Pepsi** soda shop. Here you'll also find **Tryon Palace**, where colonial history comes alive (it's like a miniature Williamsburg).

Further south and back towards the Atlantic, Historic Wilmington & NC's Cape Fear Coast encompasses the city of Wilmington and the island communities of Carolina Beach, Kure Beach and Wrightsville Beach. Wilmington's picturesque riverfront emerges from the Cape Fear River. Across the river on Eagles Island rests the majestic **Battleship NORTH CAROLINA**, a restored World War II memorial. Lights, cameras and action await you at the **Screen Gems Studios** where you can tour the studio any time of year. Then take a walking tour or carriage ride through the downtown historic district of Wilmington. There are also other museums for children or railroad buffs, and North Carolina's oldest history museum.

Home to Carolina Beach and Kure Beach, Pleasure Island embodies coastal Americana. Its gazebo, Boardwalk, piers, marinas and amusement park add to its nostalgic appeal. Take in some natural history at **Carolina Beach State Park** where you can wind your way through nature trails in search of the rare indigenous Venus Flytrap. Step back in time at a Civil War battlefield and museum (**Fort Fisher/Fort Macon**), or while away hours at the **NC Aquarium**'s state-of-the-art ocean and Cape Fear River habitats.

North of Pleasure Island is Wrightsville Beach. Enjoy a leisurely bike ride or take a harbor cruise along the Intracoastal Waterway. From sea turtle-watches to exciting watersports, there's something for those seeking a slower pace.

Sites and attractions are listed in order by City, Zip Code, and Name. Symbols indicated represent: ☐ Restaurants ☐ Lodging

FORT MACON STATE PARK

***Atlantic Beach** - 2303 East Fort Macon Road, NC Hwy 58 (milepost #0) 28512. Phone: (252) 726-3775. www.ncparks.gov/fort-macon-state-park. Hours: Daily 9:00am-5:30pm except on Christmas Day. Fort area closes at dark. Admission: FREE. Educators: The Fort Macon program introduces students to the geologic process of barrier island movement and to the plants and animals that thrive in this shifting environment: www.ncparks.gov/sites/default/files/ncparks/37/Fort%20Macon%20EELE.PDF*

Built between 1826 and 1834 to guard the entrance to Beaufort Harbor, this fort was used by Confederate and Union troops as a prison during the Reconstruction Era, the Spanish-American War, and during World War II. The fort stands as one of the finest surviving examples of military architecture and fortification. Kids notice it looks like the pentagon with its odd, strong structured walls. Exhibits and displays acquaint you with the fort's history, and restored quarters offer a look into the lives of officers and soldiers.

BIG cannons were waiting for the enemy...

Admire the fort's powder magazines, counter-fire rooms with cannon emplacements and wide moat that could be flooded to protect the fort during a siege. The fort features several original and replica cannons, a restored Hot Shot Furnace and Bake Oven. Areas of the fort depict periods of soldier occupation using selected "talking rooms". Re-enactments or musket firings are often staged on the fort's parade grounds. If you climb to the top of the fort, you'll get a wonderful view of Navy installments off Radio Island. The large park has an inviting beach with picnicking facilities and summer bathhouse. It is a favorite spot for fishing, bird-watching and shelling, too.

NORTH CAROLINA AQUARIUM AT PINE KNOLL SHORES

SE

Atlantic Beach - ***NC Hwy 58, 1 Roosevelt Drive (5 miles west of Atlantic Beach, milepost #7) 28512. Phone: (252) 247-4004. www.ncaquariums.com/pine-knoll-shores. Hours: Daily 9:00am-5:00pm. Closed only Thanksgiving, Christmas and New Years. Admission: $12.95 adult, $11.95 senior (62+) & military, $10.95 child (3-12). Note: The Aquarium also has a snack bar and a gift shop. Boat cruises, marsh explorations and other adventures (like "Get Hooked" fishing class), are available for a small additional fee. FREEBIES: Scavenger Hunts online.***

The aquarium is arranged in five themed areas: Mountain, Piedmont, Coastal Plain, Tidal Waters and Ocean. You can watch – and talk to – divers in the Living Shipwreck exhibit, meet a loggerhead turtles face to face in daily programs in the Odyssey and participate in a number of other fun activities. The aquarium's largest exhibit is the 306,000-gallon Living Shipwreck, featuring a three-quarter-size replica of the WWII German submarine, the U-352, which was sunk off of Cape Lookout. Around the sub are a variety of sea life, including a few large tiger sharks. Another popular new attraction is Queen Anne's Revenge, a 50,000-gallon depiction of the marine community and debris field of an 18th-century shipwreck discovered near Beaufort Inlet in 1996. The ship may very well be Blackbeard's flagship. Other cool finds are the Smoky Mountain waterfall, stingray touch pool and the amusing otter pools. The Little Minnows play area is soft play and dressup areas. Outdoors, the Aquarium has two nature trails, a marsh overlook, and a Fossil Hunt.

AURORA FOSSIL MUSEUM

***Aurora** - 400 Main Street 27806. www.aurorafossilmuseum.org. Phone: (252) 322-4238. Hours: Tuesday-Sunday 10:00am - 4:30pm. Mondays open only in Spring and Summer. Admission: FREE.*

Start your tour by watching the 18-minute video that traces the geological and paleontological history of the area in a setting that represents the formations as seen from the bottom of a mine. It's a great setting for kids to understand the evolution of geography and how the phosphate beds were formed that provide fossilized bones, teeth and shells found today. There are rooms with exhibits of prehistoric man in eastern North Carolina, including the Algonkian Indians who met Sir Walter Raleigh's colonists in 1584. Another display has ceremonial pipes, shell beads, pottery, axes, and grinding stones from native villages. Newer displays compare modern shark teeth with fossilized shark teeth and, everything you ever wanted to know about sharks. Kids, the perfect way to end your visit is to dig for your own fossils in the material provided from the nearby Phosphate mine. Bring a garden trowel, sifter and plastic bags. Find treasures of fossilized shark's teeth, coral and shells. The best part? You can take the findings home as a souvenir.

BALD HEAD ISLAND TOURS

***Bald Head Island (Southport)** - 1301 Ferry Road, Deep Point Marina 28401. Phone: (910) 457-5003. www.oldbaldy.org. Old Baldy Lighthouse & Smith Island Museum: Tuesday-Saturday 10:00am-4:00pm, Sunday 11:00am-4:00pm. Closed in Jan/Feb. Admission: $5.00-$8.00 per person includes museum, grounds and lighthouse. By reservation and type of tour. Historic Island Tours: Tuesday, Friday and Saturday at 10:00am. Meet at the Island Ferry landing. Cost: $40-$50.00 includes Ferry, Tour and Lunch Voucher. Note: Bald Head Island Ferry Daytrip: Cost is $22.00 per person round trip. Children 12 - under $11.00. Reservations are encouraged. (Mainland Ferry Dock, Indigo Plantation Marina at 9th Street). Does not include tours or museum.*

Take a guided historic tour of Bald Head Island, which includes a stop at the Smith Island Museum, lighthouse and lunch or dinner. Old Baldy is the state's oldest standing lighthouse built in 1817. Looking for pirates?

BEAUFORT BOAT TOURS

***Beaufort** - (Beaufort Waterfront) 28516. http://lookoutcruises.com Admission: Varies depending on cruise.*

Boy, these companies offers a lot of choices...especially for families. Lookout Cruises offers daily sailing excursions departing historic Beaufort for up to 38 passengers on a 45-foot catamaran with cushioned seating, plenty of shade and large clean restrooms on board. Here's some of the best for kids:

- DOLPHINS - Cruise inland waters in search of playful Atlantic Bottlenose Dolphin. $35.00 / $25.00
- HALF-DAY ISLAND EXCURSION - Visit Cape Lookout for shelling, swimming, surfing, fishing, hiking and birdwatching. Once on the island, take the beach "Mule Train" tour (see separate listing). $85.00 / $70.00.
- PIRATE CRUISES - Jump aboard the pirate ship "REVENGE" at 600 Front Street. Come join the crew, take part in a live pirate show, and enjoy festive music guaranteed to unleash your inner pirate. But be warned; they may enlist your expertise to man the water cannons and help defend your ship. Children receive a pirate scarf and some of the treasure to take home with them. Daily. $24.95 / $19.95. http://www.beaufortpiratesrevenge.com

SE

BEAUFORT HISTORIC SITE TOURS

***Beaufort** - 130 Turner Street 28516. Phone: (252) 728-5225 or (800) 575-7483. http://beauforthistoricsite.org/ Hours: Welcome Center: Daily, except Sunday 9:30am-5:00pm (March-November), 10:00am-4:00pm (December-February). Admission: Welcome Center, FREE. Tours: $12.00 adult, $6.00 child (age 6+). Tours: Walking: Monday-Saturday 10:00am and 2:00pm. Bus (one hour): Monday, Wednesday and Friday, Saturday - 2 times daily, Tuesday/Thursday @ 1:30pm only (April-October). Note: The Old Beaufort Shop has many fun trinkets to shop from - especially pirate stuff!*

Beaufort, an important Colonial seaport, preserves its colorful history with tours of town characterized by white picket fences, a seaside boardwalk, unique shops and restaurants. The town has been visited by patriots, privateers and pirates alike. Its residents have been fishermen, boat builders, merchants and skilled craftsmen. Tours of restored town buildings are hosted by costumed guides who also narrate tours aboard an English double-decker bus. You'll hear stories of pirates, sea captains, star-crossed lovers, Confederate spies, and the ghosts of Old Beaufort by the Sea. Enjoy a walk through historic homes, the old jail, the courthouse, the apothecary shop, the art gallery and join in a tour of the Old Burying Ground. This is a great way to orient yourself to this seaside town. Ride on top, if you're taking the bus tour!

HARVEST TIME IN OCTOBER

Beaufort - Learn through living history re-enactments about coastal Colonial times. Held for nine days in late September and early October, students learn about life in Colonial times as they press apples, quilt, cook over an open fire, make herb pillows, churn butter, tie knots, and much more. (October)

NORTH CAROLINA MARITIME MUSEUM

Beaufort - ***315 Front Street 28516. Phone: (252) 728-7317. http://ncmaritimemuseumbeaufort.com/ Hours: Weekdays 9:00am-5:00pm, Saturday 10:00am-5:00pm, Sunday 1:00-5:00pm. Admission: FREE. Educators: The Junior Sailing Program (ages 8+) uses the fun of sailing and the competition of racing to teach sailing, seamanship, navigation skills and maritime traditions. The Summer Science School has varied programs age appropriate for kids.***

> The Museum conducts curator-led field trips to nearby barrier islands, marshes, tidal flats and coastal forests for kids of all ages.

Exhibits take visitors from dugout canoes to sail rigs to traders and even pirates. Witness a giant collection of seashells, gently turn the ship's wheel of a real trading vessel from the early 1900s, watch how whales eat, touch old boats, and feel old wood sterns and rudders. Touch computer screensteach you about commercial and sport fisheries and the "strange" seafoods you can eat in North Carolina. One of the most exciting exhibits at the Museum is artifacts of the shipwreck of Blackbeard's flagship, Queen Anne's Revenge, discovered in the late 1990s near Beaufort Inlet. This is one of the most significant marine archaeological discoveries of our time. But, is it truly Blackbeard's? Investigate for yourself as you view and read about the cannons and supplies found as evidence. In the Watercraft Center, visitors can observe the construction and restoration of full-sized wooden boats and ship models. On guided tours, museum staff can take you to the top where you can see horses on the Rachel Carson Estuarine Reserve and, frequently, dolphins in the harbor. This is a very interesting and easy to understand museum that is a good introduction to an old English marine town.

SE

CAROLINA BEACH STATE PARK

Carolina Beach - ***1010 State Park Road (Hwy 421 S) 28428. Phone: (910) 458-8206. www.ncparks.gov/Visit/parks/cabe/main.php. Hours: Daylight hours, 8:00am-8:00pm (extended during summer). Closed Christmas Day. Admission: FREE. Tours: Guided tours of the Flytrap trail are given at 10:00am on Saturdays and Sundays (May-August). Note: Educators: Learn about carnivorous plants for middle grades: www.ncparks.gov/sites/default/files/ncparks/37/Carolina%20 Beach%20EELE.pdf***

The popular Interactive Carnivorous Plants exhibit (Venus Flytraps) allows visitors to experience how these fascinating plants capture their prey. Now, venture outside... ...if you dare ;)

Venus flytraps, bladderworts, butterworts, pitcher plants and sundews are waiting to be discovered on the Flytrap Trail at this park. The easy, half-mile loop trail showcases these native plants in their natural habitats. How many flytraps can you find? These plants almost seem to defy nature by consuming animal protein. Carnivorous plants are forced to get their essential nutrients from insects and tiny animals. They're really not man-eating plants as shown in the movies! The park also has five other trails, upgraded campsites, a visitor center, marina and educational programs. The visitor hall offers maze and computer games. Visitors attempt to navigate a ball, which represents an insect in the park, around a maze without taking a wrong turn and being eaten by a carnivorous plant. Their universally accessible hiking trail allows persons with disabilities, the elderly, and children to enjoy.

MICHAEL'S SEAFOOD RESTAURANT

***Carolina Beach** - 28428. 1206 N. Lake Park Blvd., www.mikescfood.com. (910) 458-7761. Right after you cross the bridge over to Carolina Beach, look to your left for a wonderful seafood lunch or dinner. Try their Samplers or Fresh Catch Special with a bowl of Captain M's Seafood Chowder (award winning chowder in rich cream base loaded w/ clams, crabmeat, scallops, veggies, potatoes, herbs & spices). If you're not in the seafood mood, try their salads or pizza. Entrees run: Light $10.00, Seafood Samplers average $20.00. Children's Menu: ~$7.00 - even steak or shrimp.* ________ ☐

ISLAND OF LIGHTS PARADE & FLOTILLA

***Carolina Beach** - Lake Park Blvd (Hwy 421).Fishing boats & pleasure crafts electrically decorated with thousands of lights present a spectacular display on the Intracoastal Waterway. The parade of boats cruise from Snows Cut to Carolina Beach Boat Basin and back. Bring your chairs, blankets & snacks. www.islandoflights.org. (first weekend in December)*

NORTH CAROLINA STRAWBERRY FESTIVAL

Chadbourn *- US Highway 74/76 and Highway 410. www.ncstrawberryfestival.com. (910) 654-3518. Strawberry Jam concerts, strawberry spitting contest, parade, crafts, food competition and rides. Hot air balloon fiesta. (first long weekend in May)*

MCAS CHERRY POINT AIR SHOW

Cherry Point *- MCAS. www.cherrypointairshow.com. Military and civilian performances and a variety of ground events combine to make this a thrilling time for the aviation enthusiast. Largest air show in the state. FREE. (first weekend in May, even years)*

MOORE'S CREEK NATIONAL BATTLEFIELD

Currie ***- 40 Patriots Hall Drive (Hwy 210) 28435. www.nps.gov/mocr/. Phone: (910) 283-5591. Hours: Daily 9:00am-5:00pm. Closed November/December. Holidays. Admission: FREE. Tours: Reservations required for guided tours. Educators: Teachers Guide online includes vocabulary, reading, historical characters and quizzes: www.nps.gov/mocr/forteachers/curriculummaterials.htm.***

The victory at the battle of Moores Creek Bridge resulted in N.C. being the first of the thirteen colonies to vote for independence.

"King George and Broadswords!" shouted the loyalists as they charged across partially Moore's Creek bridge on February 27, 1776. Just beyond the bridge nearly a thousand North Carolina patriots waited quietly with cannons and muskets poised to fire. The loyalists weren't expecting this. As the loyalists advanced across the bridge, patriot shots rang out and dozens of loyalists fell, including their commanders. The loyalists surrendered, retreating in confusion. Wagons, weapons and British sterling worth more than $1 million by today's value were seized by the patriots in the days following the battle. The battle ended the royal Governor's hopes of regaining control of the colony for the British. The park has two self-guided trails including the 1-mile History Trail (explains the battle and includes site where clash took place) and the 1/3 mile Tar Heel Trail (explains the naval stores industry during colonial times). Afternoon programs, walks, and demos are held on summer weekends.

ANNIVERSARY OF THE BATTLE OF MOORE'S CREEK

Currie *- Moore's Creek Battlefield. Activities including demos of muskets, cannon & broadswords, colonial music, surveying, cooking, military drill, blacksmithing, etc. Two militia camps portray the Loyalist and American troops who fought at Moore's Creek. A variety of children's programs are also offered, including militia drill, toy making, and surveying. Food is available. Admission is free. (last weekend in February)*

SE

COLONIAL CRAFT & TRADE FAIRE

Currie - Moore's Creek Battlefield. This weekend re-enactors demonstrate skills like gunsmithing, woodworking, blacksmithing, cooking, candle making, spinning & weaving, surveying, and colonial medicine. Each day there are presentations of Militia drill, musket firing, and historic music. Food available. (first wkend in May)

INDEPENDENCE WEEKEND AT MOORE'S CREEK

Currie - Moore's Creek National Battlefield. Celebrate the nation's independence at the battle site that convinced North Carolina to be the first state to call for the final break with England. This weekend features militia camps, musket and cannon firing, colonial medicine, and other demonstrations. (July 4th weekend)

CANDLELIGHT TOURS OF MOORE'S CREEK

Currie - Moore's Creek Battlefield. Tours leave visitor center every 15 minutes, each group is limited to 30 people. Visitors learn about events that led to the battle of Moore's Creek as they see the battlefield by candlelight. Tours free by reservation. (Dec)

JONES LAKE STATE PARK

Elizabethtown - ***113 Jones Lake Drive (NC 53 for approximately 40 miles, take a left onto NC 242 and travel north) 28337. Phone: (910) 588-4550. www.ncparks.gov/Visit/parks/jone/main.php. Hours: Daily 8:00am-dusk. Admission: FREE. Fee for camping, swimming and rentals. Educators: The Jones Lake program introduces students to the unique geology of Carolina bays: www.ncparks.gov/sites/default/files/ncparks/37/Jones%20Lake%20EELE.pdf***

View one of the greatest geological mysteries of the eastern United States - the phenomenon of the Carolina bays. Adjacent to the Bladen Lakes State Forest and home of two natural lakes, Jones and Salters lakes, the 2,208-acre park is a nature lover's delight. Bay Trail is a five-mile loop around Jones Lake, offering a chance to experience habitats of a Carolina bay. Wander through dense vegetation and over boggy soil to view lakeside flora. Large pond cypress trees, draped with Spanish moss, line the shore and grow in the shallow water. This state park is a favorite for hiking, picnicking, swimming (cool, tea-colored lake and sandy beach), fishing and camping.

CAPE LOOKOUT NATIONAL SEASHORE

Harkers Island - ***131 Charles Street 28531. Phone: (252) 728-2250. www.nps.gov/calo. Hours: Harkers Island Visitor Center 8:00am-4:30pm. Park is accessible 24 hours. FREE admission & primitive camping. Tours: Ferry to Shackleford Banks leaves daily starting at 9:00am (April-Nov). $22.00 adult, $11.00 child. Reservations suggested summers. www.islandexpressferryservices.com Transportation:***

Getting to Cape Lookout National Seashore can be an adventure! Several styles of boats are used as ferries with 16-passenger flat bottom skiffs predominating. Passengers are generally delivered directly onto the sound-side beach. The larger ferries, some carrying up to 80 passengers, make use of the docks. All are open to the elements. On windy or rainy days be prepared to get wet.

A combination of three beautifully natural islands, this area remains relatively unchanged since the pirate Blackbeard found safe harbor here 200 years ago. Accessible only by toll ferry or private boat, the seashore is the perfect destination for surf fishing, sunbathing, kayaking, beach camping and shelling. Except for the ferry landing areas, the islands are undeveloped and wild. Families can observe endangered loggerhead sea turtle, rare waterfowl and a variety of lizards, insects, crabs and clams. Vacationers looking for less action are happy with beautiful beaches, shelling, and heritage attraction sites.The beach does have picnic shelters and restrooms. What it doesn't have is drinking water, anything to buy or trash receptacles. Take all you need to eat or drink, sunscreen and bags to bring back shells, treasure and any trash that you generate. It's best to wear bathing suits under shorts and shirts when on "safari" here.

A 4-wheel drive vehicle makes searching for that good shelling, surf-fishing or camping spot easier. If you don't have your own check with ferry services for rentals

The original diamond-painted **CAPE LOOKOUT LIGHTHOUSE** and Keepers' Quarters still stand and the Quarters are available for touring April-November (Lighthouse conducts open houses only a few times/year with guides). Portsmouth Village, located on the northern end of North Core Banks, is the surviving remnant of the thriving pre-Civil War port that reached its zenith in the decade prior to 1860. Now it is practically a ghost town.

Another treasure of the Seashore is the wild **SHACKLEFORD HORSES** (www.shacklefordhorses.org). Besides small creatures, these horses are the only island residents, and they have been part of the island for more than 400 years. Brought to the Carolina Coast by colonial explorers, the wild "ponies" of Shackleford descended from Iberian stock carried by Spanish supply ships to the island of Hispaniola. The horses are believed to have swam ashore from shipwrecks, and to have been left by an abandoned Spanish colony. Today, the protected herd is managed by a tradition of the annual roundup and pony penning. The herd's lifestyle thrives with limited human contact, socialization, and intervention. The park conducts guided horse watching and beach combing trips.

One more activity is a visit to the **CORE SOUND WATERFOWL MUSEUM** next door to the visitors center. On weekends, they often conduct decoy demos.

LYNNWOOD PARK ZOO

Jacksonville - ***1071 Wells Road (off Hwy 258) 28540. Phone: (910) 938-5848. www.lynnwoodparkzoo.com Hours: Friday-Monday 10:00am-5:00pm (April-December). Admission: $10.00 adult, $8.00 child (2-12).***

Home to more than 256 types of animals - land mammals, exotic birds, water fowl, hoofed stock and reptiles. During a tour of the zoo, which takes about an hour, visitors follow hard-packed dirt trails that stay shady and cool thanks to a natural canopy of trees and vegetation. The blackbuck antelope is a native of Africa; so is the serval. The capybara, the world's largest rodent, is from South America (looks like a giant guinea pig). There's also "Cousin Mo," an emu that hails from Australia; there's "Patton" (as in the General), an ocelot, a cat on the endangered species list; and good ol' "Buzz" a 6-year-old iguana.

NEUSEWAY NATURE SCIENCE CENTER

Kinston - ***401 W. Caswell Street (On Highway 11/55 beside King Street Bridge. Off of Highway 70/258 Bypass) 28501. www.neusewaypark.com Phone: (252) 939-3367. Hours: Tuesday-Saturday 9:30am-5:00pm, Sunday 1:00-5:00pm. Admission: FREE.***

Located on 55 acres along the Neuse River, this beautiful nature-based park is full of things to do - inside and outside. Inside the Nature Center, view over 40 different types of native and exotic animals, three large aquariums, fishponds stocked with catfish and a saltwater touch tank. Outside, enjoy the 18-foot climbing rock, nature trails, camping, fishing, and canoeing. The unique site also features a lower level cave with live exhibits focusing on the Neuse River.

The Health and Science Museum is adjacent to the Nature Center, resting on the Neuse River. The second floor is home to the planetarium which includes a 32 foot dome and projector that presents star patterns, constellations and video shows. This floor includes an observation deck with a telescope. On the first floor, interact with any of the hands-on exhibits, a butterfly garden, a hummingbird habitat, a mini-replica of the local hospital, computers and a giant "Operation" game.

CSS NEUSE

Kinston - *2612 West Vernon Avenue (US 70 Business) 28502. Phone: (252) 522-2091. https://historicsites.nc.gov/all-sites/css-neuse-and-governor-caswell-memorial. Hours: Tuesday-Saturday 9:00am-5:00pm. Admission: FREE. Educators: Descriptions, vocabulary and quizzes are in the teaching packet: www.nchistoricsites.org/neuse/neuse-caswell-teaching-packet.pdf.*

The Neuse was one of 26 ironclads commissioned by the Confederate navy. The boat had a wide, flat bottom resembling a river barge and was plated with iron armor. The vast pine forests of eastern North Carolina provided the needed lumber, and local carpenters served as shipwrights.

Once used, the new ironclad ran aground en route to an attack site. It was the Confederate navy's ill-fated attempt to regain control. Shortly afterwards, the Neuse was burned by its crew, resulting in a large explosion in the port bow, which sank the ship. The Neuse remained in the river for nearly one hundred years. In the mid-1960s, the hull was raised and transported to the property where it now rests. You're looking at real remnants of a real boat built for the Civil War!

FORT FISHER STATE HISTORIC SITE & CIVIL WAR MUSEUM

Kure Beach - *1610 Fort Fisher Blvd. 28449. https://historicsites.nc.gov/all-sites/fort-fisher. Phone: (910) 458-5538. Hours: Tuesday-Saturday 9:00am-5:00pm, Sunday Noon-5:00pm (Summer Sundays only). Admission: FREE, donations welcomed. Tours: Guided tours are given at scheduled times. Educators: wonderful topical papers are available online that kids can use to research reports before/after they visit.*

> The NC Underwater Archaeology Center operates a small museum with exhibits on dive sites and maritime history dating from prehistoric to the Civil War and the present (adjacent).

Before its fall in January, 1865, Fort Fisher protected blockade runners en route to Wilmington. It was the largest earthen fort in the South and had the largest land-sea battle of the Civil War. Inside, a large lighted map follows the lines of battle by water and on the beach. Fort Fisher was a sand and wood design to defend against the blockade runners …unsuccessfully. The lifeline of the Confederacy fell into Union hands. Outside, wayside exhibits mark the tour trail, including a reproduction of a big Rifled heavy Seacoast cannon. Artillery demos are staged quarterly and are a great time to visit.

ANNIVERSARY OF THE CAPTURE OF FORT FISHER

Kure Beach - Fort Fisher State Historic Site & Civil War Museum. A large living history program featuring special tours and demonstrations interpreting the battle. Later in the evening the dramatic surrender of the last major stronghold of the Confederacy is re-created. A fireworks display follows the program. Small Donation. (third Saturday in January)

NORTH CAROLINA AQUARIUM AT FORT FISHER

Kure Beach - *900 Loggerhead Road (20 miles south of Wilmington, just beyond Kure Beach) 28449. Phone: (910) 458-8258. www.ncaquariums.com/fort-fisher. Hours: Daily 9:00am-5:00pm, except Thanksgiving, Christmas and New Year's Day. Admission: $9.95 adult, $8.95 senior (62+) & military, $7.95 child (3-12). Online discount. Note: Scavenger Hunts (download ahead of time): www.ncaquariums.com/fort-fisher/teachersstudents/scavenger-hunts. The SharkBites/TCBY snack bar, located on the food deck outside the Gift Shop.*

SE

The theme for the huge aquarium is "Waters of the Cape Fear". Visitors journey from freshwater rivers and swamps to saltwater marshes into reefs and the open ocean. The centerpiece, "Cape Fear Shoals", is a 235,000-gallon tank with sharks, barracudas, and loggerhead sea turtles. "Loggerhead Legacy" features a loggerhead sea turtle in its first year of life (baby turtles, they grow fast!). Get physical with sharks - see the inside and look at their guts. "Seahorses" showcases seahorses and their pipefish cousins. "Freshwater Wetlands of the Cape Fear" is housed in a large conservatory full of box turtles (watch some sleep and some play), gar, catfish, alligators and water snakes. If you dare, stare down a poison dart frog or venomous snake and then touch seastars, crabs and sharks! Outdoors, in the Gardens, is a new exhibit about water quality. Look for Venus flytraps naturally found in this area (look closely, though, they're low to the ground and hard to find). Listen for Conservatory songbirds. As with all NC Aquariums, this is so colorful and engaging, yet easy to manage at a fair price.

Diver shows entertain questions like: Do fish bite? Do fish eat your hair?

ISLAND OF LIGHTS NEW YEARS EVE COUNTDOWN

Kure Beach - *The Island of Lights countdown features the lowering of a giant lighted beach ball. A street dance featuring live music precedes a spectacular fireworks display to welcome in the New Year. Refreshments are available at this entertainment event for all ages. Free. www.islandoflights.org. (New Years Eve)*

CAROLINA CHOCOLATE FESTIVAL

Morehead City - *Crystal Coast Civic Center. www.carolinachocolatefestival.com. (252) 247-3883. Features chocolate specialties for sampling, dunking, buying and competing. Pudding eating contests for the kids on Saturday (hands-free eating). Also a chocolate ice cream eating (hands-free) contest on Sunday for the grown ups. The winner will receive his/her weight in ice cream (200 lb. limit). Admission. (first weekend in Feb)*

NC SEAFOOD FESTIVAL

Morehead City (waterfront) - *Seafood, music, entertainment and the cultural heritage and traditions that surround commercial fishing begin Friday night on Morehead City's downtown waterfront. Weekend events include a road race, family fishing contests, surfing and more. www.ncseafoodfestival.org. (first weekend in October)*

BIRTHPLACE OF PEPSI

New Bern - ***256 Middle Street (corner of Middle & Pollock streets) 28560. Phone: (252) 636-5898. www.pepsistore.com. Hours: Monday-Saturday 10:00am-6:00pm, year-round. Sunday Noon-4:00pm (March-December). Admission: FREE.***

The summer of 1898 was hot and humid in North Carolina. A young pharmacist,

Caleb Bradham, knew he needed to make interesting cool beverages to keep the customers coming to his soda fountain. So, he began experimenting with combinations of spices, juices and syrups. He concocted a mixture of kola nut extract, vanilla and rare oils to make a soft drink so popular, his customers began calling it "Brad's Drink". As the sale of his new drink started to grow, Caleb formed a company to market it, and so Pepsi-Cola Company, located in the back room of Caleb's pharmacy, opened its doors in 1902. Sit a spell at the old-fashioned soda fountain and enjoy a refreshing Pepsi-Cola surrounded by Pepsi memorabilia history and video clips. You can even buy anything "Pepsi" at the gift shop on site.

NEW BERN TROLLEY TOURS

New Bern - ***(departs at corner of Pollock and George Sts, Tryon Palace) 28560. Phone: (252) 637-7316. www.newberntours.com. Admission: $18.00 adult, $9.00 child (13-18). Purchase on trolley or at office. Tours: Basically twice a day, morning or early afternoon, daily (April-October). Restricted days and tours (November-March). No tours January or February.***

See a famous communion set gifted by King George at Christ Church

Explore downtown New Bern and learn about three centuries of history during this 90 minute trolley tour. Learn fascinating details of a former royal capital of North Carolina. Hear stories about duels fought and Barber Jack. Stop in the cemetery where the inventor of Pepsi is buried. When you re-embark the trolley, you'll be treated to a Pepsi. What did archeologists find in the New Bern Academy lot? We ALWAYS recommend trolley tours of historic cities.

SE

TRYON PALACE HISTORIC SITE

New Bern - ***610 Pollock Street 28560. www.tryonpalace.org. Phone: (252) 639-3500. Hours: Monday-Saturday 9:00am-5:00pm, Sunday 1:00-5:00pm. Closed New Years, Thanksgiving, Christmastime. Admission: $20.00 adult, $10.00 student (grades 1-12). Tours: Guided, costumed tours of the Palace in one-block radius. Historic houses are primarily self-guided. Last tour begins one hour before closing. Note: An audio-visual presentation is available to understand the time and place.***

Welcome. Do come in. The history of colonial America awaits you - tales of ladies and gentlemen, servants, slaves, craftsmen and apprentices. Within these walls, British rule flourished, revolution came, independence took root, and a new state capital was formed. You begin your visit in the new North Carolina History Center. History Navigator tours use portable interactive devices to make learning history high-tech. In the Family Center, step back into 1835 and explore an interactive virtual time machine village. Here, hands-on activities invite the visitor to step back in history and load and sail a ship, distill turpentine and produce naval stores, piece an electronic quilt, and help the shopkeeper find merchandise for customers in the dry goods store.

Visitors then tour the Palace rooms as they might have been arranged during the royal governor's rule. Costumed hostesses lead informative tours through the Palace and East Wing, which houses the kitchen and servant's quarters, and where craftsmen demonstrate fireplace cooking, spinning, weaving, etc. In the East Wing are the stables. If you're fortunate, you might find Governor Tryon at home, or Mrs. Tryon playing the harpsichord. On the South lawn overlooking the Trent River, some gentlemen may be playing bowls - and invite you to join them. Surry and other slave and free black characters share the stories of the large African-American population that helped to build New Bern. This is kind of North Carolina's "Williamsburg."

FOURTH OF JULY

New Bern - Tryon Palace Historic Site. Hear the Declaration read from the Palace steps by costumed characters portraying famous North Carolinians from the Revolutionary era; listen to the Tryon Palace Fife & Drum Corps; and participate in thematic and patriotic craft activities. Fireworks that evening at Union Point Park. FREE garden/outdoor activities. Buildings require tickets. (July 4th)

TRYON PALACE HOLIDAY CELEBRATION

New Bern - Tryon Palace Historic Site. See over 200 years of American Christmas traditions. Extra Admission. (December, month long)

FIREMAN'S MUSEUM

New Bern - ***420 Broad Street 28562. Phone: (252) 636-4087. www.newbernfiremuseum.com. Hours: Monday-Saturday 10:00am-4:00pm. Winter hours may vary. Admission: $7.00 adult, $4.00 student (age 6+).***

Learn about the development of the 19th century fire departments at this museum that features a collection of early fire fighting equipment, as well as Civil War relics, and steam pumpers. Hear the story of Fire Horse Fred and learn why the Dalmatian is the "Fire Dog". A rivalry between two companies left residents gathering at a blaze in anticipation of seeing which company would arrive first - competition in fire fighting?

NEW BERN CIVIC THEATRE

New Bern - ***414 Pollock Street (performances at Saax Bradbury Playhouse) 28563. Phone: (252) 634-9057. www.newberncivictheatre.org. Tickets: $10-$12.***

The theater presents dramas, comedies, musicals and even performances in sign language. Classics like "The Sound of Music", StageHands family musicals (ASL children perform) and Children's Theatre summer workshops.

OAK ISLAND NATURE CENTER

***Oak Island** - 20th Street SE & 19th Place E (end of 52nd St, park across from Yacht Drive) 28465. http://oak-islandnc.com/oak-island-nature-center/. Phone: (910) 457-6964. Hours: Seasonal, Thursday-Saturday 11am-2pm. Trails are open most days during daylight hours. Admission: FREE. Note: Oak Island Lighthouse - Located on the U.S. Coast Guard Station Oak Island in Caswell Beach. Completed in 1958, it stands 169 ft. The main light is a four light rotating fixture, reaching 24 nautical miles offshore and flashing very 10 seconds.*

Overlooking the marsh and Intracoastal Waterway, the Oak Island Nature Center offers a wide range of educational activities. The Talking Trees Walking Trail: stroll the interactive trail as trees like the Dogwood, Red Cedar, Southern Magnolia and Black Gum "talk to you". The Mineral, Rock & Animal Exhibits: Included in the animal exhibits are a ferret, prairie dog, hedgehog, guinea pig, rabbit, gecko, and moon crab. The Center also has a large touch tank with marine creatures native to the Oak Island community. The walkway spans the Davis Creek and connects to an extensive bike and walking path.

SE

NORTH CAROLINA OYSTER FESTIVAL

***Ocean Isle Beach** - (800) 426-6644. A champion oyster shucker is selected to compete in the national oyster-shucking competition with hopes of going to the international competition. There is also an amateur competition. Featuring mountains of oysters plus live music, entertainment for kids, and an oyster stew cook-off. https://ncoysterfestival.com/ Small adult admission. (October weekend)*

HAMPTON INN & SUITES ATLANTIC BEACH

***Pine Knoll Shores** - Highway 58 at Milepost 5. 118 Salter Path Road. 28512. www.hilton.com/en/hotels/oajabhx-hampton-suites-atlantic-beach The hotel offers clean, comfortable suites with pull-out couch/bed, microwave and refrigerator. Each morning a hot/cold complimentary breakfast with fresh fruit and hot food buffet is offered. Walk across the street to the public access boardwalk to the ocean/beach. Travelers enjoy magnificent beaches for swimming, surfing, parasailing, jet-skiing, or shell collecting. Afterwards, come back to the hotel and rinse off, then take a dip in the warm outdoor pool. Several mini-golf and raceway parks are on the strip and some grocery, restaurants, and shopping are within a block or two. Rates from $100.00.*

NORTH CAROLINA MARITIME MUSEUM AT SOUTHPORT

Southport - *204 E Moore Street 28461. Phone: (910) 457-0003. http://ncmaritimemuseumsouthport.com/ Hours: Tuesday-Saturday 9:00am-5:00pm. Admission: FREE.*

The museum houses a collection of memorabilia pertaining to the vast nautical history of Southport, the Lower Cape Fear, and southeastern North Carolina. Self-guided tours through 12 designated stations, or ask a knowledgeable guide to lead the way. Read Gentleman Pirate Stede Bonnet's touching pleas for clemency, before he was hanged. Test your knowledge for trivia, from the jeopardy board. The "River Pilots, Rescues and Aids to Navigation" section offers a variety of nautical instruments, including a 48" Coast Guard nun buoy. Bounce and rock on the 5' model of a turn-of-the-century "Joggle Board". On to the shipwreck "City of Houston" display of rescued treasures from the depths of the Atlantic Ocean, near the Frying Pan Shoals. Learn about hurricanes and listen to the weather forecast on marine radio; when storms are present in the Atlantic, the site tracks them on a hurricane chart.

SE

NORTH CAROLINA FOURTH OF JULY FESTIVAL

__Southport__ - Southport & Oak Island. www.nc4thofjuly.com. (910) 457-5578. Parade, fireman's games, food and fireworks over the water. There is a naturalization ceremony in which people of varying nationalities become citizens of the USA.

INGRAM PLANETARIUM

Sunset Beach - *7625 Highmarket (Village at Sunset Beach, Sunset Blvd. N) 28468. Phone: (910) 575-0033 or (910) 579-1016. www.ingramplanetarium.org. Hours: Tuesday-Saturday 2:00-8:00pm (summer). Friday, Saturday only 12:30-5:00pm (rest of year). Admission: $9.50 adult, $8.50 senior (62+) and $7.50 child (age 3-12) (includes Science Hall exhibits). Tours: Shows begin at 1:00pm, then every hour on the hour until last show beginning at 4:00pm.*

This newer, state-of-the-art planetarium offers shows (with multi-media presentations), a math and navigational display area and a gift shop. View the universe around us as you travel through space and time on Spaceship Earth. See the sky the way our ancestors did as they turn back the clock to view the constellations as they were originally recorded. Leap forward into time to witness planetary alignments as they will be seen by our childrens' grandchildren.

MUSEUM OF COASTAL CAROLINA

Sunset Beach (Ocean Isle Beach) - ***21 East Second Street (Go across the bridge and turn left at the waterslide onto Second Street) 28469. Phone: (910) 579-1016. https://museumplanetarium.org/. Hours: Thursday-Saturday 10:00am-3:00pm. Open more weekdays & Sundays late spring and summertime. Admission: $9.50 adult, $8.50 senior (60+) and $7.50 child (age 3-12). Combo pass for Ingram Planetarium & Museum of Coastal Carolina and save. Educators: Guided Nature Walks, Scavenger Hunt sheets, Questions & Vocabulary curriculum online.***

The Museum of Coastal Carolina features the natural science, environment, and cultural history of the Coastal Carolina region. Excellent dioramas include The Swamp, The Reef, and Waterfowl. Streams to the Sea explains how stormwater runoff pollutes streams and rivers from higher ground as it flows to the Carolina Coast. The Legacy of the Loggerhead is a model of a sand dune with a mother loggerhead turtle laying a nest and also hatchlings emerging from a nest. Visitors may walk through the dune to view the nests from the interior or watch a video about the life cycle of loggerhead turtles. Ringo, the Brunswick oak tree has a new look and there is an aviary for live finches. There's an always updated Touch Tank with live sea animals, too.

HAMMOCK'S BEACH STATE PARK

Swansboro - ***1572 Hammocks Beach Road (only reached by boat or ferry) 28584. Phone: (910) 326-4881. www.ncparks.gov/hammocks-beach-state-park Hours: Ferries run 9:30am-6:00pm (summer). Admission: FREE, but a fee is charged for ferry service and camping or swimming.***

This State Park is a barrier island with 3.5 miles of pristine beach. Backpack and primitive camping are allowed, as is swimming, wildlife viewing and shelling. No bikes allowed. Sand dunes on the island rise to 60 feet above sea level. Largely undeveloped, the park presently offers a bathhouse with restrooms, showers and a refreshment stand and picnic tables.

SEA TURTLE RESCUE & REHABILITATION CENTER, KAREN BEASLEY

Topsail Island - ***822 Carolina Avenue (across from the water tower in southern Topsail Beach. 28445. Phone: (910) 328-3377. Admission: $3-$5.00 is requested for tours or a visit. Hours: Thursdays & Saturdays 1-4pm. Tours: Given evenings during nesting season. www.seaturtlehospital.org.***

Topsail Island has 26 miles of coastline. Each mile

is surveyed every morning to identify sea turtle tracks and nests from May through August. The Loggerhead Sea Turtle comes ashore to nest 3 to 5 times during a nesting year (usually at night). She deposits an average of 120 eggs per nest. The eggs incubate in the sand for about 60 days. The hatchlings emerge and immediately try to make their way to sea. Only 1 in 1000 hatchlings survive their first year of life. 20-30 years later, the female turtles return to their natal beaches to nest. Volunteers stake off and protect the nests of endangered loggerhead sea turtles. The hospital also cares for sick and injured sea turtles.

> **IT'S ALIVE !!**
> Check out the TURTLE CAM. Go to: **www.topsail-island.info** and watch sea turtles go through their day.

LAKE WACCAMAW STATE PARK

Whiteville - ***1866 State Park Dr (US 74/76) 28450. Phone: (910) 646-4748. www.ncparks.gov/Visit/parks/lawa/main.php Hours: Vary by season. Adm: FREE.***

One of the most unique bodies of water in the world also contains some of the most unique plants. This park houses the native Venus flytrap, as well as pitcher plants and sundews. The best place to view the carnivorous plants is along the park's Sand Ridge Nature Trail.

BATTLESHIP NORTH CAROLINA

Wilmington - ***Battleship Drive, Eagle Island (junction of highways 17/74/76/421 across from historic district) 28401. www.battleshipnc.com. Phone: (910) 251-5797. Hours: Daily 8am - 8pm (mid-May to mid-September). Daily 8:00am-5:00pm, rest of year. Admission: $14 adult, $10 senior (65+)/military, $6 child (6-11).***

Commissioned in 1941, "The Showboat" earned 15 battle stars and participated in every major naval offensive in the Pacific during World War II. This self-guided tour allows your family to walk the decks where you visit crew's quarters, a restored bridge and WWII exhibits of crew members' personal experiences. A visit to the North Carolina is like a visit to a small city. A crew of over 2,300 worked on board in the hospital, bakery, butcher shop, print shop, general store, movie theatre or armed forces. The crews slept in metal bunks stacked five high. Look at the recipes in the galley. Pumpkin pie called for 6 cases of pumpkin, 100 pounds of sugar, etc.

Can you believe the guns could fire shells the weight of a compact car almost 23 miles against a target? Kids like the fact that you can actually turn and manipulate all of the small-to-medium sized guns on deck. Look for "Charlie" the alligator in the swamp around the boat. Maybe grab a drink from a "Scuttlebutt" drinking fountain or "gossip center".

MEMORIAL DAY OBSERVANCE

Wilmington *- Battleship North Carolina. Remember those who gave their lives in service and honor veterans at traditional Memorial Day Observance featuring a military guest speaker, an all-service Color Guard, a 21-gun salute by a Marine Corps Honor Guard, military band, Taps, and memorial wreath cast onto the waters. FREE. (Memorial Day)*

HOLIDAY LIGHTING OF BATTLESHIP NORTH CAROLINA

Wilmington *- Battleship North Carolina. A naval tradition continues as the Battleship is dressed in lights from the bow to the masts and stern. Best view from downtown Wilmington. (nightly dusk to dawn early December thru early January)*

SE

The ferocious "pretend" man-eating Venus Flytrap!

CAPE FEAR MUSEUM

Wilmington ***- 814 Market Street 28401. www.capefearmuseum.com. Phone: (910) 341-4350. Hours: Monday-Saturday 9:00am-5:00pm, Sunday 1:00-5:00pm (summer). Closed Mondays, rest of year. Admission: $8.00 adult, $7.00 senior/student/military, $5.00 child (6-17). Note: Learning Center is a place of discovery. Hands-on, facilitated activities encourage families to explore a different featured theme each month.***

The main emphasis of this museum is Cape Fear Stories: Land of the Longleaf Pine. Discover colonial Wilmington while "window shopping" in a merchant stores or watching imports come into port. See the Cape Fear waterfront as it was during the Civil War, complete with a diorama of the Second Battle of Fort Fisher (with sound and light shows). Explore regional ecology in the Michael Jordan Discovery (hands-on) Gallery. Meet a giant sloth or gaze at Michael's jersey. Make your own sand dune or peek inside trash cans. How can you make light on the beach at night without electricity? (phytoplankton plants emit cold light). A large Venus flytrap model provides children with an interactive view of how the flytrap works. Is it really man-eating? Cape Fear Museum visitors can explore watercraft people have used to get around the Cape Fear in the outdoor Maritime Pavilion. Check out the Nature-in-the-City landscape area, too.

CHILDREN'S MUSEUM OF WILMINGTON

Wilmington - ***116 Orange Street, downtown (corner of 2nd and Orange Streets) 28401. Phone: (910) 254-3534. www.playwilmington.org. Hours: Tuesday-Saturday 9:00am-5:00pm. Sunday 1:00-5:00pm. Open summer Mondays. Admission: $9.95 per person (age 1+). Senior & military discount. Note: The Toddler Exhibit is a space designed specifically for ages two and younger - and their caregivers. Museum is best for ages 1 to 10.***

Nurturing Imagination to explore and learn is their motto. Be a check-out clerk or stock the shelves to learn about the food groups, math and sorting. Pretend cook and serve a meal at the International Diner. Swab the decks maties as you pretend to be a crafty pirate aboard the ship. Next, discover the properties of sand by pouring and sifting. Meet Toothasaurus in the dental exhibit interactive. The circus area is actually run by the animals, with a lion as the ringmaster, and includes a performance ring, back stage dress-up area, clown car and a circus train carrying circus props and musical instruments as well as a tent wagon with many different types of blocks and building materials. In the Outdoor Courtyard, kids can jump like a frog, fly like a bird, climb like a monkey, creep like a spider, or wiggle like a worm as they crawl and climb in the body fitness, Animal Adventures.

HOLLYWOOD LOCATION WALK OF OLD WILMINGTON

Wilmington - ***1 Market Street (Tours Begin Riverfront At Market & Water Streets At The Black Cat Shop) 28401. Phone: (910) 794-1066. www.wilmingtondowntown.com/go/hollywood-location-walk. Admission: $13.00 for adults, $11.00 for seniors, students or military. Children ages 6 and under are FREE. Tours: 1.5 hour tours. 2:00pm Tuesday, Wednesday, Thursday, Saturday & Sunday, PLUS 10:00 am Saturdays. (Weekends only at 2:00pm Winter). Tours are rain or shine. Tours sell out quickly. Purchase tickets in advance online to assure spot.***

It's "Lights, Camera, Action!" as local actors lead visitors on a name dropping, movie & TV extravaganza through one of America's largest living film sets; Wilmington, North Carolina! Discover why, with over 400 film credits, Wilmington is known as "Hollywood East." See where some of Wilmywood's biggest movies were shot, including; Teenage Mutant Ninja Turtles, Divine Secrets Of The Ya-Ya Sisterhood, or Weekend At Bernie's.

DID YOU KNOW?

Wilmington generates more film income than any other American city except New York & Los Angeles !

Also, see real locations & actual sets where your favorite TV Shows, movies & mini-series were shot, including Dawson's Creek, One Tree Hill, several CBS series, and Matlock. Then, see where the stars like to hang-out while working, vacationing or living there. This 90 minute fun-filled walking tour will have you laughing and crying, and you better do it on cue if "*you ever want to work in this town again*"!

WILMINGTON RAILROAD MUSEUM

Wilmington - ***505 Nutt Street (corner of Red Cross and Water Streets in historic Atlantic Coast Line Center) 28401. Phone: (910) 763-2634. www.wrrm.org. Hours: Monday-Saturday 10:00am-5:00pm, Sunday 1:00-5:00pm (mid April-mid October). Only open to 4:00pm and closed Sundays, rest of year. Admission: $9.50 adult, $8.50 senior/military, $5.50 child (2-12).***

Climb aboard a steam locomotive and bright red caboose. On the FUN side are a Thomas the Tank Train play area and operating HO and O scale trains. Educationally, they trace the development of railroads in the Wilmington area as well as the careers of famous people who were involved with railroads, such as Thomas Edison and George Pullman. Learn about Wilmington's role as the center of railroad history along the coast. There are model exhibits of the Atlantic Coastline's Carolina routes from the 1940s and 50s.

CAPE FEAR RIVERBOATS

Wilmington - ***(docked at the foot of Market and Water sts at Riverfront Park) 28402. Phone: (910) 343-1611. www.cfrboats.com. Tours: See schedule. Public cruises are from April - December. Child $5.00, Adult $12.00.***

Cruise into Wilmington's historic past aboard the Cape Fear River tour boats. Vintage WWII Navy launch boats offer cruises and taxi service to the Battleship NC and the riverfront. Local wildlife, fun facts past movie and tv show sets.

THALIAN ASSOCIATION CHILDREN'S THEATRE

Wilmington - ***120 S. Second Street (Hannah Block 2nd Street Stage, Community Arts Center) 28402. Phone: (910) 251-1788. www.thalian.org.***

The Thalian Association Children's Theatre (TACT) stages four productions a year. Dozens of local children get into the act for the Thalian Association Children's Theatre productions like Beauty and the Beast or Christmas-themed juvenile productions.

WILMINGTON TROLLEY COMPANY

Wilmington - ***Forden Station 505 Cando St 28405. Phone: (910) 343-0106. www.wavetransit.com/free-downtown-trolley Admission: Free. Tours: Daily 7:00am-8:00pm, except Sundays 9am-5pm. Schedule subject to change. May be pre-empted by charters.***

The 45 minute narrated tour weaves through the bumpy brick laid streets as the guide gives life to the homes, people and events that give the town its character. The eight-mile sightseeing tour includes passing by mansions, haunted homes, TV & Movie locations, museums, birthplaces of famous locals, Civil War shipyards and some African-American historical sites. Note: Holiday Trolley Tours begin after Thanksgiving through Christmas.

The Cape Fear Historic Byway (www.ncdot.org) travels some of this route noted for its unique, exceptional historical, cultural or scenic characteristics.

AIRLIE GARDENS

Wilmington - ***300 Airlie Road 28403. www.airliegardens.org. Phone: (910) 798-7564. Hours: Daily 9:00am-5:00pm. Closed winter Mondays. Open later in the spring bloom season. Admission: $3.00-$5.00 (age 4+). $9.00 adults.***

The Butterfly House is here! Many colorful native species of butterflies take flight inside an open-air greenhouse that is open to visitors. Educational plaques focus on the butterfly life cycle and how to create your own backyard butterfly garden. The site is a combination of formal gardens, wildlife, historic structures, walking trails, sculptures, views of Bradley Creek, 10-acres of freshwater lakes, and the grandeur of the 462-year-old Airlie Oak. The Gardens are known for a collection of over 100,000 azaleas and countless camellia cultivars, which bloom throughout the winter and early spring. Displays around the Airlie Oak, Pergola Garden, and other areas bloom with continuous color year-round, as the displays are changed seasonally. While visiting, you will be able to set your own pace in the self-guided walking tour.

ENCHANTED AIRLIE: A HOLIDAY LIGHT EXTRAVAGANZA

Wilmington - Airlie Gardens. One of the largest lighting displays along the NC Coast. 40 holiday events all month long (late November - early January)

JUNGLE RAPIDS FAMILY FUN PARK

Wilmington - *5320 Oleander Drive (I-40 becomes 132 College Road. Left on Oleander Drive - US76 - one mile on right) 28403. www.junglerapids.com. Phone: (910) 791-0666. Hours: Opens at 10:00am daily. Water attractions open, seasonally, at 11:00am. Admission: Average $7.00 per person per game/activity. Range of $17.99-$25.99 for waterpark. Note: Concessions, floats and gift shop.*

This large amusement park is home to a million gallon wave pool, speed slides, tube slides and body slides, a lazy river, and a large kids' splash pool. Some of the new theme tube rides are: Sidewinder (half-pipe) and Super Bowl ("toilet bowl") rides. Inside there's a large climbing wall, laser tag, playground, arcade, and café. Also outside are the go-kart track and jungle mini-golf.

TREGEMBO ANIMAL PARK

Wilmington - *5811 Carolina Beach Rd 28403. www.tregemboanimalpark.com. Phone: (910) 791-0472. Hours: Open daily 10:00am-5:00pm (late March - Labor Day). Weekends only September, October. Admission:$12.00 adult, $8.00 child (2-11). Note: large gift shop and petting zoo area.*

Situated on five acres that create a forest-like atmosphere, this zoo features walkways that allow closeup observation of over 100 birds, mammals, and reptiles. There are some of the familiar zoo favorites like Clyde, their 24-year-old camel, a lion named Simba and Ben the bear, along with some exotic new additions including a giraffe, a zebra and a group of ring-tailed lemurs that reside on their very own Lemur Island. The Reptile, Amphibian and small Mammal building houses a tentacle snake and albino turtles. Kids will have a great time feeding the ducks and goats, offering peanuts to the monkeys and watching their amusing primate antics.

SCREEN GEMS STUDIOS / EUE TOURS

Wilmington - *1223 23rd Street North (off US 17/74, outskirts of downtown) 28405. Phone: (910) 343-3433. www.screengemsstudios.com. Admission: $12.00 adult, $10.00 students w/ ID/ military, $8.00 senior, $5.00 child (5-12). Tours: Saturdays and Sundays at Noon and 2:00pm each spring & summer and Saturdays only, other seasons (weather pending). One hour long. Reservations - call for availability.*

This is the largest movie-making studio facility east of Hollywood (a.k.a. "Hollywood East") - and your family can tour it! Filmmakers like the mild climate, beautiful beaches, diverse architecture, varied landscapes and history along the Cape Fear River. The guided tour includes a visit to the sound stages, prop warehouses, and sets from current television series taped here. Most of the props you see are real. How do they use showers and kitchen sinks without the water hooked up? See a stairway to nowhere. Tour a locker room in a pretend high school or the many bedrooms on set. The tour changes as productions change so each one is different. Visit the actual set of the current WB hit show. Dream Stage 10 features a 50-foot indoor "tank" of water. The studio is always adding new props and items from the movies to Stage 1, which consists of items such as a jail cell (from "Matlock"), a "MINE" stamping machine (from "Elmo in Grouchland"), "Under the Dome", "Iron Man 3" movie, and set pieces from the "Dawson's Creek" series. A taste of "behind-the-scenes" Hollywood.

Lights...Camera...Action !

POPLAR GROVE PLANTATION

Wilmington - ***10200 US 17 North (10 miles north of Wilmington) 28411. Phone: (910) 686-9518. www.poplargrove.org. Hours: Monday-Saturday 9:00am-3:30pm. Closed Thanksgiving Day. Closed the week of Christmas, reopens first Monday in February. Admission: $12.00 adult, $10.00 senior/military, $6.00 child (6-15). Tours: Daily guided tours by costumed interpreters on the hour. Note: Picnic area, restaurant and playground.***

SE

"A peanut here, a peanut there, pretty soon it adds up to some serious peanuts." Featuring outbuildings and crafts typical of an 1800s working community, this peanut plantation features a house, farmer's cabin, blacksmith's shop, and a peanut/agricultural exhibit building. Some of the discoveries made from the peanut were peanut butter, paint, salves, bleach, tan remover, wood filler, washing powder, metal polish, paper ink, plastics, shaving cream, rubbing oil, linoleum, shampoo, axle grease and others. Because of George Washington Carver, more farmers in North Carolina started planting peanuts instead of cotton. Today, peanuts are North Carolina's fifth largest cash crop. In the craft shops you can learn about basket making and weaving. They also have geese, goats, sheep, chickens and turkeys, and horses.

CHRISTMAS OPEN HOUSE

Wilmington *- Poplar Grove Plantation. Sip some yuletide punch and nibble on a Christmas cookie in the warmth of a "Victorian Christmas" Manor House. You'll be back in antebellum times; stroll the decorated plantation, see the blacksmith or weaver creating their treasures, or visit the farm animals. FREE. (first Sunday in December)*

NORTH CAROLINA AZALEA FESTIVAL

Wilmington - The Festival is a celebration of Wilmington's exceptional artwork, gardens, rich history and culture during its five days of entertainment that includes: a parade, street fair, circus, concerts, pageantry, and all that is Southern. Call (910) 794-4650 for more information. Various Locations. www.ncazaleafestival.org (five days in April)

JULY 4TH CELEBRATION

Wilmington - Riverfront, downtown. (910) 251-5797. Fireworks launched from the Battleship NC. Battleship Blast. Harbor cruises for fee. Best view from downtown. FREE.

RIVERFEST

Wilmington - Downtown Wilmington, Riverside - Water Street. Riverfest celebrates life and culture on the Cape Fear River with a variety of family-friendly events and activities, including a street fair, outdoor entertainment, ship tours, the Invasion of the Pirates Flotilla, and fireworks. www.wilmingtonriverfest.com. (910) 452-6862. (first long weekend in October)

COLONIAL CHRISTMAS AT BURGWIN-WRIGHT HOUSE

SE

Wilmington - Burgwin-Wright House Museum. www.burgwinwrighthouse.com. 224 Market Street. The house is decorated in the 1700's Christmas tradition during this two day event. Visitors are entertained by musicians playing 18th century music, food in colonial times is held in the colonial kitchen, hot wassail is served. A colonial surgeon is also available to demonstrate life during the colonial period, colonial dancers in authentic costumes dance and see weaving and spinning in the craft room above the kitchen. The old dungeon can be viewed in the cellar area. Admission. (second or third weekend before Christmas in December)

BLOCKADE RUNNER BEACH RESORT

Wrightsville Beach - 28480. 275 Waynick Blvd. www.blockade-runner.com. (910) 256-2251 or (800) 541-1161. Located right on Wrightsville Beach Island, the resort fronts the Atlantic Ocean with a sandy beach and an Intracoastal Waterway on the other side. The largest guest rooms on the coast of North Carolina also have refrigerator wet bars in every room. The "SeaEscape" beach snack bar is surrounded by beach volleyball, sunbathing, surfing and swimming. A heated indoor channel leads to a heated outdoor pool, jacuzzi and sauna. They seasonally offer "Sand Campers" day and night activity programs. Average $150 per night w/ some rates starting at $100.00! Complimentary full American hot breakfast weekdays.

WRIGHTSVILLE BEACH SCENIC CRUISES & WATER TAXI

Wrightsville Beach - ***(across from Blockade Runner resort) 28480. Phone: (910) 200-4002. https://wrightsvillebeachscenictours.com/ Tours: Harbor: Monday-Saturday Noon, 1:30pm & 3:30pm. (weather permitting). Make reservations. Other theme cruises are available at additional cost.***

Narrated cruises around Harbor Island and nature excursions include funny stories about people who have anchored here. Also, hear stories about hurricanes and the story about a house with natural air-conditioning. See spots where movies have been filmed and famous stars live. Treasure Island is here (where Blackbeard hid his treasures). Someone has since found the Spanish gold but others still look for more. Go under a drawbridge and then learn the amusing story of the "Palm Tree Island" parking meter.

- ISLAND PIRATE ADVENTURE: Join a costumed pirate storyteller on a 2.5 hour narrated voyage of Money Island on the Intracoastal Waterway. Meets at Wrightsville Beach Museum of History - 303 West Salisbury Street. $35.00/$30.00
- ISLAND ECO TOUR: This eco-minded tour explores Masonboro Island, NC. Masonboro Island is state owned wildlife sanctuary area. Here visitors, guided by a trained naturalist, can experience first hand the pristine ocean beaches, dunes and saltmarsh eco-system. Learn crabbing. Shelling. 2 hours. Adult $45.00 / $30.00 child.

CAPE FEAR KITE FESTIVAL

Wrightsville Beach *- Shell Island Resort. Come watch as they paint the Cape Fear Sky! Flyers from all over join in for the Annual Cape Fear Kite Festival, held on Wrightsville Beach, in front of Shell Island Oceanfront Suites. See the sky filled with color from countless kites of unbelievable sizes and styles! www.capefearkitefestival.com. Free. (first weekend in November)*

NORTH CAROLINA HOLIDAY FLOTILLA

Wrightsville Beach *- Banks Channel. www.ncholidayflotilla.org. (800) 222-4757. A floating parade of brightly lit and wildly decorated boats of all shapes and sizes combine with a fireworks display at the beginning. A holiday fair, children's art show, rides, food and performing artists add to the festivities. (Saturday after Thanksgiving in November)*

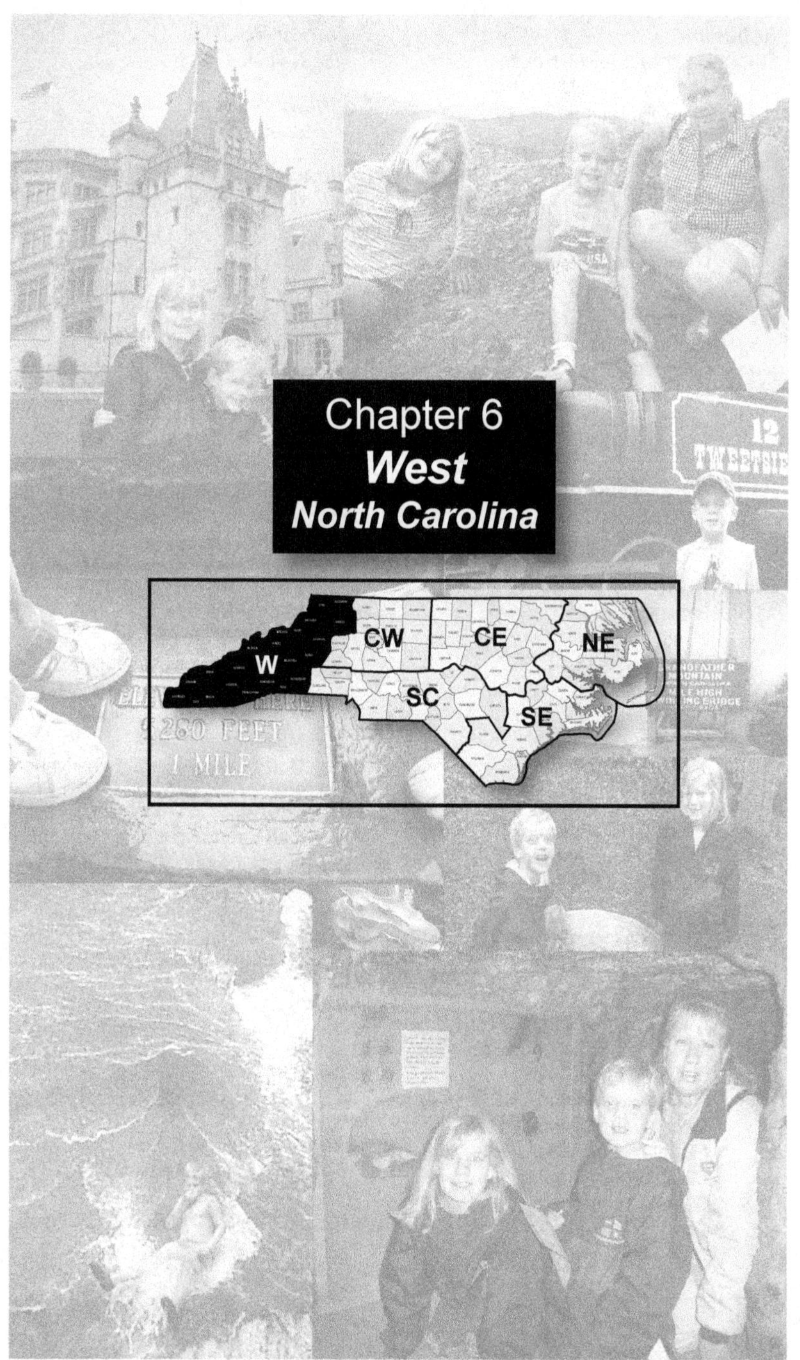
Chapter 6
West
North Carolina
CW
CE
NE
W
SC
SE
12
TWEETSIE
5280 FEET
1 MILE

Asheville
- Smith-McDowell House
- Thomas Wolfe Memorial
- Asheville Historic Trolley Tours
- Asheville Science Museum
- Biltmore House
- Blue Ridge Parkway Visitor Center
- Folk Art Center
- Hampton Inn Tunnel Road
- Western North Carolina Nature Center
- North Carolina Arboretum
- Goombay! Festival
- National Gingerbread House Competition
- Kwanzaa Celebration

Asheville (Weaverville)
- Vance Birthplace State Historic Site

Blowing Rock
- Blowing Rock
- Mystery Hill
- Tweetsie Railroad

Boone
- Dan'l Boone Inn Restaurant
- Horn In The West

Bryson City
- Great Smoky Mountains RR
- Smoky Mountain Trains Museum

Burnsville
- Mount Mitchell State Park

Cherokee
- Holiday Inn Of Cherokee
- Museum Of The Cherokee Indian
- Oconaluftee Indian Village
- Oconaluftee Visitor Center/ Mountain Farm Museum - Great Smoky Mountains
- Santa's Land Theme Park & Zoo
- Unto These Hills Outdoor Drama

Chimney Rock
- Chimney Rock Park

Connelly Springs
- South Mountains State Park

Cullowhee
- Mountain Heritage Day

Fletcher
- NC Mountain State Fair

Fontana Dam
- Fontana Village

Franklin
- Scottish Tartans Museum
- Franklin Gem & Mineral Museum
- Nantahala National Forest / Mountain Water Scenic Byway
- Sheffield Mine
- Wilderness Taxidermy Museum

Hendersonville
- DuPont State Forest
- Holmes Educational State Forest
- Mineral & Lapidary Museum
- Western North Carolina Air Museum
- North Carolina Apple Festival

Hendersonville (Flat Rock)
- Carl Sandburg Home National Historic Site
- Flat Rock Playhouse

Hiddenite
- Hiddenite Gems

Highlands
- Highland Area Waterfalls

Jefferson
- New River State Park

Lake Lure
- Lake Lure Tours And Beach / Water Works
- Rumbling Bald Resort On Lake Lure

Lenoir
- Tuttle Educational State Forest

Linville
- Grandfather Mountain

Linville Falls
- Linville Gorge Wilderness Area

Maggie Valley
- Wheels Through Time Museum

Marion
- Linville Caverns

Marion (Nebo)
- Lake James State Park

Old Fort
- Mountain Gateway Museum And Heritage Center

Pisgah Forest
- Cold Mountain
- Cradle Of Forestry In America
- Sliding Rock - A Natural Water Slide
- Blue Ridge Corn Maze

Roaring Gap
- Stone Mountain State Park

Rosman
- River Adventures

Rutherfordton
- Kidsenses Children's Interactive Museum

Sapphire
- Gorges State Park

Sparta
- Blue Ridge Parkway Homesteads / Doughton Park

Spruce Pine
- Gem Mountain

Spruce Pine (Little Switzerland)
- Emerald Village
- Orchard At Altapass

Tryon
- Foothills Equestrian Nature Center (Fence)

Valdese
- From This Day Forward Outdoor Drama

Waynesville
- International Festival Day
- Apple Harvest Festival
- A Night Before Christmas

West Jefferson
- Ashe County Cheese Factory

A Quick Tour of our Hand-Picked Favorites Around...

Western North Carolina

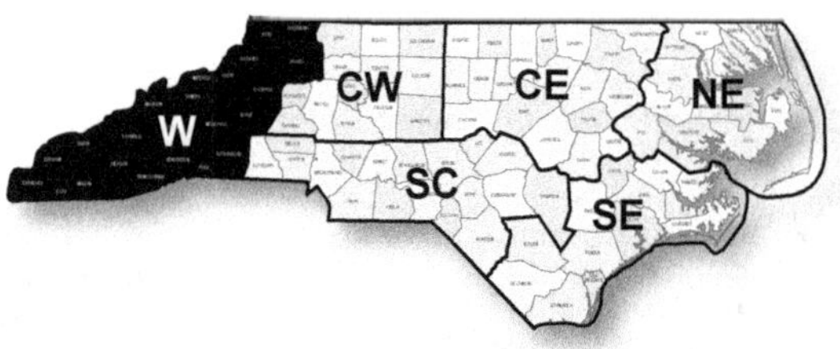

The Appalachian mountain chain runs through the western part of the state, forming the peaks and valleys of the region. The Great Smoky Mountains in southwestern North Carolina are one of the country's top natural destinations, and visitors can enjoy 250 miles of the world-famous Blue Ridge Parkway winding through North Carolina's mountains. Ride both a train and a ferris wheel at one park – **Tweetsie Railroad**. Traveling the Parkway in the rainy spring or fall months, you might feel you're on a cloud at **Grandfather Mountain** with its famous Mile High Swinging Bridge. Next, prepare to be elevated at **Chimney Rock**! Made famous in the movie *The Last of the Mohicans*, traverse a cool tunnel and then take the fast elevator up a 26-story shaft blasted through solid granite!

With the highest mountain peaks east of the Mississippi and some of the lowest average temperatures, outdoorsy families are provided with outstanding snow sports; a cool oasis for hiking, biking trails through enchanted Forests in the spring and summer; and an amazing season of fall foliage. Whitewater paddlers, anglers, hikers, mountain bikers and gem miners alike will find something fun to do here in this lush wilderness. In the summer, try a site at mountains base called **Lake Lure**. Taking a boat tour around the mountain lake, rafting or just splashing at the beach waterpark are all easy recreation activities at this resort town away from it all.

Ready for adventure? Indians once roamed these hills – and still do. Visit the **Cherokee Heritage Center** and the **Museum of the Cherokee Indian** and see the outdoor drama, **Unto These Hills** to learn more about the proud heritage of these Native Americans. While in the forest, visit The **Cradle of Forestry in America**. Pretend you're wildlife crawling the forest floor or don a swimsuit and swoosh down a natural 60-foot water slide called **Sliding Rock**.

And the great indoors is just as exhilarating as the outdoors. Spend an afternoon exploring America's largest home, at the **Biltmore Estate.** Be sure to ask for the scavenger hunt sheet to complete while you tour. Only the little detectives in your family may be able to "eye spy" everything on the list and win a prize! Nearby the **Asheville Science Museum** keeps young minds engaged and little hands busy.

Have an aspiring author or poet in your family? Writers and actors have always found the North Carolina mountains inspiring. Author **Thomas Wolfe** made his home in Asheville, while Historic Hendersonville and Flat Rock were home to poet **Carl Sandburg** (biography of Lincoln fame). Both homes will engage your kids literary senses – or maybe yours!

Sites and attractions are listed in order by City, Zip Code, and Name. Symbols indicated represent: ☐ Restaurants ☐ Lodging

SMITH-MCDOWELL HOUSE MUSEUM

***Asheville** - 283 Victoria Road (campus of Tech College) (off Hwy. 25 south of downtown, follow the signs to A-B Tech College) 28801. Phone: (828) 253-9231. www.wnchistory.org. Hours: Wednesday-Saturday 10:00am-4:00pm. Closed major holidays. Admission: $5.00-$10.00 (age 5+).*

A wealthy businessman by the name of James McConnell Smith built the mansion in 1840. He was the first child-settler born west of the North Carolina mountains. This National Register property was once the home of mayors, a Confederate Major, and friends of the Vanderbilts at nearby Biltmore Estate. While touring, notice much of the woodwork is original. Other interesting sights within the house include a journey through time including an 1840s kitchen, 1850s bedroom, 1880s parlor and 1890s dining room. Period furnishings are appropriate for each of the rooms. In addition, the museum offers a variety of educational programs and exhibits throughout the year.

VICTORIAN EASTER CELEBRATION

***Asheville** - Smith-McDowell House Museum. The town's oldest mansion is decorated with Easter baskets, old-fashioned bunnies and chicks, hand-painted eggs and colorful spring flowers. (end of March thru mid-April)*

CHRISTMAS AT THE SMITH-MCDOWELL HOUSE MUSEUM

Asheville *- Smith-McDowell House Museum. Come visit the Smith-McDowell House Museum and see how popular culture effected trends and styles from the 1840s through 1890s. Each room in this restored circa 1840 mansion and local history museum is authentically decorated with fresh trees, garlands, ornaments, and toys of the Victorian Age. Admission. (mid-November thru New Years week)*

THOMAS WOLFE MEMORIAL

Asheville ***- 52 North Market Street (I- 240, take the Merrimon Avenue Exit (5A) 28801. Phone: (828) 253-8304. https://wolfememorial.com/. Hours: Tuesday-Saturday 9:00am-5:00pm. Admission: $2.00-$5.00 per student/adult. Educators: Wealth of biographical editorials online.***

Portrayed as Dixieland in Wolfe's most famous novel, Look Homeward, Angel, the boarding house is the author's boyhood home (named Altamont in the book). A classic of American literature, Look Homeward, Angel has never gone out of print since its publication in 1929, keeping interest in Wolfe alive and attracting visitors to the setting for this great novel. Wolfe's writings were closely based on "characters" from his home town. Locals either despised or loved him for this "too close to home" approach. Kids learn the process of writing from a struggling, yet famous, author. The Visitor Center has a short video, plus numerous displays. Lots of biographical information online.

W

ASHEVILLE HISTORIC TROLLEY TOURS

Asheville ***- 36 Montford Avenue (I-240 exit 4C) Asheville Visitor Ctr., center of downtown OR Grove Park Inn) 28802. www.ashevilletrolleytours.com. Phone: (828) 669-8046 or (888) 667-3600. Admission: $32.00 adult, $30.00 senior/AARP, $12.00 student (5-11). Admission includes discounted Wolfe house tour. 2nd day free. Tours: Monday-Saturday 8:30am.-4:40pm, Sunday 12:30-3:30pm. Closed January-February (except for special group bookings). Allow 75 minutes for the full tour. Departures: Every 90 minutes from each stop. See schedule on web.***

See the best of Asheville aboard a vintage trolley and enjoy the narration covering all major points of interest in Asheville including: the Grove Park Inn, Biltmore Village, the downtown shopping and restaurants district, the Thomas Wolfe Memorial, the Asheville Museum and Art Gallery district, the Asheville Visitors Center and much more. Learn how "Biltmore" got its name. Pass a house that celebrates Christmas every day. Your guide will combine humorous stories and historical information into a fun-filled experience. Disembark the trolley at any of the many convenient stops, then re-board and continue the tour.

ASHEVILLE MUSEUM OF SCIENCE

***Asheville** - 43 Patton Avenue 28801. Phone: (828) 254-7162. https://ashevillescience.org/. Hours: Monday-Saturday 10am-5pm, Sunday 1-5pm. Admission: $8.00 adult, $7.00 student/senior/child (age 4+). Note: Monthly Homeschool, & After School classes offered.*

Scratching soft minerals into powder...

Before you start, ask for an exploration guide and fill in the blanks to win a prize "gem" at the end. Now, start in The Hall of Minerals featuring specimens such as an amethyst crystal cluster; a green fluorite from a North Carolina mine; and a ruby in zoisite from Tanzania. The Gem Room includes a 220 carat blue topaz from Brazil and a 2,405.5 carat boulder opal from Australia. The North Carolina Gallery favorites include itacolumite (the bending rock) from Stokes County and an emerald crystal from the Old Plantation Mine in Cleveland County. Walk through an authentic replica of a gem mine next. The hands-on gallery explores the forces that shape the Earth such as the rock cycle, volcanoes, earthquakes, and plate tectonics. Highlights include a touch screen computer program on plate tectonics and large scale models of a volcano and the Earth. Visitors can investigate Weather, Climate and You - finding clues to the science behind weather reports. What happens when wind hits a mountain or floods rock the Piedmont. Fossils, Florescent Minerals and Crystals round out the collection. Throughout the museum, hands-on study areas include: Sand digging, water play, Picking up a light rock (pumice) vs. a heavy rock (scoria), or even make your own powder from scraping a soft stone.

BILTMORE HOUSE

***Asheville** - 1 Approach Road (Take I-40 West to Exit 50-B on US 25. Take US 25 exit of Blue Ridge Parkway) 28803. www.biltmore.com. Phone: (828) 225-1333 or (800) 624-1575. Hours: Daily 9:00am–5:00pm. Some outdoor areas and shops open later. Gate Price: $69 adult, Half Price for youth (ages 10-16). Children 9 and younger are admitted free year-round with a paying adult. Access to the House and Gardens self guided tour, Antler Hill Village, and a wine tasting. Pricing differs for Christmas at Biltmore (November-early January). Extra $25.00 for Behind the Scenes or Rooftop tours. Tours: Self-guided hike or bike maps available at the Outdoor Center. Also at the Center, guided raft, kayak, trail, and carriage rides thru the property for an additional fee.*

Tailor your Biltmore House visit to your child's attention span and energy level. Take a breather and visit the Ice Cream Parlor or Bake Shop for a quick snack or water break. Run wild! Burn off pent-up energy with a race to the top of the Vista in front of Biltmore House.

BILTMORE HOUSE (cont.)

Educators: Top notch Student Resource Guides, Workbooks and Teacher Lesson Plans online. Note: Grab lunch in the Stable Café, once used to house the horses and carriages on the Estate. Family carriage rides and river float tours, too.

Imagine the awe on your child's face at the first sight of this real-life castle! This was the home of "Richie Rich" in the movie of the same name (watch it before you go to get into the mood). In the 250-room Biltmore House, kids can imagine what it might have been like to live in a home with its own bowling alley and swimming pool. After you're greeted by the butler "Welcome Home", you'll take yourself on a self-guided visit through four floors of Biltmore House filled with art and antiques (look, don't touch), including the giant Banquet Hall (why are the acoustics so good?), the infamous Library (look for the secret stairway), the kitchens (with walk-in refrigerators), and servants' quarters. Stroll through century-old gardens designed by America's first landscape architect. Meet friendly farm animals in the Farmyard at the River Bend Farm. Plan to spend half the day indoors, half outdoors on a hike or trail ride. Get the free Commodore's Treasure Hunt guide for your kids and explore upstairs, downstairs, and all around (they get a sticker prize if they complete the hunt). Another great way to increase the kids' interest in visiting this amazing house is to read The Mystery of Biltmore House, by Carole Marsh.

W

EASTER AT BILTMORE HOUSE

Asheville - *Biltmore House. Spring arrives at Biltmore Estate with Easter egg hunts held on the front lawn of Biltmore. Children ages 2-9 can participate in several hunts throughout the day with prizes, magic shows and visits/breakfast with Biltmore's 19th Century Easter Rabbit. Admission to home required. (Saturday of Easter weekend)*

CHRISTMAS AT BILTMORE ESTATE

Asheville - Biltmore House. See dozens of trees dressed with glittering lights and elaborate ornaments, including a 34-foot Fraser fir that graces the Banquet Hall. Your senses will be thrilled with the spicy scent of evergreen and yuletide tunes from the Banquet Hall organ. Candlelight Christmas Evenings capture the magic of the holidays with candlelight and firelight, tinsel and glass ornaments, and choirs and musicians that fill the house with good cheer. Admission. (first weekend in November thru day after New Years)

BLUE RIDGE PARKWAY VISITOR CENTER

Asheville - ***195 Hemphill Knob Road (milepost 384) 28803. Hours: 9:00am - 5:00pm daily. www.blueridgeheritage.com or www.nps.gov/blri/.***

The Blue Ridge Parkway is ranked "America's most scenic drive" by leading travel writers. The Parkway follows the mountain crests from Shenandoah National Park in Virginia to the Great Smokey Mountains National Park in North Carolina and Tennessee. This environmentally friendly facility has native plants growing from a sod roof and glass panels in front to collect heat to warm the building. Inside, volunteers and staff assist visitors with trip plans. An expansive, interactive map covers an entire wall of the structure. As visitors move a monitor across the length of the map, videos and photographs pop up with relevant travel information. Exhibits at the center focus on recreation, natural and cultural diversity and the economic strength of the region; a focus on the chestnut tree and its impact on Southern Appalachia is also there. To get the best "feel" for traveling the Parkway, watch the 25-minute movie. In addition, ten kiosks provide tickets to participating regional attractions, outdoor activities and tours.

With the highest mountain peak in the Eastern United States, the oldest river in North America, some of the oldest mountains in the world, the deepest gorge east of the Grand Canyon, the highest waterfall east of the Rockies and the two most visited National Park lands in the country, the natural heritage of the North Carolina Mountains is surpassed by none. Now that you're equipped with maps in hand, go out and explore! Note: most of our listings indicate what milepost on the Parkway to exit.

FOLK ART CENTER

Asheville - ***PO Box 9545 (I-40 exit 55 or milepost 382 on the Blue Ridge Parkway) 28805. Phone: (828) 298-7928. www.southernhighlandguild.org. Hours: Daily 9:00am-5:00 or 6:00pm. Closed Thanksgiving, Christmas and New Year's Days Admission: FREE.***

Didn't get enough crafters? Head west a little ways on US70 (940 Tunnel Rd, www.stuartnye.com) to the Stuart Nye Hand Wrought Jewelry studio. Here, they hammer and shape flower designs out of metal.

A Center representing the crafts culture of the Southern Appalachians. Works of Art guild members are displayed and sold and artisans frequently demonstrate their craft (March-December). We watched a quilter and a basket weaver (ever seen garlic and onion baskets?). Also a bookstore and Information center are on the premises.

HAMPTON INN TUNNEL ROAD

***Asheville** - 28805. 204 Tunnel Road, http://hamptoninn3.hilton.com/en/hotels/north-carolina/hampton-inn-asheville-tunnel-rd-AVLTUHX/index.html or (800) 426-7866. I-240 exit 7. Close to most attractions, this comfortable hotel has a warm indoor pool, whirlpool, expanded continental breakfast, and a fireplace lobby serving tea and cookies nightly.* ☐ ____________________

W

WESTERN NORTH CAROLINA NATURE CENTER

Asheville - ***75 Gashes Creek Road (I- 40, take exit 53B. From I- 240, take exit 8) 28805. Phone: (828) 298-5600. www.wildwnc.org. Hours: Daily 10:00am-5:00pm. Closed Thanksgiving, Christmas, New Years and MLK day. Closed winter Wednesdays. Admission: $10.95 adult, $9.95 senior (65+), $6.95 child (3-15). Discounts for residents. Note: Trillium Outdoor Exploring Trail has boardwalk & dirt paths (takes ~30 minutes to hike). Petting area with goats and sheep. FREEBIES: Download a Nature Center Scavenger Hunt before you visit. Ask for a Wild Child Pack once you're there. Backpacks full of nature tools and activity booklet (ages 6-16). www.wncnaturecenter.com/SchoolsandGroups/EducationResources.aspx***

Indoors, the Nature Center welcomes you with a hands on greeting. Children and adults are encouraged to get a feel for the outdoors by touching, feeling, and examining articles of mountain area natural history. Touch actual bear fur (the closest you'll ever get) or see turtles burying themselves in the sand. By utilizing the microscope and magnifying glass stations, you can zoom in on everything from a rattlesnake fang to a butterfly wing. Get up close and personal with a native reptile by handling harmless snakes or Box Turtles. Experience the world of night in the Nocturnal Hall. Screech owls make their calls into the night.

Pretend to be an otter as you slide down the very slippery otter slide. (CAUTION: Fast!)

You may hear these creatures at night, but how often do you see them? Meet the Skunk, Opossum, Deer Mice, Bats, Flying Squirrels, and frogs. When you head outside, you'll want to walk the trail of predators like cougars, wolves and bobcats, oh my! Then enjoy the antics of river otters in their own special habitat (above and below water). In the barns, you may get a close look at baby animals.

NORTH CAROLINA ARBORETUM

Asheville - ***100 Frederick Law Olmstead Way (UNC campus, I-26 east to exit 33/ Hwy 191 south Blue Ridge Pkwy, look for signs) 28806. www.ncarboretum.org. Phone: (828) 665-2492. Hours: Grounds open 8:00am-sunset. Visitor Education Center: Daily 9:00am - 5:00pm. Greenhouse: Monday - Friday 8:00am - 2:00pm. Closed state holidays. Admission: Charge is $14.00 per personal vehicle. Note: Café and gift area.***

Located at the edge of the Pisgah National Forest, the 424-acre site features a Visitor Education Center, state-of-the-art greenhouse complex, an array of gardens, a loop trail and a variety of ongoing special programs. Stop by the Information Desk to pick up a brochure listing each month's educational programs, tours, garden demonstrations and workshops. Kids will like to visit during the Arbor Day or Bonsai Expo.

GOOMBAY! FESTIVAL

Asheville *- YMI Cultural Center and downtown. www.facebook.com/AshevilleGoombay/ Goombay emerged during slavery days in Bermuda. Both music and rhythm were brought from Africa and the West Indies. The original dancers used a skin-covered drum that was called "Gombey" meaning rhythm. Goombay dancers wear colorful costumes and high headdresses topped with feathers and, at times, masks. After watching performers, enjoy an authentic Caribbean meal at the Island of Delight Café. Street vendors sell everything from ice cream to third world crafts. Admission. (mid-September weekend)*

NATIONAL GINGERBREAD HOUSE COMPETITION

Asheville *- The Grove Park Inn Resort. (828) 252-2711 or www.groveparkinn.com. See more than 20 gingerbread works of art from all over the country. Houses will be on display throughout the holiday season. This month long event includes over 25 uniquely decorated trees. Enjoy themed areas, garlands, poinsettias, an elves' playhouse and much more. (day after Thanksgiving thru December)*

W

NAVITAT CANOPY ADVENTURES

Asheville (Barnardsville) - ***242 Poverty Branch Road (Parkway mileposts 376.6 to 393.6) 28607. Phone: (828) 626-3700. www.navitat.com. Tours: $99.95 every day. Must weigh at least 90 lbs. Spring thru end of November.***

Consistently called one of the best zipline canopy tours in the nation, Navitat is a fully guided, 100-percent tree based tour that showcases the beauty of North Carolina's Blue Ridge Mountains. The course includes two sky bridges, two rappels, three short hikes and 10 exhilarating ziplines – including one that soars more than 200 feet above the forest floor, and some that reach speeds up to 40 mph. Glide past dense forest, amazing trees and jaw-dropping views in all directions.

VANCE BIRTHPLACE STATE HISTORIC SITE

Asheville (Weaverville) - ***911 Reems Creek Road (U.S. 19-23 north to New Stock Road OR Blue Ridge Pkwy milepost 375/376) 28787. Phone: (828) 645-6706. www.facebook.com/VanceBirthplaceNCHS/ Hours: Tuesday-Saturday 9:00am-5:00pm. Admission: FREE.***

Historic homestead of North Carolina's Civil War governor, Zebulon B. Vance. The state historic site depicts early pioneer life in the mountains during the 1800s. Also included is the history of Vance's famous political mountain family. As the War Governor of the South, Vance's untiring efforts made on behalf of the soldiers and their families, provided every possible comfort to them during the famine and sadness of war. These actions ensured his place in the minds and hearts of the people he served. Nearby, the visitor center houses exhibits portraying the life of Vance and a 15 minute slide presentation. Best visited during spring and fall living history weekends.

CHRISTMAS CANDLELIGHT TOURS

Asheville (Weaverville) *- Vance Birthplace. Candlelight tours with living history. Admission. (mid-December Saturday)*

BLOWING ROCK

Blowing Rock - ***PO Box 145 (Hwy 321 South of Blue Ridge Parkway, follow 321 Bypass) 28605. Phone: (828) 295-7111. www.theblowingrock.com. Hours: Daily 9:00am-5:00pm; Daily 8:30am-7:00pm (April thru October). Closed Tuesday, Wednesday in January - March. Closed Thanksgiving and Christmas Day. Admission: $9.00 adult, $7.00 senior (60+), $3.00 child (5-12). $2 off winter hours. Note: Walking the self-guided trail takes an average of 15 to 25 minutes.***

The Blowing Rock is an immense cliff 4,000 feet above sea level overhanging Johns River Gorge 3,000 feet below. The phenomenon is so called because the rocky walls of the gorge form a flume through which the northwest wind sweeps with such force that it returns light objects cast over the cliff. Visible from "The Rock" down the gorge to the southwest are Hawksbill Mountain and Table Rock.

To the west are Grandfather Mountain (the highest peak in the Blue Ridge chain) and Mount Mitchell (the highest peak east of the Rockies). The Blowing Rock's mysterious winds cause even the snow to fall upside down. Lookout points have great views of the layers of mountain regions below. Enjoy the scenic views and observation tower, gardens, small garden waterfall and unique gift shop. On a clear day, this is picture taking mecca!

MYSTERY HILL ENTERTAINMENT COMPLEX

Blowing Rock - ***129 Mystery Hill Lane (Hwy. 321 between Boone and Blowing Rock. Pkwy exit 291) 28605. Phone: (828) 263-0507. www.mysteryhill-nc.com. Hours: Daily 9:00am-5:00pm. Open until 8:00pm (June - August). Admission: $9.00 adult (13-59), $8.00 senior (60+), $7.00 child (5-12). Includes museums and mystery hill. Note: On the premises is the Appalachian Heritage Museum (set up as it might have been in 1910 w/ crafters occasionally) and its walls are filled with Native American Relics.***

Things that make you wonder. This area attraction defies gravity. In the Mystery House, visitors stand at a 45 degree angle, water flows up hill and anyone can throw a curve. There is a stronger than average pull to the north which causes some of our basic laws of physics to work differently than normal. What causes this unexplained pull? Optical illusions are in the Hall of Mystery but there's also Mystery Rocks, Puzzles and giant Bubbles. Over 40 "experiments" to have fun with - watch, it may tickle your funny bone.

TWEETSIE RAILROAD

Blowing Rock - ***300 Tweetsie Railroad Lane (US 321, BRPkwy exit milepost 291, Boone exit) 28605. Phone: (828) 264-9061. www.tweetsie.com. Hours: Daily 9:00am-6:00pm (Memorial Day week-mid August). Long weekends only (early April, Late August-October). Admission: $52.00 adult, $33.00 child (3-12). Admission includes railroad, live entertainment, rides and Deer Park.***

Be a cowboy, cowgirl, Indian or an engineer. Stroll down Main Street, learn to clog, pan for gold or visit with deer and goats in Deer Park. Be sure to ride the chair lift or hike up Miner's Mountain. Tweetsie also has amusement rides for all ages and venues throughout the park performing live. The main feature, though, is the famous historic train ride. Hop aboard for a fun-filled three-mile Wild West journey through scenic mountains. Funny skits (kids love 'em) abound. If you cooperate, you might even get a souvenir bullet. Of course, you should be on the lookout when you walk around the park because you may meet Calamity Jane or get caught helping the posse look for the gold shipment from Fort Boone. Visitors get involved in most all the "shows" - they know how to keep the family amused and smiling. Plenty of good eatin', too - from hearty western-style meals to their Tweetsie Fudge for dessert.

4TH OF JULY

Blowing Rock - *Tweetsie Railroad. Park is open until 8:00pm. Parking $5.00. Be sure to bring a tailgate picnic. Event is for park guests only. Fireworks display.*

DAN'L BOONE INN RESTAURANT

Boone - *130 Hardin Street 28607. Historic downtown. www.danlbooneinn.com (828) 264-8657. Family style dining in a historic property. For over 40 years, Dan'l Boone Inn has been serving Boone and the high country delicious homecooked meals, just like you remember at grandma's house. Family style meals begin with a salad in the summer and soup in the winter. Three meats and five vegetables are served along with biscuits, preserves, dessert and beverage. A full family style breakfast is served on Saturdays and Sundays. Really gets you in the mood to see the outdoor drama. Go hungry, there is tons of food! ($5.95-$19.95).* ______ ☐

HORN IN THE WEST

Boone - ***591 Horn in the West Drive (Powderhorn Theatre) 28607. Phone: (828) 264-2120. www.horninthewest.com. Hours: Nightly except Monday at 8:00pm (late June through mid-August). Admission: ~$30.00 adult, child admission is half price. Note: Other shows include matinees with young themes.***

This outdoor drama is a tale of tragedy and triumph, happiness and heartbreak, all set in the context of a new wide-open America. Enjoy the three-stage story of Daniel Boone and the courageous settlers in their journey to the west. Specifically, follow the Stuart family as they discover things about themselves and their fellow journeymen. Learn about the Blue Ridge, Appalachia, Moravians, and the Cherokee. It keeps the kids entertained with a simple story-line, action, song and dance. You'll enjoy the lovable characters of the preacher and the widow. Look for the fire dance scene. Start in the late afternoon with a picnic, then enjoy the **HICKORY RIDGE HOMESTEAD LIVING HISTORY MUSEUM**. Costumed live interpreters give visitors a taste of pioneer life. Living history is recreated by docents in traditional costume, working with traditional tools, engaged in hearth baking, candle-making, weaving, tin-smithing and other activities among original mountain cabins. Located on the premises of the Theatre, the cost is included in your price of admission to the drama. Also open weekends each spring and fall.

HICKORY RIDGE HOMESTEAD APPLE FESTIVAL

Boone - *See living history museum cabins and taste all of the apple goodies including: homemade apple butter, pies, cider, and fritters. (early weekend in October)*

GREAT SMOKY MOUNTAINS RAILROAD

Bryson City - ***226 Everett Street 28713. Phone: (800) 872-4681. www.gsmr.com. Admission: $51.00-$58.00 adult, $29.00-$34.00 child (2-12). Tours: Mornings, Afternoon and Sunset tours generally last about 2 1/2 to 4 hours round-trip. Depart from Dillsboro (US 441 & Front Street) and Bryson City. Daily, March - December. Weekends only, January-February. Note: Box lunch options can be purchased at time of reservation or eat at restaurants in the gorge during layover. Also, foods can be purchased in the Conductor's Car during the excursion.***

Enjoy scenic train journeys across fertile valleys, through tunnels and across river gorges in the Great Smoky Mountains, pulled by diesel-electric and steam locomotives. Over the last several years the trains have played a part in several motion pictures: The Fugitive starring Harrison Ford and Tommy Lee Jones; Digging to China with Kevin Bacon; and Forces of Nature with Sandra Bullock and Ben Affleck.

Guests ride in comfortable, reconditioned coaches, crown coaches, club cars, dining cars, and open cars that are ideal for viewing the scenery and taking pictures. Experience the ride of your life with one of their Locomotive Cab Rides. Dillsboro Departures feature a scenic journey along the Tuckasegee River traveling alone side farmland. Bryson City Departures travels into the Nantahala Gorge known for its white water activity.

RAILFEST

Bryson City *- Great Smoky Mountains Railroad. Three days of railroad fun! Railroad enthusiasts world wide gather in town to see and ride historic railroad equipment, Motor car display and musical performances. (mid-September long weekend)*

PEANUTS™ - EASTER BEAGLE EXPRESS

Bryson City *- Great Smoky Mountains Railroad. Peanuts™ - The Express departs Dillsboro Depot at 3:30pm. This 4-hour round trip special event train departs the historic Bryson City Depot at 11:00am, and will travel along the Tuckasegee River to the quaint town of Dillsboro, North Carolina for a 1 ½ hour layover of activities. Passengers will join Snoopy, Lucy, Charlie Brown and our Easter Bunnies for old fashioned Easter fun! Festivities include an on-going Easter egg hunt, crafts, coloring sheets, temporary tattoos, and snacks with Snoopy and more.*

POLAR EXPRESS™, THE

W

Bryson City *- Great Smoky Mountains Railroad. The Polar Express comes to life when the train departs the Bryson City depot for a journey to their "North Pole". Guests on board will enjoy hot chocolate and treats while listening and reading along with the magical story. Experience the joy of watching the children's faces when the train arrives at the "North Pole," where Santa Claus will be waiting. Santa boards The Polar Express and greets each child, presenting them with a special memento. Holiday carols are sung on the return trip to Bryson City. Families will want to make this a holiday tradition! Special fare and online reservations required. (begins long weekends in November, then almost daily in December thru a few days before Christmas)*

SMOKY MOUNTAIN TRAINS MUSEUM

Bryson City ***- 100 Greenlee Street (US 74 exit 67, north on Veterans, east on US 19, north on Greenlee) 28713. www.gsmr.com/smoky-mountains-trains-museum. Phone: (866) 914-5200. Hours: Daily 9:00am-5:00pm. (June-December). Admission: $9.00 adult, $5.00 child (age 3+). Museum admission FREE with all GSMR Regular Train Excursion tickets.***

More than 7,000 Lionel locomotives and cars dating back to 1918 are on display. Over a mile of track on three levels with six trains running simultaneously. Visit the freight yard with more than 400 cars, see the five-foot waterfall and 12 animated scenes. There's an operating roundtable with roundhouse and a live cascading five-foot waterfall. There are also various wooden train tables to play with in the activity center and a retail shop. The museum recently added to their vast collection of model trains. What is different is that you (or the kid in you) and the kids can push buttons and operate the trains and over 20 accessory items. If small trains aren't enough for you, walk over to the Bryson City depot of the Great Smoky Mountain Railroad (same owners).

MOUNT MITCHELL STATE PARK

Burnsville - ***2388 SR 128 (Blue Ridge Parkway milepost 355) 28714. Phone: (828) 675-4611. http://ncparks.gov/Visit/parks/momi/main.php. Hours: Visitor Center: Daily 10:00am-6:00pm (May-October). Admission: FREE.***

Mount Mitchell is the highest peak (6,685 feet) in the eastern United States. The park offers easy access from the Blue Ridge Parkway with a restaurant, tent camping area, museum and picnic area, as well as hiking trails connecting to the Pisgah National Forest. The Exhibit Hall, located near the mountain's summit, offers visitors insight into the mountain's natural, cultural and historical faces. Exhibits include: An interactive weather station, (punch in your birthday to find out the weather conditions on Mount Mitchell's summit on that date); A life-size wood carving of "Big" Tom Wilson, the mountain guide who led a search for the person who first calculated Mount Mitchell to be the highest peak on the east coast; a replica of "Big" Tom's cabin with historical artifacts and buttons that allow visitors to listen to four different stories about his life; a three-dimensional topographic map of the Black Mountains with interactive buttons; a geology section with a hands-on demonstration of a rock fault and four samples of the different rock types in the state park; and dioramas that depict animal life in the state park.

W

HOLIDAY INN OF CHEROKEE

Cherokee - *376 Paint Town Road, 28719. US Highway 19 south. (828) 497-9181 or www.holidayinn.com/hotels/us/en/cherokee/chrnc/hoteldetail. Located in the Smoky Mountain range. Take a dip in the outdoor or indoor pool. Grab a bite to eat in the Chestnut Tree Restaurant (featuring home-style cooking). Entertainment for the kids includes a cute outdoor playground, pool table, air hockey, and game room. Complimentary hot breakfast included with stay. From $145/night.*

☐

MUSEUM OF THE CHEROKEE INDIAN

Cherokee - ***778 Drama Road (Hwy 441 & Drama Road, center of town) 28719. Phone: (828) 497-3481. www.cherokeemuseum.org. Hours: Opens daily at 9:00am except on Thanksgiving, Christmas and New Year's Day. Museum closes between 5:00-7:00pm. Admission: $12.00 adult, $7.00 child (6-12), FREE pre-schooler (under 6). Educators: A traditional Cherokee story lesson is online.***

As the keepers of tradition, Cherokee storytellers played an important role in tribal life. As your guide through thousands of years of the Cherokee experience, the storyteller (shown through holograms and spoken voices) will help the interactive museum come to life. Travel back to a time of mastodons and atlatls - prehistoric time. Step forward where you'll meet a dramatic chieftain, see and hear a medicine man and play the centuries old butter bean game. You'll learn what happened when white men first appeared on their land. Later, you'll pass by the Revolutionary War and the creator of the brilliant Cherokee alphabet, Sequoyah. Finally, travel along the infamous Trail of Tears, and back to the present. Modern, engaging displays work to tell the story in many formats.

OCONALUFTEE INDIAN VILLAGE

Cherokee - ***218 Drama Road (US 19 west to Hwy 441, center of town) 28719. Phone: (828) 497-2315 or (828)-497-2111 (Off Season). www.cherokeesmokies.com/oconaluftee_village.html. Hours: Daily 10:00am-5:00pm (mid-April to mid-November). Tours: $20 adult, $12 child (6-13) - guided.***

W

Making of blow guns from

Shiyo! (Hello! In Cherokee) The Oconaluftee Indian Village is an authentic recreation of an 18th century Cherokee Indian village. Here you will see the model of a Cherokee village from over 225 years ago. Cherokee guides in native costume explain their history, the culture and life-style of their ancestors, and answer your questions. The tours (leaving about every 10 minutes) provide simple, quick explanations of each craft. We especially liked the fact that real Cherokee are crafting. Carefully watch the demos of river cane and mountain cane used to make large and small blow guns or arrows. Then, see men chipping flint creating sharp arrowheads for hunting or fighting. Next, a villager demonstrates the blow gun with a target. Move on to various housing units. The Sweat House was used for a hospital...how? It was so interesting to see how Indians took a giant log and burned a canoe out of it. The Ceremonial Square is where prayer dances were held. Cherokee did not worship idols and nature, just one Creator (God). Cherokee use slow dances to worship or pray. How did they make rattles? Water drums? Hear Cherokee spoken and interpreted. This Village is highly recommended before attending the drama. You'll learn more than you can imagine about their people. Maybe even learn some Cherokee to impress your friends.

OCONALUFTEE VISITOR CENTER/ MOUNTAIN FARM MUSEUM - GREAT SMOKY MOUNTAINS

Cherokee - *(2 miles north of town, on US 441 , Great Smoky Mtn. National Park) 28719. Phone: (828) 497-1900. www.nps.gov/grsm. Hours: Open all year during business hours 8:30am-4:30pm. Great Smoky Mountains National Park is open 24 hours a day, 365 days a year. However some secondary roads, campgrounds, and other visitor facilities close in winter. Admission: FREE.*

The Smokies offer activities for visitors of various ages and interests. Recommended activities include camping, hiking the park's more than 800 miles of trails, picnicking, sightseeing, fishing, auto touring, nature viewing, and photographic opportunities. Guided horseback rides are available in season at four horse stables in the park in Tennessee and North Carolina.

The Mountain Farm Museum has a collection of southern Appalachian farm buildings assembled from different locations throughout the Park. Visitors can explore a chestnut log farmhouse, barn, hen house, apple house, springhouse, and blacksmith shop.

Salamander Capital of the World !
At least thirty species of salamanders live in the Great Smoky Mountains park.

The farmstead even has crops in the field and live farm animals during the summer. Seasonally, park staff and volunteers give demonstrations of some traditional mountain ways like black-smithing, plowing, and syrup making. The Mingus Mill near Oconaluftee (open spring thru fall) exhibits a turbine-powered grist mill and the opportunity to chat with a miller some afternoon.

SANTAS LAND THEME PARK & ZOO

Cherokee - *571 Wolfetown Rd. (east of downtown on US 19) 28719. Phone: (828) 497-9191. www.santaslandnc.net. Hours: Daily 10:00am-5:00pm (May-October). Admission: Average $24.00 per person (age 2+).*

A family Theme Park and Zoo, Santa's Land is a small enchanted Christmas theme park young kids will love as a diversion. Enjoy riding the Rudi-Coaster, train, and kiddie rides. Ride the paddle boats to Monkey Island while viewing some of the largest gold fish you've ever seen. Pet domestic animals, visit with Santa, his elves and reindeer, or browse their Christmas shops. Bring a picnic lunch or eat at one of their establishments.

UNTO THESE HILLS OUTDOOR DRAMA

Cherokee - ***PO Box 398 (off Hwy 441 North, Mountainside Theater) 28719. Phone: (866) 554-4557. www.cherokeesmokies.com/unto_these_hills.html Hours: Nightly, except Sunday at 8:30pm (late May to mid-August). Length of Performance - 2hrs 15min. (Pre-show entertainment begins at 7:30pm) Admission: $25.00 adult, $15.00 child (6-12). Reserved seats are $28 per person, $18 child. $3.00 parking.***

"Unto These Hills" is the tragic and triumphant story of the Cherokee. Set against the backdrop of the Great Smoky Mountains, the compelling story opens with the arrival of the Spanish (Hernando DeSoto in 1540), and builds to a climax with the cruel removal of all but a remnant of Cherokee on the infamous "Trail of Tears." This drama recreates the inspiration of the great Sequoyah and other leaders. Cherokee descendants, whose ancestors were forcefully driven out of the mountains and marched 1,200 miles to Oklahoma, play important roles in the drama and in the many dances, highlighted by the colorful and world-famous Eagle Dance or the Wedding scene (learn where the saying "Tie the Knot" comes from). They mix dramatics with humor and choreographed dance and fighting scenes to keep the play interesting. A great way to study Cherokee history and the events that led to the removal of most Cherokee from this land. Backstage tour is $5.00.

The Cherokee were forcibly removed from their ancestral home in 1838-39. After the Trail of Tears, the few Cherokee who remained formed the Eastern Band of the Cherokee.

W

CHIMNEY ROCK PARK

Chimney Rock - ***PO Box 39 (I-26 east to exit 18A, or just follow US 64/74A east towards Lake Lure) 28720. www.chimneyrockpark.com. Phone: (828) 625-9611. Hours: Daily 8:30am-5:30pm, weather permitting. Winter hours 10:00am-4:30pm.***

Except Thanksgiving, Christmas, and New Year's Day. Ticket office closes 1 1/2 hours before closing. Admission: $17.00 adult, $8.00 child (6-15). Reduced rates for very inclement weather (we recommend mid-spring to early fall). Climbing Tower, $5.00 extra. Note: Sky Lounge patio accessible to strollers and wheelchairs. Nature Center. Old Rock Café at park entrance. Picnic/grill areas.

Prepare to be elevated! Made famous in the movie "The Last of the Mohicans", traverse a cool tunnel and then take the fast elevator up a 26-story shaft blasted through solid granite! Then it's just a short distance across the clear-span bridge to the stairs to the Chimney. Imagine the Indian warriors and early settlers who climbed and explored this same rock (but, with no guard rails!). Hickory Nut Falls, one of the highest waterfalls east of the Mississippi River (404 feet), can be reached by hiking along the Skyline-Cliff Trail Loop (mostly on the edge of cliffs - 90 minutes) to its top or by taking the gentler walk via the Forest Stroll (1.5 mile round trip) to a platform at its bottom.

Wait 'til a squirrel finds this GIANT acorn...

The Great Woodland Adventure is an interactive, half-mile trail. Search for clues about creatures that live in the park. Grady the Groundhog offers challenges at each of the 12 discovery stations. Along the way, try to jump as far as spiders, sit on a giant acorn or climb inside a large turtle shell (great photo ops!). Life-size sculptures draw you in. Beware of the mother bear - look for the baby cub nearby! This park is a different adventure for every family member - an experience not to be missed!

W

SOUTH MOUNTAINS STATE PARK

Connelly Springs - ***3001 South Mountains State Park Ave. (SR 1904) (from I-40, turn south on NC 18, travel nine miles and make a right turn onto SR 1913 - Sugarloaf Road. Follow signs) 28612. www.ncparks.gov/Visit/parks/somo/main.php. Phone: (828) 433-4772. Hours: Daily 8:00am-dusk. Admission: FREE, fee for camping. Educators: The South Mountains program introduces students to stream and watershed ecology, focusing on the aquatic life, water quality, indicator species, biotic index, watershed and stewardship of Jacob's Fork River: https://files.nc.gov/ncparks/37/South%20Mountains%20EELE.pdf Note: Trout fishing and camping.***

With a variety of trails (over 48 miles) designated for mountain bikes and equestrian or hiking activity, this is trailblazer country. The most popular trail, High Shoals Falls Loop Trail, travels one mile along the Jacob Fork River to the base of High Shoals Falls, a beautiful crystal-clear waterfall. The trail then continues to the top of the falls before looping around and returning to the picnic area. The terrain can be rugged, so be observant of the trail and wear sturdy shoes. An easier trail, originating near the park office, is the Hemlock Nature Trail. This .74-mile wheelchair-accessible loop travels along the Jacob Fork River and through a forest. Eleven display areas along the trail explain the environment of South Mountains State Park and describe its plants and animals.

MOUNTAIN HERITAGE DAY

Cullowhee *- Western Carolina University campus. (828) 227-7129. Mountain Heritage Day is a combination old-fashioned mountain fair and showcase for authentic Southern Appalachian folk arts. Kids play pioneer games, crafters demonstrate their skill and sell their wares, and there are live dance and music performances all day. www.mountainheritageday.com. FREE. (last Saturday in September)*

NC MOUNTAIN STATE FAIR

Fletcher *- Western North Carolina Agricultural Center, 1301 Fanning Road. www.mountainfair.org. A 10-day celebration of Western North Carolina heritage blended with games and entertainment. Admission. (wkend after Labor Day for 10 days in Sept)*

W

FONTANA VILLAGE

Fontana Dam - ***50 Fontana Road (Hwy 28 North, off US 129) 28733. Phone: (828) 498-2211 or (800) 849-2258. www.fontanavillage.com.***

"Tail of the Dragon" with its 318 curves in 11 miles is considered the nation's #1 motorcycle and sports car road - use caution if you're prone to motion sickness.

Historic Fontana Village, set amid this perfect panorama of the Smokies, is a destination resort area. The Village has a wide range of accommodations, including inn rooms, suites, cabins, and even RV and tent camping. Other resources include restaurants, outfitters, a bike shop, pools, marina, horseback riding, miles of on-site trails suitable for mountain biking and hiking, ropes course and more. Some of the exciting destinations in the area are the famous Blue Ridge Parkway, Great Smoky Mountains National Park, Nantahala Gorge whitewater rafting, skiing in Maggie Valley, gem mining in Franklin, jet boat rides, or local mountain heritage at Stecoah Valley Center. Fly-fishing and biking on the village trails are favorites for Dads and kids. The Fontana Dam (Visitors Center: 800-470-3790) is 480 feet high, and 2,365 feet long - the highest concrete dam east of the Mississippi.

SCOTTISH TARTANS MUSEUM

Franklin - ***86 East Main Street 28723. http://scottishtartans.org/museum/aboutus.php. Phone: (828) 524-7472. Hours: Monday-Saturday 10:00am-5:00pm. Admission: $2.00-$4.00 donation (age 10+).***

This museum contains the official registry of all publicly known tartans and is the American extension of the Scottish Tartans Society in Edinburgh, Scotland. See displays on the culture, dress, customs, military, and history of Scotland. The evolution of the kilt can be easily seen from the mannequin displays. Learn the difference between tartan and plaid, kilt and philabeg, pleating to sett and stripe. Watch the kilt transform from a simple woolen blanket to the tailored garment a man can own today. The museum's staff offers help to visitors in locating their family tartans.

TASTE OF SCOTLAND

Franklin *- A Taste of Scotland Festival takes place each June in downtown Franklin, featuring a parade of clans and tartans, Scottish food, crafts, music, children's highland games, and border collie demonstrations. (second weekend in June)*

W

FRANKLIN GEM & MINERAL MUSEUM

Franklin - ***25 Phillips Street 28734. Phone: (828) 369-7831. www.fgmm.org. Hours: Monday-Saturday Noon-4:00pm (May - October). Saturday only (rest of year) Admission: FREE.***

The museum may provide inspiration to become a rockhound when you see the wealth of gems mined from these mountains in Western NC. It occupies the Historic Old Jail of Macon County that was built in 1850. There are 6 rooms dedicated to the preservation of gem and mineral specimens from around the world as well as those found in North Carolina and Macon County - home to the famous Cowee Valley where Rubies and Sapphires have been found for over 100 years. Our favorites were the fluorescent stones and a replica of Aaron's Breast Plate using the same stones as mentioned in the Bible.

NANTAHALA NATIONAL FOREST / MOUNTAIN WATER SCENIC BYWAY

Franklin - *(US 64, SR 1310 - Wayah Road, and US 19) 28734. Phone: (828) 524-6441. http://ncnatural.com/NCUSFS/Nantahala/scenic.html.*

The Mountain Waters Scenic Byway is a 61.3-mile drive that winds through southern Appalachian hardwood forest, two river gorges, and rural countryside. Part of this nationally-recognized byway coincides with two State scenic routes. Much of the byway travels through the Nantahala National Forest. At overlooks and side routes, you may see signs of forest management activities. Here is a sample of attractions along the route:

- **CLIFFSIDE LAKE & VAN HOOK GLADE**: Cliffside Lake Recreation Area is 4.4 miles west of Highlands and then 1.5 miles off U.S. 64. This area offers picnicking, swimming, fishing and hiking. You can camp nearby at Van Hook Glade.
- **CULLASAJA FALLS**: US 64 East. This beautiful waterfall is located on the Cullasaja River at the lower part of the Cullasaja Gorge and cascades for 250 feet over moss-covered stones.
- **WAYAH BALD**: A side trip to Wayah Bald is well worth the effort. From Wayah Gap, journey 1.3 miles up gravel Forest Road (FR) 69 and see the Wilson Lick Ranger Station. Continue another 3.2 miles up FR 69 to Wayah Bald. Take the short, paved trail to the historic Wayah Bald Fire Tower. The tower provides a great view of the southern Appalachian Mountains in Georgia, Tennessee, and both Carolinas. You can picnic nearby at the Wayah Bald Picnic Area. Two long-distance trails, the Appalachian Trail and the Bartram Trail, cross the mountain at the tower.
- **NANTAHALA LAKE**: Located about 6 miles west of Wayah Gap, this lake has 29 miles of shoreline and offers fishing and boating. Boat ramps are available.
- **NANTAHALA RIVER**: This mountain river offers great trout fishing in its upper and lower reaches. The stretch of river above the powerhouse has excellent catch-and-release fishing from spring until early summer.
- **NANTAHALA RIVER GORGE**: The river draws more than 250,000 boaters who enjoy whitewater rafting, canoeing, and kayaking. From a wooden walkway, spectators get a thrilling view of the wild ride over the final series of rapids, including Nantahala Falls.
-

SHEFFIELD MINE

Franklin - ***385 Sheffield Farms Rd. (only follow detailed directions on website) 28734. Phone: (828) 369-8383. www.sheffieldmine.com. Hours: Open daily at 10:00am (April-October). Last customer accepted between 2:30-3:00pm. Admission: Buckets range from $3.00-$100.00. Note: Be prepared. Wear old clothes & old shoes. This is a wet and dirty adventure. Cash only, no credit cards.***

This place uses terminology like Squeakers and Honkers. To find Rubies & Sapphires requires a lot of patience, perseverance, scrubbing and rinsing the rocks in your tray. The average person needs to Scrub-Rinse about 4-5 times per tray load, otherwise you will NOT get the rocks clean enough to discover that some of those rocks are actually RUBIES & SAPPHIRES. They don't look like gems. Instead, look for peeks of colorful rock and purple coloring. Hunting for Rubies and Sapphires takes a minimum of 2 hours - so plan your trip accordingly and don't get here too late. No matter what your age, when it comes to rocks and dirt, we are all kids again.

WILDERNESS TAXIDERMY MUSEUM

Franklin - ***5040 Highland Road 28734. www.wildernesstaxidermy.com Phone: (828) 524-3677. Hours: Monday, Tuesday, Thursday, Friday 8:00am-5:00pm, Saturday 8:00am-Noon. Admission: FREE.***

A unique facility that features a museum, a wildlife art gallery, and a working studio. Animals are tastefully mounted in dioramas in their natural surroundings. Even see a "stuffed" zebra or lion. You can also watch demonstrations of the process of Taxidermy while at the facility (not for weak stomachs).

DUPONT STATE FOREST

Hendersonville - ***Dupont Road (from Asheville/Brevard via US64 and Little River Rd) 28718. Phone: (828) 877-6527. www.dupontforest.com.***

The DuPont State Forest is located in the Blue Ridge Mountains. Most first time visitors want to see falling water, and DuPont State Forest probably has as much per square mile as any public land in the Southeast. The large falls are on the Little River - High Falls and Upper Triple Falls - and they are but 20 to 30 minutes from the trail head. The property is presently open to hunting, fishing, hiking, horseback riding and mountain biking. The Forest lies in an upland plateau of the Little River Valley, with large sections of gently rolling land bordered by moderately steep hills and mountains. Most all of the ridges have exposed granite slabs and domes.

HOLMES EDUCATIONAL STATE FOREST

Hendersonville - ***1299 Crab Creek Road (Rte. 4, southwest of town) 28739. Phone: (828) 692-0100. www.ncesf.org/holmes.html Hours: Daily daylight hours (mid-March to late November). Admission: FREE.***

Holmes is located in the Blue Ridge Mountains. With rugged terrain, numerous rock outcroppings, and scenic vistas, it also offers a rich mixture of mountain hardwoods, rhododendron, flame azaleas, and a variety of wildflowers. These features are accessible by a series of well-marked trails which are accented by exhibits and displays (talking trees) depicting the ecology of the managed forest. Picnic areas and hiking trails are available.

MINERAL & LAPIDARY MUSEUM

Hendersonville - ***400 North Main Street (south of downtown, US 64) 28792. Phone: (828) 698-1977. www.mineralmuseum.org. Hours: Monday-Friday 1:00-5:00pm, Saturday 11:00am-5:00pm. Admission: FREE.***

"The Geode Cracking Museum" has a collection of gems, minerals, fossils, and, yes, geodes. They even have two large petrified logs and a fluorescent display. Children can touch a dinosaur egg nest from China for FREE; adults pay a one dollar fee. If you want to find the secret beauty inside the ugly outside rock of your choice - let them crack open a geode for you to purchase as a souvenir.

W

WESTERN NORTH CAROLINA AIR MUSEUM

Hendersonville - ***1340 Gilbert Street (adjacent to Hendersonville airport) 28793. Phone: (828) 698-2482. www.wncairmuseum.com. Hours: Wednesday, Saturday and Sunday Noon - 5:00pm. Weather permitting. Admission: FREE.***

Home of a collection of airplanes and memorabilia celebrating state aviation history, specifically Western North Carolina air history. Chat with the aircrafts' owners or watch these vintage machines in action in good flying weather. They display at least 12 different airplanes at any one time in their hanger and just outside.

NORTH CAROLINA APPLE FESTIVAL

Hendersonville - *Downtown. www.ncapplefestival.org. (828) 697-4557. Apple breakfast, parade, recipe contests, orchard tours, street fair and rides, and local music and dance. FREE. (Labor Day weekend)*

CARL SANDBURG HOME NATIONAL HISTORIC SITE

Hendersonville (Flat Rock) - *1928 Little River Road (US 26E to exit 53 south. Upward Rd. turns into Highland Lake Rd. Turn west onto US 25 south, make a right onto Little River) 28731. Phone: (828) 693-4178. www.nps.gov/carl Hours: Daily 9:00am-5:00pm, except Christmas Day. Admission: Free for grounds, trails and barn; no park entrance fee. Tours require fee. Tours: 30-minute house tours are offered for $8.00 adults (age 16+), $5.00 seniors (62+) and children are FREE. Each tour is restricted to 15 visitors. You must walk up a steep hill path to get to the house. If unable, use the phone at the visitor display (near the parking lot) to call up for assistance. Note: From June until mid-August, live performances of Sandburg's Rootabaga Stories and excerpts from the Broadway Play, The World of Carl Sandburg, are presented at the park amphitheater. Educators:*

Home of the famous poet and biographer Carl Sandburg, the site preserves and protects over 260 acres of land (on which the Mrs. raised champion goats), historic structures (check out the goats in the barn - babies in April/May) and over five miles of trails where Sandburg spent the last 22 years of his life.

Around the curve, past the pond, up the long hill...you'll find inspiration...

Mr. Sandburg used to take his chair out to some of the rock outcroppings along the trail to sit and write. The house and farm are open to the public for guided tours. Explore the goat barn on your own and meet some of the relatives of Lilian Sandburg's herd. The Sandburg Home was built in 1838 and now houses his collection of 10,000 books, notes and papers. On tour, notice there were books in every room and hallway! Besides being an author, he was also a folksinger and winner of two Pulitzer Prizes. The collection of walking canes and the guitar are noted by kids in the living room. Famous for biographies about President Lincoln, he provided enduring 20th century insight into the circumstances and spirit of the everyday working person. Are you a night owl? Sandburg always wrote at night.

Note: While the grounds and trails are free to wonder, families with tweens to teens would best appreciate the house tour. Rangers and volunteers are on hand, outdoors each summer, to share the fascinating story about goats and Mrs. Sandburg's dairy goat operation while others are on the tour.

FLAT ROCK PLAYHOUSE

Hendersonville (Flat Rock) - *2661 Greenville Hwy 28731. Phone: (828) 693-0731. www.flatrockplayhouse.org.*

Considered one of the ten best seasonal theater companies in the country, the Vagabond Players perform a variety of hits each summer featuring comedies, American classics, musicals, farces and whodunits. Sit back and enjoy spectacular matinee and evening performances from late May through mid-October. The comfortable atmosphere is ideal for families, vacationers and touring groups.

FLATROCK - AROUND TOWN - As you enter town, you'll notice The Historic Village of Flat Rock provides some of the finest examples of Southern aristocracy. The community was founded about a century and a half ago. In order to escape the sweltering heat and the epidemic of yellow fever and malaria, affluent Charlestonians, Europeans and prominent plantation owners of the South's Low Country built large summer estates in Flat Rock. With many of these homes still on their original sites, the entire district of Flat Rock is included in the National Register of Historic Places.

EMERALD HOLLOW MINE

Bring a large margarine or Cool Whip container with the child's name on it for their gemstone collection they will find.

W

Hiddenite - *P.O. Box 276 28636. www.emeraldhollowmine.com. Phone: (866) 600-GEMS. Hours: Friday-Sunday 8:30am-sunset. Only closed on Thanksgiving, Christmas Eve and Day. Admission: General, $10.00/$5.00; Sluicing/Creeking Combo $18.00/$8.00, Sluicing/Creeking/Digging Combo $25.00/$8.00. Tours: Field Trip Reservations and Information: (828) 635-0556. Wear old play clothes. Plan on getting soil on you! Bring a change of clothes and shoes, and maybe a hand towel to dry your feet if you're creekin'.*

The Emerald Hollow Mine is the only emerald mine in the world that is open to the public for prospecting. Try your luck at prospecting for valuable gemstones in one of two large "state of the art" sluiceways where you may wash buckets filled with ore taken directly from the mine. Prospecting in the creek can be very rewarding. It is most productive to work the creek gravels with a screen, although some prefer the easier method of just "eyeing" the thousands of rocks in the creek bed, hoping to catch a glimpse of a nice gemstone. Digging at the mine can be hard work, but many mother lode finds are made chasing veins. For those who prefer easier prospecting, there is also lots of bare ground for surface collecting in the mining area.

HIGHLAND AREA WATERFALLS

Highlands - *(see below) 28741. Phone: (828) 526-2112.*

- BRIDAL VEIL FALLS: US 64 West, On the South Side of the Fraser River. Cars can drive under this spectacular 120 foot fall that tumbles over a smooth rock face, creating a veil-like effect. Picnicking and hiking are available in the adjacent, scenic day-use area.
- DRY FALLS: US 64, Between Franklin and Highlands. Take an easy walk on a well marked path with a hand rail behind this 75 foot curtain of rushing water that is located on the Cullasaja River, named after the Cherokee word for sugar water.
- GLEN FALLS: South of Highland, Highway 106 South. A steep one mile trail leads down to the falls that are composed of three waterfalls that drop approximately 60 feet, each on the east fork of Overflow Creek in the scenic Blue Valley area.
- WHITEWATER FALLS: NC 281 at the North Carolina State Line, Approximately 20 miles from Highlands. A very impressive cascade, Whitewater Falls, arguably the highest in the eastern United States, is called the "king of waterfalls" No other waterfall in the east has the combination of water volume, height and visibility. The upper falls of this cascade falls 411 feet. The lower falls cascade for 400 feet.

NEW RIVER STATE PARK

Jefferson - ***1477 Wagoner Access Road (After driving through Jefferson, turn right on NC 88 east. Cross the New River and turn left on Wagoner Access Road - SR 1590 - 28640. Phone: (336) 982-2587. http://ncparks.gov/Visit/parks/neri/main.php. Hours: Daily 8:00am-dusk. Admission: FREE, fee for camping.***

Canoe more than 26 miles of the National Wild and Scenic South Fork of the New River. Easy paddling and spectacular scenery make the New River a natural canoe trail for inexperienced paddlers. Its shallow, gentle waters and mild rapids are perfect for beginners, families and groups. Besides good canoe access, the Wagoner Road entrance features a couple of good, easy hiking trails that allow you to learn about the river environment. The most diverse habitats of the park can be found along the Farm House Loop Trail at Alleghany Access Area.

Our favorite way of enjoying the New River is atop a tube. Local outfitters abound near the parks, so it is easy to rent a tube or canoe. It's hard to beat a lazy float down the scenic New from the Waggoner Road put-in to the US 221 take-out area. So, float this spring and summer in America's oldest river, the New. Three access points, primitive camping, fishing, hiking, mountain scenery and wildlife are other activities.

LAKE LURE TOURS & BEACH/ WATERWORKS

Lake Lure - ***2930 Memorial Hwy. (25 miles southeast of Asheville on Hwy 64/74A. Or, I-26 east to exit 18A) 28746. Phone: (877) FUN-4-ALL. www.lakeluretours.com. Hours: Beach and the Works: Daily daytime (Memorial Day weekend through Labor Day weekend). Admission: Boat Tours: $16.00 adult, $14.00 senior (62+), $7.00 child (4-12). Beach/WaterWorks: $7.00-$9.00 (age 4+). Tours: Scenic one-hour boat tours, sunset and dinner cruises are available. Daily March through early December (hourly tours from 10:00am to twilight). Early spring and late fall hours vary according to weather (mostly Friday-Sunday afternoons only).***

Discover why National Geographic named Lake Lure "one of the ten most spectacular man-made lakes in the world." The one-hour lake tour includes a visit to the site of a popular film. Passengers hear the story of Snake Island, and delight in the legend of the church said to be in the center of the lake...100 feet down. Look for blue heron and fawns along the shore. Did you know the lake is shaped like a cross? Visitors may rent canoes, kayaks, paddle boats, electric boats and pontoon boats as well. Splash at the beach or play at the Fun Center with family-oriented, interactive games and activities. The Beach Water Works has soaking-wet games, bumper boats, water balloons cannons, water wars and water slides. A great spot to have fun getting wet!

W

RUMBLING BALD RESORT ON LAKE LURE

Lake Lure - 112 Mountains Road 28746. I-40 exit 81 south. Stay on Sugar Hill Road, turn right onto Bills Creek Road, then right onto Buffalo Creek Road or follow Rte. 64/74A east past The Beach to the other side of the Lake. www.rumblingbald.com. (828) 694-3000. Once known as Lake Lure Golf & Beach Resort, the resort is nestled at the base of the majestic 2,800-foot Rumbling Bald Mountain on the north end of beautiful Lake Lure. This resort offers a variety of lodging options. They have everything from studio villas to two and three bedroom condos. Most units have a kitchenette. Weekly summer events include beach cookouts, barbeques, storytellers, live bands and dance nights. The Mountain Kids Program runs weekdays each summer. Everything from Kids Night Out to crafts and outdoor play to nature hikes. Restaurants of all styles are on the property, as is a fitness center, spa, arcade, tennis, bingo, and swimming pools (indoor/outdoor) - one with a floating lazy river. ______________________________ ☐

TUTTLE EDUCATIONAL STATE FOREST

Lenoir - ***3420 Playmore Beach Road (I-40 to Hwy. 18-64 north to west on SR 1611) 28655. Phone: (828) 757-5608. www.ncesf.org/TESF/home.htm. Hours: Daily spring thru fall. Closed Mondays. Admission: FREE.***

Located in the foothills of the Blue Ridge Mountains, Tuttle boasts a wide variety of pines and hardwoods plus rolling terrain and clear streams. These features are accessible by a series of well-marked trails accented by talking tree exhibits and displays which explain the ecology of the managed forest.

GRANDFATHER MOUNTAIN

Linville - ***2050 Blowing Rock Hwy. (US 221 south & Blue Ridge Parkway, near Rte. 105 & Rte. 221) 28646. www.grandfather.com. Phone: (828) 733-4337 or (800) 468-7325. Hours: Daily 9:00am-6:00 to 7:00pm. Closed Thanksgiving and Christmas Days. Open weather permitting in winter. Admission: $22.00 adult, $20.00 senior (60+), $9.00 child (4-12). Note: Great gift shop, restaurant and Outdoor Exploring center. Picnic tables and grills scattered throughout the park. Bicycling is not permitted on the roadways or on the trails. Pets on a leash are welcome.***

The Mountain features environmental habitats with native wildlife, numerous hiking trails, the famous swinging bridge and an Outdoor Exploring museum and theater. The Mile High Swinging Bridge was built to give visitors easy access to the breath-taking view from Linville Peak (an adventure mini-hike!). The 228-foot suspension bridge spans an 80-foot chasm at more than one mile in elevation. Exhibits at the Museum include: a North Carolina Amethyst (The 165-pound cluster is considered the finest amethyst ever discovered in North America), Gems & Minerals of North Carolina (see them "before and after" they're polished), North Carolina Gold (including largest gold nugget on display in NC), and Indians and Daniel Boone at Grandfather Mountain. When you see the Black Birch Burl Bowl (a 64" x 46" x 34" bowl made from a 3,200 pound piece of black birch), you may think it looks like an "Outdoorsman's bathtub". Outside in the Outdoor Exploring Center Habitat, you'll be most attracted to the river otters and the best "authentic" bear habitat we've ever seen! Along the way up the mountain look for The Split Rock & Sphinx Rock (two rocks the size of houses). In great weather, plan to spend the day here as there are both indoor and outdoor sites to see and more than 12 miles of maintained trails (some, easy nature walks). Pack a picnic lunch or grab a picnic-to-go from the restaurant. For the best value, pick a nice day in mid-spring through early fall.

On a foggy day, we couldn't see

HIGHLAND GAMES & GATHERING OF SCOTTISH CLAN

Linville - Grandfather Mountain. Over 120 Scottish clans gather for parades, music and games. This is the New World event with the most variety of Scottish families. Admission. (mid-July Thursday-Sunday)

LINVILLE GORGE WILDERNESS AREA

Linville Falls - ***Kistler Memorial Hwy (NC 1238) 28647. Phone: (828) 652-2144. www.fs.usda.gov/recarea/nfsnc/recarea/?recid=48974 Hours: Daily during daylight hours. Admission: FREE. Note: See their online brochure for trail maps. The gorge trails are for the seasoned rough campers and hikers, folks.***

The Grand Canyon of the East – Linville Gorge Wilderness. It covers 12,000 acres and the gorge descends more than 2,000 feet to the Linville River below. Wild and isolated, the Linville Gorge Wilderness offers the primitive camper the ultimate in scenic beauty and tranquility. Pack your fishing rod along with your tent, so you can tangle with smallmouth bass and native trout. Hike or camp near rock formations such as Sitting Bear, Hawksbill, Table Rock, or The Chimneys of the Blue Ridge landscape. At the top of the gorge, and just off the Blue Ridge Parkway is Linville Falls, a spectacular three-tiered waterfall plunging into the wilderness area. This is the most accessible area to vehicles.

W

WHEELS THROUGH TIME MUSEUM

Maggie Valley - ***62 Vintage Lane (I-40 West to exit 27 (Maggie Valley). Exit on to US 19/74 North (exit 103 right) 28751. www.wheelsthroughtime.com. Phone: (828) 926-6266. Hours: Thursday-Monday 9:00am-5:00pm (April-November). Admission: $15.00 adult, $12.00 senior (65+), $7.00 child (6-14). Note: The new Time Machine online video page offers visitors the opportunity to watch folks magically restore rare machines.***

They offer the world's largest collection of rare American motorcycles and cars from each of the 10 decades of America's automobile history. From the early years of 1900 - 1928, motorcycles emerged from a motor powered bicycle to a form of reliable sport and transportation. Over 250 rare antique American Motorcycles unite the "art of the motorcycle" with a new generation of American freedom.

LINVILLE CAVERNS

Marion - ***19929 US 221 North (Hwy. 221 N) 28752. Phone: (828) 756-4171 or (800) 419-0540. www.linvillecaverns.com. Hours: Daily 9:00am-4:30pm (November-March, except December, January, February- Weekends Only); Daily 9:00am-***

5:00pm (April, May, September, October); Daily 9:00am-6:00pm (June-Labor Day). Admission: $9.00 adult, $8.00 senior (62+), $7.00 child (5-12). Tours: The guided tours through the caverns leave every few minutes, and last about half an hour. Mostly level walkways (partially wheelchair, but not stroller, accessible). Please note that the caverns are often drippy and maintain a constant 52 degrees so you may want to bring a jacket.

Deep inside of Humpback Mountain lie the Linville Caverns, North Carolina's only caverns. These caverns were first explored by the white man over 100 years ago. It is said that in 1822 a fisherman noticed trout swimming in and out of the mountain and he began looking for a way to see where they were going. Linville caverns remain active as mineral deposits continue to form stalactites and stalagmites. The water, produced by this mountain, with its carbon dioxide, created the cavern's natural passageways. A highlight at the end of the tour is the Bottomless Lake, gauged to be 75m deep. A metal bridge allows visitors to gaze deep into the clear water, which is lighted. During the winter and early spring you may get to view an Eastern Pipistrelle Bat, which hibernates here, hanging from the ceiling. The owners approach these formations from a Creationist's point of view: "Although we do not believe any rock is millions of years old, these formations are still very unique and show the majestic work of an awesome GOD."

LAKE JAMES STATE PARK

Marion (Nebo) - ***2785 Hwy 126, Lake James Road (I-40, take the Nebo/Lake James exit (exit 90) 28761. Phone: (828) 652-5047. www.ncparks.gov/Visit/parks/laja/main.php. Hours: Daily 8:00am-dusk. Admission: FREE. Educators: The Lake James program, Aquatic Critters (an Environmental Educational Learning Experience) introduces students to the lakeshore environment, focusing on the plants and animals that live there: https://files.nc.gov/ncparks/37/Lake%20James%20EELE.pdf***

Tucked away in rolling hills at the base of Linville Gorge is Lake James, a 6,510-acre lake with more than 150 miles of shoreline. Try swimming and sunbathing or enjoy a picnic along the lakeshore. Boat, water ski or fish in cool mountain waters, or take a walk and enjoy an abundance of wildflowers and wildlife along park trails with lake overlooks. Two one-way footpaths travel along the shoreline of Lake James. A half-mile trail leads to Sandy Cliff Overlook, and a 1.5-mile trail leads through the campground to Lake Channel Overlook. Fox Den Loop Trail is the park's longest trail at 2.2 miles. Nature programs presented by rangers.

MOUNTAIN GATEWAY MUSEUM AND HERITAGE CENTER

Old Fort - *102 Water Street (corner of Water and Catawba) 28762. Phone: (828) 668-9259. http://ncmuseumofhistory.org/osm/mgw.html. Hours: Monday Noon -5:00pm. Tuesday-Saturday 9:00am-5:00pm. Sunday 2:00-5:00pm. Admission: FREE. Note: Pioneer Day is last Saturday in April.*

The Heritage Center near Asheville interprets the Mountain region's history. Visit the state-run museum complex with its two century-old cabins and an excellent collection of early photographs, tools and house wares. An indoor exhibit on early water systems using techniques of dowsing, divining, pumping and wells are displayed. Public programs are held outdoors throughout the growing season to demonstrate the techniques and methods used by farmers in the 19th & 20th centuries. At harvest time, programs include demonstrations on early food preservation methods such as drying and canning.

COLD MOUNTAIN

Pisgah Forest - *1001 Pisgah Highway (from Asheville, drive south along the Parkway past Mt. Pisgah to milepost 411) 28768. www.romanticasheville.com/coldmountain.htm*

Based on Asheville-area native Charles Frazier's best-selling Civil War-era novel Cold Mountain, set in the mountains of Western North Carolina. The easiest place to see it is along the Blue Ridge Parkway just past Wagon Road Gap (mentioned in the book). There, visitors will find a large, weathered, wooden National Park Service sign, not unlike those found at all of the other Parkway overlooks. Visitors can strategically place themselves next to the sign with the now-famous mountain looming in the distance.

CRADLE OF FORESTRY IN AMERICA

Pisgah Forest - *11250Pisgah Hwy. Ranger Station (I-26E to exit 40, NC280 West. When in Pisgah Forest, turn right on Hwy 276 & go 11 miles. Near Parkway milepost 412) 28768. Phone: (828) 877-3130. http://cradleofforestry.com. Hours: Daily 9:00am-5:00pm (mid-April to early November). Admission: $6.00 adult, $3.00 youth (4-12). Note: Café and gift shop. Nearby is the Pisgah (pronounced Piz-gah) Center for Wildlife Education (828-877-4423). Events most every weekend promote visiting often.*

The Birthplace of the Forestry Service. At this magnificent facility, start with the Forestry movie. Learn how Vanderbilt purchased this land and hired, now famous, foresters. Now, stay indoors for a while to explore the Discovery

Center. Walk through re-created scenes from a typical forest with sound effects. Next, crawl through a tunnel (parents too!) as you explore where creatures burrow underground. This is also the best area to begin finding clues on your Scavenger Hunt game sheet (prizes awarded for completion). At the edge of the "forest", climb inside a life-size Fire-fighting Helicopter Simulator ride. It's so cool! You actually ride along as the pilots complete a "water drop". Head outside on guided trails to historic cabins with cultural interpreters and an interactive map called: The Adventure Zone. Stop at the original Forestry School, the store and a boarding house. Groups of children get to do some chores (like churning butter or washing clothes) while others watch a toy maker, a weaver, a baker, or a quilter. Another trail leads to the 1915 logging train and antique saw mill. Even though preservation was important here, logging was also part of the mix. We were impressed - very engaging, but make sure you watch the video to better understand the offerings here.

Climb aboard a life-size helicopter simulator

SLIDING ROCK - A NATURAL WATER SLIDE

Pisgah Forest - ***(US 276, about 7.5 miles south of Blue Ridge Pkwy (or 7 miles north off of US 280) 28768. http://ncnatural.com/NCUSFS/Pisgah/lkglass.html. Phone: (828) 877-3265. Hours: Daily 10:00am-5:30pm (Memorial Day to mid-August) Admission: $1.00 per person upon exiting. Note: Lifeguards on duty. Pools of water are very cold, even in the summer. Because rocks are slippery and some are jagged, wear swim socks. The bottom pool water is 8 feet deep. Must be able to swim or be accompanied by an adult. They do allow life jackets.***

The king of swimming holes in the mountains near Asheville, this 60-foot natural water slide down a well-worn slab of rock was providing summertime entertainment long before water slides became standard fare. What a "hoot & holler" to race down as a family. A worthwhile find in Forest country. Transylvania County calls itself "Land of Waterfalls" with good reason. Many waterfalls of various sizes are found in the Pisgah Forest. On your way into the Forest, take an observation look (or even a dip!) in LOOKING GLASS FALLS... very impressive. It's 35 feet wide and drops 65 feet! You can view it from the observation deck or you can walk to its base.

Wear your old blue jeans or cut-offs to sit and slip down the rock into the pool below, where 60-degree water beats summer heat.

W

You might recognize this waterfall from the movie Last of the Mohicans, which was filmed in this and several other beautiful spots in NC. Other falls of note in the area include Turtleback Falls, a favorite swimming spot, Moore Cove Falls, which spills over a tremendous granite shelf, creating a falls you can walk behind, and Twin falls, which features two falls. As a word of caution, always be careful around waterfalls! Mossy covered rocks are VERY slippery and fatalities occur every year on the waterfalls. Particularly stay away from the tops of falls.

BLUE RIDGE CORN MAZE

Pisgah Forest - Blue Ridge Corn Maze, 570 Everitt Road (Hwy 64 east, south on Crab Creek, west on Everitt). http://blueridgecornmaze.com. (828) 884-4415. The Blue Ridge Mountains are a great backdrop for the corn maze. 6 acre corn maze plus contests, prizes, food, drinks, souvenirs, hay rides, local produce and crafts. Admission. (Friday nights & weekends in September and October)

STONE MOUNTAIN STATE PARK

W

Roaring Gap - ***3042 Frank Parkway (I-77, turn west onto US 21. Veer left onto Traphill Road - SR 1002 - follow signs) 28668. Phone: (336) 957-8185. http://ncparks.gov/Visit/parks/stmo/main.php. Hours: Daily 8:00am-dusk. Admission: FREE. Educators: rock cycle, geology for grades 3-6: https://files.nc.gov/ncparks/37/Stone%20Mountain%20SP%20EELE.pdf***

It's a strenuous three quarters of a mile hike on the Stone Mountain Loop Trail to the 2,305-foot summit. This magnificent 600-foot granite dome is well worth the wait.

You'll likely see turkey vultures and red-tail hawks wheeling overhead. Wild goats clamber up the hillsides, and wildlife ranging from deer to bobcats may be seen throughout the park. If you are not prepared for the tough climb to the summit, go across the park's meadow and take the more sedate portion of the trail to Stone Mountain Falls. It's also a great place to spread out the blanket. Check out the park's old-time still, loom and other historical artifacts in the Mountain Culture Exhibit in the park office building. Other exhibits include animal pelts and a full-body black bear mount. Walk through one of the park's historic sites, the Hutchinson Homestead. The homestead is complete with a log cabin, barn, blacksmith shop, corncrib, meat house and original furnishings. Visitors can play recordings that explain how different aspects of the farm were run. The park includes camping and views of waterfalls.

RIVER ADVENTURES

Rosman - ***P O Box 145 (intersection of North & West Forks of the French Broad River & Hwys. 64 & 915) 28772. www.headwatersoutfitters.com. Phone: (828) 877-3106. Hours: April-October. Tube Run (mid-May thru mid-September). Weather permitted. Admission: Generally $20.00-$40.00 per person.***

They shuttle you to the river, then let the scenic mountain waters gently float you to Lyon Mountain Bridge where you're transported back to the main depot (1-2 hours). Canoe and Kayak trips (3 hours) paddle you down the old river, meandering and twisting thru Outdoor Exploring along the riverbanks.

KIDSENSES CHILDREN'S INTERACTIVE MUSEUM

Rutherfordton - ***172 N. Main Street 28139. www.kidsenses.org. Phone: (828) 286-2120. Hours: Tuesday-Saturday 9:00am-5:00pm. Admission: $8.00 general.***

Imagine the excitement of kids as they create a castle, act as a TV commentator, or explore the streets of a fun city just for them. The layout is bright but not overwhelming. Look around some and then interact in a kid-size Dental Office, Grocery, TV station, Factory, or Stage. Climb the Big Climber or play small in the Alphabet Trail area. Play with Science and Art, too. Many kids museums have a grocery store but this one has a Café: a play restaurant where children become a chef, waiter or greeter. There's even a room dedicated to Bubbles.

GORGES STATE PARK

Sapphire - ***Hwy 281 (from I-26, taking exit 9 onto NC 280 and traveling west toward Brevard. Turn west on US 64, follow signs) 28774. Phone: (828) 966-9099. www.ncparks.gov/Visit/parks/gorg/main.php. Hours: Daily 8:00am-dusk. Admission: FREE.***

Rugged river gorges, plunging waterfalls, sheer rock walls and one of the greatest concentrations or rare species in the eastern United States are found within the park. With a 2,000 foot elevation, combined with abundant rainfall, the environ creates a temperate rain forest and supports numerous waterfalls. Being a new park, administration is still planning and building new facilities.

BLUE RIDGE PARKWAY HOMESTEADS / DOUGHTON PARK

Sparta - *Blue Ridge Parkway MP 241 28675. Phone: (336) 372-8877. www.nps.gov/blri/planyourvisit/doughton-park-trails.htm*

This landscape of open meadows is a place to view wildlife and get a feel for the lives of those who lived here long ago. Doughton Park is one of the best places along the motor road to view white-tailed deer, raccoons, red and grey foxes, and bobcats, as well as spectacular shows of flame azalea and rhododendron in the late spring. Bluffs Lodge is open during the summer season along with a restaurant and gas station. There is a campground with ranger talks during the summer season. Hiking opportunities range from a short hike at Fodder Stack Trail to the strenuous 7.5 mile Bluff Mountain Trail. Visit the Brinegar Cabin 1885 (MP 238.5) - the home of Martin Brinegar and his family. Brinegar was a cobbler as well as a farmer. His home is open on summer weekend afternoons. Hand-loom weaving and other craft demonstrations are often given during the summer months. Or, hike into Basin Cove to view the Caudill Family Homestead (MP 241). The Northwest Trading Post at Milepost 258.6 has a wide variety of craft items and souvenirs for sale from this part of North Carolina.

GEM MOUNTAIN

Spruce Pine - ***Hwy 226 (milepost 331 off Blue Ridge Pkwy, just up the road from NC Museum of Minerals) 28777. Phone: (888) 817-5829. www.gemmountain.com. Hours: Daily 9:00am-5:00pm (March-December). Open later in summer. Admission: FREE. Mining Buckets start at $20.00. Tours of the Brushy Creek Aquamarine Mine are conducted on weekdays and Saturdays through October weather permitting. $35.00-$70.00. Note: Appalachian General Store & Museum.***

Panning. Just place a scoop of rough material on the screen... then rinse with clear water. The Gem Stones, when wet, will reveal colors and crystal shapes. Use the identity chart to compare and name your finds. Larger gems can be cut into jewelry.

EMERALD VILLAGE

Spruce Pine (Little Switzerland) - ***McKinney Mine Road (off Blue Ridge Pkwy, take exit 334, US 19E northwest) 28749. www.emeraldvillage.com. Phone: (828) ROK-MINE. Hours: Daily 10:00am-4:00pm (April-October). Extended hours May-October, especially weekends. Open in the winter by reservation. Admission: Gem mining: $10-$20 per bucket. Mine & Museums tours: $6-$8.00 (age 6+).***

In this famous historical mining area, 60 different rocks & minerals have been found including Aquamarine, Emerald, Garnet, Smoky Quartz as well as Uranium and Fluorescent minerals (glow in the night) - all here in this little village. Historical preservation of these mines and the opportunity to prospect for your own gems make Emerald Village a center of North Carolina Gem collecting activities. Explore the historic Bon Ami Mine with its authentic mining equipment, mine for gemstones in a fresh water flume, watch artisans cut and mount jewelry and then picnic in indoor or outdoor picnic areas. While here take in the many free displays such as the Antique Music Museum, the Homestead (farm display), Gallery of Minerals, and Crossings of the Blue Ridge Railroad. When gem panning, you are guaranteed a gem find every time and can keep what you find.

ORCHARD AT ALTAPASS

Spruce Pine (Little Switzerland) - *1025 Orchard Road 28749. Phone: (888) 765-9531. www.altapassorchard.org. Tours: Hayrides are offered every Saturday and Sunday, late May through October, at 1pm, 2:30pm & 4pm for $5.00/person.*

The 30-minute journey begins by following the path of the Revolutionary War mountain soldiers called the Overmountain Men. The hay wagon swings through the orchard itself, past old and young trees. The scenery is spectacular for the entire route, and the stories are entertaining and educational for all ages. This ride lasts 45 minutes. Stories are geared to the audience, but cover subjects such as the early settlers, the coming of the railroad, the March of the Overmountain Men in the Revolutionary War, the Flood of 1916, and more delightful tales by people whose families date back hundreds of years in these parts. A coffee shop and entertainment are available each weekend.

FOOTHILLS EQUESTRIAN NATURE CENTER (FENCE)

Tryon - *3381 Hunting Country Road (off I-26, just north of South Carolina state line) 28782. Phone: (828) 859-9021. www.fence.org. Hours: Daylight hours. Admission: FREE.*

Five miles of hiking and riding trails thread their way through the property, including a hard-paved trail for the physically challenged. The trails are equipped with information stations and shelters. A nature pond with an observation boardwalk serves as an outdoor classroom for observing wildfowl and native plant species.

The Equestrian Center comprises three lighted show rings with all-weather footing, stabling for over 200 horses and spectator seating. The nationally-famous Block House Steeplechase, is run each Spring. Hunter/Jumper competitions, cross-country events, dressage and carriage driving are among the equestrian disciplines which make use of the Center.

FROM THIS DAY FORWARD OUTDOOR DRAMA

Valdese - Fred B. Cranford Old Colony Amphitheatre, Church Street. This is the story of the Waldenses, a religious sect that arose in southeast France in the 1100s, and their struggle to survive persecution in their homeland and their eventual arrival in North Carolina to establish a colony in 1893 at Valdese. The show, directed by John Hogan, includes music and dance. www.oldcolonyplayers.com/. (828) 874-0176. (8:00pm Friday-Saturday in July and first two weekends in August)

APPLE HARVEST FESTIVAL

Waynesville - Main Street. (828) 456-3517. Live mountain music and dance, craft and demonstrations booths, apples, cider, fresh fried pies and everything apple. (third Saturday in October)

A NIGHT BEFORE CHRISTMAS

Waynesville - (828) 456-3517. Beginning with the Christmas Parade, come share the caroling, handbells, live music, a live nativity, pictures with Santa, old-fashioned wagon rides, storytelling, poetry and streets lined with luminaries. (2nd Saturday evening in December)

ASHE COUNTY CHEESE FACTORY

West Jefferson - ***106 East Main Street (SR 163 in town) 28694. Phone: (336) 246-2501. www.ashecountycheese.com. Hours: Monday-Saturday 8:30am-5:00pm. Admission: FREE. Tours: Self-guided viewing window. They post a monthly cheese-making schedule online. Check before making a special trip.***

Ashe County Cheese is open to visitors year-round who often come in to watch through a viewing room to see just how the cheese is made. The viewing window allows people to watch some of the procedure and see the milk running into the vat along with some of the other things that are done. Ashe County Cheese is the only cheese making plant in the area of its kind and possibly the only one in the state. Around 50,000 pounds of cheese are made a week at the factory. Sample some of the more than 50 varieties of cheese in the gift shop. One of the favorites, cheese curds, are available in the gift shop as well. *Always better fresh!*

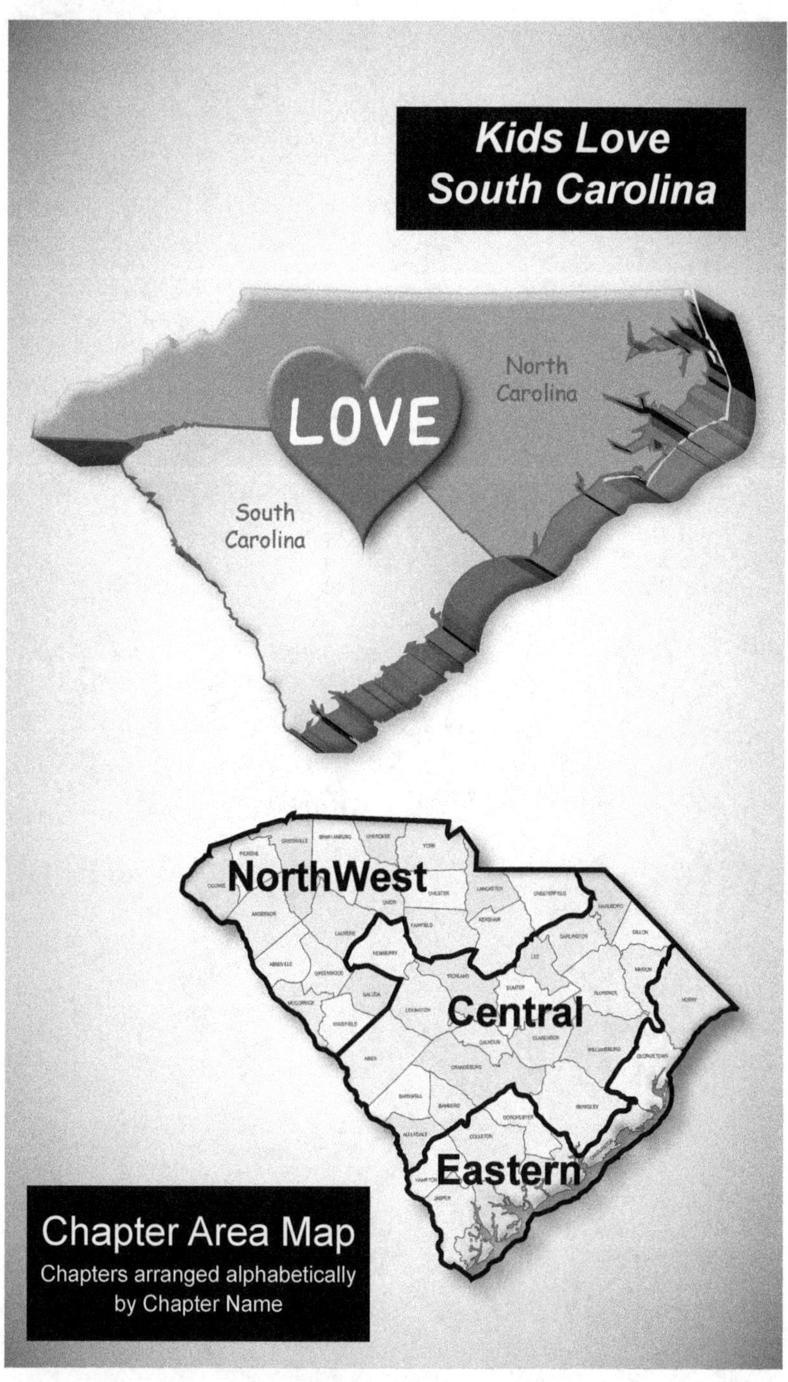
Kids Love
South Carolina
LOVE
North
Carolina
South
Carolina
NorthWest
Central
Eastern
Chapter Area Map
Chapters arranged alphabetically
by Chapter Name

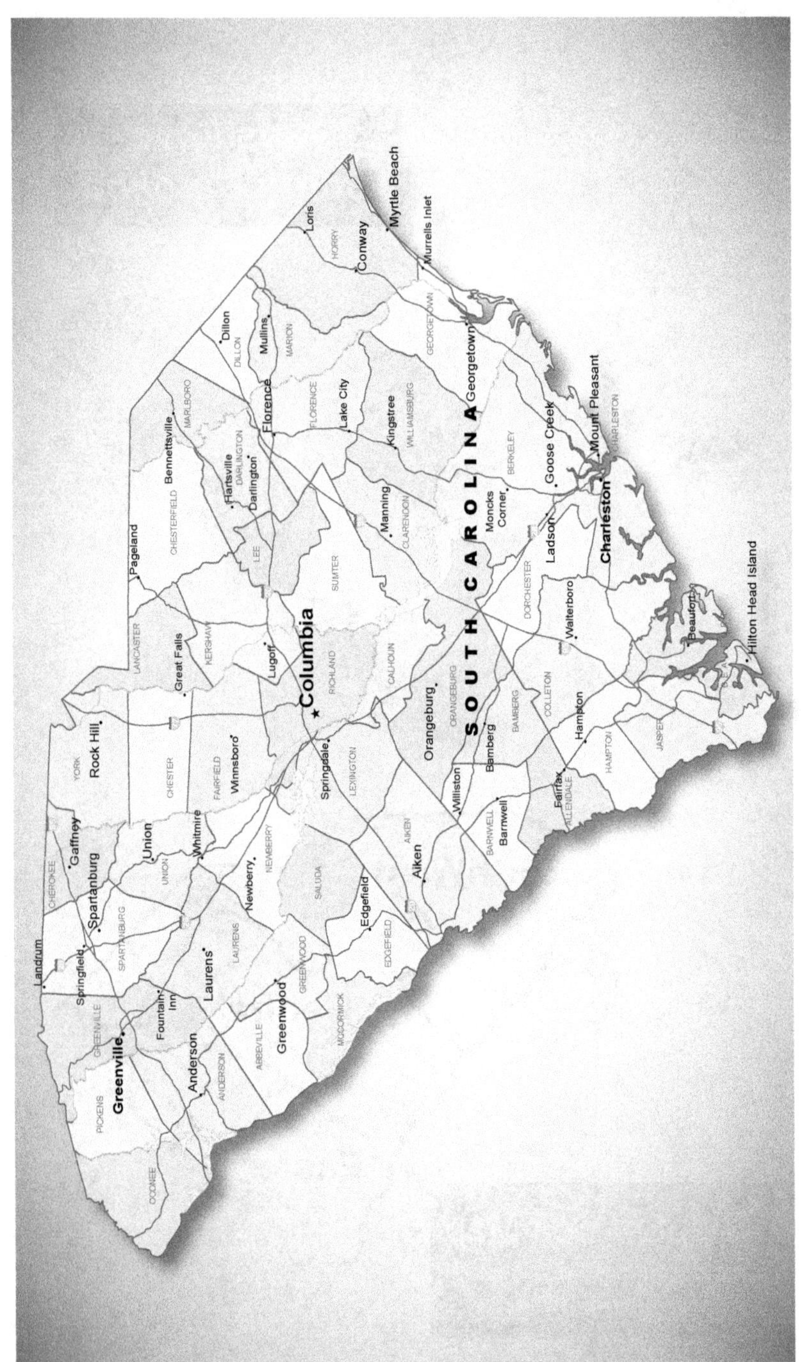
SOUTH CAROLINA
Columbia
Greenville
Spartanburg
Charleston
Myrtle Beach
Murrells Inlet
Loris
Conway
Dillon
Mullins
Florence
Lake City
Kingstree
Georgetown
Bennettsville
Hartsville
Darlington
Manning
Moncks Corner
Goose Creek
Mount Pleasant
Ladson
Pageland
Lugoff
Great Falls
Rock Hill
Winnsboro
Springdale
Orangeburg
Bamberg
Williston
Walterboro
Beaufort
Hilton Head Island
Hampton
Fairfax
Barnwell
Aiken
Edgefield
Newberry
Whitmire
Union
Gaffney
Landrum
Springfield
Fountain Inn
Laurens
Greenwood
Anderson

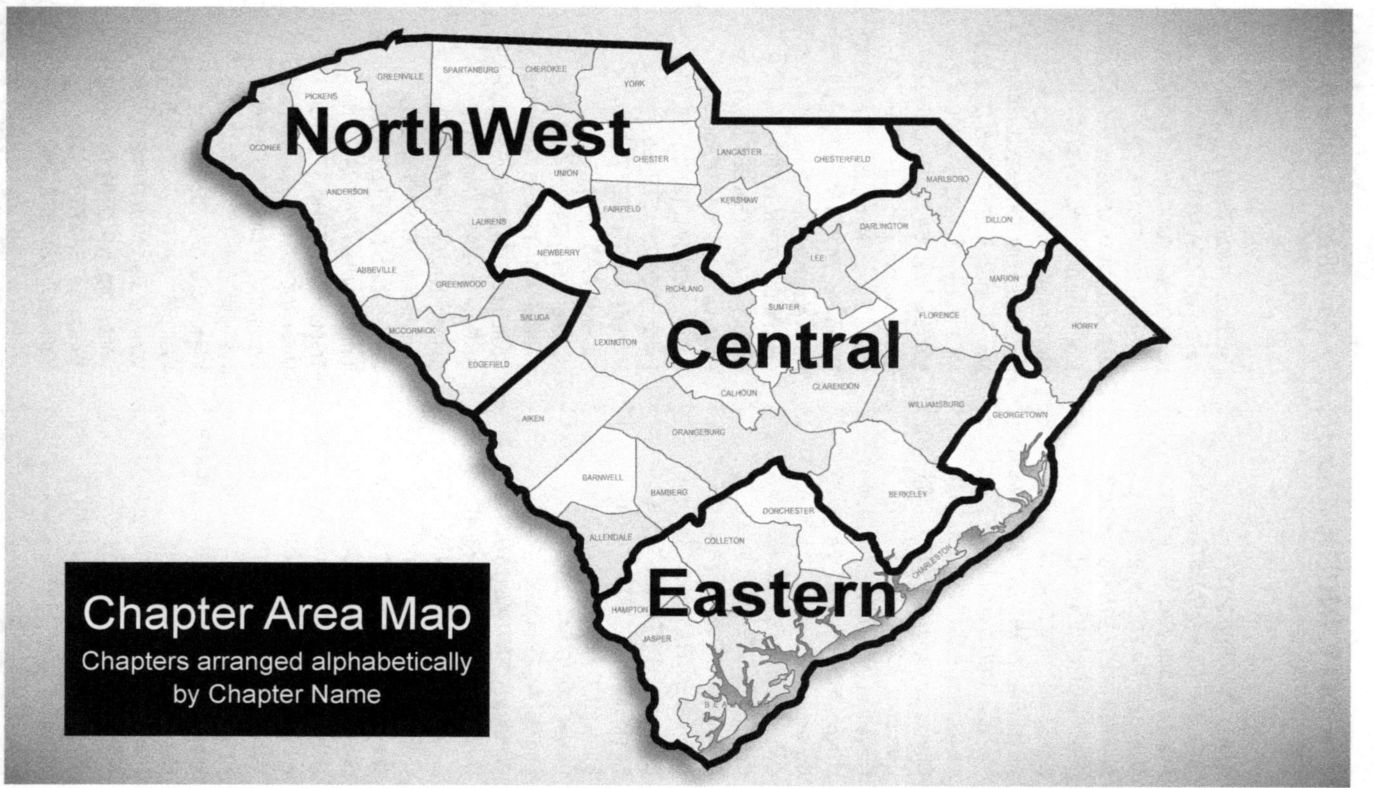
NorthWest
Central
Eastern
PICKENS
GREENVILLE
SPARTANBURG
CHEROKEE
YORK
OCONEE
CHESTER
LANCASTER
CHESTERFIELD
UNION
ANDERSON
MARLBORO
KERSHAW
FAIRFIELD
LAURENS
DARLINGTON
DILLON
NEWBERRY
LEE
ABBEVILLE
MARION
GREENWOOD
RICHLAND
SUMTER
FLORENCE
SALUDA
HORRY
MCCORMICK
LEXINGTON
EDGEFIELD
CLARENDON
CALHOUN
WILLIAMSBURG
GEORGETOWN
AIKEN
ORANGEBURG
BARNWELL
BERKELEY
BAMBERG
DORCHESTER
ALLENDALE
COLLETON
CHARLESTON
HAMPTON
JASPER
Chapter Area Map
Chapters arranged alphabetically
by Chapter Name

CITY INDEX *(Listed by City, Area, Page Numbers)*

General State Agency & Recreational Information

Call *(or visit websites)* for the services of interest. Request to be added to their mailing lists.

- South Carolina Beaches: www.SCBeaches.travel provides up-to-date travel information on three distinct areas – the Lowcountry and Resort Islands, Historic Charleston and Myrtle Beach & the Grand Strand – along with interactive games for kids, weather, maps and a photo album.
- South Carolina Department of Natural Resources: www.dnr.sc.gov
- South Carolina State Parks: www.SouthCarolinaParks.com
- South Carolina Farm Markets: www.sc-heritagecorridor.org
- South Carolina Pumpkin Patches: www.pumpkinpatchesandmore.org/SCpumpkins.php
- South Carolina Hot Deals: www.schotdeals.com - Vacation travel deals, updated frequently
- South Carolina Tourism: www.discoverSouthCarolina.com
- Columbia/Lake Murray Tourism: www.scjewel.com
- Myrtle Beach Tourism: www.visitmyrtlebeach.com
- Low Country Tourism (Charleston/HiltonHead): southcarolinalowcountry.com
- Pee Dee Country Tourism: www.peedeetourism.com
- Santee Cooper Country Tourism: www.santeecoopercountry.org
- Upcountry Tourism: www.theupcountry.com
- South Carolina Campgrounds: http://koa.com/where/sc/ or http://camping.about.com/od/cgwebpagessc/South_Carolina_Campgrounds_with_Web_pages.htm

PLANETARIUMS

Ever looked at the night sky on a clear evening and wondered more about what lights of our solar system you were staring at? Take that curiosity to a nearby planetarium and get answers. These special domed theaters have "star projectors" that recreate the night sky, including constellations, planets, and special effects such as comets, auroras, shooting stars and lunar eclipses. Each planetarium plans programs that differ in time and admission. Contact each facility for details:

- **Central** - DOOLEY PLANETARIUM - Cauthen Educational Media Center- Francis Marion University. Florence 843-661-1381. The Dooley Planetarium is full of surprise answers, supported by space travel simulations, NASA footage and all kinds of unexpected phenomena.

PLANETARIUMS *(cont.)*

- **Central** - STANBACK PLANETARIUM & NASA EDUCATOR RESOURCE CENTER - South Carolina State University. Orangeburg 803-536-7174. The state's second largest planetarium focuses on providing free programs for area school children. The public is admitted to all regularly scheduled programs on a first-come, first-served basis, including December's Christmas specials "A Star for Santa's Tree" and "Star of Wonder."
- **Northwest** - DUPONT PLANETARIUM - Ruth Patrick Science Education Center, USC Aiken. 803-641-3654. This cozy theater puts you closest to the star field by displaying more than 9,000 stars down to the eighth magnitude. Besides all this high- tech, you'll find some impressive low-tech features as well, including Egyptian obelisk and Roman wedge sundials, and the world's only known camera obscure (a large, rare pinhole camera) that projects images from outside onto a planetarium dome.
- **Northwest** - HOWELL MEMORIAL PLANETARIUM - Bob Jones University. Greenville. (864) 242-5100. BJU's planetarium produces and presents a variety of educational programming that is not only scientifically accurate but also consistent with Biblical teachings and a Christian worldview. Even the planetarium's setting is heavenly, with mural-covered walls depicting the solar system and other astronomical objects.
- **Northwest** - SETTLEMYRE PLANETARIUM - Museum of York County. Rock Hill 803-329-2121. With an extensive collection of African animals and artifacts, complemented by a changing schedule of innovative astronomical programs, this public planetarium offers weekend shows year-round.
- **Northwest** - T.C. HOOPER PLANETARIUM / SCIENCESPHERE - Charles Daniel Observatory. Roper Mountain Science Center. Greenville 864-281-1188. Starry Nights, held every Friday evening, and monthly second Saturday programs are the public's opportunity to see this dramatic astronomical facility. Recently named a Star Center One™ partner site, the center is one of only 60 U.S. sites chosen to help build awareness of the International Space Station. Once you're ready to come back down to Earth, visit the lush nature trails, arboretum and butterfly gardens.

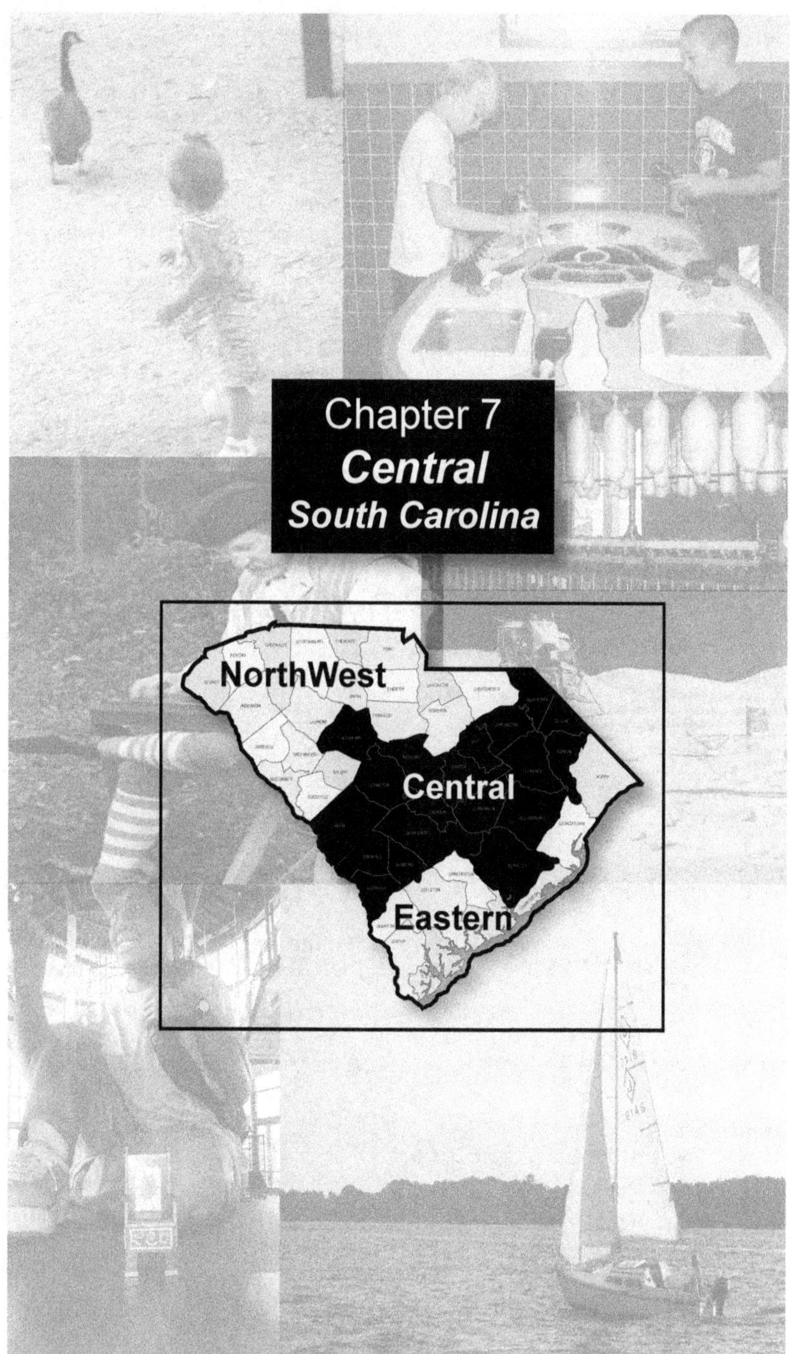
Chapter 7
Central
South Carolina
NorthWest
Central
Eastern

Aiken
- Battle Of Aiken

Beech Island
- Redcliffe Plantation State Historic Site

Bishopville
- South Carolina Cotton Museum

Camden
- Historic Camden Revolutionary War Site

Columbia
- Maurice's Barbeque
- Columbia Marionette Theatre
- Edventure Children's Museum

Columbia
- Riverfront Park
- South Carolina State House
- South Carolina State Museum
- Staybridge Suites - Columbia
- Pawleys Front Porch
- Riverbanks Zoo
- Frankies Fun Park - Columbia
- South Carolina State Fair
- Holiday Lights On The River

Columbia (Irmo)
- Lake Murray
- Southern Patriot On Lake Murray
- Okra Strut - Irmo

Darlington
- Darlington Raceway & Stock Car Museum

Dillon
- Little Pee Dee State Park
- South Of The Border

Ehrhardt
- Rivers Bridge State Historic Site

Elloree
- Elloree Heritage Museum & Cultural Center

Florence
- Hilton Garden Inn - Florence
- Pee Dee State Farmers Market
- Redbone Alley Restaurant
- The Drive In
- Young Pecan Plantation

Gilbert
- Lexington Cty Peach Festival

Hartsville (McBee)
- McLeod Farms

Hopkins
- Congaree National Park

Lexington
- Flight Deck Restaurant
- Lexington County Museum

Manning
- Swamp Fox Murals

North Augusta
- Berry Plantation
- Living History Park

Olanta
- Woods Bay State Natural Area

Pelion
- Peanut Party - Pelion

Santee
- Clark's Inn & Restaurant
- Lone Star Barbecue
- Santee State Park

Summerton
- Santee Indian Mound & Fort Watson Site (Santee National Wildlife Refuge)

Sumter
- Swan Lake Iris Gardens

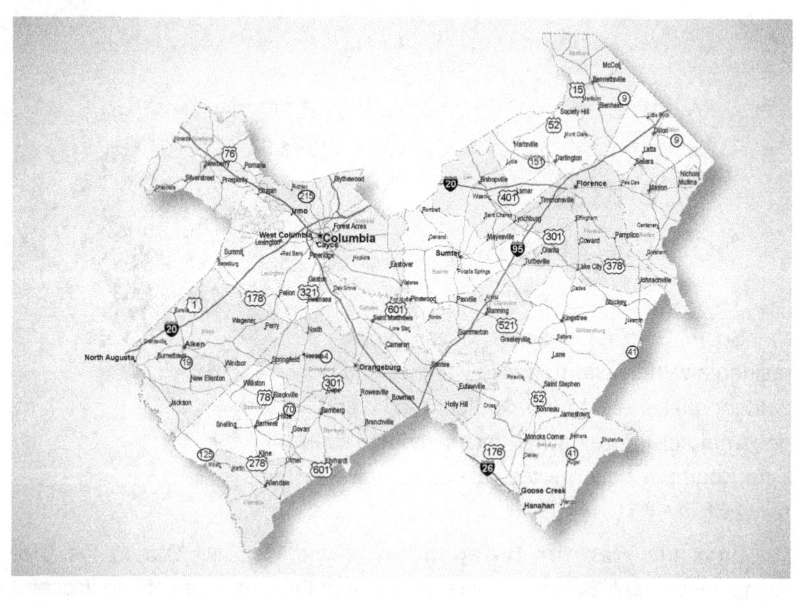

Travel Journal & Notes:

A Quick Tour of our Hand-Picked Favorites Around...

NorthWest
Central
Eastern

Central South Carolina

South Carolina beacons visitors and residents with its warm, gentle weather and outdoor pleasures to its comfort foods and good-natured guides at fun museums and tours. This Southern belle invites guests to settle in and stay awhile.

From the **War for Independence** and the Civil War to the Civil Rights movement, South Carolina has been at the center of both conflict and resolution throughout America's history. **Battlegrounds** dot the fields of the Midlands – ones you can visit, dress up and "march" on today.

South Carolina's other historical sites including **military sites** along with a range of historical festivals and celebrations, reveal fascinating stories you won't find in history books.

Up and down Carolina lakefronts, guests can arrange day or weekend trips that include fishing, looking out for **Purple Martins**, or just cruising at sunset. Some locations have preserved nature with great care and offers fantastic places to go biking, fishing, boating, horseback riding, and nature walking. The **Central** portions of the state offer boardwalk trails through **swamps**!

Wishing for a little fresh water? From **Lake Murray** in the Midlands, the action never stops on South Carolina lakes. These are some of South Carolina's best family vacation spots, offering a wide range of accommodations and virtually every activity you can imagine. It's a great way to create an inexpensive family vacation you won't forget...maybe in a **lakeside cabin** in the middle of the woods. **Santee State Park** area may be the perfect spot to take in all of this.

Whether you're looking for a fun way to spend a rainy afternoon, or just want to have a play date with your children, South Carolina's **children's museums** will help spark a love of learning for your child... and create memories along the way.

South Carolina cuisine has been inspired by their unique cultural heritage, and thus includes European, African, Caribbean and American frontier influences. From South Carolina BBQ to **Gullah** shrimp & cheesy grits, food is serious business. They even divide the state by **barbecue** regions. Mustard-based in the Midlands, vinegar-based on the coast and in the Pee Dee. And visitors quickly learn: Many of the best places are mom-and-pops and Mom and Pop are typically open only Wednesday or Thursday through Saturday. Sometimes Sunday. That means South Carolina is perfect for everyone from a family on a budget to the serious foodie-but be sure they're open!

For those who prefer food and wildlife resources up close and personal, stroll through one of South Carolina's **State Parks** or numerous **Farm Festivals**. With a great climate and long growing season, South Carolina is acclaimed for its mouth-watering **peaches** and huge **watermelons** in summer, juicy mountain-grown apples in fall and vine-fresh berries in spring.

Millions of travelers drive across South Carolina each year en route to the beach, and for those willing to wait just a minute, there's a lot for them to see and do just off the interstate on their way to Hilton Head, Charleston and Myrtle Beach. Thriving cities full of attractions are in greater **Columbia** and **Florence** communities, right off interstates. History, theme parks, zoos and family friendly farms loaded with produce and fun are just some of the attractions.

Sites and attractions are listed in order by City, Zip Code, and Name. Symbols indicated represent:

☐ Restaurants ☐ Lodging

BATTLE OF AIKEN

Aiken - The Battle of Aiken, in which Joe Wheeler and his men, greatly outnumbered and outgunned, sent Maj. Gen. Hugh Judson Kilpatrick's men running for cover and even captured old "Killer's" hat. For three days, reenactors eat, sleep, live and fight in a painfully recreated version of the world in 1865. The Civil War battle has grown from a few hundred men with muskets to a full-blown Civil War festival. In addition to battle reenactments, there are authentic 19th-century military encampments and reproductions of medical facilities. Admission. www.battleofaiken.org (last weekend in February)

REDCLIFFE PLANTATION STATE HISTORIC SITE

Beech Island - 181 Redcliffe Rd (I-20 exit 1) 29842. Phone: (803) 827-1473. http://southcarolinaparks.com/redcliffe/introduction.aspx Hours: Grounds: Thursday - Monday 9:00am-6:00pm. Admission: $5.00- $10.00 (age 6+). Tours: House Museum Tours are held Thursday through Monday at 11am, 1pm & 3pm.

"Cotton is King!" Those words resounded through Congress and then the nation in a fiery speech by South Carolina Sen. James Henry Hammond in the years leading up to the Civil War. Completed in 1859, Redcliffe's Greek-Revival mansion was the home of James Henry Hammond and three generations of his descendants. Hammond, whose political career included terms as a United States congressman, governor of South Carolina, and United States senator, was perhaps best known during his lifetime as an outspoken defender of slavery and states' rights.

CHRISTMAS IN THE QUARTERS

Beech Island *- Redcliffe Plantation State Historic Site. Explore the holidays at Redcliffe Plantation from the perspective of the enslaved women, men, and children that were owned by the Hammond family. Participants will be guided through the slave quarters and hear stories about 19th century Christmas rituals. Admission. (mid-December weekend)*

SOUTH CAROLINA COTTON MUSEUM

Bishopville - 121 W Cedar Lane 29010. www.sccotton.org Phone: (803) 484-4497. Hours: Monday-Saturday 10:00am-4:00pm. Admission: $3.00- $6.00 per person (age 6+).

Central

This museum preserves the history of South Carolina's cotton culture. How much do you really know about Cotton? Learn how seed cotton is transformed into usable cotton fiber. Find out about the evil boll weevil bug or the wonderful modernization of using ring spinners that form hundreds of spools of thread in minutes. See an original plantation spinner, a 130-year-old loom, a three-foot tall boll weevil, original tools and more. Interactive exhibits and amusing stories in an authentic setting allow you to experience a way of life long gone yet very much a part of the present.

HISTORIC CAMDEN REVOLUTIONARY WAR SITE

Camden - 222 Broad Street (I-20 exit 98. North on Hwy 521) 29020. Phone: (803) 432-9841. www.historiccamden.org Hours: Tuesday-Saturday 10:00am-5:00pm; Sunday 1:00-5:00pm. Admission: Full tour of Kershaw-Cornwallis House - $4.00-$5.00 per person (age 7+). FREE admission: lower grounds and nature trail.

Spend a few peaceful hours where the British spent a rough year. After the siege of Charleston, Lord Charles Cornwallis and 2,500 British soldiers marched to Camden and set up their main backcountry supply post. For the next 11 months the town was occupied. The 107-acre outdoor museum complex includes the 18th-century town site, the furnished 1785 Craven House, two restored log cabins with exhibits, partial reconstruction of British military fortifications and the reconstructed and furnished Joseph Kershaw House, headquarters for Lord Cornwallis. There's also a blacksmith exhibit and a .6 mile Nature Trail. Check out the 16-minute orientation film. Guided and self-guided tours are available and focus on Camden's Colonial and Revolutionary eras. The Old Camden Trace is a 3.5 mile walk through Historic Camden.

MAURICE'S BARBEQUE

Columbia - (several exits off interstate near Columbia - look for signs on highway logo boards). Barbeque joints that don't appear that nice are typically the best tasting. So is true here. Nothing to look at inside or out but you're greeted by a friendly face who can tell a newbie 100 yards away. They first tell you about their homemade sauce, then offer you a sample of some on some meat to try. This sauce looks different than regular BBQ sauces because it's Golden - made that distinctively different color from a mustard base. We tried all sorts of meats but the brisket with that Golden Regular was the perfect combo. Once you get over how great the odd sauce is, be sure to try something regional as a side - hash over rice. Not the hash you may think - more like a smooth stew over rice - very good. They are cooking every day making fresh hickory pit-cooked ham, pork, chicken, beef and ribs. Like the sauce a lot? Take some of their heirloom recipe home with you. www.piggiepark.com

Central

COLUMBIA MARIONETTE THEATRE

Columbia - 401 Laurel Street 29201. http://cmtpuppet.org. Phone: (803) 252-7366. Shows: Performances are every Saturday at 11:00am and 3:00pm (excluding major holidays) and the third Monday of each month at 10:00am. Admission: $5.00 per person (children 2 and under are free). You do not need reservations. Simply purchase your tickets at the door.

The mission of this theater is to expose children and adults throughout the state to the long-standing tradition and artistry of marionette puppetry.

Puppets, ranging from Tinkerbelle's 12 inches to Zeus' 5 feet, appear on a 30-foot stage. All productions are created entirely in house -- the script is written, the puppets are made, the soundtrack is recorded and the sets are painted. Productions range from folk tales to science and historical fiction.

Meet Eddie, the World's Largetst Child!

EDVENTURE CHILDREN'S MUSEUM

Columbia - 211 Gervais Street (anchors of a two-mile riverfront development in Columbia's city center) 29201. Phone: (803) 779-3100. www.edventure.org Hours: Daily 9:00am-5:00pm. Closed Easter, Thanksgiving, Christmas Eve, Christmas Day. Admission: $11.95 adults and children; $10.95 seniors (age 62+) & military with ID; children under 2 free. Note: "Blooming Butterflies", an enclosed outdoor nature exhibit featuring more than 20 species of butterflies (May - October). It is filled with dozens of species of trees and plants that support hundreds of butterflies from more than 20 different species native to the Southeast United States. Be sure to check out the Bloom Room and observe chrysalises and emerging butterflies.

EdVenture Children's Museum in Columbia is the largest museum for kids in the Southeast. Designed for children 12 and younger, Eddie, the world's largest child, is the centerpiece of the museum. A 40-foot tall structure made primarily of molded plastic, Eddie weights 35,000 pounds and is large enough for everybody to climb in, on and through. You can climb his vertebrae to his brain, crawl through his heart, bounce around inside his stomach and slide out his intestines. Flexible parents - you can climb along with your kids, too.

EdVenture is divided into six sub galleries, each with a different theme. While there you can talk to a skeleton, anchor the news, drive a fire truck, build a town, and explore how people work. One gallery is the World of Work, which offers a look into what really goes into some of the state's more well-known jobs. Future farmers will enjoy collecting eggs from chickens, milking a cow and driving a tractor through a field while city slickers can learn the skills necessary to manage a grocery store. As expected, they also have a "Backyard" devoted to wee ones, live critters, art or computer stations, and a water table outside for all to share. We loved all of it - especially Eddie!

RIVERFRONT PARK

Columbia - 312 Laurel Street 29201. www.sctrails.net/trails/trail/riverfront-park Phone: (803) 545-3100. Hours: Daily 7:00am-9:00pm. Admission: FREE.

This 167-acre park was the site of the original waterworks for the City of Columbia. This was also the site of the world's first electrically operated textile mill and the hydroelectric plant, the oldest one in the state, is still operating. A popular jogging/walking trail runs two and one half miles along the linear park and offers wonderful views of the river. There is also a beautiful brick amphitheater as well as a self guided walkway by the old parts of the water plant. The park hosts several events annually such as Riverfest, Greekfest and several smaller concerts. Fish ladder tours are at Riverfront North. Find out how migratory fish use the passage to travel upstream to spawn. Every Friday at 4:00pm through May.

SOUTH CAROLINA STATE HOUSE

Columbia - 1100 Gervais Street (and Main St) 29201. Phone: (803) 734-2430. https://southcarolinaparks.com/education-and-history/state-house. Hours: Monday-Saturday 10am-4pm Closed all state holidays. Admission: FREE. Tours: offered each day (except Sunday), 4 times/day starting at 9:30am. FREEBIES:https://southcarolinaparks.com/education-and-history/coloring-sheets

One of the nation's first planned communities, Columbia was established in 1786 as a centrally located state capital. Much of the city was destroyed in a spectacular fire after the undefended city surrendered to Union Gen. William Tecumseh Sherman and his troops on Feb. 17, 1865, the same day Confederate troops evacuated Charleston in the final weeks of the war. Completed in 1907, the copper-domed granite building today wears six bronze stars to mark hits from Sherman's cannons.

Tours of the State House, the seat of South Carolina's legislative and executive branches of government can be taken guided or self-guided. Things to look for: the Ordinances of Secession (1st state to secede) and the crescent moon similar to the one on the state flag. Why is it straight up vs. tilted?

SOUTH CAROLINA STATE MUSEUM

Columbia - 301 Gervais Street (beside the historic Gervais St. Bridge and just a few blocks west of the State Capitol) 29201. www.scmuseum.org. Phone: (803) 898-4921. Hours: Monday - Saturday 10:00am-5:00pm, Sundays Noon - 5:00pm. Closed: Easter, Thanksgiving, Christmas Eve and Christmas Day Admission: $8.95 adult, $7.95 senior (62+), $6.95 child (3-12). Infants 2 and under: FREE. Planetarium & 4D shows are extra fee. Note: They have a large museum store with products made in or for South Carolina. Crescent Café has sandwiches and snacks plus the museum's fresh, on-site made fudge in dozens of flavors. Educators:Lessons/Activities:www.southcarolinastatemuseum.org/educational_programs/LessonsAtGlance.aspx.

More astronauts came from South Carolina than any other state.

This state museum is a refreshing combination of four floors of exhibits, many of them hands-on, focusing on the arts, history and technology. Climb aboard the "Best Friend of Charleston" train. Stroll along a boardwalk at the beach diorama. Be thrilled by the accomplishments of S.C. astronauts. Learn how a South Carolinian invented the laser. The museum itself is located inside its largest artifact, the world's first totally electric textile mill, which opened in 1894. Families with young children can learn and play together in the Stringer Discovery Center on the first floor or the Science Center on the top floor is ideal for older kids to recreate science experiments. Along the way, there are plenty of mini-movie corners to sit, watch and rest.

Museum goers looking for the unusual can find the little people in permanent exhibit murals on the museum's three upper floors. All told, there are nine of the little guys—six on the natural history floor, one on the science and technology floor and another two on the cultural history floor. They can be found in all kinds of locations and situations, from a river-bottom swamp to the surface of the moon! Looking for the little gnomes is a good way to engage the whole family to observe everything interesting.

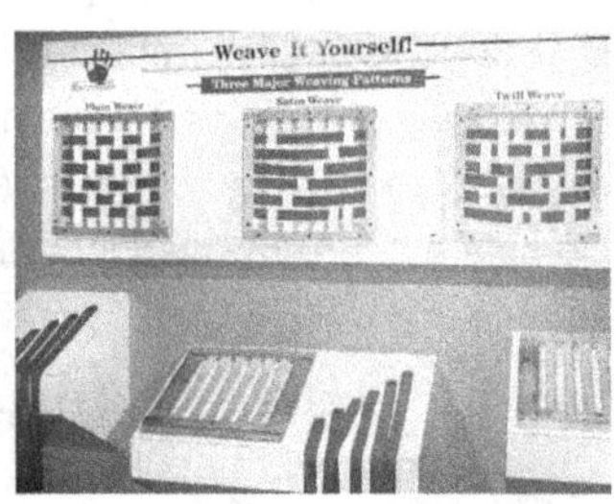

Try you hand at weaving....

STAYBRIDGE SUITES - COLUMBIA

Columbia - 1913 Huger Street (I-126 exit Huger Street) 29201. Phone: (803) 451-5900. www.staycolumbiasc.com. At the Staybridge Suites Columbia, discover the best of Southern charm and hospitality with modern amenities. The newly constructed residential hotel offers spacious suite accommodations with kitchens/utensils and family-friendly features, including indoor pool and daily complimentary hot breakfast for guests. Several weekdays the staff also serve a catered light dinner, too. The downtown hotel location puts you just 1 mile from the University of South Carolina's main campus and blocks from downtown restaurants and museums. Children always stay free, and sleeper sofa beds in every room are perfect for kids and groups. Rainy days? Try a museum nearby or hang out at the indoor pool. Don't miss breakfast in the lobby. Great way to start your family touring days around Columbia or over to Lake Murray.

PAWLEYS FRONT PORCH

Columbia - 827 Harden Street 29205. www.pawleysfrontporch.com Phone: (803) 771-8001. Pawleys Porch is a fresh addition to the strip of restaurants in the Five Points area of Columbia (near the University). The burger joint, featured on the Food Network's "Diners, Drive-ins and Dives", serves creative burger combinations all named after South Carolina coastal cities or themes. The Fripp Island burger with Southern salsa, boursin cheese (creamed five cheese blend) and a fried green tomato is a must-try. Or how about the Isle of Palms burger with housemade pimento cheese with jalapeno bacon. Mmm…Non-adventuresome kids can just order a plain beef burger, chicken sandwich or chicken tender wrap. Pawleys smokes their own bacon, grinds their meat in-house and makes their own pickles. This makes the half-pound burgers even better. Oh, and they serve your burger plate with a steak knife dug into the middle of the burger - it's so thick, you may need to cut it into small bites! Daily Lunch and Dinner. Moderate pricing.

☐ ____________________

RIVERBANKS ZOO

Columbia - 500 Wildlife Pkwy (just off I-126 at Greystone Blvd.) 29210. Phone: (803) 779-8717. www.riverbanks.org. Hours: Daily, 9:00am-5:00pm; special hours for Lights Before Christmas and Boo at the Zoo. Holidays Closed : Thanksgiving and Christmas Admission: $19.95 adult, $17.95 senior & military, $16.95 child (2-12). Online discount. Tram Tours: Tram stops are located beside Kenya Café and in front of the Garden Visitors Center. Zipline is extra fee.

Riverbanks is home to more than 2,000 fascinating animals and one of the nation's most beautiful and inspiring botanical gardens. The lush 170-acre site features dynamic natural habitat exhibits, scenic river views, spectacular valley overlooks and significant historic landmarks.

Areas we feel are best to explore:

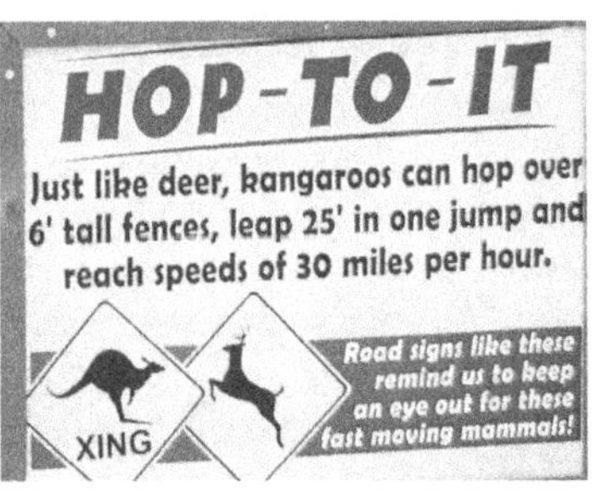

Ndoki Forest - esp. the gorillas and meerkats; African Plains - here's where you can hand feed giraffes!; Conservation Outpost - fun monkeys and tree kangaroos; Birdhouse at Riverbanks - penguins, flamingos and a place to feed the Koi fish; Koala Knockabout - down under creatures plus sweet feed treats for the lorikeets; Riverbanks Farm - feed goats, ride ponies or meet llamas; and finally, the amusing lemurs on Lemur Island. From a diving expedition on the Indo-Pacific coral reef to a safari through the plains of Africa, there's so much to do at the Zoo.

Riverbanks Zoo and Garden is also caretaker to a number of Civil War era historic sites located within the Zoo on both sides of the river including: Saluda Factory Interpretive Center, Covered Bridge Abutments, Camp Sorghum, Saluda Factory Historic District and Sherman's Rock. Little placards by the sites briefly describe their significance to wartime events.

LIGHTS BEFORE CHRISTMAS

Columbia *- Each evening from 5:00-9:00pm experience Columbia's longest running holiday tradition at Riverbanks Zoo and Garden. Explore the Zoo illuminated by nearly one million twinkling lights and more than 350 handcrafted images. Take your photo with Santa, roast marshmallows at the Jingle Bell Bonfire and be sure to wear your hat – it snows nightly at Riverbanks during the Lights Before Christmas. Admission is free for Riverbanks members and general admission is $9 for children ages 2 – 12 and $8 for adults. (mid-November thru New Years Day)*

FRANKIES FUN PARK - COLUMBIA

Columbia - 140 Parkridge Drive 29212. https://frankies.com/columbia/. Phone: (803) 781-2342. Hours: Monday-Thursday 10:00am - 10:00pm, Friday-Saturday 10:00am - midnight (September - May); daily 10:00am-midnight (June - August) Closed: Thanksgiving, Christmas. Admission: based on activity, ~$7.00 each.

A 14-acre family oriented amusement center serves up great rides, food and good times. Go-Karts, miniature golf, bumper boats, amusement rides, laser tag, batting cages and an awesome arcade are part of a mega mix of fun.

SOUTH CAROLINA STATE FAIR

Columbia - State Fairgrounds @ Rosewood & Assembly Sts (across from Williams-Brice football stadium). Rides, games, animal exhibits, fried food and music at the State Fairgrounds. www.scstatefair.org. Admission. (runs 11 days mid-to-late October)

HOLIDAY LIGHTS ON THE RIVER

Columbia - 5605 Bush River Road, Saluda Shoals Park. The Midlands Largest Drive-Through Lights Display! Holiday Lights features over 300 themed light displays on a two-mile loop of the park! In addition to old favorites, look for the Wetland Wonderland walking area, a bigger, better dazzling, Dancing Forest. Take a ride on the Red-Nose Express Hayride, or enjoy a leisurely trip through the lights in a horse-drawn carriage. Young children can see the lights while riding on the Saluda Shoals Choo-Choo. Try your hand at tubing without the snow and take a slide down the Winter Wonder Ride. Concessions, crafts to make & take home, roasting marshmallows, and a special photo and visit with Santa are additional highlights. www.icrc.net Admission for each activity. (Thanksgiving thru December)

LAKE MURRAY

Columbia (Irmo) - 29063. Marina: (803) 781-1585 or lakemurraymarinasc.com. www.lakemurraycountry.com. Note: The state's official fish is the striped bass and Lake Murray has plenty. You can catch them with shad as your bait.

The biggest Fish ever captured on Lake Murray was a 298-pound sturgeon by four young men on April 28th, 1956. The fish was 9 feet long!

Lake Murray, near Columbia, is one of the state's many lakes and rivers offering excellent fishing with the lure of striped bass, blue catfish, trout or bream. The lake draws thousands of users each day to this recreational paradise. Boaters love it, whether its canoeing or kayaking in clam waters or rapids, navigating sails through cutting winds or leisurely cruising in a power or fishing boat. Nationally sponsored fishing tournaments are held. The largest event held on Lake Murray is the Lake Murray July 4th Celebration.

There are so many coves and curves of the lake, finding your favorite spot is difficult. We'd suggest stopping by the marina first. Grab a seafood snack at the bar and grill and wander around a bit to get a feel for the layout (or put in your boat and head out to chart your own day).

Central

SPIRIT ON LAKE MURRAY

All of the black specks in this photo are thousands of purple martins...

Columbia (Irmo)* - *(dock: 1600 Marina Road, Lake Murray Marina) 29063. (803) 749-8594. www.lakemurrayadventures.com. Hours: Purple Martin Departures: July & August 6:45pm to 9:15pm. Cruises available on Sunday's and Mondays only. Purple Martin Cruises: $35.00 Per person (Light supper - ex. chicken fingers, picnic sides & lemonade/sweet tea, narration is included) Cruises depart from Lake Murray Marina.

The Southern Patriot is a 65 foot double deck cruise boat located on beautiful Lake Murray, just a few miles north west of Columbia. The Southern Patriot can carry up to 100 passengers and is suitable for any type of event.

Purple Martin Cruises: A phenomenon you have to see to believe. This 2 ½ hour cruise takes you out to historic Bomb Island, where hundreds of thousands of birds (Purple Martins) circle and roost on the largest Purple Martin sanctuary in North America. As the sun sets, you'll see maybe a few 100 birds. Then they come and flock in mass of 1000s and start dancing and chirping near dark. During this cruise you will hear narration about the Purple Martins and about the historic significance of how this island was used for bombing practice by Jimmy Doolittle prior to his raid on Tokyo during WWII.

By day purple martins nest in gourds or man-made compartment birdhouses similar to condos!

Note: July and August are the months to see this natural phenomenon, the largest such roosting sanctuary of its kind in North America. By September, the birds head off to South America on their winter migration.

Central

OKRA STRUT - IRMO

Columbia (Irmo) *- Community Park, 7507 Eastview. The town of Irmo hosts two days of all things okra. Green pod lovers of all ages will enjoy "Okryland" kids' area, okra-eating and -growing contests and musical entertainment and hundreds of crafters. The festival boasts an array of food from traditional festival fare to the famous "fried okra" deliciously seasoned by The Lake Murray-Irmo Women's Club. 50,000-70,000 attendance. www.theokrastrut.com Small fee for adults. (last weekend in September)*

DARLINGTON RACEWAY & STOCK CAR MUSEUM

Darlington - 1301 Harry Byrd Hwy. (exit 164 west on Hwy 52, then two miles west of the city of Darlington on highway SC 151) 29540. Phone: (843) 395-8499. www.darlingtonraceway.com. Hours: Monday-Friday 10:00am-4:00pm. Admission: $5.00 for adults, and FREE for kids under the age of 12.

The late Dale Earnhardt once said, " ... there's no victory so sweet, so memorable, as whipping Darlington Raceway."

In 1950, when the idea to build a track was conceived, the original landowner, farmer Jack Ramsey, had just one request — don't disturb his fishing pond. Thus, Brasington was forced to change the design from a geometrically correct oval to more of an egg-shape. In doing so, he not only preserved the fishing hole, he made Darlington Raceway one of the most challenging tracks in the country. Over the years, Darlington Raceway has earned a reputation as "the track too tough to tame." Fans can watch the pros squeeze through the narrow third and fourth turns (remember the pond?) from the comfort of updated grandstands and infield.

MUSEUM: Here you can view a priceless collection of historic race cars, including Johnny Mantz's No. 98 Plymouth that won the first race back in 1950. Kids can push buttons near each display and it will play an audio history of each driver. Occupying a prominent spot in the back is Darrell Waltrip's 1991 Chevy Lumina, which rolled eight times in the '91 Pepsi 400 in one of the most fearsome crashes in stock car history. Waltrip walked away from the incident, and the car stands as an impressive witness to stock car safety. Stop at the museum and gift shop, have lunch in the picnic area, then walk out on the track and just take in the ambiance of the place. If you're a NASCAR fan, it really is awesome, even when there isn't a single car running.

LITTLE PEE DEE STATE PARK

Dillon - 1298 State Park Road (exit 193 onto Hwy9 thru Dillon. Right onto Hwy 57 for several miles. Left onto CR22) 29536. Phone: (843) 774-8872. https://southcarolinaparks.com/little-pee-dee Hours: Daily 9:00am-6:00pm (extended to 9:00pm during Daylight Savings Time). Admission: FREE.

Little Pee Dee State Park is a setting for fishing the still waters of 54-acre Lake Norton. Visitors can explore the park's river swamp, examine features of the Sandhills region and admire an example of the mysterious geological depression unique to the Atlantic Coastal Plain, the Carolina Bay. The Beaver Pond Nature Trail can be accessed from the park road or from the campground. This 1.3-mile trail to a beaver pond loops back to the original point of entry. Jon boats, canoes and kayaks with life jackets and paddles are available for rent. Guests also enjoy the park's campground and picnic area.

SOUTH OF THE BORDER

Dillon - mm 198, right at NC/SC border off I-95 & US 301 N) 29536. Phone: (843) 774-2411. www.thesouthoftheborder.com. Hours: Daily, hours for venues varies but generally 7:00am-11:00pm. Note: Pedros Rockey City has oodles of fireworks - big ones, too. Sombrero Restaurant serves Mexican food and 3 other restaurants are on the premises.

Pedro straddles the South of the Border entrance, 97 feet tall, "the largest freestanding sign east of the Mississippi."

The auto trip from the Northeast to the sunny shores of Florida via I-95 takes some driving. Halfway there, a huge alien sombrero nearly 200 feet high suddenly appears. After an onslaught of 120 billboards for 200 miles, this is what you've waited to see. Drive under Pedro, the attraction's mascot, into a world of Mexico Americana. South of the Border is so named because it is just "south of the border" – the border between the states of South Carolina and North Carolina. This attraction offers an amusement park with bumper cars, a Ferris wheel, parachute drop, miniature golf and more. If you like things that crawl, stop by Reptile Lagoon. SOB has both RV campgrounds and 300 motel rooms spread over its 135 acres. And staying here allows access to Pedro's Pleasure Dome, with its indoor pool, steam room, and Jacuzzi. Kids will want to use their spending money at the Gift Shops as quantity is king and the hardest decisions are which of the handfuls of different souvenirs should you get? You can take a ride in the glass elevator to the top of Pedro's 200-foot tall Sombrero Tower! They say this is an oasis and once you've looked off the top of the tower, you'll see why - nothing, nowhere.

RIVERS BRIDGE STATE HISTORIC SITE

Ehrhardt - 325 State Park Road (I-20 exit 18. follow signs) 29081. Phone: (803) 267-3675. www.southcarolinaparks.com/riversbridge/introduction.aspx Hours: Daily 9:00am-6:00pm. Admission: FREE.

Rivers Bridge is the site of one of the Confederacy's last stands against General William T. Sherman's sweep across the South. The still-intact earthen fortifications bear silent witness to the fierce battle that raged there on Feb. 2-3, 1865. The outnumbered Southerners held on for two days, marking the only major resistance the Union army encountered on its march south, which culminated later with the burning of Columbia. The war itself ended soon after. The Battlefield Interpretive Trail is a self-guided trail about 3/4 of a mile with interpretive wayside panels. Ranger-guided tours and special programs help educate visitors about the battle and military life during the Civil War.

ELLOREE HERITAGE MUSEUM & CULTURAL CENTER

Elloree - 2714 Cleveland Street (exit 98 west; Rte 6 west right into town, left on Cleveland) 29047. Phone: (803) 897-2225. www.elloreemuseum.org. Hours: Wednesday -Saturday 10:00am-5:00pm Admission: $3.00- $6.00 (ages 6+).

The town of Elloree is most known for its quaint streets and shops. Rich in history, the Heritage Museum explores a plantation cotton gin house and how cotton is grown, picked and ginned today. Next, stroll Cleveland Street as it appeared in 1900, with recreated stores, bank and hotel. Further down the exhibit hall is the 18th century Snider cabin and farm yard where you can meet "William J. Snider" and learn the plan for his new town. You can walk into many of the exhibits back here. Try to find the canned peaches or the kitty cat. Look closely around a corner for the outhouse. This is really one of the cutest small town museums we've seen. Nice way to see what it takes to build a southern town from scratch.

Two blocks away, Joe Miller Park offers picnic tables and playground spaces. Each March the town is the setting for the Elloree Trials Horse Race for thoroughbreds and quarter horses. The town is also home to the bi-annual trash and treasures sales, the annual Winter Lights festival, and a Pork Fest.

HILTON GARDEN INN - FLORENCE

Florence - 2671 Hospitality Blvd. (I-95 Exit 160 A to first light. Turn right on Radio Drive. Turn left at next light onto Hospitality Blvd. Hotel is on the left) 29501. Phone: (843) 432-3001. www.florence.stayhgi.com. This family hotel offers friendly service and easy access to I-95 and I-20. Best features: Complimentary high-speed Internet and evening room service. Work out in the fitness center, relax in the whirlpool or take a plunge in the indoor heated pool. For your family's comfort and convenience they offer a Children's Menu, high chairs, cribs and playpens. A freshly prepared breakfast is offered daily in the Great American Grill® restaurant, and dinner is also available. All of their chicken dishes are really flavorful. The Pavilion Pantry® convenience mart offers sundries, an assortment of beverages and ready-to-cook meals bound for the in-room microwave oven or refrigerator. Oh, and after traveling all those highway miles, you'll enjoy their Sleep Deep beds. ☐ ______________________________

PEE DEE STATE FARMERS MARKET

Florence - 2513 W. Lucas Street (US Hwy. 52) (just head about one mile west off the exit 164. Market is on right.) 29501. http://agriculture.sc.gov/divisions/agency-operations/state-farmers-markets/pee-dee-state-farmers-market/ Phone: (843) 665-5154. Hours: Monday-Saturday 8am-6pm. Admission and parking are FREE. Note: Vending machines and restrooms.

The Pee Dee Farmers Market includes fresh produce for sale plus a 100-year-old barn which houses a pecan kitchen, potter's shop and a café. Elijah Thomas spends a few hours each day at his potter's wheel in his studio at the Red Barn. His "Confederate Cup" and "Batter Bowl" are two of the popular items he sells. Visiting with him is a delightful experience.

REDBONE ALLEY RESTAURANT

Florence - 1903 W Palmetto Street (exit 160A east a few miles on I-20. Left on US 76) 29501. www.redbonealley.com. Hours: Daily lunch & dinner.

Want to visit an outdoor Charleston café - indoors? This restaurant's theme looks very much like a theatrical set. And, it has a children's area with an ice cream truck (stocked with free ice cream treats) smack dab in the middle of a playspace for toddlers and kids' arcades. This space has the diversions you've been looking for while you wait for your food. (note: if you're a family with kids, you'll most likely get seated in this lively area). The staff start every day early by gathering the day's ingredients -- produce bought directly from local farmers -- honey gathered by South Carolinian beekeepers, Darlington County rice, freshly caught Atlantic seafood and the highest quality aged Western beef flown in daily. The menu really is influenced by French, Mediterranean,

African, English and West Indian cooking. Their entrees have a dramatic twist: Low Country Shrimp and Grits or Fried Green Tomatoes & Blackened Shrimp w/ Cajun sauce. Trust me, this northern girl now loves grits - Redbone grits, that is! If that's too odd for the kids, go with traditional Chicken Planks seasoned w/ one of 3 different batters. And, there's some form of ham in half the dishes so the flavor is familiar. If you just want traditional Kids menu items, they've got them: eight items - all for just $5.00. Average lunch $10.00, Average dinner $18.00. Still have room for dessert? How about a grilled pound cake panini "sandwich" made from an heirloom recipe. What an ending to an explosion of new tastes! Named after the owner's daughter's Red Bone coon hound, each restaurant also offers live entertainment and a clothing line featuring the Redbone Alley hound. ______ ☐

How cool..getting to play ICE CREAM TRUCK...

THE DRIVE-IN

Florence - 135 E Palmetto Street (I-20 to end, left onto US 76, just a couple blocks past intersection of US 52) 29501. Phone: (843) 669-5141. www.thebestdrivein.com. Hours: Monday-Saturday 10:30am-11:00pm. This renovated restaurant in downtown Florence has been serving some of the best hot dogs, burgers and shakes since 1957. Though the 50s-style restaurant now flaunts its modern architecture, the outside curb station still exists. The Drive-In is said to have the best fried chicken in the Pee Dee. We think it's very moist-probably the moistest we tasted in the Carolinas. One thing The Drive-in has now that wasn't around in the 50s is Wi-Fi. Bring your laptop and enjoy a smooth, cool milkshake for lunch. You're in for a good ol' fashion nostalgic treat and a twist, if you like. Since the owners are Greek, add a gyro and a piece of baklava (cinnamon-y) to your order. ______ ☐

Central

YOUNG PECAN PLANTATION

Florence - 2005 Babar lane (exit 164 west on US 52 west one half mile) 29501. Phone: (843) 66-2452. www.youngplantations.com. Hours: Monday-Friday 9:00am-5:00pm, Saturday 10:00am-4:00pm. Extended Christmas-time hours.

Pecan trees, fresh shelled pecans and candy coated pecans are all available from the retail sales shop at Young Pecan Plantation. These delectable treats are shipped around the world from South Carolina. Our favorite part of the visit is the Sampler Bar - a long counter full of samples of every type of flavored nut including some unique ones: Butter roasted and lightly salted (local fav), Double-Dipped Chocolate, Honey Crisp or Butterscotch. Don't like nuts? Have some ice cream or lunch instead. Once you've chosen your favorite flavors to purchase to take on the road, wander around the store and discover other homemade, and very unusual products. Pick up a few of their homemade ciders...blackberry, peach, strawberry, blueberry, and yes, apple. Wow, the peach is so refreshing!

LEXINGTON COUNTY PEACH FESTIVAL

Gilbert - (I-20 east exit Rte 37 north). South Carolina is the second largest grower of peaches in the country, behind California and ahead of Georgia. Events include a parade, arts and crafts, entertainment, the Peach Queen Contest and fireworks. And for refreshments? How about peach ice cream, peach slush, peach tea, peach parfaits and peach cobbler? www.lexingtoncountypeachfestival.com (July 4th)

MCLEOD FARMS

Hartsville (McBee) - 29247 Hwy 151 South (4.5 Miles South Hwy 151). www.macspride.com

"Life's a peach" is more than a slogan for the McLeod family of McBee, South Carolina. The McLeods operate one of the largest peach orchards in the area, growing 22 varieties on 650 producing acres on sandy loam. But when it comes to peaches, the family recommends everyone try the Cary Mac variety developed exclusively by them – a delicious delight from the Carolinas.

- PEACH FESTIVAL is held in July (usually weekend after July 4) during peak of peach harvest. www.macspride.com.
- FALL EVENTS - Corn maze - Read the clues taken from a 3rd grade history book and see if you can make it through the 7 acre corn maze. Children and adults will enjoy an old timed horse drawn wagon tour that will take you on a site seeing adventure. On your wagon ride you will be able to look across acres of peach trees, vegetable beds, and other varieties of produce grown at McLeod Farms. You can also choose to take a hayride to the pumpkin patch to pick your fall pumpkin. Fall Festival late October features all this plus live entertainment, pumpkin chunkin, games and homemade food.

CONGAREE NATIONAL PARK

***Hopkins** - 100 National Park Road 29061. www.nps.gov/cong. Phone: (803) 776-4396. Hours: Harry Hampton Visitor Center: Daily 9:00am-5:00pm. Closed Federal Holidays. Admission: FREE.*

Congaree National Park preserves the largest remnant of old-growth floodplain forest remaining on the continent! Experience national and state champion trees, towering to record size amidst an astonishing array of plants and animals. Congaree is home to a family-friendly exhibit area within the Visitor Center and a 2.4 mile boardwalk loop trail (crossing 8 feet above the ground). Other popular activities within the park include canoeing, kayaking, fishing, birding, nature study and more. Before you embark on your adventures, watch the introductory film and get the latest information about conditions in the park. A little more adventuresome. There's no better way to see the park than by canoe, and the Park offers FREE ranger guided canoe tours most Saturdays and Sundays. Or, if you have kids who don't fidget on long walks, try a guided Tree Trek tour in the afternoon or a weekend evening flashlight Owl Prowl. On the boardwalk trail, your kids exclaim it looks prehistoric! However, instead of dinosaurs, you will find plenty of squirrel and salamander - we even saw a blue salamander cross our path!

See GIANT Cypress Trees...

FLIGHT DECK RESTAURANT & BAKERY

***Lexington** - 109 Old Chapin Road (I-20 Hwy 378 exit. Intersection of Hwy 1 (Main St) & Hwy 378 (Columbia Ave) 29072. www.flightdeckrestaurant.net. Phone: (803) 957-5990. Hours: Mon-Thurs 11am-9pm, Fri-Sat 11am-10pm, Closed Sundays. This place is great for families with children; the arcade and displays really keep them occupied while waiting for food to be served. Their specials for hearty appetites include Steak or Meatloaf for dinner and the Blue Plate Express. The Express special offers a choice from nine entrees and 20 sides. Comes with a choice of entree, two veggies, and tea for $9.95. Their mac n cheese side is amazingly like grandmas, meatloaf moist and gravy is poured over most entrées. Because the theme is airplanes, their menu is named appropriately: Wing and a Prayer wings, Bombardier Patty Melt, or Tailgunner chicken. Kids menu with 6 basic items under $6. They have a whole page devoted to sweets. Oh, and if you like Greek food - try their Gyro or Baklava. Price range: $5-$15.*____ ☐

LEXINGTON COUNTY MUSEUM

Lexington - 231 Fox Street (I-20 exit 61, Rte. 378 west) 29072. Phone: (803) 359-8369. www.facebook.com/LexingtonCountyMuseum Hours: Tuesday - Saturday 10:00am-4:00pm, Sunday 1:00-4:00pm. Admission: $5.00 adult, $2.00 child.

Some of the historic structures include the original Lexington County post office, the oldest documented house in Lexington, and the house where the traditional song "Give Me That Old Time Religion" was composed. Most notable among the buildings is the ten-room, two-story John Fox House that was built in 1832. Originally a plantation home, the John Fox House is furnished and decorated with period pieces from Lexington County that truly evoke pre-Civil War living conditions. Costumed guides offer tours of the complex as they combine learning with fun. At times, kids are asked to sit on the floor, up close, and listen to stories about old-fashioned artifacts. They might then go outside and play with toys or participate in games.

SWAMP FOX MURALS

Did you know?
The number of Revolutionary War engagements in SC is about equal to the combined total of all engagements fought in the other twelve colonies.

Manning - Office: 19 N Brooks St, Clarendon County Chamber of Commerce (historic US 301 best at exit 119 & 132 east) 29102. www.clarendonmurals.com. Phone: (803) 435-4405. Hours: Daylight hours. Admission: FREE. Note: Victory at Fort Watson Encampment and Reenactment - Late March.

Art museums sound boring? Try this alternative, "drive thru" art promoting history with Historic murals (in Manning, Paxville, Summerton & Turbeville): The Swamp Fox, General Francis Marion and his engagements with the British in 1780-81 in St. Mark's Parish, now Clarendon County. Every mural tells a story of the events of the American Revolution in South Carolina.

Central

See 22 historic murals in Manning (7 murals), Paxville (1 mural), Summerton (8 murals) and Turbeville (6 murals). A favorite - Ox Swamp Mural, is at the corner of Boyce & Boundary, In Manning, Brits gave chase but Marion slips away into Ox Swamp to set an ambush. British gave up the chase and said, "as for the old fox, the devil himself could not catch him." Thus, General Francis Marion became known as the "Swamp Fox". The

Tearcoat mural has a lot of different activities going on - this still picture seems to portray action - US 301 in Turbeville, exit 132). Kids gravitate to the action scenes so be sure to view Swamp Fox and Tearcoat murals first.

BERRY PLANTATION

North Augusta - 345 Briggs Road 29860. www.gurosiksberryplantation.com. Phone: (803) 292-3621. Hours: Monday-Friday 10:00am-6:00pm, Saturday 8:00am-5:00pm. Opening date: early April. Tours: can be scheduled Monday-Friday for $7/person (early April - mid May).

Gurosik's Berry Plantation is a true family farm. April thru July is prime strawberry season and the farm market is bursting with berries in all forms for sale. They also have u-pick options that are fun adventures in the fields and save money. And, if you call ahead and arrange a group tour (or ask to be part of another), educational tours last approximately 1.5 hours and include: u-pick a quart of fresh strawberries while learning about plant growth and production; a delicious strawberry smoothie; kids get a "Berry Time" activity booklet; tour a working bee hive; observe and feed 1000s of catfish; and end it all with your own picnic lunch.

LIVING HISTORY PARK

North Augusta - 299 W Spring Grove Avenue 29861. www.colonialtimes.us/. Hours: Daily daylight hours. Public events are held every last Saturday of the month (except winter months). Admission: FREE.

The Living History Park serves citizens from a two state area (South Carolina and Georgia). This 7.5 acre park with natural springs provides a children's hands-on educational experience into the history of this area. Public events are held every last Saturday (January - October) - the Cabin will be bustling with activities of the 18th century from 10:30am to early afternoon. October has a pumpkin theme, Christmastime is for the Birds. While you are there, don't miss a chance to see South Carolina's state heritage horse -- the Marsh Tacky. These horses' ancestors came to SC shores when Spanish ships landed in the Carolinas as early as 1500, bringing with them colonists and small, fine-boned horses. Find out more about them at: www.marshtacky.org

COLONIAL TIMES

North Augusta - Living History Park. The nation's Colonial past comes to life through demonstrations including cannon firing, tombstone carving and lacemaking. Visitors experience re-enactors representing individuals such as frontiersman Daniel Boone, the event features demonstrations in pottery, weaving and spinning, frontier trading, quilting, blacksmithing, meat curing, gold and silversmithing, candle making, and much more. Musicians play music on colonial period instruments. FREE. (third wkend in Oct & another in April)

WOODS BAY STATE NATURAL AREA

Olanta - 11020 Woods Bay Road (SR 53 east to SR 597 south to SR48 southeast, 3 miles west of Olanta) 29114. Phone: (843) 659-4445. www.southcarolinaparks.com/woodsbay/introduction.aspx Hours: Park is open daily 9:00am-6:00pm. Nature Center is only open sporadically - mostly weekends. Note: Some guest enjoy canoeing & rentals, hiking, fishing, and birding. They have nice shaded picnic spots.

Woods Bay features a geologic formation known as a Carolina bay. A sand rim is most characteristic with these formations and is most visible along the southeastern edge. This elliptical depression in its swampy habitat is a mystery. Try to solve the mystery as you study the historical placards along the trail - with Spanish moss drizzling down from above and flecks of on-target bugs in flight skip across the swamp water below. Just stopping to stretch your legs? The park's 500-foot boardwalk and canoeing trail offers a closer view of this rare resource. You actually walk into the Black Swamp! The Mill Pond Nature Trail is an easy 3/4 mile loop.

PEANUT PARTY - PELION

Pelion - The annual edition of the peanut party celebrates the gift of goober to this farm community not far from Columbia. Governor Mark Sanford, in 2006, officially signed into law, H.4585 making the boiled peanut South Carolina's official state snack food. However, the South Carolina Peanut Party has been going nuts over boiled peanuts for over 30 years! Peanut Butter Sandwich Eating Contest, and, of course, Boiled Peanuts! Be sure to visit the tents for a variety of old-fashioned peanut candies, flavored dry-roasted peanuts and handmade peanut art. Rides, booths, car show and are part of the fun. www.facebook.com/pages/category/Community-Organization/Pelion-Peanut-Party-

441999206173788/ (second weekend in August)

CLARK'S INN & RESTAURANT

Santee - 114 Bradford Blvd. (I-95 exit 98 west on Rte. 6) 29142. Phone: (803) 854-2141. www.clarksinnandrestaurant.com. In the heart of Santee, this historic Inn & Restaurant first opened in 1946 and is renowned for its warm Southern Hospitality. Clark's Restaurant offers delicious Southern meals: Roast Pork, Baked Chicken, Catfish and Fried Green Tomatoes. Try some Million Dollar Bread for an appetizer and save room for dessert - decades old recipe Apple Crisp or Pecan Pie are king here. They have guest rooms, two-room suites with microwaves and refrigerators, as well as luxury suites with full kitchens. Our room was spacious with a cute feature - bookshelves lined with an interesting assortment of novels. Most folks I talked to had signed up for one of their golf or fishing vacation packages. ______________________

LONE STAR BARBECUE

Santee - 2212 State Park Road (exit 98 west on Hwy 6 less than one mile from Santee) 29142. Phone: (803) 854-2000. www.facebook.com/SanteeBBQplusmore/?__tn__=HHH-R Hours: Lunch & Dinner buffets. Only serving Thursday-Sunday. These 100-year-old authentically restored country stores feature original counters and showcases, old drink boxes, candy jars, vintage displays, old photographs and a wide variety of other antiques. Kids won't recognize half the stuff but will have fun trying to figure it out. Look for an old outhouse and a smokehouse. A country-style lunch buffet is served, with evening specials like Thursday quail & fish fry, Friday barbecue ribs, and stewed shrimp & grits on Saturday. Basic buffet includes: Pork barbecue, rice, barbecue hash, fried chicken, cole slaw, macaroni made with plenty of strong cheese and banana pudding. Come hungry because at Lone Star, it's always "all you can eat"! ______________________

SANTEE STATE PARK

Santee - 251 State Park Road (1 mi. W. of the town of Santee on Hwy 6, exit 98 west) 29142. www.southcarolinaparks.com/santee. Phone: (866) 345-PARK. Hours: Daily 6:00am-10:00pm. Admission: $2.00 adults over age 16. Tours: Fisheagle Lake & Swamp Tours depart from the fishing pier within the park for approximately two hours on Wednesdays, Fridays, Saturdays (times may vary). The Fisheagle travels up Lake Marion to one of the cypress swamps that has become a wildlife haven. Tour Prices are: $30.00 adult, $28.00 senior, $20 child (ages 3-11). Note: If you head east off the exit and go 8.2 miles to Eutawville, turn left on Redbank Road to INDIAN BLUFF PARK. The park offers a fishing pier, deep-water boat ramp, picnic tables and grills, children's play area, boardwalk, restrooms and bathhouse for your leisure and stretching your legs.

Rent some bicycles, kayaks or fishing gear to explore this park. Or, take the FISHEAGLE BOAT TOUR (800-9-OSPREY or www.fisheagle.net) into the lakes to witness the natural beauty of waterfowl including eagles and osprey. Come face-to-face with alligators or enjoy the lake wildflower gardens. Accommodations include ten pier-based cabins, 20 lakefront vacation cabins, and 158 lakeside campsites on Lake Marion. The pier cabins are octagon shaped and so close to the lake, you literally walk out your door and fish off the pier. Cabins have two bedrooms (sleep 6) with full kitchen, bath and heat or A/C. Outdoorsy folks of all ages enjoy the fishing pier, biking and hiking trails and picnic areas with playgrounds.

SANTEE INDIAN MOUND & FORT WATSON (SANTEE NATIONAL WILDLIFE REFUGE)

Summerton - 2125 Fort Watson Road, Santee Nat'l Wildlife Refuge (exit 102 Rte. 301/15. Follow signs to Visitors Center Of Refuge 29148. Phone: (803) 478-2217. www.fws.gov/santee/. Hours: Refuge: Daily dawn to dusk. Center: Tuesday - Friday 8:00am-4:00pm. Closed federal holidays. Admission: FREE. Note: Fishing on the Refuge: All areas open to boating are also open to fishing, as well as the Scott's Lake Public Fishing Beach. These areas produce largemouth bass, catfish and bream.

THE SANTEE INDIAN MOUND is over 3,000 years old and served as a prehistoric ceremonial and subsequent burial for the Santee Indians. It is the largest ceremonial center found on the coastal plain. Be the first to climb it to the top. Perhaps the mound's greatest notoriety comes from its use as a British fort during the American Revolution. This outpost was built by the British and was at least 30 feet high. Gen. Francis Marion, the Swamp Fox, and Light Horse Harry Lee laid siege to the post April 15-23, 1781,

by erecting a tower of logs under the cover of night enabling them to fire into the British stockade. This brought about the surrender of the fort cutting off the main British supply line to Camden, forcing Lord Rawdon to withdraw from that position. The Battle of FORT WATSON is one of the murals featured on the Swamp Fox Murals Trail (see separate listing). From an observation point at the top of Indian mound, visitors can get a panoramic view of Santee Cooper and the countryside.

THE VISITOR'S CENTER has window viewing of wildlife (esp. good if weather outside isn't pleasant); an aquarium with fish found in the area's lakes plus some animal dioramas and a "touch table".

THE SANTEE NATIONAL WILDLIFE REFUGE offers notable wildlife tours and exhibits. A walk along the one-mile Wrights Bluff Trail affords families the chance to observe songbirds, wading birds, and several species of waterfowl along swampland and the beautiful lake. Santee just happens to be located in the flyway from Canada to the tropics so birds abound certain times of year.

SWAN LAKE IRIS GARDENS

Sumter - 822 West Liberty Street (exit 135 west to US 378/76 west to SR 763 exit straight into town and just past) 29151. www.sumtersc.gov/community/swanlake Phone: (800) 688-4748. Hours: Gardens daily, 7:30am-dusk; Visitor Center: Monday-Friday 8:30am-5:00pm Admission: FREE. Note: Although the birds are generally friendly, they may exhibit territorial behavior during the mating season and should be approached with reasonable caution.

The black waters of Swan Lake form a setting for Iris Gardens. The lake is dotted with colorful islands, wildlife is abundant and it is the only public park in the US to feature all eight swan species. It's a little enchanting to see many elegant swans (like the Trumpeter Swan or Mute Swan, the swans of fairy tales) to noisy swans like the Whooper Swans. Beside the swans are groupings of Canada geese, mallards, wood ducks, herons and egrets. If you're thinking this is a quiet retreat - think again. Some ducks may be louder than your kid's giggles and squeals as they chase them around in circles. A leisurely 3/4 mile stroll around the lake reveals even more groupings of duck families, and, if you're lucky, some impromptu duck races. More adventure is had along a boardwalk stretching deep into the cypress swamp.

The 150-acre garden also is home to plantings of Japanese iris, which bloom yearly from mid to late May through the beginning of June. Did you know the garden was started by accident? The original owner discarded iris bulbs that had failed and they took root! Every December, the holiday season blazes into life with the Swan Lake Fantasy of Lights.

IRIS FESTIVAL

Sumter - *Swan Lake Iris Gardens. South Carolina's oldest continuous festival and is ranked among the top festivals in the Southeast. It runs for three days and includes concerts, an arts and crafts show, a flower show, a food tasting and contests. Kids Area, where children up to age 12 can play on inflatable and mechanical rides -- for free. (last long weekend in May)*

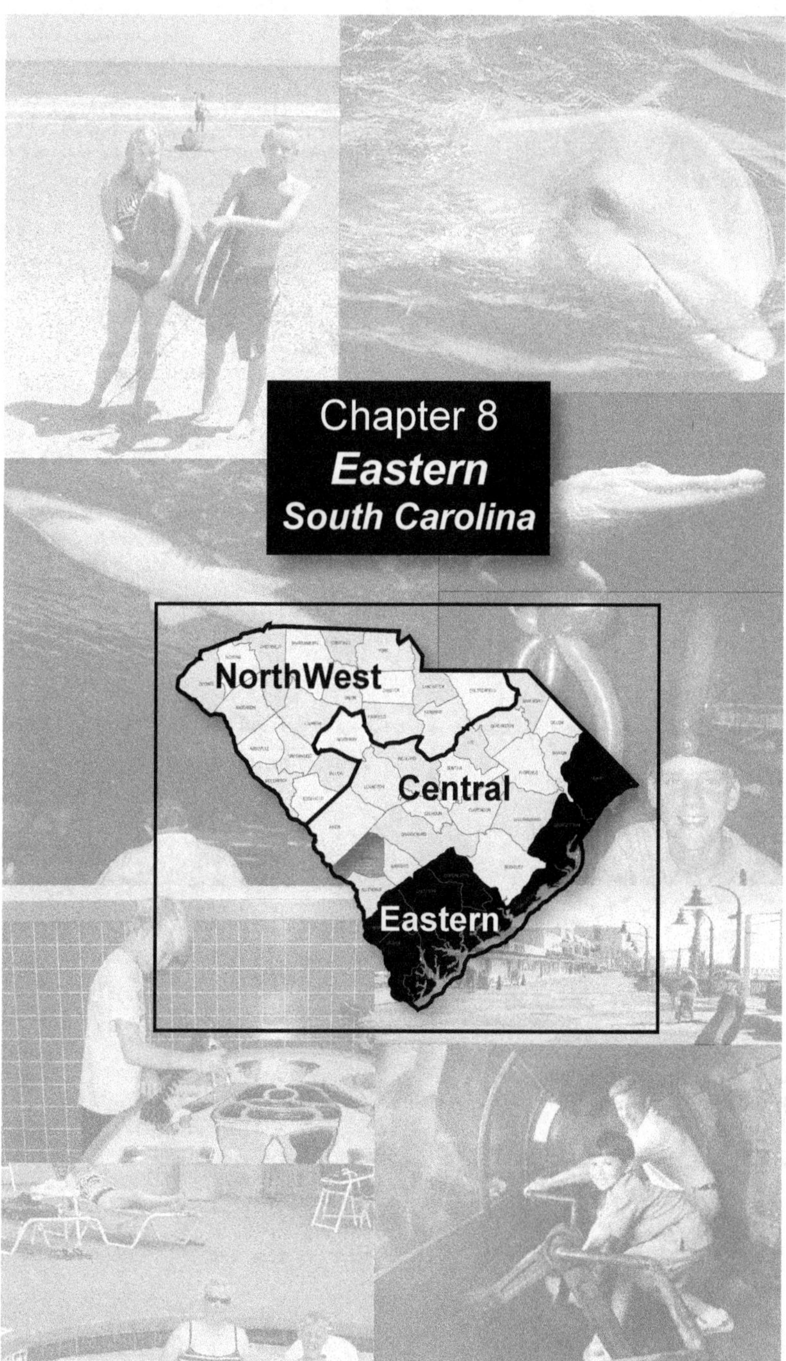
Chapter 8
Eastern
South Carolina
NorthWest
Central
Eastern

Atlantic Beach
- Gullah/Geechee Festival

Awendaw
- Seewee Restaurant

Beaufort
- Beaufort River Tour & Dolphin Watch
- Verdier House

Beaufort (Hunting Island)
- Hunting Island State Park

Charleston
- Charleston Boat Tours
- Charleston Candy Kitchen
- Charleston Carriage Companies

Charleston
- Charleston Pirate Tours
- Fort Sumter
- Old Exchange & Provost Dungeon
- South Carolina Aquarium
- Aiken-Rhett House
- Charleston Museum
- Children's Museum Of The Low Country
- Charles Towne Landing State Historic Site
- Adventure Harbor Tours
- Drayton Hall
- Magnolia Plantation
- Middleton Place
- Holiday Festival Of Lights
- Wild Blue Ropes

Charleston (Mt Pleasant)
- Patriots Point Naval & Maritime Museum
- Boone Hall Plantation
- Boone Hall Pumpkin Patch

Charleston (Wadmalaw Island)
- Charleston Tea Plantation Tours

Charleston, North
- Hunley Submarine
- Charleston County Waterparks

Coward
- Old Plantation Syrup Making

Edisto Island
- Edisto Beach State Park

Georgetown
- Carolina Rover Boat Tours
- Lowcountry Plantation Tours
- Rice Museum

Hampton
- Watermelon Festival

Hardeeville
- Savannah River National Wildlife Refuge

Hilton Head Island
- Coastal Discovery Museum
- Skull Creek Boathouse
- Adventure Cruises
- Harbour Town Lighthouse
- Palmetto Bay Sun Rise Café
- The Sandbox Children's Museum
- Hilton Head Island

Mcclellanville
- Hampton Plantation State Historic Site

Moncks Corner
- Cypress Gardens
- Old Santee Canal Park

Moncks Corner / Charleston
- Gilligan's Steamer And Raw Bar

Myrtle Beach
- Amusements
- Camping - Myrtle Beach
- Riverside Café
- Kingston Plantation Resort
- Myrtle Beach State Park Nature Center
- Children's Museum Of South Carolina

Myrtle Beach (cont.)

- Family Kingdom Amusement And Water Park
- Jimmy Buffett's Margaritaville Restaurant - Myrtle Beach
- Myrtle Beach
- NASCAR Speedpark
- Ripley's Aquarium
- Theatre Shows
- Wheels Of Yesteryear
- Waccatee Zoo
- Sun Fun Festival
- Beach, Boogie & BBQ Festival
- Christmas At Myrtle Beach

Myrtle Beach (Murrells Inlet)

- Huntington Beach State Park
- 4th Of July Boat Parade (Murrells Inlet)

Myrtle Beach (Pawleys Island)

- Brookgreen Gardens

Myrtle Beach, North

- Alligator Adventure

Ravenel

- Caw Caw Interpretive Center

St. George

- World Grits Festival

Summerville

- Colonial Dorchester State Historic Site

Walterboro

- Duke's Barbecue

Walterboro (Cottageville)

- Bee City Honeybee Farm, Petting Zoo & Café

Yemassee

- Low Country Visitors Center & Museum

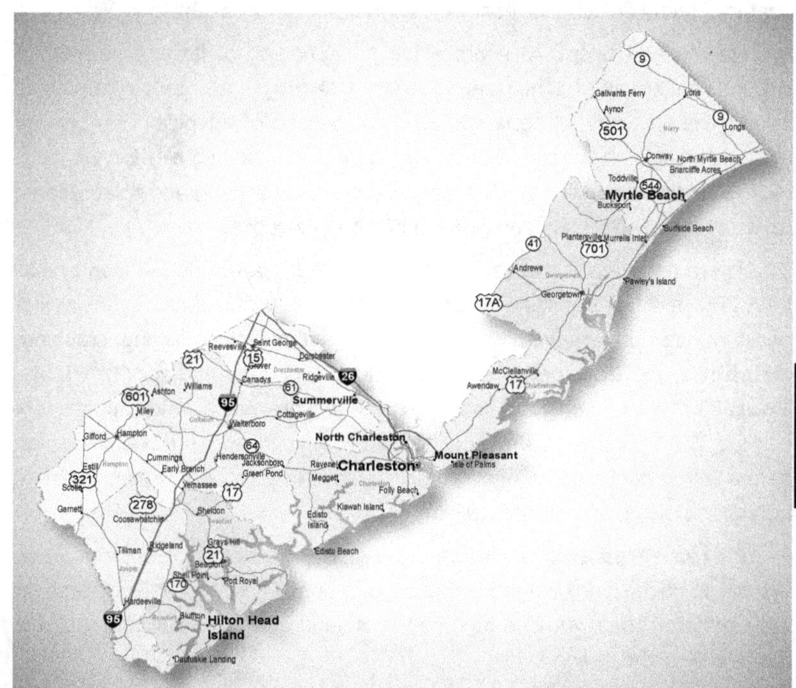

A Quick Tour of our Hand-Picked Favorites Around...

NorthWest

Central

Eastern

Eastern South Carolina

South Carolina beacons visitors and residents with its warm, gentle weather and outdoor pleasures to its comfort foods and good-natured guides at fun museums and tours. This Southern belle invites guests to settle in and stay awhile.

One of the 13 original colonies, South Carolina became the eighth state to ratify The Constitution in 1788, the first to secede from the union in December 1860 and the site of the first shots fired in the Civil War, at **Fort Sumter** in **Charleston** Harbor in April 1861. From the **War for Independence** and the Civil War to the Civil Rights movement, South Carolina has been at the center of both conflict and resolution throughout America's history.

Having had over 340 years since the founding of its first permanent English settlement – **Charles Towne Landing**, kids today can climb aboard the ship Adventure, a life-size reproduction of a typical 17th-century trading ship. South Carolina's other historical sites including **military sites**, **rice plantations**, along with a range of historical festivals and celebrations, reveal fascinating stories you won't find in history books.

There are warm breezes that blow from the Atlantic Ocean along more than 200 miles of coastline in South Carolina. Up and down the Carolina coast, guests can arrange day or weekend trips that include fishing, crabbing, **dolphin watching**, or just cruising at sunset. Our favorite activity: **Pirate Tours**! Inshore and offshore fishing expeditions are available in almost every city along the coast, as are boat rentals. Some locations have preserved nature with great care and offer fantastic places to go biking, fishing, boating, horseback riding, and nature walking.

Hilton Head Island, South Carolina is well known for its palm trees, live oaks and tall pines elegantly draped with Spanish moss. While walking on the sandy beaches, you can feel the warm sand between your toes and see the beauty of the ocean.

It's hard to talk about any South Carolina family vacation destination without talking about **Myrtle Beach**. It might seem odd to head to a water park when the ocean -- the world's largest "water park" -- is just short trip away, but your kids will probably think differently after their first exhilarating plunge down a slide in one of the Grand Strand's three **water parks**.

This is the home of America's #1 **family beaches**...but great beaches are just the beginning! From **musical shows** and **crazy museums** to fishing piers, mini-golf and countless other family-friendly attractions, Myrtle Beach is made for family fun. **Entertainment on the boardwalks and piers** is the highlight of a warm summer evening.

Whether you're looking for a fun way to spend a rainy afternoon, or just want to have a play date with your children, South Carolina's **children's museums** will help spark a love of learning for your child... and create memories along the way. Love pretty fish? The state's **aquariums** cater to the kids allowing them to press close to the glass floor-to-ceiling tanks and touch tanks full of interesting creatures.

South Carolina cuisine has been inspired by their unique cultural heritage, and thus includes European, African, Caribbean and American frontier influences. From South Carolina BBQ and Charleston's She-Crab soup to **Gullah** okra gumbo, shrimp & cheesy grits to fresh caught mountain trout, food is serious business. They even divide the state by **barbecue** regions. Mustard-based in the Midlands, vinegar-based on the coast and in the Pee Dee, ketchup- and tomato-based in the Upstate. And visitors quickly learn: Many of the best places are mom-and-pops and Mom and Pop are typically open only Wednesday or Thursday through Saturday. Sometimes Sunday. That means South Carolina is perfect for everyone from a family on a budget to the serious foodie-but be sure they're open!

For those who prefer food and wildlife resources up close and personal, stroll through one of South Carolina's State Parks or numerous **Farm Festivals**. With a great climate and long growing season, South Carolina is acclaimed for its mouth-watering **peaches** and huge **watermelons** in summer, juicy mountain-grown apples in fall and vine-fresh berries in spring.

Dreaming of screaming? Then climb aboard a rollercoaster at one of South Carolina's family **amusement parks**. From waterparks and kiddie rides to the thrill of Myrtle Beach's NASCAR Speedpark, they've got all the excitement you and the kids can handle!

Sites and attractions are listed in order by City, Zip Code, and Name. Symbols indicated represent: Restaurants

GULLAH TOURS

Originally descended from African slaves who worked the Southern plantations, the Gullah people of the Lowcountry and nearby coastal areas of South Carolina and Georgia are the most culturally distinctive African-American population in the United States. Due to isolation from the mainland, the people of the Sea Islands developed a distinct language and culture of their own. The Gullah people developed a unique culture based on folktales, superstitions and a distinct cuisine (gumbo, lowcountry boil and hoppin n' jon).

- **GULLAH-N-GEECHIE MAHN TOURS** - St. Helena Island (Beaufort). (843) 838-7516 or www.gullahngeechietours.net. On tour you will experience: the Penn Center & Museum - first school in South to educate "newly freed" slaves; Brick Baptist Church - built by slave labor in 1855; The Oaks Plantation - used for growing of the Sea Island cotton and other crops during the Slave Trade; and a Praise House - built on the grounds of the plantation, these were small slave dwellings converted into places of worship for the slaves. "Cum jine we ont we tour!" (Translation: "Come and join us on our tour!"). Three times daily Monday-Saturday. $39 per person air-conditioned mini-bus tour.
- **GULLAH HERITAGE TRAIL TOURS** - Hilton Head Island. (843) 681-7066 or www.gullaheritage.com. Take a pleasant narrated travel through several neighborhoods, established during the Civil War (1862) long "before the bridge" (1956) to the mainland. Travel through hidden paths of the subtropic traditional landscape of Hilton Head Island. Hear fourth generation Gullah Family members relate first hand stories of traditional food ways, family life and the Gullah language. At halfway point you will have a 15-20 minute rest stop at one of the Public Beach accesses allowing for a casual stroll over a boardwalk to view the Atlantic Ocean and refresh. Departs from the Discovery Museum @70 Honey Horn Drive (north end of island) twice daily on Wednesday thru Saturday and Noon on Sunday. Fares: $15-$32.

- **GULLAH TOURS** - Charleston. www.gullahtours.com or (843) 763-7551. White, rich, aristocratic history is everywhere in Charleston. Gullah tours is the black history of Charleston. Black people built Charleston and they were mostly slaves and some "Freemen" artisans... Funny, interesting tour about "the other side" of Charleston. 2 hour tour on air-conditioned bus. Tours depart twice daily (Monday-Saturday) from the African American Art Gallery at 43 John Street. $20 per seat.

WATERSPORTS

Sailboat, Jet Ski, canoe and kayak rentals are offered up and down the Atlantic coast. Other above-water activities along the beach include parasailing, surfing, boogie-boarding, windsurfing and kite surfing.

Hilton Head -

- **H2O SPORTS** - 149 Lighthouse Road (Harbour Town Marina) Sea Pines Plantation. 29928. www.h2osports.com. (843) 671-4FUN. Everything you need to go boating, water skiing and parasailing. They offer two-hour charters, and their captains are Coast Guard licensed and are very conscious about safety.
- **PALMETTO DUNES OUTFITTERS** - www.palmettodunes.com. Paddle the saltwater lagoon system around Palmetto Dunes. No experience is necessary, and it's easy and safe enough for young kids to participate.

Myrtle Beach -

- **CAPTAIN SMILEY CHARTERS** - www.captainsmileyfishingcharters.com. (843) 361-7445
- **DOWNWIND SAILS** - www.downwindsailsmyrtlebeach.com. (843) 448-7245
- **EXPRESS WATERSPORTS** - www.expresswatersports.com. (866) 566-9338
- **FISHHOOK CHARTERS** - www.fishhookcharters.com. (843) 283-7692
- **LITTLE RIVER FISHING FLEET** - www.littleriverfleet.com. (843) 249-1100
- **LONGWAY FISHING CHARTERS** - www.longwaycharters.com. (843) 249-7813
- **MYRTLE BEACH WATERSPORTS** - http://myrtlebeachwatersports.com (843) 651-9915
- **OCEAN WATERSPORTS** - www.parasailmyrtlebeach.com. (843) 445-7777
- **SHALLOW MINDED INSHORE CHARTERS** - www.fishmyrtlebeach.com (843)-458-3055

GULLAH / GEECHEE FESTIVAL

Atlantic Beach - *This August festival celebrates the history and culture of the Gullah/ Geechee heritage- descendants of slaves from the west coast of Africa. Soul food and tasty Southern dishes are served to visitors in Atlantic Beach, while various activities and lectures give a glimpse into the rich culture of the Gullah /Geechee people. For more information call (843) 663-1433.*

SEEWEE RESTAURANT

Awendaw - *4804 US Hwy 17N 29429. Phone: (843)-928-3609. www.facebook.com/SeeWeeRestaurant/. This place looks like an old store because it was one. The building dates back to the 1920s when it was a general store. Reopened in 1993 as SeeWee Restaurant, the place serves Lowcountry cruise in, fresh local seafood and desserts. Entrees are served with three sides which can include collard greens, red rice, fried mushrooms, butter beans, sweet potato casserole, fried okra, mac-n-cheese, or steamed squash. For starters, there are fried green tomatoes, fried clam strips, fried calamari rings and fried pickles. Their grits and shrimp cakes and she-crab soup get lots of raves from parents. Kids like the old-fashioned motif and the bottles of Coke or Nehi Grape soda you can purchase at the counter. Lunch, Dinner, Brunch. Live entertainment some nights.*

BEAUFORT RIVER TOUR & DOLPHIN WATCH

Beaufort - 1006 Bay Street, downtown marina of Beaufort 29902. Phone: (843) 812-2804. www.beaufortrivertours.com. Tours: 1.2 hour tour Daily except major holidays. See website for current schedule. Tours run $20.00 adult, $12.00 child (under 12).

Eastern

Departing daily from the Downtown Marina of Beaufort, this 1.25 hour tour aboard the Prince of Tides offers you a scenic tour of Beaufort and the Beaufort River that you won't see anywhere else. Fully narrated, passengers are provided information about the ecology, the wildlife and the homes of the planters as you make your way up river past the historic Old Point neighborhood to Pleasant Point Plantation. Playful dolphins vie for your attention, though, as the stately osprey soars overhead. During sunset tours, you can easily see why explorers have found these sea islands irresistible.

VERDIER HOUSE

Beaufort - 801 Bay Street 29902. www.historicbeaufort.org. Phone: (843) 379-6335. Tours: The Verdier House is open for tours Monday-Saturday from 10:00am-4:00pm (last tour at 3:30). There is a guided tour, with an admission fee of $5.00 which supports the ongoing interpretation of the house.

The Verdier House is Beaufort's only historic house regularly open to the public as a museum. Built 1800-1805 by John Mark Verdier, a prosperous merchant and planter, it is one of the finest examples of a Federal-style home. During its history, the Verdier House served as the post headquarters for Union soldiers during the Civil War and was the site of the first telephone exchange in Beaufort.

HUNTING ISLAND STATE PARK

Beaufort (Hunting Island) - 2555 Sea Island PKWY (I-95 to Hwy 21 E toward Beaufort. Drive 42 miles straight to park) 29920. Phone: (843) 838-2011. www.southcarolinaparks.com/hunting-island. Hours: Daily 6:00am-6:00pm (extended to 9:00pm during Daylight Savings Time) Admission: $8.00 adult, $5.00 senior, $4.00 child (6-15). Tours: There is a $2.00/person charge to climb the lighthouse and you must be at least 44" tall to do so. Lighthouse open daily from 10:00am, with the last climb at 4:45pm. (March-November)

Hunting Island is South Carolina's most popular state park, attracting more than a million visitors a year. Animals are attracted to the semitropical barrier island too. Wildlife such as loggerhead sea turtles, alligators, dolphins and pelicans flock here. The lagoon is home to such unexpected species as seahorses and barracuda. Everyone enjoys the five miles of beach, 1000s of acres of marsh, tidal creeks and maritime forest, a saltwater lagoon and ocean inlet.

- HUNTING ISLAND STATE PARK LIGHTHOUSE: Adding to the natural history of the big park is a piece of man-made history: South Carolina's only publicly accessible historic lighthouse. Dating from the 1870s, the Hunting Island Lighthouse shoots 170 feet into the air, giving those who scale its heights a breathtaking view of the sweeping Lowcountry marshland and the Atlantic Ocean. Amenities: fishing pier, campsites and cabins.

CHARLESTON BOAT TOURS

- CHARLESTON WATER TAXI - www.charlestonwatertaxi.com. Leaves from 10 Wharfside St. $12 all day pass.
- SCHOONER PRIDE - The Pride is an authentic 84-foot Tall Ship that sails in Charleston's historic harbor. They offer two hour harbor cruises, each one is unique, depending on the wind. On this scenic cruise you will see the Charleston Harbor with the aircraft Carrier Yorktown; the four forts: Castle Pinckney, Ft. Sumter, Ft. Johnson and Ft. Moultrie plus the beautiful Battery. Departs from Aquarium Wharf. www.schoonerpride.com.
- CHARLESTON HARBOR TOURS - Harbor of History tour aboard the 250-passenger vessel the Carolina Belle. See the "holy city" from a new perspective and take in over 300 years of history on a 90-minute, non stop tour. See the forts that helped shape history: Fort Moultrie, Fort Johnson and Fort Sumter. Waterfront mansions, Sullivan's Island and cruising past the USS Yorktown, too. Goes under the new Ravenel Bridge. Refreshments on board. www.charlestonharbortours.com. Tours 3 times daily from mid-February thru November.

CHARLESTON AROUND TOWN

- RAVENEL JR. BRIDGE - This is the new bridge from historic Charleston to Mt. Pleasant. You can walk, bike or drive over it with no tolls. The views from the second observation tower beat any view from downtown---just jaw-dropping views. Bring your camera.
- CHARLESTON WATERFRONT PARK - Green public space overlooking the coast. Great for picnics and walks. Folks really like the swings that go out above the water, too. Kids often play in the fountains - one is shaped like a giant pineapple. The park is near restaurants on East Bay.

SAVANNAH'S CANDY KITCHEN

Charleston - 32 N Market Street 29401. www.savannahcandy.com.

Kids love to stop in and watch the old-fashioned taffy being made in one corner. Across the room, you can watch as candy makers craft pecan pralines, peanut brittle and chocolate gophers by hand. It's hard to find a kid who can resist the barrels and barrels full of individual candy. And the gourmet pretzels dipped in chocolate and topped with kid-friendly treats like crushed Oreos - kids can't resist using some personal funds to make themselves a goodie bag. If you like taffy - it's everywhere.

CHARLESTON CARRIAGE COMPANIES

Charleston - (lined up just off Market Street) 29401. $25 adult, $15 child (3-11). Kids 2 and younger are free on their parent's laps.

- **PALMETTO CARRIAGE WORKS**: Relax on a coach pulled by two mules. While you wait in the barn, you can see where and how the mules are cared for. (You also can drop a quarter in a machine to get a handful of food for the two goats who live there) It's a great way to get an overview of the peninsula, and pick up a few tidbits of history. It's an hour-long trip on one of three routes through the historic district. The guides are typically lifelong Charlestonians. They keep the kids engaged with stories about ghosts, duels and pirates and the adults with info about the beautiful old homes you pass by. In between they fill the tour with compelling storytelling and facts about architecture and history. www.palmettocarriage.com. (departs from the Red Barn off Market St).
- **OLDE TOWNE CARRIAGE CO**.: 20 Anson St., (843) 722-1315, see http://mycharlestoncarriage.com.
- **CLASSIC CARRIAGE**: 10 Guignard St., www.classiccarriage.com. (843) 853-3747

CHARLESTON PIRATE TOURS

Charleston - 79 Cumberland Street (Powder Magazine) 29401. www.charlestonpiratetour.com. Phone: (800) 442-7299. Admission: $20.00 adult, $18.00 senior & military, $13.00 kids (4-12). Charleston Pirate Tour: Monday-Saturday 10am, Sunday at 2pm. Children's Scavenger Hunt: Daily at 10:30am (White Point Gardens - $12 adult, $16 child includes swords, treasure, balloons, & pirate flags) Because it's a walking tour, dress for the weather and bring a water bottle. Note: the Powder Magazine is part of this tour.

South Carolina is famous for its pirates - from Blackbeard to Bonnet. Charleston Pirate Tours are walking adventures around town, showing you the sites where pirates roamed back in the Golden Age of Piracy from the 1600s until 1730. Storytellers (in full pirate garb) and Capt. Bob (the blue and gold macaw) walk the streets of Charleston, telling of the days of Blackbeard, Bonnet, Richard Worley and Anne Bonny. They will fill you in on Blackbeard's blockade of Charleston harbor and tell you the real story about why pirates wore eye patches. Find out why male pirates might wear a dress or females dress like men - a disguise! He will show you the hangouts and burial spots of the pirates, who made Charleston one of their ports of call. This may be the best way to tour historic Charleston with kids.

FORT SUMTER

Charleston - Liberty Square (340 Concord Street) 29401. Phone: (843) 883-3123. www.nps.gov/fosu/ ferry: www.fortsumtertours.com Hours: Daily 10:00am-4:00pm. Longer Spring and Summer hours. Shorter winter hours. The Visitors Center is open daily 8:30am-5:00pm except New Years, Thanksgiving and Christmas. Admission: FREE admission to Fort & Visitor Center. 30-minute ferry ride tickets run: $19.50 adult, $17.00 senior, $12.00 child (6-11). Tours: Boats are clean, safe and equipped with snack bars and restrooms. Narrated. Depart two to three times daily - at least once in the morning and once in the afternoon. With each arriving ferry, families should listen to a 10-minute ranger history talk before beginning their self-guided tour. Note: A snack bar is available on board the ferry boat, and a water fountain is located inside the fort. Picnicking is not permitted inside Fort Sumter. Educators: Lesson Plans & Teachers Guides are plentiful: http://www.nps.gov/fosu/forteachers/lessonplansandteacherguides.htm.

Did you know the United State's bloodiest war started with a battle in which hardly anyone died? The Civil War, a conflict that would end with about 620,000 fatalities, began at Fort Sumter on April 12, 1861.

At that time, without a single Southern state electoral vote, Lincoln became president. To Southerners, it was a sure sign their slave-holding days were short. The Confederate States of America had formed but not acted. However, all but one federal southern fort was run by Southern "rebels." The one that remained was Fort Sumter. Confederates wanted to control it and shots fired when federal ships tried to resupply it. Conflict. The battle lasted 34 hours. On April 14, Anderson and his men marched out of Fort Sumter, boarded a Union ship and headed to New York. While stationed at the fort, these men were never defeated and never surrendered - in doing so keeping the Southern resolve strengthened. The fort was also used in the Spanish-American War and WWI. Because the fort is situated in the middle of Charleston Harbor, it is only accessible by boat. The Fort Sumter Visitor Education Center in downtown Charleston is the main ferry-departure site. Once at the fort, visitors have one hour to check out the ruins. While the Visitor Center introduces the story leading up to the war, the fort is mostly outdoors and exhibits bring the history of the fort up to modern times. Most young kids love "playing" around the fort property, so you probably will have complaints from them when they're told they have to board the boat back to the inland.

- **FORT MOULTRIE VISITOR CENTER** (1214 Middle Street, Sullivan's Island) museum exhibits trace the story of American seacoast defenses from 1776-1947. A 20-minute orientation film is offered on the hour and half-hour from 9:00am with the last film starting at 4:30pm. A bookstore offers interpretive items relating to Fort Moultrie's history. The rest of the site is primarily outdoors. This historic site is on land and accessible by vehicle. Guided (by reservation) and self-guided tours.

OLD EXCHANGE & PROVOST DUNGEON

Charleston - 122 East Bay Street (I-26 exit 221B. The Old Exchange building is straight ahead where Broad Street ends at East Bay) 29401. Phone: (843) 727-2165. www.oldexchange.com. Hours: Daily 9:00am-5:00pm. Admission: $10.00 adult, $5.00 students (6-12). Many membership discounts available. Note: Waterfront Park, behind the Old Exchange Building, is an ideal location for picnic lunches during nice weather.

One of the three most historically significant colonial buildings in the United States, the Exchange and its Provost Dungeon played host to a number of 18th-century pirates awaiting execution. And, Colonial leaders declared independence from Great Britain from the steps of the Exchange in 1776. Tours and programs are designed to highlight and reinforce various aspects of 17th and 18th century Colonial history, Revolutionary War history, the history of the United States Constitution, and for fun, a bit of Charles Town pirate history. Experienced docents will lead you through its eerie confines and animatronic storytellers--the Deputy Collector, Mister Mate and Tom the Stockman--will entertain you and your family with wonderful tales of pirates and patriots.

SOUTH CAROLINA AQUARIUM

Did you know that alligators can go through 2000 teeth in a lifetime?

Charleston - 100 Aquarium Wharf 29401. www.scaquarium.org. Phone: (843) 720-1990. Hours: Daily 9:00am-4:00pm (later spring and summer). Admission: $29.95 adult, $22.95 child (3-12). Closed Thanksgiving Day, December 25, and 1/2 day December 24 (open 9:00am-Noon). FREEBIES: Keep your students actively involved throughout their Aquarium tour with Scavenger Hunts: http://scaquarium.org/field-trips/ Educators: Fact Sheets are found on this link page also. For excellent, grade-based curriculum: http://curriculum.scaquarium.org/

Get up close to over 6,000 animals including sharks, penguins and river otters at Charleston's #1 attraction. Explore new worlds at Shark Shallows or go behind the scenes at the Sea Turtle Hospital and discover how injured sea turtles are cared for every day. Watch as aquatic animals dive underwater, learn about colonies, and discover what makes otters so playful.

Other exhibits explore the Mountains and Piedmont of South Carolina. Camp Carolina is an outdoor adventure of the mountain regions. Check in at the general store, hike the hills, stop by the stream brimming with fish, then settle in at the camp site. Catch live dive shows in the Great Ocean Tank. Parents can take in great views of the Charleston Harbor while kids run around in play areas or the touch tank featuring sting rays. Alligators do entice kids - maybe it's all their teeth?

AIKEN-RHETT HOUSE

Charleston - 48 Elizabeth Street (2 blocks from the Charleston Visitor Ctr) 29403. Phone: (843) 723-1159. www.historiccharleston.org/house-museums/aiken-rhett-house/ Hours: Daily 10:00am-5:00pm. Admission: $12.00 adult, $5.00 child (6-16). Educators: Pre-and-post visit lessons online here: www.historiccharleston.org/ Education/. Part of that lesson is a Scavenger Hunt which would be helpful to print off and complete while any family is touring.

The Aiken-Rhett House stands alone as the most intact townhouse complex showcasing urban life in antebellum Charleston. Built in 1818 and greatly expanded in the 1830s and 1850s, the house has survived virtually unaltered since 1858. The house tour is a unique audio/mp3 tour so families can go at their own pace. How would people who lived in this house entertain themselves? The Aiken-Rhett House is unique in that the slave quarters and work buildings still stand on the property. This provides the opportunity for visitors to look back in time at the lives of enslaved African Americans living in Charleston during the nineteenth century. How did slaves entertain themselves? What were some of the themes of their songs? Compare and contrast the lives of enslaved African Americans and the Aiken family. Family tours Thursdays.

CHARLESTON MUSEUM

Charleston - 360 Meeting Street (across the street from the Charleston Visitor Center) 29403. Phone: (843) 722-2996. www.charlestonmuseum.org. Hours: Monday-Saturday 9:00am-5:00pm, Sunday 1:00-5:00pm. Admission: $12.00 adult, $5.00 child (3-12). FREEBIES: Ask for their Scavenger Hunt or Matching worksheet to complete as you tour.

The Charleston Museum, America's first museum, showcases a variety of cultural and natural history artifacts that tell the story of the South Carolina Lowcountry. It's a small museum that gives a nice overview of the history of the town. Visitors go back in time viewing ancient fossils and an enormous whale skeleton (from a whale that swam into the harbor in 1880) to elegant costumes and Charleston silver. There's a replica of the Hunley submarine.

Families enjoy Kidstory, a hands-on exhibit for children. Lowcountry Stories features an interactive storytelling station with video clips of local storytellers telling tales of Charleston, Gullah people, Native Americans, and more. Join Rosa as she tells visitors about live oak trees, Spanish moss, and the marsh. At the lighthouse, help James turn on the light to guide ships into Charleston's harbor. Rummage through crates and barrels to see what was coming and going through the port of Charleston. Go through toy chests and play with toys like a colonial girl had.

CHILDREN'S MUSEUM OF THE LOW COUNTRY

Charleston - 25 Ann Street 29403. http://explorecml.org/. Phone: (843) 853-8962. Hours: Tuesday-Saturday 9:00am-5:00pm, Sunday Noon-5:00pm. Admission: $12.00 per person (ages 1+). SC residents save $2.00.

Feel like waterman at Charleston's Children's Museum of the Lowcountry, casting nets and counting the catch, steering the boat through stormy waters, cooking dinner and hearing the sounds of ocean life on a 30-foot Shrimping Trawler... the only thing missing is the smell of that salty sea air.

Across the way, switch eras completely and check out life as a medieval duke or duchess at Castle Stories, where you can dress up in medieval costumes, put on a puppet show or explore the shadow wall. Toddlers can twist and turn and slide through the tunnels in the Totally Toddler area. Kids create, make and take home projects of their imagination in Creativity Castle, aka The Art Room, where three different themed activities are featured each week. The center is designed just for children ages 3 months to 12 years and their families.

CHARLES TOWNE LANDING STATE HISTORIC SITE

Charleston - 1500 Old Towne Rd I-26 E: Take Cosgrove Road exit 216A onto Hwy. 7 (Sam Rittenberg Blvd.) bear left onto Hwy. 171 (Old Town Rd.) 29407. Phone: (843) 852-4200. https://southcarolinaparks.com/charles-towne-landing Hours: Daily 9:00am-5:00pm. Admission: $12.00 adult, $7.50 senior, $7.00 youth (6-15). Note: There are no overnight facilities at this Park. 7 miles of Interpretive Trails and Picnicking areas are available.

Here a group of English settlers landed in 1670 and established what would become the birthplace of the Carolinas colony, the plantation system of the American South and one of the continent's first major port cities.

Begin with the 12-room, interactive museum in the Visitors Center that includes a "digital dig". Then walk the self-guided history trail, using the MP3 players that add an audio tour to the experience. Learn about the threats that faced the first Charles Towne residents. Next, visit a natural habitat zoo that is home to animal species that were indigenous to Carolina at the time of the settlement such as bison, black bear, puma, elk, otter and more. Talk to archaeologists at work. Discover some of the many aspects of maritime trade and travel during the 17th century. See some of the tools used by sailors and some of the products they shipped. Visit the Adventure, Charleston's only 17th century replica sailing ship, and the authentic experimental crop garden.

ADVENTURE HARBOR TOURS

Charleston - 56 Ashley Point Dr (Charleston Maritime Center) 29464. Phone: (843) 442-9455. www.adventureharbortours.com. Admission: $55.00 adult, $30.00 child (3-12). Tours to Morris Island go daily, starting at 9:00am, and then every hour after that. Bring coolers, snacks, towels. Note: if the weather is hot, bring water bottles. Bring several bags to "share the load" of shells and such you collect.

These tours are usually voted the #1 thing to do with kids in Charleston. Combine a boat, some dolphins and a little history and you've got a good combination. The 2.5 hour boat excursions head to Morris Island. Morris Island is an unspoiled, undeveloped piece of land with the finest shell and shark's teeth hunting beach in Charleston. The guide shares details of what makes Morris Island so special, while helping you find treasure on the beach...all the while looking out at Fort Sumter and wading in the tidal pools. Can you imagine all of the pirates and soldiers that passed through this harbor island on their way to raid Charleston? Observe dolphins on the way there and back. And guess what - you can even bring your dog!

WILD BLUE ROPES ADVENTURE PARK

Charleston - 1595 Highland Ave (just off Folly Road - less than 10 minutes from Downtown Charleston and Folly Beach) 29412. wildblueropes.com Phone: (843) 225-1555. Admission: $19.00 (age 5+). Explorers Gateway. Tours: last approximately 60 minutes. Hours: Wed/Thurs 2-6pm. Sat/Sun 10am-6pm.

The WBR Explorers Gateway is an entry level course designed with our younger patrons in mind. Easy to navigate, balance & climb, participants make their way through 7 obstacles on a continuous loop. The Explorers Gateway is part of the lower level of the WBR Challenge Course, and stands 15ft. tall.

DRAYTON HALL

Charleston - 3380 Ashley River Road 29414. www.draytonhall.org. Phone: (843) 769-2600. Hours: Daily 9am-5pm. Admission: $32.00 adult, $15.00 youth (8-14), Tours: last approximately 30-60 minutes and begin on the hour. Gates open at 9:30am-4:00pm. Earlier/Later in the summer. Note: River Walk - there are woods and a tidal marsh to walk outside.

If these walls could talk...Families walk on the very ground where real people walked and tour rooms these people knew. Tour guides point out changes that occurred during the almost three centuries the house has stood. The main cash crops were rice and indigo in the 18th century and rice and cotton in the 19th century. What plantation job would you want? Brick-layer, carver, plasterer, potter, farmer, cooper, cook, or driver? Was there time to play games?

MAGNOLIA PLANTATION

Charleston - 3550 Ashley River Rd 29414. www.magnoliaplantation.com. Phone: (800) 367-3517. Hours: Daily 8:00am-5:30pm. Winter hours vary slightly. Admission: The Gardens and Grounds ticket is the basic admission and must be purchased to buy tickets for the House, Nature Train, Nature Boat, and/or the Slavery to Freedom Tours. The basic admission is $10-$20.00 per person (including kids ages 6+). This allows you access to the gardens and grounds (nice if you like gardens - most kids don't). Each tour is an additional $8.00 per person. Note: Peacock Café.

Magnolia Plantation and Gardens, founded in 1676 by the Drayton family, is the oldest public tourist site in the Lowcountry, and the oldest public garden in America. The plantation offers a historic house tour, nature tram, nature boat, a maze, petting zoo, and an award winning program focusing on plantation slavery. While the nature tram is interesting to kids (you'll see alligators), most families spend the money to come here for the "From Slavery to Freedom" tour. As the guide explains the origins of the original slave population here, he further shows how their descendants, some of whom still work on the grounds and lived in the cabins, stuck around. You'll see how vital slaves were to the success of a plantation. Young ones may just want to wander the maze and petting zoo (included with basic admission).

MIDDLETON PLACE

Charleston - 4300 Ashley River Road 29414. www.middletonplace.org. Phone: (843) 556-6020. Hours: Daily 9:00am-5:00pm except Christmas Day. Admission: $28.00 adult, $15.00 student, $10.00 child (6-13) covers grounds, gardens, stables and slave/craft areas.

Small additional fee charged for 30 minute guided tours of the House Museum and 45 minute Carriage tours. Save $ online. Note: weather in late summer is hot and humid - best to visit spring and fall...esp. during Special Events like Plantation Days. Strollers are permitted on garden paths but not in the House Museum. As a courtesy, adults with active or restless young children are asked to take turns touring the House. A café and restaurant are on the property.

Middleton Place is an 18th century rice plantation and National Historic Landmark comprising 65 acres of America's oldest landscaped Gardens, the Middleton Place House Museum and the Plantation Stableyards. While kids don't favor gardens, this one has 200 year old oak trees, swans, interesting wildlife, and Spanish moss hanging everywhere to make it look ancient. There are carriage tours that lead to the main house tour. Here, a guide takes you through the reconfigured home with great detail. The original home was burned down during the Civil War. May be boring for kids except for the interactive area where you can see and speak with people taking care of farm animals or making crafts. We noticed during the house tour they talk about plantation family life but not much about slavery life. Peak season, craft artisans are stationed by their trades. The Blacksmith, Potter, Cooper and Carpenter demonstrate the working life of many slave men and women on the plantation.

GRAND ILLUMINATION: CHRISTMAS 1782

Charleston - Middleton Place. Step back in time to Christmas 1782. Stroll thru gardens illuminated by torchlight, candlelight and starlight. Hear costumed guides tell stories of this joyous holiday season when the British evacuated Charleston and the Middleton family was reunited near the end of the Revolutionary War. House seasonally decorated and glowing in candlelight, enjoy a warm fire, live music and a buffet dinner in the Pavilion. Special admission. (mid-December weekend)

HOLIDAY FESTIVAL OF LIGHTS

Charleston - James Island County Park, 871 Riverland Drive. www.ccprc.com/1546/Holiday-Festival-of-Lights More than two million enchanting lights adorn James Island County Park. Come experience the three-mile driving tour and see a wide array of dazzling designs for the holidays. Create your own light display at the Lakeside Lights activity center or take a leisurely stroll through the Enchanted Forest. Phone: 843-795-4386. Admission per vehicle. (Evenings mid-November thru New Years)

PATRIOTS POINT NAVAL & MARITIME MUSEUM

Charleston (Mt Pleasant) - 40 Patriots Point Road (just over the Arthur Ravenel Bridge) 29464. Phone: (866) 831-1720. www.patriotspoint.org. Hours: Daily 9:00am-6:30pm. Admission: $24.00 adult, $19.00 senior/active duty military, (in uniform-FREE), $16.00 child (6-11). Parking $5.00 a day. Tours: Guided Tours last approximately 1 ½ hours and are highly recommended for visitors on a tight schedule. Note: Fighting Lady Cafe serves lunch Monday-Saturday.

This big museum houses all sorts of ships. You can explore on your own, or tag along on one of the 90-minute guided tours. The centerpiece is the aircraft carrier USS Yorktown, a decorated warship that played a key role in the Pacific during World War II. You'll also see war planes used during conflicts from World War II to Desert Storm. The planes are located aboard the Yorktown's 40,000 square foot hangar bay and atop the 888 foot flight deck. It even includes the National Congressional Medal of Honor Society's museum, a Navy submarine and a Coast Guard ship. Giant ships with small crannies are ideal for a little kid's imagination.

BOONE HALL PLANTATION

Charleston (Mt. Pleasant) - 1235 Long Point Rd. (Hwy 17 south. Turn right onto Long Point Road. Follow signs. 8 miles from downtown Charleston) 29464. Phone: (843) 884-4371. www.boonehallplantation.com. Hours: Monday-Saturday 9:00am-5:00pm; Sunday 1:00-4:00pm (Labor Day to late March). Extended hours earlier & later from late March to Labor Day (spring/summer). Closed Thanksgiving Day & Christmas Day. Admission: $24.00 adult, $21.00 senior (65+), $12.00 child (6-12). Includes admission to all seasonal tours, plantation house tour and grounds coach tour. Tours: Boone Hall Plantation presents live presentations that cannot be found on any other plantations in the area. However, these shows are seasonal...so check in advance for performance dates and times (example: Black History, Gullah Culture, House Tours, Slave Street). Educators: clever, hands-on worksheets and programs were designed to teach and engage the kids: www.boonehallplantation.com/education.php. Click on the links provided in each program description (ex. Slavery, cash crops, history, nature).

In 1743, the son of Major John Boone, planted live oak trees, arranging them in two evenly spaced rows. These same moss-draped trees still form the spectacular approach to his home you can visit today. Learn about the beginning of Boone Hall and the workings of a Carolina Plantation. Three main cash crops were planted on this plantation between 1681 and the early 1900s. Indigo, cotton and pecan trees supplied the plantation with all of the wealth it could afford. View some of the buildings and learn what happened in them. Discuss how a plantation ran and what crops were grown on it. Kids may get to de-seed cotton. The slave cabins along Slave Street were built between 1790 and 1810. They were made of the damaged or cast-off brick from the kilns on the plantation. They housed the "elite" slaves of the plantation meaning those who were skilled (seamstress, cooks, carpenter, blacksmith, etc.) They are the only known brick slave cabins still in existence in the Charleston area.

BOONE HALL PUMPKIN PATCH

Charleston (Mt. Pleasant) - Boone Hall Plantation. A yearly event with over 25,000 people of all ages visiting. They feature the largest jumping pillow in the state, a hay mountain, slide tower (two stories tall), corn maze, rope maze, play area, goat tower, hayride, and pick your own pumpkin patch. Separate admission for pumpkin patch from plantation admission. http://boonehallplantation.com/fall_festival.php (Daily in October)

CHARLESTON TEA PLANTATION TOURS

Charleston (Wadmalaw Island) - 6617 Maybank Highway 29487. Phone: (843) 559-0383. www.charlestonteaplantation.com. Tours: The Factory Tour is FREE! It begins every 15 minutes on the quarter hour and can be accessed at the top of the stairs in the Gift Shop. Trolley Tour tickets are $10 adult, $5 child (12 and under). The Trolley Tour may last 25 to 30 minutes and departs several times daily. Note: on your way here, be on the lookout for Angel Oak, a live Oak tree that is believed to be over 1,500 years old. While at the Gift Shop help yourself to all of the iced American Classic Tea you can drink.

Just south of Charleston on Wadmalaw Island is America's only tea plantation. The Charleston Tea Plantation is home to thousands of tea plants and a processing factory to tour.

- FACTORY TOUR: The Bigelows themselves, via flat screen televisions guide you down a glass tourway overlooking the factory. You will learn about the history of tea, the harvesting and production of the American Classic Tea and the story of the Charleston Tea Plantation. During peak season you may witness all stages of the production process. You can see tea leaves being withered, macerated, oxidized and dried all in one day. How do they use static electricity to sort teas?

- TROLLEY TOUR: Enjoy a scenic ride around the 127 acre tea farm. Tea expert William Barclay Hall educates you about the history of America's only tea garden while challenging your knowledge of tea. See more than 320 varieties of tea plants in various stages of growth. During harvesting season, you may even witness the Green Giant, a custom tea plant harvester, in action. Why is this the only tea plantation in the United States?

See Giant augers processing tea leaves...

HUNLEY SUBMARINE

Charleston, North - 1250 Supply Street, Building 255, old Charleston Navy Base (Warren Lasch Conservation Center) 29405. www.hunley.org. Phone: (843) 744-1488. Tours: Hunley tours are available every Saturday from 10:00am - 5:00pm, Sunday Noon – 5:00pm (except Easter Sunday). Generally, they run about $10-$18.00 per person for the tour. Last tour begins at 4:40pm. Tours not available on weekdays so scientists can continue their work preserving the Hunley.

The World's first successful combat submarine is open during Saturday and Sunday public tours. The guided tour of the lab includes viewing the Hunley in her 90,000 gallon conservation tank...in an active archaeological site. Everything from video scopes, x-ray machines, and computers, to a wide spectrum of archeological supplies will be required throughout every phase of the project. It's a lesson in history, forensic science, archeology and conservation. You will also view artifacts found on board during excavation of the submarine, films and interactive exhibits.

CHARLESTON COUNTY WATERPARKS

Charleston, North - 888 University Blvd 29406. www.ccprc.com/index.aspx?nid=10. Phone: (843) 572-7275.

Get soaked each summer at your Charleston County Waterparks!

Charleston's three family waterparks are the hottest spots in town during the summer months, and each facility offers a fun, family adventure at a reasonable price. (~$7.99 per person/day - daylight hours, seasonally)

- **SPLASH ISLAND WATERPARK** - Tucked within Mt. Pleasant Palmetto Islands County Park, is a water playground designed for toddlers to pre-teen children. Water slide, otter slide, geysers, sprays, Cyclone 10 minute swirling water ride, pool, concessions, showers. Palmetto Islands County Park. 444 Neddlerush Pkwy. Mt. Pleasant. (843) 884-0832.
- **SPLASH ZONE WATERPARK** - Taste of Caribbean with the island-style play structures and slides at James Island County Park. Tube slide, open slide, Caribbean play structure, sprays, lazy river, pool, concessions, showers. 871 Riverland Drive, Charleston, SC 29412. (843) 795-7275.
- **WHIRLIN WATERS ADVENTURE WATERPARK & WANNAMAKER COUNTY PARK** - This scenic park offers over 1,000 acres of woodlands and wetlands, with a freshwater lagoon for pedal boating and bicycling. Other features include a water sprinkler, two playgrounds, a play hill, paved and unpaved trails, a park center, and picnic areas. The area's largest waterpark offers over 15 acres with an otter bay, lily pad lagoon for toddlers, twisting slides, mat racers, a big kahuna wave pool, tree house and more.

OLD PLANTATION SYRUP MAKING

Coward - 1059 W Old Number Four Hwy (Russ Brothers Farm). Cane syrup production has a long and storied history in South Carolina. To watch how the "Sweetener of the South" has been made for centuries, stop by the Cane Syrup Days. Breakfast is served featuring pancakes with cane syrup, sausage and biscuits. There are also demonstrations of how cane syrup is made. (843) 389-3383. https://agriculture.sc.gov/agritourism-farms/russ-brothers-farm-and-old-plantation-syrup/ (mid-November Saturday)

EDISTO BEACH STATE PARK

Eastern

Edisto Island - 8377 State Cabin Road (From Hwy. 17: Take Hwy 174, 28 mi. to entrance of the town of Edisto Beach) 29438. Phone: (843) 869-2756. www.southcarolinaparks.com/edisto-beach Hours: Daily 8:00am-6:00pm (extended during Daylight Savings Time). Admission: $4.00- $8.00 per person (age 6+).

An oceanfront campground on a palmetto-lined beach famed for its shelling is just one highlight of Edisto Beach State Park. The park also offers the state's longest system of handicapped-friendly hiking and biking trails, including one leading to a mysterious, 4,000-year-old shell midden alongside a secluded bend on a tidal creek. Who were these prehistoric inhabitants? The park offers not only beach and hiking but also camping, cabin rentals, fishing, boating.

With the theme "Choosing to Protect Our Coast," the Edisto Interpretive Center helps promote the wise use of coastal resources, including a touch tank. The Interpretive Center is open Tuesday through Saturday from 9:00am-4:00pm. If you're lucky, you may arrive when they're feeding the aquarium animals.

CAROLINA ROVER BOAT TOURS

Georgetown - 735 Front Street 29440. http://roverboattours.com. Phone: (843) 546-8822. Admission: $30.00-$38.00 per person. Tours: They plan tours so that they can put guests onto the beach at the best possible time for finding shells. Call for exact schedule.

The Carolina Rover takes guests on a three-hour environmental eco-tour to North Island at the mouth of Winyah Bay for shelling, sightseeing and the North Island lighthouse (c. 1809).

LOWCOUNTRY PLANTATION TOURS

Georgetown - 701 Front St (behind the Town Clock, on The Front Street HarborWalk) 29440. Phone: (843) 477-0287. www.lowcountrytours.com. Tours: Most run $38.00 adult, $30.00 child. 3 hours (Monday-Saturday).

Cap'n Rod Singleton brings a lifetime's experience of tales and folklore to Lowcountry Plantation Tours. A native of the lowcountry, Cap'n Rod weaves into his tours a magical mixture of antebellum history, lowcountry legends and personal experiences on the water. The year-round tours offer a unique opportunity to experience coastal South Carolina in ways never seen by the land-bound visitor. The tours offer visitors a relaxing glimpse into the history and stories of the past as you view majestic Rice Plantations, slave cabins and giant oaks. Tours include: Plantation River Tour, Lighthouse Shell Tour and the Ghost Story & Harbor Tour.

The Lowcountry Plantation Tour Boat is a safe, comfortable 56-foot pontoon boat, offering shaded deck seating and clean, modern restrooms. It is fully USCG certified, and handicap accessible.

RICE MUSEUM

Georgetown - 633 Front Street 29442. www.ricemuseum.org. Phone: (843) 546-7423. Hours: Monday-Saturday 10:00am-4:30pm. Admission: $7.00 adult, $5.00 senior (60+), $3.00 students (6-21).

A 60-minute guided tour takes visitors through these buildings, both of which date from 1842. The story of the rice culture in Georgetown County is captured here. Through maps, dioramas, artifacts and other exhibits, visitors to the museum gain a knowledge and understanding of a society based on one crop. The museum is located in the Old Market Building, erected in 1842. In the adjacent Maritime History Gallery is Brown's Ferry Vessel, a 50' river freighter built in 1710, sunk around 1730 and the oldest boat in North America! Other exhibits include history of the Kaminski Hardware Company; Gullah history of the S.C. low country; Miss Ruby Forsythe, one of South Carolina's great educators; and Joseph Hayne Rainey, the first African American elected to the U.S. Congress. The Kaminski Building tour continues with a 17-minute video presentation of "The Garden of Gold," a history of rice in Georgetown County.

WATERMELON FESTIVAL

Hampton - Lake Warren State Park. A family fun day at Lake Warren State Park, pet shows, watermelon judging and eating contests, pageants and other events fill the week-long schedule. The parade is one of the largest in the state. www.hcmelonfest.org. (third week of June)

SAVANNAH RIVER NATL WILDLIFE REFUGE

Hardeeville - 763 Alligator Alley 29927. www.fws.gov/savannah/. Phone: (912) 652-4415. Hours: Daily dawn to dusk. Admission: FREE.

Established in 1927, the 22,940-acre refuge lies along the Savannah River, protecting numerous kinds of wildlife, from Whitetail deer to alligators. Evidence of the rice industry is found in the refuge with its rice levee remains, foundations of slave quarters, old mill sites and small graveyards. A four-mile driving tour along the refuge levees is open to the public. The tract is known as one of the outstanding refuges along the Atlantic Flyway, which extends from Canada to the Caribbean.

COASTAL DISCOVERY MUSEUM

Hilton Head Island - 100 William Hilton Pkwy (Hwy 278) (mile marker #1) 29926. Phone: (843) 689-6767. www.coastaldiscovery.org. Hours: Monday-Saturday 9am-4:30pm, Sunday 11am-3pm. Tours: Critter or History tours offered Spring-Fall for $10 adult/$5 child. Note: If your summer plans include a trip to Hilton

Head Island, here's a little bit of advice: Get bikes. The resort island is a bicycling family's dream, with 25 miles of paved bike paths ideal for easy rides.

As you're racing across the bridge to the Island, stop long enough to take a look inside this museum. It has two locations. The location on Hilton Parkway features a small exhibition gallery and a gift shop. It's the perfect way to acquaint yourself with the area you're about to visit. There is also a location at Honey Horn, a 68-acre historic property that features salt marshes, open fields and some majestic live oaks. This is a good way to get an overview of what's on the island (both history and nature) without being bored with guided tours. Don't pass up a visit to the butterfly discovery area. Or a hands-on salt marsh discovery, where you'll learn how to trap and harvest blue crabs.

SKULL CREEK BOATHOUSE

__Hilton Head Island__ - 397 Squire Pope Road 29926. www.skullcreekboathouse.com. Phone: (843) 681-3663. A local place with indoor/outdoor dining - right on the water. Their huge menu appears overwhelming but the wait staff can recommend what's best for your family. Have someone in your party order the Lowcountry Throwdown - steamed shrimp, sausage, potatoes and corn in a seasoned broth (runs ~$25). Just for the Little Shuckers…coloring pages and a kids menu just for them. Kids Plates range from fried fish or chicken to steak & shrimp to classics like burgers and pasta (avg $7).

ADVENTURE CRUISES

Hilton Head Island - Dock C - Shelter Cove Harbour (Business Hwy. 278 directly across from Palmetto Dunes Resort) 29928. www.hiltonheadisland.com/adventure. Phone: (843) 785-4558. Tours: Dolphin: $20.95 adult, $11.00 child (3-12). Dolphin = one hour, 45 minute narrated cruise. Cash only. Crabbing: $22.00 adult, $16 child (3-12), $5 infants.

- **DOLPHIN CRUISE**: Round trip narrated cruise features bottle-nose dolphins, salt water marshlands, Wexford Plantation, Broad Creek, Tides, Cross Island, Spanish Wells, Oyster Beds, Shrimp boats, Buck Island, Statue of Liberty, Daufuskie Island, wading birds and Harbour Town. Times vary daily year-round (closed in January) with more cruises offered April - October.
- **CRABBING CRUISE**: motor out to the calm waters of Broad Creek. Along the way watch dolphins play. Anchor in the shallow water right next to the salt marsh and fish for blue crabs. (April-early September). 843-422-5110 for reservations.
-

HARBOUR TOWN LIGHTHOUSE

Hilton Head Island - 149 Lighthouse Road (Hwy 278 east to the Island traffic circle and turn onto Greenwood Drive) 29928. www.harbourtownlighthouse.com. Phone: (866) 305-9814. Hours: Daily 10am - sunset.

The 90-foot, red-and-white striped tower of the Harbour Town Lighthouse on Hilton Head Island is the visual centerpiece of the popular Sea Pines. Families can venture to the top of the lighthouse for only $4.95/person. Take the steps for a self-guided Legends Tour while looking at artifacts from the creation of the lighthouse, ancient items found while building it and a recently added Civil War era display. The Shop At The Top is a nautical gift shop at the top of the lighthouse selling Harbour Lights Lighthouses, jewelry and other collectibles. http://harbourtownlighthouse.com/pages/webcab is where to find the view from the top anytime.

PALMETTO BAY SUN RISE CAFÉ

__Hilton Head Island__ - 86 Helmsman Way (near Palmetto Bay Marina) 29928. Phone: (843) 686-3232. www.palmettobaysunrisecafe.com Hours: Daily 6:00am-2:00 or 3:00pm. At this cozy café, you can enjoy a hearty breakfast until 3:00pm, giving you enough time to sleep in on your Hilton Head family vacation. If it's busy, they offer coffee while you wait. Parents love the made to order omelets or the Eggs Benedict (suggestion: Crab Cake Benedict or Shrimp Hash). Kids go crazy for the apple cinnamon pancakes or french toast. Prices start at $6.99 and most plates are under $12. Lunch menu available after 11:00am but breakfast is their thing.

THE SANDBOX CHILDREN'S MUSEUM

Hilton Head Island - 18A Pope Avenue (behind St. Andrew By Sea Methodist Church) 29928. Phone: (843) 842-7645. www.thesandbox.org. Hours: Tues-Sat 10am-5pm. Open Mondays in April, June, July and August. Admission: $6-$8 (ages 1+). Note: Strollers are not allowed in the museum.

Designed for the 8-and-younger set, this hands-on museum is educational and fun. Kids can put their imaginations into high gear as they shop, buy and prepare exotic meals in the International Bazaar or play with magic sand in the Loggerhead Sandcastle. They can take a trek across the rock challenge course to track a T-Rex or paint and play music in the Rhythm and Hues room. Find their Passport to the World in the international airport terminal with a plane ready for little pilots to fly.

HILTON HEAD ISLAND

Hilton Head Island - 29938. www.hiltonheadisland.org.

Hilton Head Island is a foot-shaped barrier island located off the Atlantic Coast of South Carolina, approximately 45 miles north of Savannah, GA. The 12-mile long and 5-mile wide island was the first Eco-planned destination in the United States. The island is known for its pristine natural environments with relaxing, hospitable atmosphere with subtle signage and no neon lights.

- RECREATION - There are 12 miles of beach with public access and metered parking available. You'll see bikers, dog walkers, sand-castle builders, and kite flyers. Dolphins play out in the distance, ghost shrimp and clams make their holes in the sand and pelicans dive into the water in search of prey. Activities: biking, watersports, fishing and crabbing, horseback riding, nature-based tours, mini golf, swimming, etc.
- ACCOMMODATIONS - Hilton Head Island has an array of accommodations, from resorts to RV spots. Options include more than 6,000 villas; 3,000 hotel/motel rooms; 1,000 timeshares; two RV resorts and one campground (off-Island). Many Resorts offer kids camps and kids programs from supervised recreation to specialized adventure watersports camps during the day. Look for half and whole day programs at places like: Westin Resort, Crowne Plaza Resort and Sea Pines Resort.
- MINIATURE GOLF - Pirate's Island Adventure Golf: Adventure Cove: laser tag, bumper cars, video arcade, an indoor play room, miniature golf and more.
- LEGENDARY GOLF
- DINING - Those wishing to sample the local fare should visit an Island restaurant specializing in Lowcountry cuisine, where dishes such as She-Crab Soup and Frogmore Stew - a savory South Carolina blend of shrimp, hot sausage, potatoes and corn on the cob - capture the flavor of the region. A visit to Hilton Head also wouldn't be complete without sampling the famous local seafood, including shrimp, sweet blue crab and briny oysters. Fast food restaurants also are available for those who want food on the go, but they may not look familiar. All Island restaurants must conform to a strict building code requiring construction to blend with the local environment.
-

HAMPTON PLANTATION STATE HISTORIC SITE

McClellanville - 1950 Rutledge Road (Travel N on Hwy 17 for approximately 35 miles. Turn left onto Rutledge Rd) 29458. Phone: (843) 546-9361. www.southcarolinaparks.com/hampton Hours: Grounds open daily 9:00am-6:00pm. Admission: $10 adult, $6.00 SC senior, $5.00 child (age 6+). Tours: The mansion is open for tours Friday, Monday & Tuesday at Noon & 2:00pm and Saturday and Sunday at 10am, noon and 2:00pm. Tours are about 40 minutes long. Note: Enjoy fishing for catfish, bream and bass in Wambaw creek. A valid South Carolina fishing license required. Pets allowed in most outdoor areas.

Hampton is a colonial-era rice plantation. The plantation's Georgian-style mansion and well-kept grounds serve as an interpretive site for the system of slavery that helped build such plantations into the greatest generators of wealth in early American history. They also tell the story of the freed people who made their homes there for generations after emancipation. A historic kitchen building, huge live oaks, camellia gardens and archaeological sites also tell the story of Lowcountry rice culture.

- MANSION TOURS: Several prominent families of Colonial & Antebellum South Carolina lived at Hampton Plantation. Today, the mansion stands as a testament to the wealth and power of these families as well as the craftsmanship of the builders. Tours include a study of the architecture and evolution of the house, as seen in the open walls and unfurnished rooms, as well as personal insight into the people that called Hampton home.
- INTERPRETIVE TRAILS: The two-mile Nature Trail encircles an inland rice field. Look out upon Wambaw Creek at the remains of rice fields that once stretched as far as the eye could see.

CYPRESS GARDENS

Moncks Corner - 3030 Cypress Gardens Road (northeast on US 17A towards Moncks Corner) 29461. Phone: (843) 553-0515. www.cypressgardens.info. Hours: Daily 9:00am-5:00pm. Last entrance at 4:00pm. Admission: $10.00 adult, $6.50 senior, $5.00 child (ages 6-17). FREE parking. Guided boat tours are $5.00 per person. Self-guided boats no additional fee, limited to availability. Note: Picnic shelters and a gift shop are other amenities at the park. FREEBIES: printable Scavenger Hunts online on the Educational Programs page/Teacher Resources.

This 175-acre swamp/garden (once part of Dean Hall, one of the most prosperous Cooper River rice plantations) offers a walk-thru Butterfly House with free-flying butterflies, beautiful plants, tropical birds and more. A Swamparium features native fish, reptiles and amphibians. An International Reptile Center houses giant exotic constrictors and native venomous snakes. Visitors can spy on endangered crocodilians in the Crocodile Isle exhibit. During the proper seasons, wood ducks, hawks, herons, egrets, various woodpeckers, songbirds and even the occasional Wood Stork or Bald Eagle can be spotted. The swamp garden is easily accessible with 4.5 miles of walking paths.

We highly recommend the boat rides (either guided or rentals). Boat rides through the swamp offer visitors a mesmerizing journey through the water forest. Is the water really black or is it a trick on your eyes? The reflections of the tall bald cypress and tupelo trees are mirrored in the calm, dark water. Notice the alligators are even black. Did you encounter any gators on your swamp journey? Scenes from the movie "The Notebook" are easy to find. The swamp garden was also featured in "The Patriot" starring Mel Gibson. Some fake props are still left from the set.

The swamp comes to life with a boat tour....

OLD SANTEE CANAL PARK

Moncks Corner - 900 Stony Landing Road (Rte. 6 east thru town, then left on Byp 52 and right onto Stony Landing) 29461. www.oldsanteecanalpark.org. Phone: (843) 899-5200. Hours: Daily 9:00am-4:30pm. Gates lock at 5:00pm. Closed: New Years Day, Easter, Thanksgiving, Christmas Eve/Day. Admission: $2.00-$3.00 general (ages 7+). Includes Berkeley county & Heritage Center Museum. Note: the Little David Children's Garden has SC State Seal & Symbols scattered about the garden. Educators: Excellent short "unit studies" are found by clicking on the Programs link.

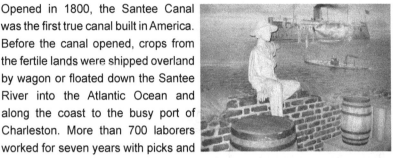

Opened in 1800, the Santee Canal was the first true canal built in America. Before the canal opened, crops from the fertile lands were shipped overland by wagon or floated down the Santee River into the Atlantic Ocean and along the coast to the busy port of Charleston. More than 700 laborers worked for seven years with picks and shovels to complete the project. The finished canal was 22-miles long, 30-feet wide and only 5.5 feet deep. Boats and barges full of cotton and other goods were pulled down the canal by mules and horses using 10-foot wide towpaths cut on both sides. Sadly, the completion of the railway between Columbia and Charleston in 1840 left the canal hardly in use.

The Interpretive Center houses exhibits. As you walk up the entrance to the door, notice the walkway is actually a canal lock gate. The Center includes displays that go back to 4000 BC with early hand tools. A model of the canal and scale model of the Little David, a semi submersible Confederate torpedo boat built here, is on display. Look through the eyes of a child at Charleston Harbor under siege of war. If you have time, ask to see a film about the area.

Four miles of boardwalks with observation decks and trails provide an up-close view of the park's natural beauty and wildlife. Canoe rentals are available to explore Biggin Creek and the southern terminus of the Santee Canal. A 19th-century plantation house and picnic facilities are on site.

Also at the park is the BERKELEY MUSEUM, which tells the story of 1000s of years of the region's history focusing on the Swamp Fox, American Indians, Colonial Life, the Civil War, Rural Electrification and the Black Swamp lands. Special programs and events are held throughout the year.

GILLIGAN'S STEAMER AND RAW BAR

Moncks Corner / Charleston - 582 Dock Road (many locations in and surrounding Charleston) 29461. Phone: (843) 863-2244. www.gilligans.net. Hours: Daily lunch and dinner. Note: Want to watch the amazing shrimp peeling machine live, in action? Gilligan's main location on North Market Street in historic Charleston has it on display, in action. We had a coupon for free Shrimp Dip and crackers so we ordered that first. It is so fresh and so good! Is it the secret spices? (the dip runs $9.99 and well worth it) Next, entrees. If you're smart and you like seafood, go with any of their Favorites. Other choices are beef or chicken usually paired with pasta. Even the kids can try Fried Popcorn Shrimp, Fried Fish fingers and all the regular pizza and sandwich choices are available for ~$5. The Kid's Menu doubles as a coloring & activity sheet but most families head out to the docks *to watch fishing boats. Lunch plates run ~ $8-$10. Dinner $16-$20. All entrees come with hush puppies that are so good, you can buy it now to take-n-make at home. The hush puppies work on puppies and noisy kids, too.*

AMUSEMENTS - MYRTLE BEACH

MYRTLE WAVES WATER PARK - South Carolina's largest water park offers 20 acres of themed attractions and more than one million gallons of water. There is also a giant wave pool, lazy river and interactive Saturation Station, along with concessions, volleyball, group facilities, and more. For additional information, call (843) 913-9269, or visit www.MyrtleWaves.com.

WILD WATER AND WHEELS THEME PARK - This 16-acre park is packed with more than 33 exciting rides, including high-speed flumes, waterfalls, a wave pool, Adventure River Ride, kiddie slides and many other high-energy attractions. There's also miniature golf, a video arcade, food court, picnic facilities and a separate racetrack complex with rides for all ages. For additional information, call (843) 238-3787, or visit www.Wild-Water.com.

PUTT PUTT: MINIATURE GOLF - Golf fans of all ages can choose from a myriad of miniature golf themes, from man-eating dinosaurs and lava-spewing volcanoes, to high-seas adventures aboard pirate ships. The Grand Strand is considered the miniature golf capital of the world with 50 miniature golf courses to choose from.

CAMPING - MYRTLE BEACH

Myrtle Beach - Sleep Under the Stars - The Myrtle Beach area offers campers and outdoor enthusiasts a choice of nearly a dozen campgrounds, two state parks and more than 7,000 camping sites, all located in close proximity to the beach and other attractions and amenities along the Grand Strand. Some locations include:

- **MYRTLE BEACH STATE PARK**: Located in the heart of Myrtle Beach and boasts an impressive beach, fishing pier, 350 campsites, cabins, picnic shelters, activity center, nature center, hiking trails and free nature programs with admission to the park. For more information, call (843) 238-5325 or visit SouthCarolinaParks.com.
- **HUNTINGTON BEACH STATE PARK**: The diverse natural environment of the South Carolina coast consists of freshwater lagoons, salt marshes, nature trails along the fabulous stretch of beach. The park has 133 campsites, picnic areas with shelters, nature programs and the historic castle Atalaya, once the winter home of sculptor Anna Hyatt Huntington and her husband, Archer. For more information, call (843) 237-4440 or visit SouthCarolinaParks.com.
- **OCEAN LAKES FAMILY CAMPGROUND**: Visitors will enjoy beachfront camping on the eight fresh water lakes. On-site amenities include

the Four Seasons Center with heated pool, and a 17,000-square-foot recreation center – plus nearly 900 campsites, 250 rentals units and over 2,000 annual lease sites. For more information, call (877) 510-1413 or visit OceanLakes.com.

- **LAKEWOOD CAMPING RESORT**: Offers visitors the choice of oceanfront or lakefront campsites or villa accommodations; with available amenities including golf cart rentals, on-site telephones, heated swimming pool, three-acre recreation complex, and oceanfront amphitheater and meeting rooms for clubs and rallies. For more information, call (877) LAKEWOOD or visit www.LakewoodCampground.com.
- **PIRATELAND FAMILY CAMPING RESORT**: For nearly 40 years, PirateLand campground has been accommodating family travelers with more than 700 campsites, a heated indoor swimming pool, two- and three-bedroom vacation rentals, golf packages and a beautiful, wide span of beach. For more information, call (800) 443-CAMP or www.Pirateland.com.

√ *RIVER CITY CAFÉ*

Myrtle Beach - www.rivercitycafe.com. (5 locations - N 21st St and Barefoot Landing most popular). An inexpensive dining hangout where you eat peanuts and throw the shells on the floor. They have a few specialties but probably the best bets are their sandwiches - specifically their many burger varieties. Most everything is round $7.00, add $2.29 for fries and coleslaw. And, if your kids dare, people can write on the walls, tables, chairs here - go ahead! Lunch and dinner served. ___

KINGSTON PLANTATION RESORT

Myrtle Beach - 9800 Queensway Boulevard (US 22 to M.Beach area. Take Kings Rd. exit right. 1.2 miles on left) 29572. www.kingstonplantation.com. Phone: (843) 449-0006. Note: This oceanfront Myrtle Beach Resort is located on the north end of Myrtle Beach. Once on the property, park, secure a map, and take advantage of the free shuttle service around the resort and outlying restaurants and shopping. Nightly rates hover around $200+ per night. Condos are typically cheaper than Embassy and provide more space.

This oceanfront hotel complex is located on 145 beautifully landscaped acres on approximately a mile of pristine beach, just 12 miles from Myrtle Beach International Airport and minutes from restaurant row.

- KINGSTON PLANTATION CONDOS: individually owned and decorated casual upscale multi-bedroom condos are in towers on either side of the Embassy or Hilton Hotel Resort.

- EMBASSY SUITES OCEANFRONT: All of the luxurious two-room suites feature a spacious bedroom with one king bed or two double beds, plus a separate living area with mini refrigerator and microwave, and a private balcony with ocean views. Suites are fully equipped with two 32" LCD televisions, a sleeper sofa, and a well lit dining/work table.
- RESORT DINING: Complimentary Breakfast - All registered guests of the Embassy Suites enjoy a complimentary breakfast buffet daily. Other resort guests can pay for the buffet. The restaurant offers great views of the ocean and pool complex. Before you leave home, go to www.embassykids.com for online games and offline printable activity sheets. Fish Eye Grill features daily fresh fish specials, along with regional Calabash style cuisine.

- RECREATION: Splash! Water Park is open seasonally. This 50,000 pool area is the main feature for fun in the water. It offers water jets, water pumps, water slides and the "bucket". The bucket is a 500 gallon bucket which fills with water and dumps every two minutes on participants below. Or, Enjoy one of 9 swimming pools at the resort. Relax in the Lazy River. Fun for kids and adults alike. The large complex also offers a golf course, tennis and a huge Sport and Health Club. And, of course, the Beach - softsand, great body board surfing, and the Apache Pier with fishing and nightly entertainment during summer.

Easy place to make friends around the pool, set up a family tent on the beach or prepare light meals back at the room. This resort is perfect for safe family fun with plenty of leisure activities available. We highly recommend it!

MYRTLE BEACH STATE PARK NATURE CENTER

Myrtle Beach - 4401 S Kings Hwy 29575. www.southcarolinaparks.com/myrtle-beach. Phone: (843) 238-5325. Hours: Daily 6:00am-10:00pm (March-November). Daily 6:00am-8:00pm (December-February) Admission: $3.00-$5.00 per person (ages 6+). Educators: engage your students to learn beyond the classroom with www.discovercarolina.com - a hands on, curriculum based school field experience with pre-and post activities and a scavenger hunt.

Myrtle Beach State Park is a natural retreat, home to one of South Carolina's last stands of easily accessible, oceanfront maritime forest. This traditional state park was built by the Civilian Conservation Corps in the 1930s. The park has a small but very active nature center that educates visitors about the natural beauty and diversity of Myrtle Beach. Saltwater aquariums, live reptiles and fun, interactive natural history displays help visitors understand the inhabitants of the park. A backyard wildlife habitat complete with bird feeders, bird houses, bird baths, water garden containers, nature sculpture and seasonal butterfly garden are available for viewing even when the center is not open. The park includes a campground, cabins, nearly a mile of beach, picnic areas, a fishing pier and nature center. In addition, a nature trail provides a rare opportunity to see one of the last stands of maritime forest on the northern coast of South Carolina.

EDVENTURE

Myrtle Beach - 3061 Howard Avenue (Market Common) 29577. www.edventure.org/myrtle-beach. Phone: (843) 839-0475. Hours: Monday-Saturday 10:00am-6:00pm, Sunday Noon-6pm. Closed: Most major holidays. Admission: $8.00 per person (age 2+).

EdVenture is a learning playground of interactive exhibits that invite touching, exploring and playing. Take a trip through a space ship; play house on the moon; draw, cut, color and paint at the Makers Space make and take station. Older kids will have fun learning aeronautics with airway tubes and a flight simulator.

FAMILY KINGDOM AMUSEMENT AND WATER PARK

Myrtle Beach - 300 S. Ocean Blvd (Ocean Boulevard and 3rd Avenue South) 29577. Phone: (843) 626-3447. www.familykingdomfun.com. Hours: Waterpark is open from 10:00am-6:00pm seasonally. Amusement Park - Admission: FREE admission into park. Individual Ride Tickets are available for $1.15 plus tax each and range from 2 to 5 tickets per ride. Ticket options include each park wristband runs $20-$30.00 - Combo tickets for one day at the water park and one day at the amusement park are $40.00 plus tax. Note: Free parking can be difficult to find, although there are nearby lots where you can pay to park.

This is the Grand Strand's only oceanfront park - two parks - the waterpark oceanside and the amusement park complex across the street. You'll notice they have more Family & Kiddie rides vs. high thrill, screaming rides- a pleasant throw back to old-fashioned amusement fun. Come in and enjoy all of the sights and sounds for free! (tickets required for rides).

Family Kingdom Amusement Park is home of the legendary Swamp Fox wooden roller coaster, the largest Ferris wheel in the state of South Carolina (and, it overlooks the ocean) plus over thirty other great rides and attractions for all ages. The Park also offers midway games, family entertainment and traditional park temptations such as funnel cakes and cotton candy.

Family Kingdom Water Park features three serpentine water flumes each with a drop of greater than a 100 feet, two speed slides and two intermediate slides, all with a stunning view of the Atlantic Ocean. Families can also enjoy a Lazy River that stretches out more than 400 feet along the seashore. Splash pools feature two rain trees, a multi-tiered waterfall and eight kiddie slides. There are seating areas with lounge chairs. Saving tip: Adults can get into the waterpark free if they just want to watch their children and not go on a slide.

JIMMY BUFFETT'S MARGARITAVILLE RESTAURANT

Myrtle Beach - 1114 Celebrity Circle Broadway at the Beach 29577. Phone: (843) 448-5455. www.margaritavillemyrtlebeach.com Note: Be prepared for a 2 to 3 hour wait during peak season. Put your name in and then browse the shops. They will call your cell phone when your table is ready. After a fun-filled day with the kids on the beach, you may not want to lose that tropical feeling. Kids have their own menu including chicken fingers, a "Cheeseburger In Paradise" or pasta but also fun tropical drinks plus other selections. Margaritaville's specialties include chicken, shrimp and fish entrees often served with Island rice and your choice of mango salsa, Jerk BBQ or Island butter. Key lime pie or their Chocolate Hurricane make a great dessert. Average entrée $18, burger plate $10. Although their food is fun, folks really come for the atmosphere. While you wait for your meal to be served, a pirate on stilts makes balloon hats. Once an hour, a tropical storm brews and there's a hurricane indoors! Lunch and Dinner served daily..

MYRTLE BEACH

Myrtle Beach - (Pier 14 located at 14th Avenue North to the Second Avenue North pier) 29577. www.visitmyrtlebeach.com/boardwalk Note: Biking & pets are only allowed on the Boardwalk during restricted hours early morning making biking on the "strip" difficult with kids during the day. If you're staying at a resort complex or beach house (north or south of main hub), there's a better chance you can bike ride for miles as a family.

The launch of the Myrtle Beach Oceanfront Boardwalk & Promenade in summer 2010 breathed new life into the Grand Strand beachfront. From souvenir shops and arcades to an oceanfront park near the 2nd Avenue Pier, the 1.2-mile (1.9-kilometer) walkway is now the town's hub of activity, with live entertainment each summer evening, including roaming stilt walkers, jugglers, bagpipers, living statues, and a weekly fireworks display.

The 1.2 mile-long Myrtle Beach Oceanfront Boardwalk and Promenade traverses through the sand from the 14th Avenue to 2nd Avenue Piers in Myrtle Beach. The boardwalk provides oceanfront views of the pristine beachline, numerous shops and restaurants along its path, and is divided into three different sections:

- The northernmost portion winds down from the 14th Avenue North Pier to Plyler Park.
- The mid-section is located from Plyler Park to the former Pavilion Amusement Park site at 8th Avenue North and encompasses more of a carnival-like atmosphere with oceanfront dining and businesses.
- The southernmost end of the boardwalk leading up to the 2nd Avenue pier has a meandering oceanfront park.

<u>HOTELS</u> - Early morning ocean breezes, breakfast in bed, indoor/outdoor water parks, swimming pools, spas, private balconies and, of course, sun-drenched beaches. It's the little things that add up to a memorable vacation, and when you're with the kids, where you choose to stay is as important as where you choose to play. That's why the Myrtle Beach area's grand beaches and communities are strung with luxurious resorts, roomy condos, cozy cottages, quaint motels and beach houses catering to every budget and lifestyle. Nearly 90,000 rooms are available.

<u>DINING</u> - Calabash buffets – the most famous being the Original Benjamin's Calabash Seafood – line Highway 17 for miles, offering guests hundreds of delicious options to choose from; everything from crab to flounder and shrimp or hushpuppies...with all-you-can-eat prices. Many calabashes now offer a variety of meats and a playplace area for kids. Advice: look for discount coupons (earlybird) and come hungry.

<u>BOARDWALK</u> - Peaches Corner is a landmark. The restaurant across the street from the site of the old Pavilion amusement park has been serving up foot-long chili dogs, cheeseburgers and fries since 1937. The Pavilion might be gone, but the blue-and-white building in the heart of Myrtle Beach is still serving seven days a week. www.peaches-corner.com.

Venture further south and travelers will find themselves in the heart of Low Country, where chefs utilize local ingredients such as Carolina rice, stone-ground grits, shrimp, blue crab, grouper and country ham, in traditional recipes handed down from the Gullah community.

GOLF - The Grand Strand has more than 50 miniature golf courses. Tickets run $8.00 - but most courses offer discounts if you play during the day. During fall and spring, you'll find more people on the golf course than on the beach. www.golfholiday.com. Most of the 100 regulation golf courses are public.

BROADWAY GRAND PRIX

Myrtle Beach - 1820 21st Avenue North (Highway 17 Bypass at 21st Avenue North-Broadway at the Beach) 29577. http://broadwaygrandprix.com/. Phone: (843) 918-8725. Hours: Generally opens at 10:00am or Noon and closes at 8:00pm. Opens earlier and closes later summers. Admission: FREE admission into complex. Unlimited wristbands $22-$32.00.

NASCAR Speedpark features 26 acres of family thrills with 7 different difficulty level tracks (one just for young families), sky coaster, miniature golf, kiddie rides, indoor rock climbing, arcade, bumper cars, and more.

✓ RIPLEY'S AQUARIUM

Myrtle Beach - 1110 Celebrity Circle (Broadway at the Beach) 29577. Phone: (843) 916-0888. http://myrtlebeach.ripleyaquariums.com/. Hours: Open Sun-Thurs 9am-7pm (until 9:00pm Friday & Saturday). Admission: Adults (12 years and older) $34.99; Children (Ages 6-11) – $24.99, Child (2-5) $14.99. Discount coupons online. Combo prices, too. Note: Broadway on the Beach Entertainment Complex: dozens of themed restaurants, unique shops and old-fashioned fair foods and kiddie rides round out this large area a mile from the beach between North 21st & 29th streets.

The huge building is home to 1000s of colorful fish. Travel through the 750,000 gallon Dangerous Reef tunnel on a moving glide path surrounded on all sides by sharks up to 10 feet long. The Discovery Center - an interactive area with a horsehose crab touch tank - is the hands-on section of the building along with 30 new interactive and live displays. "Babies" is devoted to nature's incubators - featuring baby sharks, seahorses, frogs, jellyfish and dinosaur eggs. Ray Bay and Friendship Flats are inhabited by a variety of stingrays and small sharks.

Rainbow Rock has a stunning display of 1000s of brilliantly colored tropical Indo-Pacific fish. Educational casual aquatic talks and dive shows are scheduled throughout the day. After the kids look at and touch a variety of ocean creatures, they can play oceanographer in the lower level playground. The winding, dark and mysterious shark tunnel is our favorite area in this place.

The "Touch Tank" will have the kids talking for sure...

- **RIPLEY'S ODDITORIUM** - www.ripleys.com. Featuring more than 500 unusual and macabre exhibits, Ripley's Believe It or Not Museum will stimulate the mind and senses, from a roller coaster made of matchsticks to vampire skulls! Even the outside of the building is designed to look like a hurricane-ravaged building about to fall to pieces. $17.99 / $8.99.
- **RIPLEY'S MARVELOUS MIRROR MAZE** - Ripley's Marvelous Mirror Maze puts a new spin on the traditional house of mirrors. The walk-through attraction features hundreds of floor-to-ceiling mirrors that create nearly 2,000 square feet of mirrored paths, corners and dead ends. With multiple pathways throughout the maze, visitors can experience something new each time. $9.99 everyone.
- **RIPLEY'S 4D MOVING THEATER** - Experience film like never before! Ripley's 4D Moving Theater system combines a high impact 70mm film experience with computer controlled hydraulic seats that move in sync with the action taking place on the screen. The dynamic surround sound system and extra large screen bring the ride to life – making viewers feel like they are a part of the picture. $12.99/$9.99.

THEATRE SHOWS

Myrtle Beach - 29577.

- **PALACE THEATRE** - "Broadway at the Beach" Entertainment Complex. The Palace Theatre plays host to some of the most spectacular live entertainment shows, Broadway theatre productions and musicals from around the world, including its resident show Cirque. From a human chandelier to acrobats climbing chairs to the sky, this show really displays the dance art and human strength of gymnastics beyond what you think the body can do. Summer Series in King's Suite Showroom includes shows like Alice in Wonderland, Narnia, and a changing Christmas production.

Phone: (843) 448-9224. www.palacetheatremyrtlebeach.com. Shows: April thru October evening shows at 8pm (Monday-Saturday). Matinees are the following: Wednesday at 10:00am and Thursday at 2:00pm. Kids (ages 3-12) are always $10-$12. Adult prices range from $35-$45 per show. Around $20-30 for matinees and plays. King's Suite Showroom shows vary but usually evening shows at 6:00pm plus many that are daytime showings.

- **ALABAMA THEATRE** - Gaylord Entertainment presents ONE The Show at the Alabama Theatre, featuring multi-talented entertainers performing America's favorite music including country, Broadway, bluegrass and gospel, as well as comedy, dance and more. The theatre showcases touring acts such as Merle Haggard, Clint Black, Loretta Lynn, Little Richard, Engelbert Humperdink, George Jones and many others. They have a Christmas show, too. (800) 342-2262 or visit www.Alabama-Theatre.com. 4750 Hwy 175, North Myrtle.
- **CAROLINA OPRY** - Calvin Gilmore Presents The Carolina Opry. Guests will enjoy a variety of stellar music, dance and comedy acts performed by professional artists including "All That!" of NBC's "America's Got Talent." Joining the Opry's repertoire on select nights is Good Vibrations, in which the Carolina Opry cast turns out hits from the '60s, '70s and '80s. Also, an annual Christmas Show. (800) 843-6779 or visit www.TheCarolinaOpry.com. 8901 North Kings Hwy.
- **PIRATES VOYAGE DINNER & SHOW** - Pirates battle each other on deck, in the water and sky above on their full size pirate ships in a 15-foot deep lagoon. Plus live animals, acrobatics, plus 4 course feast. http://piratesvoyage.com. 8901 North Kings Hwy.
- **LEGENDS** - The show features state-of-the-art lighting, sound and technical equipment and a cast of dynamic tribute artists portraying such show business greats as Frank Sinatra, Barbara Streisand, Rod Stewart, Elvis Presley and a host of others. For more information, call (800) 960-7469 or visit https://legendsinconcert.com/locations/myrtle-beach-sc/ 2925 Hollywood Drive.
- **MEDIEVAL TIMES** - At Medieval Times Dinner & Tournament, the glory and chivalry of the Middle Ages come to life amid pageantry and thrilling tournament action. Guests enjoy a four-course banquet while six knights compete in medieval games of skill astride magnificent Andalusian stallions. For more information, call (888) WE-JOUST or visit www.MedievalTimes.com. 2904 Fantasy Way.

WHEELS OF YESTERYEAR

Myrtle Beach - 413 Hospitality Lane (Hwy 501 and Hwy 31) 29579. Phone: (704) 604-4664. www.wheelsofyesteryearmb.com. Hours: Daily, 10:00am-6:00pm, Extended summer hours. Admission: $10.50 adult, $7.35 child (6-15). 5 and under are FREE.

Wheels of Yesteryear features over 45 classic cars and trucks collected and painstakingly restored by automobile enthusiast Paul Cummings. Cummings' collection consists of over 100 accurately and fully-restored cars which will all be featured in the auto showcase on a rotating basis, year-round. The collection primarily consists of Chrysler/Dodge/Plymouth MOPAR cars, commonly referred to as American Muscle, some Ford Motor Company, GM Division, and AMC Corporation examples of muscle and classic cars of yesteryear. The cars the kids will hover over the most are the winged warriors and nostalgia drag cars.

WACCATEE ZOO

Myrtle Beach - 8500 Enterprise Road 29588. www.facebook.com/pages/Waccatee-Zoological-Farm/113464532020431. Phone: (843) 650-8500. Hours: Daily 10:00am-5:00pm, weather permitting. Admission: $12.00 adult, $5.00 child (1-12).

Waccatee Zoological Farm is 15 minutes from Myrtle Beach with 100 species of animals in a nature themed walkway with cages. You can go at your own pace and there's shade from trees on most of the trails. For the best kid-friendly experience, purchase a bag of feed for a few bucks. There are lots of farm animals like horses, ducks, goats and even exotic animals to feed like monkeys, emus and ostrich. There are bears, lions, donkeys, ducks, zebras, nutria, turtles, fish, snakes and many other animals as well as the first 'zonkey' and a two headed turtle. Note: this zoo is privately owned and the environment is set up as cages, not vast open prairies like large community zoos. Still, you get up close to the animals - even giant rodents (capybara) and a porcupine.

Eastern

SUN FUN FESTIVAL

Myrtle Beach *- The first Sun Fun Festival in 1951 was conceived to attract vacationers during the period between the end of the school year and the July 4th holiday. Almost sixty years later the area's official kick-off to summer is still going strong, drawing upwards of 35,000 attendees each year. The festival is held the first weekend of June at Grand Park across from The Market Common on the former Myrtle Beach Air Force Base. Sun Fun features live entertainment, a Kids Zone, food and arts/crafts vendors and much more. For more information, call (800) 356-3016 or www.sunfunmb.com.*

BEACH, BOOGIE & BBQ FESTIVAL

Myrtle Beach - The "grand finale" of summer, this Labor Day weekend festival, which draws between 50,000 and 60,000 visitors, features the official barbeque competition of South Carolina, car shows, live entertainment and Kids Zone among other events held at Grand Park across from The Market Common. For more information, call (800) 356-3016 or visit www.BeachBoogieBarbequeFestival.com.

HUNTINGTON BEACH STATE PARK

Myrtle Beach (Murrells Inlet) - (off US 17 south of Myrtle Beach strip) 29576. Phone: (843) 237-4440. http://southcarolinaparks.com/huntington-beach. Hours: Daily 6:00am-10:00pm. Admission: $4.00- $5.00 (age 6+).

If the family wants a pristine Grand Strand beach, sea-breezy camping, fishing and some of the finest bird watching on the East Coast, this is the place. Huntington Beach State Park boasts a lagoon, maritime forest, salt marshes and three miles of the most well-preserved beach on the Grand Strand.

The lush park environment provides prime habitats for wildlife including alligators and more than 300 recorded species of birds. Other park amenities include a campground, boardwalks with many observation decks, and nature trails. The Education Center has touchtanks with horseshoe crab, stingray, etc. to pet plus little dioramas that clearly highlight the creatures that reside in the park like live turtles, fish, alligator and birds. Next, head back outside to hike up and down the 3 miles of protected beach. When visiting the beach, be sure to include your road bicycle, beach bike, or mountain bicycle. They have a 26 mile trail from Huntington to Litchfield Beach that is safe and well guarded. There were bikes and kids everywhere during our visit. Extremely family-oriented.

Guided Coastal Exploration programs are held from March through November. Programs are free with park admission and include alligator walks, ghost tours, beachcombing and birding expeditions. Call the Education Center for program information: (843) 235-8755.

4TH OF JULY BOAT PARADE (MURRELLS INLET)

Myrtle Beach (Murrells Inlet) - Each Independence Day, decorated boats sail down the parade route with festival goers watching from equally decorated docks of the Murrells Inlet Marshwalk and picturesque restaurants. The day concludes with a spectacular firework display in the Inlet, and awards for the best boat and dock decorations. For more information call (843) 651-5675 or visit www.facebook.com/MurrellsInletBoatParade/

BROOKGREEN GARDENS

Myrtle Beach (Pawleys Island) - 1931 Brookgreen Dr (U.S. 17 between Myrtle Beach and Pawleys Island) 29585. Phone: (843) 235-6000. www.Brookgreen.org. Hours: Daily from 9:30am-5:00pm. Closed on Christmas Day. Admission: $18.00 adult (13-64) $16.00 senior (65+) $10.00 child (4-12). Tours: Guests can visit varied ecosystems and historic sites via boat or aboard Springfield tidal creek excursions and Trekker back-roads excursions for an extra fee. Note: As your kids navigate the gardens and low country trails, they will notice an emphasis on the Gullah culture. Want to learn more, from a kids' perspective? Go to this fun website: www.gullahgullah.com. Exploring the Sculpture Garden? Be sure to pick up Brookgreen Detectives booklet for kids to make this garden a scavenger hunt. WARNING: Many sculptures here are the classic style - human body figures, unclothed. If you're sensitive to that, concentrate on the Zoo and Lowcountry Trails (separate parking available out front) which feature sculpture but more history and animals.

Considered the finest outdoor presentation of American figurative sculpture in the world, Brookgreen Gardens was created in the early 1930s by Archer and Anna Hyatt Huntington on the site of four former rice plantations. Brookgreen Gardens is home to more than 900 works (550 currently displayed) by 300 of the greatest names in American sculpture, past and present.

- **LOWCOUNTRY HISTORY AND WILDLIFE PRESERVE** - are rich with evidence of the great rice plantations of the 1800s and the Gullah culture of the enslaved Africans who sustained it. While walking along "The Lowcountry Trail," students learn about being children of the Plantation Owner, the Overseer, the Enslaved African Male, and the Enslaved African Female. The Audio Tour winds along the Ricefield Overlook and adjacent rice field and is free with garden admission. A 30-minute fictional story about life on Brookgreen Plantation unwinds progressively as listeners move through Listening Stations.
- **CHILDREN'S DISCOVERY CENTER** - Every one of the discovery stations has something to do with an aspect of Brookgreen heritage and history. At some stations, children complete projects they may carry home with them.
- **WHISPERING WINGS BUTTERFLY EXPERIENCE** - houses dozens of species of butterflies native to the Southeast. The butterfly house is open daily to the public spring through October each year. (small fee)
- **ZOO** - features a collection of animals native to the woods, swamps and waters of the Lowcountry, along with domestic animals of the plantation and cypress aviary. The zoo's reflection of its native environment provides visitors with an experience that is truly unique.

ALLIGATOR ADVENTURE

Myrtle Beach, North - (Barefoot Landing, Hwy 17) 29582. Phone: (843) 361-0789. www.alligatoradventure.com. Hours: vary, call ahead. Admission: $26.99 adult, $24.99 senior, $18.99 (4-12).

One of the largest exotic reptile parks in the world features live shows, nature exhibits, zoological gardens, and a serpentarium. Highlights include albino alligators, river otters, squirrel monkeys, bears and Utan, the largest crocodile to come to the United States. Families can get the best value by focusing on the frog, lizard, turtle house and the alligators - cold-blooded creatures. Make sure you go on a day/time of feeding as that is the main attraction for kids.

CAW CAW INTERPRETIVE CENTER

Ravenel - 5200 Savannah Highway 29470. www.ccprc.com/index.aspx?nid=53. Phone: (843) 889-8898. Hours: Tuesday - Sunday 9:00am-5:00pm. Admission: $2.00/person. Canoe rentals are $10.00 per canoe. Note: We suggest bringing insect repellent in the summer as flies and mosquitoes can be common. Follow safety signs about reptiles you may encounter on trails and how to avoid them.

The Caw Caw Interpretive Center was once part of a 5,500-acre rice plantation that flourished in the late 1700's and early 1800's. The land was home to enslaved Africans who applied skills in agriculture to carve highly successful rice fields out of this cypress swamp. Still evident are the earthen dikes, water control structures, and visible canals. The Park features 6 miles of interpretive trails including over 1200 feet of boardwalk winding through 9 different habitats. The Exhibit & Learning Center sheds light on the history and science of rice plantation growth in the south. Kids always become more interested in the site when they learn that "flooding the fields" is actually a good thing. Careful where you step...often little critters like to use the trail path, too.

WORLD GRITS FESTIVAL

St. George - (I-95 exit 77). Join in on this three-day celebration of that celebrated Southern icon: GRITS. Event includes a parade, rolling-in-the-grits contest, grits meals, crafts, grits grinding, street dancing, clogging, gospel music, carnival, live bands, grits eating contest and more. www.worldgritsfestival.com (mid-April long weekend)

COLONIAL DORCHESTER STATE HISTORIC

Summerville - 300 State Park Road (15 miles upriver from Charleston on the Ashley River, I-26 exit 199) 29485. Phone: (843) 873-1740. www.southcarolinaparks.com/colonial-dorchester. Hours: Daily 9am-6pm. Admission: $1.00-$3.00 per person (age 16+). Note: Pets (leashed) are allowed.

An archaeological treasure, the park rests on the site of Dorchester, a trading town that flourished on the Ashley River inland from 1697 through the Revolutionary War. Intact remains of the old town include the brick bell tower of St. George's Anglican Church, a fort made of the oyster-shell concrete called tabby, and part of a log wharf visible at low tide. Visitors can observe and even participate in archaeological digs revealing preserved building foundations, street systems and other evidence of colonial life in the old town. A kiosk and interpretive trail offer exhibits and waysides on the history of the village and the process of discovery through archaeological and historical research. Hands-on educational programs are held regularly on weekends.

DUKE'S BARBECUE

Walterboro *- 949 Robertson Blvd (just follow the signs with big arrows after exit 57 east off I-95) 29488. Phone: (843) 549-1446. Hours: Duke's is open for lunch and supper only on Thursday, Friday, Saturday and Sunday. Duke's is stark...on purpose. Everything about this place is designed to help you concentrate on the hickory-smoked barbecued pork. It is served in big chunks at a cafeteria line that also includes rice, hash (a stewlike mixture made from pork shoulders), a choice of red sauce that is four-alarm hot or yellow mustard sauce that is sweet and tangy (unique to central South Carolina), and pickles. The drink of choice is sweet tea and each table is outfitted with a few loaves of Sunbeam bread, which is just the right thing for mopping a plate of all its good sauce. Please note the limited hours. In the tradition of the old-time pig-pickin', South Carolinians consider a meal like this a weekend celebration. www.dukesbarbque.com*

BEE CITY HONEYBEE FARM, PETTING ZOO & CAFÉ

Walterboro (Cottageville) - 1066 Holly Ridge Lane (three miles north of Givhans State Park on Hwy. 61. I-95 exit 68 south) 29435. Phone: (843) 835-5912. www.beecity.net. Hours: Tuesday-Saturday 9:00am-5:00pm (weekends open until 6:00pm) (summer). Weekends only (September-May). Admission: $7.00 petting zoo admission (age 3+). Tours: Tuesday-Saturday. Scheduled with groups of 15 plus. $4.00 each for regular. Hands on tours cost $9-$12.00 a program.

Eastern

Near the beautiful Edisto River is a farm that focuses on educating the public on the importance of honeybees. View a glass observation bee hive and actually get a closer look at the workers, drones and the queen. If you've never seen bees in action, it is really amazing to see all the different "jobs". The petting zoo consists of domestic and exotic animals, which include deer, monkeys, lemurs, wallabies, alpacas and llamas. The nature center features reptiles like snakes, turtles, lizards and alligators. The gift shop is full of everything bees and honey. The café serves homemade lunches - all around $5.00 a plate.

- FIELD TRIPS: The $9.00 Field Trip includes bottling an 8 oz. honey bear, and pouring a beeswax figurine with melted beeswax. The $12.00 field trip includes all of the above as well as an additional activity where the participants roll a pair of honey comb candles out of a sheet of beeswax. Some of the younger children can handle this with a little help. All field trips include a tour of the petting zoo and nature center.

LOW COUNTRY VISITORS CENTER & MUSEUM

Yemassee - 1 Lowcountry Lane (I-95 exit 33 & US 17) 29945. www.southcarolinalowcountry.com. Phone: (843) 717-3090. Hours: Daily 8:30am-5:00pm. Admission: FREE.

Housed in the historic Frampton Plantation House, c. 1868, the Lowcountry Visitors Center and Museum features a recreated 1900s plantation parlor, complete with antique furnishings and displays from the region's 10 museums and the SC Artisans Center. Our favorite room was the Parlor room and the Gullah items. It's clever how they mix artifacts with items you can purchase and brochures. Kids like the old-fashioned toys and trinkets plus the free samples of fruit cider made right here in Low Country. Outside, they offer a small walking trail, picnic tables under the huge live oaks, and even a pet walk. Before you leave, be sure to ask if there's a festival going on. They have a festival to celebrate nearly everything: the endangered Gopher Tortoise, watermelons, catfish, rice, harbors and water, shrimp, chili and even more.

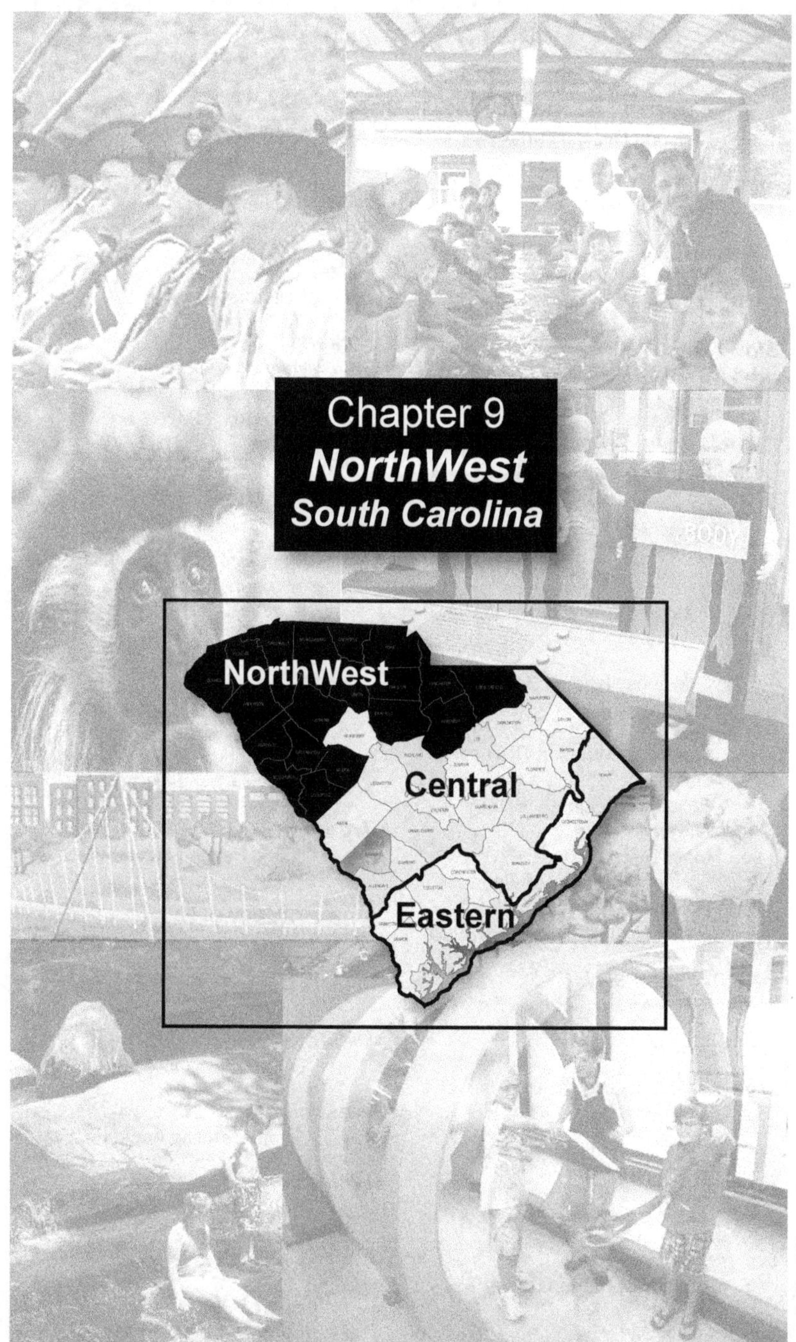
Chapter 9
NorthWest
South Carolina
NorthWest
Central
Eastern
BODY

Anderson
- Split Creek Farm
- Sadlers Creek State Park Rec Area
- Balloons Over Anderson

Blacksburg
- Kings Mountain State Park

Clemson
- '55 Exchange
- Bob Campbell Geology Museum

Cleveland
- Caesars Head State Park / Mountain Bridge Wilderness

Clinton
- Musgrove Mill State Historic Site

Edgefield
- Historic Oakley Park

Enoree
- Stewart Farms Corn Maze

Gaffney
- Cowpens National Battlefield

Greenville
- Children's Museum Of The Upstate
- Falls Park & Liberty Bridge
- Greenville Zoo
- Mast General Store
- Upcountry History Museum
- Greenville Games
- Roper Mountain Holiday Lights

Greenville (Greer)
- Suber Mill

Greenwood
- Emerald Farm

Johnston
- Peach Museum

Lancaster
- Andrew Jackson State Park

Long Creek
- Chattooga Ridge Canopy Tours

McCormick
- Heritage Gold Mine

Ninety Six
- Lake Greenwood Area
- Ninety Six National Historic Site

Pageland
- Watermelon Festival - Pageland

Pelzer
- Fall Farm Festival @ May-Lan

Pickens
- Hagood Mill Historic Site & Folklife Center
- Table Rock State Park

Rock Hill (McConnells)
- Historic Brattonsburg

Seneca
- Duke Energy's World Of Energy
- Tokeena Angus Farm

Spartanburg
- Spartanburg Parks - Cleveland Pk
- Beacon Drive In
- Spartanburg Regional History Museum
- Spartanburg Science Center
- Carolina Panthers Training

Trenton
- Ridge Peach Festival

Union
- Rose Hill Plantation Site

Walhalla
- Oconee Station Historic Site

Wellford
- Hollywild Animal Park

Westminster
- South Carolina Apple Festival

Winnsboro
- South Carolina Railroad Museum

York
- Apple Harvest Festival
- Planetariums

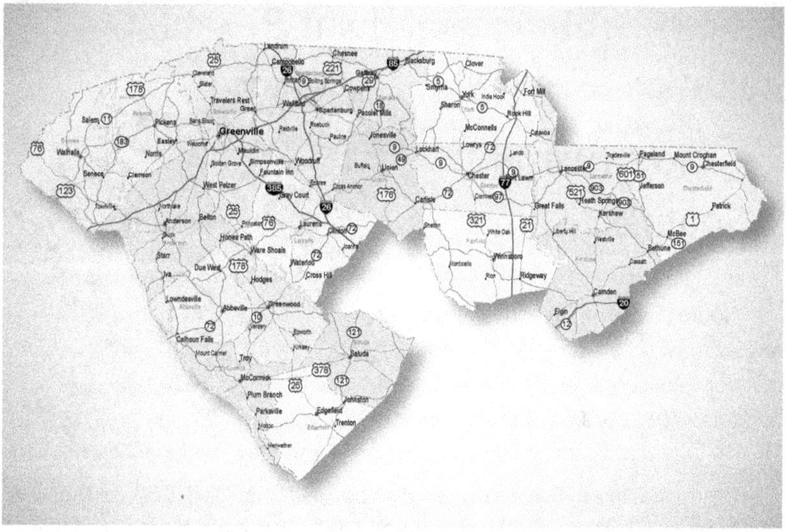

Travel Journal & Notes:

A Quick Tour of our Hand-Picked Favorites Around...

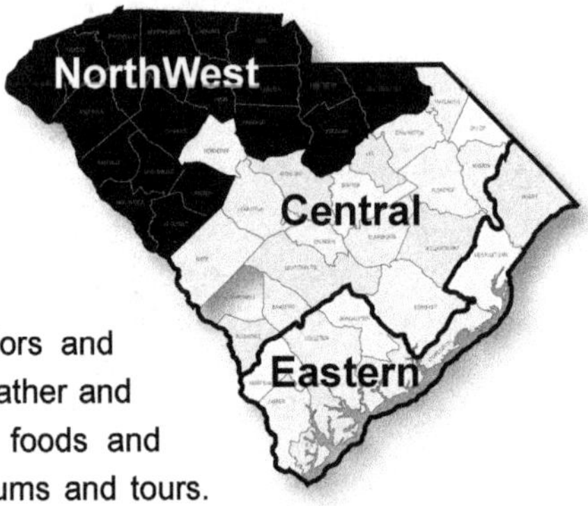

NorthWest South Carolina

South Carolina beacons visitors and residents with its warm, gentle weather and outdoor pleasures to its comfort foods and good-natured guides at fun museums and tours. This Southern belle invites guests to settle in and stay awhile.

From the **War for Independence** and the Civil War to the Civil Rights movement, South Carolina has been at the center of both conflict and resolution throughout America's history. **Battlegrounds** dot the fields of the Upcountry – ones you can visit, dress up and "march" on today.

South Carolina other historical sites including **military sites** along with a range of **historical festivals** and celebrations, reveal fascinating stories you won't find in history books.

Got mountains on your mind? The **Northwest South Carolina foothills** of the Blue Ridge are among the prettiest you'll find for fishing, camping, hiking, rafting, horseback riding...you get the picture.

Whether you're looking for a fun way to spend a rainy afternoon, or just want to have a play date with your children, South Carolina's **children's museums** will help spark a love of learning for your child... and create memories along the way.

South Carolina cuisine has been inspired by their unique cultural heritage, and thus includes European, African, Caribbean and American frontier influences. From South Carolina BBQ to fresh caught mountain trout, food is serious business. They even divide the state by **barbecue** regions... ketchup- and tomato-based prevails in the Upstate.

For those who prefer food and wildlife resources up close and personal, stroll through one of South Carolina's **State Parks** or numerous **Farm Festivals**. With a great climate and long growing season, South Carolina is acclaimed for its mouth-watering **peaches** and huge **watermelons** in summer, juicy mountain-grown apples in fall and vine-fresh berries in spring.

Dreaming of screaming? Then climb aboard a rollercoaster at one of South Carolina's family **amusement parks**. From **Carowinds** and the new "Intimidator" to the thrill of local amusement centers, they've got all the excitement you and the kids can handle!

Millions of travelers drive across South Carolina each year en route to the beach, and for those willing to wait just a minute, there's a lot for them to see and do just off the interstate on their way to Hilton Head, Charleston and Myrtle Beach. Thriving cities full of attractions are in cities like **Greenville**, right off the interstate. History, theme parks, zoos and family friendly farms loaded with produce and fun are just some of the attractions.

Sites and attractions are listed in order by City, Zip Code, and Name. Symbols indicated represent: Restaurants

SPLIT CREEK FARM

Anderson - 3806 Centerville Road 29625. www.splitcreek.com. Phone: (864) 287-3921. Hours: Stores: Monday-Saturday 9:00am-6:00pm, Sunday 2:00-5:00pm. Tours: Since this is a working farm and a great deal of time is spent daily with milking, feeding and processing cheese, visitors are encouraged to schedule a tour for a better look at the farm and how it is operated. Tours cost $5.00 per person and last approximately 1-1/2 to 2 hours. A minimum of ten people is required to schedule a tour. If you do not have that many in your group, they may be able to work you in with another scheduled tour.

The dairy maintains about 350 goats as well as other farm animals. The Grade A Dairy is in a barn designed and built by the owners to include the milking and cheese operations and a kid nursery. A retail gift shop featuring goat milk products and folk art is open to the public. On a tour you will learn about the different breeds of dairy goats and Split Creek's management of the goat herd. An explanation and observation of the farm's guardian dogs and herding dogs will follow. You tour the milking parlor as well. The tour ends with the sampling of the cheeses, fudge and milk produced at the farm and an opportunity to browse through the farm shops. Spring is a popular time of year when the kids (baby goats) are being born. Since this is a real farm, wear clothes and shoes you wouldn't mind getting dirty.

SADLERS CREEK STATE PARK REC AREA

Anderson - 940 Sadlers Creek Road (12 mi SW of town off SC 187 & I-85 exit 14) 29626. http://southcarolinaparks.com/sadlers-creek. (864) 226-8950. Hours: Daily sunrise to sunset. Admission: $1.00-$3.00 per person.

Outdoor water recreation and wildlife observation are popular activities at this 395-acre park that is on a peninsula providing access to Lake Hartwell. The park features a lakeside campground, fishing, picnicking, hiking, and boat access to 56,000-acre lake. Visitors can enjoy viewing glimpses of deer, turkey, and other wildlife.

BALLOONS OVER ANDERSON

Anderson *- 3027 MLK Blvd (Anderson Sports & Entertainment Complex). You will love the show with flying aircrafts by the Fire Tower Flyers remote control airplane club and the Flying Tigers Skydiving Team. Five flights are scheduled and one dedicated tethered balloon will be giving balloon rides all weekend. Two evening glows are planned, Friday and Saturday. Entertain the kids with the Bouncin'Roo inflatables and the Wounded Wolf Bungy Trampoline. Kids can also learn the art of making paper airplanes. FREE. http://balloonsoveranderson.org (first long weekend in November)*

KINGS MOUNTAIN STATE PARK

Blacksburg - 1277 Park Road (I-85 exit 8 onto Hwy 161 across SC/NC state line) 29702. www.southcarolinaparks.com/kings-mountain. Phone: (803) 222-3209. Hours: Daily 8:00am-6:00pm (extended from 7:00am-9:00pm during Daylight Savings Time). Admission: $1.00- $3.00. Tour and Programs Information: Self-guided tours of the Historical Farm are available from 9:00am-5:00pm from Memorial Day through Labor Day and on weekends in April, May, September and October. Weekend living history events. Note: park is adjacent to Kings Mountain National Military Park, site of a pivotal Revolutionary War battle. Camping.

Kings Mountain has miles of trails, equestrian facilities, group camping barracks, campgrounds, two fishing lakes with boat rentals and the popular Living History Farm. The farm is a realistic replica of a typical Piedmont farm from the early to mid 1800s. Buildings include a house, barn and gin, and there are gardens and animals, including cows, chickens and a bunch of friendly cats. Enjoy fishing for bass, bream, crappie and catfish from a rental jon boat in the park's 65-acre Lake York. Private boats are not allowed. Nature Trail: easy 1.2-mile loop trail begins at the picnic area in Kings Mountain State Park and is one the whole family would enjoy. There are various interpretive signs along the trail, which will educate you about the local wildlife, vegetation, and history.

'55 EXCHANGE

Clemson - Hendrix Student Center, Clemson University 29634. Phone: (864) 656-2215. www.clemson.edu/icecream/ Hours: Weekdays 11:30am-6pm. Weekends 1-6pm. Varies on game days. Closed on Academic Holidays. This shop sells Clemson University's famous ice cream, blue cheese and other products. Established in 2005 by a generous gift from Clemson's Class of 1955, the '55 Exchange is a student run enterprise that was created to preserve the Clemson Ice Cream Experience. An exciting feature of the '55 Exchange is the Tiger Slab, where customers create their own unique ice cream flavor using traditional Clemson Ice Cream and an assortment of special mix-ins.

BOB CAMPBELL GEOLOGY MUSEUM

Clemson - 103 Garden Trail (Clemson Univ campus, SC Botanical Garden) 29634. Phone: (864) 656-4600. www.clemson.edu/public/geomuseum Hours: Daily 10am-5pm. Closed University holidays. Admission: FREE. Donations suggested .

The museum houses an impressive variety of minerals and gems including one of the largest faceted gem collections in the southeast. Fossils, meteorites, and terrestrial rocks are also on display. A large walk-in darkroom showcases minerals that fluoresce under ultraviolet light. The life-size 'smilodon,' a saber-tooth cat skeleton, is the only one of its kind in the southeast.

CAESARS HEAD STATE PARK / MOUNTAIN BRIDGE WILDERNESS

Cleveland - 8155 Geer Hwy (US 276 access, just over NC/SC state line) 29635. Phone: (864) 836-6115. www.southcarolinaparks.com/caesars-head. Hours: Daily 9:00am-6:00pm (extended to 9pm during daylight savings time). Admission: Trail access fee: $1-$3.00 per person (age 16+).

Set against the Blue Ridge outcrops, this park offers breathtaking views year-round, especially when fall sets the hardwoods ablaze (late October, early November). At 3,208 feet above sea level, Caesars Head provides a panoramic view of the mountain country. Hiking trails ranging from easy to challenging circle and traverse Caesars Head and adjoining Jones Gap state parks, which together form the Mountain Bridge Wilderness. One of the most popular trails (moderate, 2-mile trail) leads to 420-foot Raven Cliff Falls, where a suspension bridge offers one of the two publicly accessible overlooks to the falls as they splash deep into the mountain cove below. Picnicking and wilderness trailside camping available. The park also leads to some prime trout fishing areas in the state-designated scenic Middle Saluda River.

HAWK WATCH

Cleveland - Caesars Head State Park. Each fall, timed to allow visitors to marvel at the unforgettable sight of hundreds of soaring, swirling migrating raptors – hawks, kites, falcons, eagles and more – from the park visitors' perch at 3,200 feet above sea level.

MUSGROVE MILL STATE HISTORIC SITE

Clinton - 398 State Park Road (I-385 to I-26E to exit 52 for Hwy 56 Clinton for 6 miles) 29325. www.southcarolinaparks.com/musgrove-mill. Phone: (864) 938-0100. Hours: Daily 9:00am-6:00pm. Admission: $1.00-$3.00 (ages 6+).

In the summer of 1780 a group of roughly 300 loyalist partisans and 200 British Provincials set up camp at the home of Edward Musgrove on the Enoree River. Retreat was impossible, a frontal assault suicidal. So the Patriot forces took a strong defensive position and lured the Loyalists into a fierce fight that turned into a near rout after the British attack collapsed.

The park's visitor center is filled with interpretive exhibits which focus on the Battle of Musgrove Mill. The park's nature trail highlights Horseshoe Falls, where legend has it Mary Musgrove, the mill owner's daughter, hid a Patriot soldier from the British. The park also offers picnicking and a popular fishing pond. Scenic Horseshoe Falls is a small, but beautiful waterfall easily accessible by an ADA walkway and scenic overlook. The site also maintains a canoe and kayak launch on the Enoree River. Musgrove Mill has nearly 2.5 miles of interpretive trails, including a 1.2 mile trail through the battlefield north of the Enoree River that marks where much of the fighting took place.

HISTORIC OAKLEY PARK

Edgefield - 300 Columbia Road (off US 25) 29824. Phone: (803) 637-4027. http://south-carolina-plantations.com/edgefield/oakley-park.html. Hours: Thursday-Saturday 10:00am-4:00pm. Admission: $3.00- $5.00 students and adults.

Named for the oak trees on the land, Historic Oakley Park was built in 1835 by Daniel Byrd, a Virginian who came to Edgefield and became a very successful cotton planter. The beautiful mansion later was the home of Gen. Martin Witherspoon Gary, a fiery Confederate politician and father of the Red Shirt movement that assured the election of Wade Hampton as governor in 1876.

WILD TURKEY CENTER

Edgefield - 770 Augusta Road, along Hwy 25 29824. Phone: (803) 637-7626. www.nwtf.org/about/hunting-heritage-center/wild-turkey-center. Hours: Monday-Friday 9am-4:30pm, closed summer Fridays. Admission: $5.00 adult, $2.00 child. Purchase comes with 4 Laser Shot coins. Note: Take them outside on a series of nature trails past streams, ponds, and of course, turkeys.

A gobbling good time is had by all in the little town of Edgefield - home to the National Wild Turkey Federation. Their museum is all about the natural and cultural history of America's favorite game bird - the wild turkey. Interactive exhibits include an actual helicopter where visitors can sit inside and watch a fascinating, lifelike video through the cockpit windows of a vivid prescribed forest "burn" used to keep a suitable habitat for creatures and flora alike. An animated, life-like, old-time storyteller sits in a rocking chair and tells stories about the history of the NWTF, turkey hunting and conservation. Also featured is an animated Cherokee Indian, who shares legends and stories about wild turkeys. Can you make a good turkey call?

STEWART FARMS CORN MAZE

Enoree *- 6600 SC 92. It's geared to ages 7 and up and offers the chance to work on your sense of direction. Just remember: Getting lost is part of the fun. A visit includes information on how farmers create the maze, a passport to help you navigate the paths and a stroll through corn stalks. It's open from Friday evenings, 10:00am-10:00pm Saturdays and 2:00-8:00pm Sundays. Stewart Farms also features a pick-your-own pumpkin patch (opening Sept. 18) and wagon rides for the whole family. www.stewartfarms.net. Admission. (Starts late September and running through Halloween)*

COWPENS NATIONAL BATTLEFIELD

Gaffney - 4001 Chesnee Highway 29341. www.nps.gov/cowp/index.htm. Phone: (864) 461-2828. Hours: Daily 9:00am-5:00pm. Closed Thanksgiving, Christmas and New Year's Day. Admission: FREE. Educators: www.nps.gov/cowp/learn/education/otherresources.htm covers the War of Independence.

Famous for the January 17, 1781, battle where Daniel Morgan led his outnumbered troops against British troops, Cowpens offers interpretive facilities, a visitors center with exhibits, a tour road and a walking trail through the battlefield. Each year on the weekend closest to January 17, the park celebrates the anniversary of the battle with firing demonstrations and a living history encampment. About once a month they hold family activities at the Scruggs House. Start your visit in the Visitors Center watching the 18-minute show titled: "Cowpens: A Battle Remembered".

The Battle of Cowpens, fought by the Americans and British on January 17, 1781, lasted less than an hour.

Another visual is the fiber-optic Map illustrating the Southern Campaign of the American Revolution and the battle tactics employed by Daniel Morgan. There's another area where kids can pretend play "battles" using figures and landscapes. Finally, be sure to get the walking or auto route maps before you depart out onto the battlefield.

CHILDREN'S MUSEUM OF THE UPSTATE

Greenville - 300 College Street (Heritage Green, downtown) 29601. Phone: (864) 233-7755. www.tcmupstate.org. Hours: Tues-Sat 9am-5pm, Sunday 11am- 5pm. Admission: $10 adult, $9 child (ages 1-15).

This children's museum is like many in the state - they sneak in areas of surprise around each corner. How about starting in a Garage where you rock. Next, become an anchor on WTCM studios, blast off into space, shop at the market, analyze x-rays, dig and build, or play with lasers. The wonders of water play are around the Reedy River Bend for the big kids (Lily Pond for the toddlers). Grandma Betty's Farm is another area of pretend play - but just for preschoolers and babies.

FALLS PARK & LIBERTY BRIDGE

Greenville - 206 S Main Street, downtown (enter park at Main St & West Camperdown Way or East Camperdown & Falls St) 29601. www.fallspark.com. Hours: Open daily 7:00am-9:00pm. FREEBIES: Pick up a copy of the Falls Park activity book during your visit (one per family) or download www.greenvillesc.gov/DocumentCenter/View/10457/Falls-Park-Guide-and-Activity-Book?bidId=.

This downtown property feels like a slice of the country. The spotlight: Liberty Bridge. a 355-foot long, 12-foot wide pedestrian bridge with a concrete reinforced deck supported by a single suspension cable. It spans the Reedy River in Greenville, overlooking the waterfall and gardens at Falls Park. Take a walk over it. Your family might feel as if they are floating over the park.

Bring a picnic basket and enjoy a meal on the grounds or at the park picnic shelter. Visitors may also choose to eat in one of the park's two restaurants: Mary's Restaurant at Falls Cottage and Passerelle Bistro. Each season brings different events: from Duck races to a Chautauqua.

GREENVILLE ZOO

Greenville - 150 Cleveland Park Drive (I-385 exit 42. E Washington St.) 29601. Phone: (864) 467-4300. www.greenvillezoo.com. Hours: Daily 10:00am-4:30pm. Closed Thanksgiving, Christmas and New Years. Admission: $9.75 adult, $6.50 child (3-15). Note: Concession stand. Safari gift shop. The Swamp Rabbit Trail connects downtown Greenville, Furman Univ & Travelers Rest to the Zoo.

The Greenville Zoo is a 14-acre facility featuring hundreds of wildlife from all over the world including giraffe, monkeys, giant tortoises and elephants. They're monkeying around here. Two colobus monkeys are residents here - and they're fun to watch. Or, check out one of its newest residents, a young red panda named Firecracker. His future mate - Scarlett. And because the zoo is really into "coupling", look for Mojo the male brown-headed spider monkey to be a companion for Jasmin, a female.

MAST GENERAL STORE

Greenville - 111 N Main Street 29601. www.mastgeneralstore.com. Phone: (864) 235-1883. Hours: Monday -Saturday 10:00am-6:00pm (open until 9:00pm on Friday/Saturday), Sunday Noon-6:00pm.

Like nostalgia? Looking for items that bring back memories of your childhood... or your parent's childhood? In operation since 1883, the Mast Store has not changed all that much - it still offers the down-home feeling associated with a country general store. Take a stroll through Mast General Store for a walk down memory lane. Remember Teaberry Gum (tastes a little like mint Pepto Bismol) or Dick and Jane readers, Moon Pies, little wax bottle candy or red wagons? There are plenty of gadgets and toys to view and purchase and they don't require batteries. You'd be surprised how much your kids are amused by toys that never go out of style.

UPCOUNTRY HISTORY MUSEUM

Greenville - 540 Buncombe Street 29601. www.upcountryhistory.org. Phone: (864) 467-3100. Hours: Tuesday-Saturday 10:00am-5:00pm; Sunday 1:00-5:00pm. Admission: $3800- $10.00 per person (age 5+). FREEBIES: Scavenger hunts are available at the admission desk to help reinforce what students learn on their "walk through time". Check out their Homeschool Fridays.

Experience three centuries of Upcountry South Carolina history through state-of-the-art interactive touchscreen and motion-activated exhibits at the Upcountry History Museum. Their theme: Common Threads. Uncommon Stories. 19th century to today. Go on a mini "dig" to discover artifacts from the Cherokee and Catawba Indian tribes. Learn what needs Civil War soldiers had while they were at war and how groups of ladies at home helped to fill those needs. And finally, how did sharecroppers and mill workers create a textile industry boom in Upcountry South Carolina?

ROPER MOUNTAIN SCIENCE CENTER

Greenville - 402 Roper Mountain Road (off I-385) 29615. Phone: (864) 355-8900. RoperMountain.org. Roper Mountain Science Center is only open to the public for select events throughout the year, including Friday Starry Nights and Second Saturdays. Outdoor facilities including the nature trails and arboretum are open to the public Monday – Friday from 9 a.m. to 5 p.m. during the school year.

Families can attend numerous events throughout the year including Friday Starry Nights, Second Saturdays and the ever-popular Butterfly Adventure. Generally admission is between $5.00-$6.00 per activity.

GREENVILLE SCOTTISH GAMES

Greenville - The Upstate of South Carolina is home to one of the highest concentrations of Scots-Irish descendants in the country. The Greenville Games pay tribute to the Highlands of Scotland, featuring pipe bands, athletic competitions, crafts, border collie demos and dancing. Children have their own mini Scottish village. At Wee Scotland, the kids get their own crafts, athletic events, and "mountains" to climb. The Friday evening parade and music takes place in downtown Greenville. The all-day Saturday event is on the Furman Univ campus. gallabrae.com. (Memorial Day wkend)

SUBER MILL

Greenville (Greer) - 2002 Suber Mill Road 29650. Phone: (864) 877-5616. www.scmills.com/subers.php. Hours: Monday-Friday 8:00am-5:00pm.

The mill, built circa 1908, still grinds corn using water power. Suber's Corn Mill is just one of a handful of grist mills still operating in South Carolina. Suber's rests on the slope of a hardwoods-covered hill in the Upcountry. Watch water from a holding pond above pours down a wooden chute and spills onto the paddles of a large vertical wheel, keeping it in a steady, rhythmic spin. Shelled corn is fed into a chute on top and gravity sends it tumbling to the crushing millstones below. One floor down, the fine white powder emerges where it is bagged and stacked for sale. Stop by and see the mill at work and buy a bag of freshly ground corn meal.

EMERALD FARM

Greenwood - 409 Emerald Farm Road 29646. www.emeraldfarm.com. Phone: (864) 223-2247. Hours: Visits welcome Monday-Saturday 9:00am-5:00pm. Train tours: Only $2.75 for an individual. Second ride at reduced rates. Ride Weekdays by appointment only & all day Saturdays. Guided Tours by appointment.

The Zahn family love growing natural foods and products and are more than willing to share their stories of organic farming on tours. The Emerald Express runs around the farm with authentic RR signs, the Village, tunnels, and more. Feed the fish and buy the healthy goat soap products at the natural food store. Alternative foods are available for those with diabetes, lactose intolerance, and those with allergies to products such as wheat or corn. Ever had goat milk? Their fresh milk is the product of Saanen goats from Switzerland; first bred hundreds of years ago to produce the finest milk for drinking and making cheese. This nutritious milk is collected at the farm for use in their soap making operations. You can view/tour the soap factory and the forming, molding and drying stages of soap production. Before you leave, shop in the depot store full of hobby toys.

PEACH MUSEUM

Johnston - 416 Calhoun Street (inside the Edgefield County Chamber of Commerce bldg) 29832. www.villageprofile.com/southcarolina/edgefield/03/topic.html. Phone: (803) 275-0010. Note: Just for kids page of coloring sheets and kid-friendly recipes: www.scpeach.com/kids.htm. Enjoy the Johnston Peach Blossom Festival the first weekend in May.

Johnston and Edgefield County have been central to the peach industry's development in South Carolina and throughout the region. Once dominated by the Piedmont region, peach production has shifted to the Ridge area of the state – Saluda, Edgefield and Aiken counties. Nearly all the commercial peaches are freestone varieties grown for the fresh market.

The exhibits present the history of the peach, pioneers of the industry, and peach production of yesterday and today. Learn why South Carolina is "The Tastier Peach State." See displays on how peaches are cleaned, sized and boxed for sale.

While visiting, you can purchase real peach preserves. During the peach growing season, from the blooming of the trees to the picking of peaches (March - August), you can head out into Edgefield's spectacular countryside to visit a myriad of colorful roadside peach and vegetable stands.

ANDREW JACKSON STATE PARK

Lancaster - 196 Andrew Jackson Park (I-77 north exit Hwy 9E toward Richburg) 29720. www.southcarolinaparks.com/andrewjackson/introduction.aspx. Phone: (803) 285-3344. Hours: Park open daily 8:00am-6:00pm. Museum open weekend afternoons only 1:00-5:00pm. Schoolhouse open many weekends spring thru fall. Admission: $1.00 - $3.00 (age 16+).

The only park in the system dedicated to a U.S. president, Andrew Jackson State Park features a museum that details the boyhood of the nation's seventh president, who grew up here in what then was known as the Waxhaws of the South Carolina backcountry. The museum tells the story of Jackson's boyhood experiences during the Revolutionary War and highlights life in the South Carolina backcountry from Andrew Jackson's birth in 1767 until he left South Carolina in 1784.

The park also has a replica of a late 18th-century one-room schoolhouse, an amphitheatre that serves as home to a well-attended bluegrass festival, as well as a campground, fishing lake, picnicking facilities and trails.

CHATTOOGA RIDGE CANOPY TOURS

Long Creek - 1251 Academy Road 29658. www.chattoogaridgecanopytours.com. Phone: (864) 647-9587. Note: this company is part of Wildwater Ltd. Rafting adventures whitewater, canoeing and kayaking excursions.

Located on the Historic Long Creek Academy campus, this 3 hour tour takes you on a flight through the trees to experience the exhilaration of soaring with a birds eye view of native trees, wildflowers, historic buildings and 4 crossings over Academy Lake. Ten zip lines and 4 "sky bridges" included in the tour with 2 "Canopy Rangers" to share stories & monitor safety. Flyers must be at least 10 years old and between 70 and 250 lbs. Don't worry, moms, this is really safe and fun - even for the "less flexible." Rates: $89 per person. Flights several times/day.

HERITAGE GOLD MINE

McCormick - Dorn Mine, just head into town, signs and townspeople will direct you 29835. Phone: (864) 852-2835 (visitors center). www.heritagegoldmine.com. Hours: 9:30am-4:30pm, 2nd and 4th Saturdays, May through October plus Spring Bonanza (mid-April) and Gold Rush Day (mid-September). Mine Tour: $3.00, under 5 free. Gold ore: $5.00 per 1 gallon bucket. Gemstones: $5.00 per 1 gallon bucket. Cash or check only.

Area resident William B. Dorn discovered gold here and developed this mine which produced a yield of $72,000 from 1857 to 1859. The mine was later owned by Cyrus Hall McCormick, inventor of the reaper, for whom the town of McCormick is named. The mine operated at intervals until as late as the 1930s. Today you can tour the mine and pan for gold. Original features of the 1850's mine include the open trench, several pits and vertical shafts, dewatering piping, and a horizontal tunnel. After your guided or self-guided tour, pan for gold or screen for gemstones and keep what you find. Celebrate your finds with an ice cream at Strom's Drug Store in downtown McCormick.

LAKE GREENWOOD STATE RECREATION AREA (THE DRUMMOND CENTER)

Ninety Six - 302 State Park Road (I-26 exit 74 to Hwy 34 towards Newberry) 29666. www.southcarolinaparks.com/park-finder/state-park/926.aspx. Phone: (864) 543-3535. Hours: Museum open 9:00am-5:00pm (extended to 8:00pm during daylight savings time). Admission: $1.00- $3.00 (age16+).

The park occupies a series of peninsulas on Lake Greenwood, which itself offers 212 miles of shoreline and 11,400 acres of boating and fishing opportunities year-round. The Civilian Conservation Corps Museum is home to an extensive set of interactive exhibits describing the life and times of the men of the CCC who built this park and 16 others across South Carolina during the 1930s. Amenities: Camping and hiking lakeside.

NINETY SIX NATIONAL HISTORIC SITE

Ninety Six - 1103 Highway 248 29666. Phone: (864) 543-4068. www.nps.gov/nisi. Hours: Grounds daily, dawn to dusk; Visitor Center 9:00am-5:00pm. Admission: FREE, donations accepted. Educators: The American Revolution Teachers Guide: www.nps.gov/revwar/educational_resources/teachers.html.

This is an actual battle site. Here settlers struggled against the harsh backcountry to survive, Cherokee Indians hunted and fought to keep their land, two towns and a trading post were formed and abandoned to the elements, and two Revolutionary War battles that claimed over 100 lives took place here. The site features a visitor center, interpretive trail, periodic archaeological digs and insightful restorations. Ninety Six National Historic Site saw the first land battle of the Revolution in the South November 19-21, 1775, when Maj. Andrew Williamson's force of Patriots was besieged by Loyalists. In 1780 Ninety Six fell into the hands of the British, who fortified the town extensively and made it one of their major outposts. From May 22-June 19, 1781, the Loyalist garrison held out against Gen. Nathanael Greene's entire force of Continentals, until Lord Rawdon marched with 2,000 British troops to the relief of the post. Ninety Six is one of the best preserved battle sites of the Revolution: the Star Redoubt has survived intact for 200 years, and archeologists have uncovered the remains of other parts of the fortifications.

WATERMELON FESTIVAL - PAGELAND

Pageland - Downtown on Pearl Street. www.facebook.com/pagelandchamber.org. Pageland is known as the Watermelon Capital of the World. See one of the largest parades on Saturday morning. Savor the delicious variety of foods as the beautiful wares of the crafters lure you. Children's Stage located in Moore's Park. And don't forget the old fashion seed spittin' and watermelon eatin' contests for all ages. classic car show and admire the talents displayed at the festival rodeo. Then gather to enjoy music and entertainment of live bands. (mid-July weekend).

FALL FARM FESTIVAL @ MAY-LAN TREE PLANTATION

Pelzer - 156 Cooley Bridge Road. Come take a hayride tour through the land of the broomhead and pumpkin people, navigate a maze, visit our barnyard buddies and more! Prepare for your fall decorating by purchasing pumpkins, gourds, squash and May-Lan grown mums. Activities are for families with children 2nd grade and below. Phone: (864) 243-3092. Admission. http://maylanfarms.com (month of October)

HAGOOD MILL HISTORIC SITE & FOLKLIFE CENTER

NorthWest

Pickens - 138 Hagood Mill Road 29671. www.facebook.com/hagoodmill. Phone: (864) 898-2936. Hours: Wednesday-Saturday from 10:00am-4:00pm to tour the grounds and to pick up those "mill products."

This restored 1845 grist mill is listed on the National Register of Historic Places and is the only mill in SC grinding with original wheel components. The site includes a reproduced Cherokee home site, blacksmith shop, 1791 Murphree cabin, 1830s Hagood cabin and more. The mill is open during daylight hours to picnic and hike and the third Saturday every month for folklife festivals with demonstrations, living history and musical entertainment. These monthly "corn grinding" days became mini-festivals of traditional arts, folklife and music. .

TABLE ROCK STATE PARK

Pickens - 158 E Ellison Lane (near SC 11) 29671. Phone: (864) 878-9813. www.southcarolinaparks.com/table-rock. Hours: Daily 7:00am -9:00pm. Winter hours slightly shorter. Admission: $1.00-$3.00 per person (age 16+).

Table Rock Mountain provides a towering backdrop for an upcountry retreat at the edge of the Blue Ridge Mountains. This is also where the visitors center serves as a regional headquarters for sightseers – and Caesars Head, the latter offering a panoramic view from 3,000 feet above sea level. For a real-time look at what's happening on the Blue Ridge, there's also the Web cam at Table Rock, a site to see in the fall and even in the winter when snow-starved lowlanders enjoy taking a rare peek at the white stuff in South Carolina. Table Rock State Park features two lakes, a campground, mountain cabins, meeting facilities and its historic, renovated lodge.

HISTORIC BRATTONSBURG

Rock Hill (McConnells) - 1444 Brattonsville Road (I-77 exit 73. SR 901N to SR 322W to SR 165) 29726. Phone: (803) 684-2327. www.chmuseums.org/brattonsville. Hours: Monday-Saturday 10:00am-5:00pm. Sunday 1:00-5:00pm. Admission: $8.00 adult, $7.00 senior (60+), $5.00 youth (4-17). FREEBIES: Scavenger Hunt of Brattonsburg: http://myupkeep.com/chmuseums/kids_and_families/files/Scavenger_Hunt_for_Brattonsville.pdf. Note: Living History Saturdays are best for family visits.

Historic Brattonsville has flourished to become one of the largest restoration and living history sites in the Southeast. The 775-acre Revolutionary War battlefield site features 29 historic structures and programs chronicling Carolina Piedmont development from the 1750s through the 1840s. Its focus includes the African American story. Explore a log cabin, visit the vegetable garden, and join in games of the 1700s. The self-guided walking tour at Historic Brattonsville is often complemented by the presence of costumed interpreters demonstrating historical skills such as cooking, farming, gardening and woodworking and every Saturday features Living History with a variety of changing activities. Several buildings at Historic Brattonsville were used in filming the Revolutionary War epic "The Patriot" in 2000. Also available: hiking, bicycling and horseback riding trails.

DUKE ENERGY'S WORLD OF ENERGY

Seneca - 7812 Rochester Hwy (Oconee Nuclear Station) 29672. Phone: (800) 777-1004. www.duke-energy.com/worldofenergy. Hours: Monday-Friday 9:00am-5:00pm. Closed on holidays. Admission: FREE.

Great, you made it to the beginning of the Story of Energy! To begin your tour, touch the hand print on the wall to your left.
Please watch your step and stay alert on your journ

Discover how electricity is generated using water, coal and uranium by journeying through a self-guided tour and by playing hands-on computer games. The self-guided tour lets you explore at your own pace; it takes 30 to 45 minutes to complete. Watch waterways, push buttons to turn coal into a source of energy, and finally, step into a fission chamber to learn how energy is made from tiny particles called atoms. Afterwards, children can enjoy testing what they learned on their video games. Children also enjoy observing the fish in several indoor ponds and aquariums. The facility is located on the beautiful shores of Lake Keowee - the lake is a source of hydroelectric power. Outside, you can walk the garden trail (look for butterflies), fish from the dock, or have a picnic.

TOKEENA ANGUS FARM

Seneca - 320 Coyote Lane 29678. Phone: (864) 247-7843. www.tokeena.com.

Tokeena Angus Farm is home of an historic angus herd. There are several buildings on the grounds that date back to the turn of the century as well as a display of family farming artifacts from the early 1900's through the Great Depression. Tours of a working farming operation are welcome to visit and see what goes into the production of all natural, forage fed beef. Beef is available for sale on the farm. Call ahead to schedule a visit or tour of the farm.

SPARTANBURG PARKS - CLEVELAND PARK

Spartanburg - 121 N Cleveland Park Drive. 29303. https://sc-spartanburgcountyparksandrec.civicplus.com/Facilities/Facility/Details/Cleveland-Park-169

Cleveland Park offers the finest in leisure amenities, including Picnic Shelters, a lakeside Promenade and Amphitheater, an Island Gazebo, spacious playground, and walking trails. Cleveland Park is home to 2 miniature trains named Sparky and Sparkles. The trains are open to riders of all ages from April through October on the following schedule: Friday and Saturday 10:00am-

5:00pm and Sunday from 1:00pm-5:00pm. Tickets are $1.00/rider.

BEACON DRIVE-IN

Spartanburg - 255 John B. White, Sr. Boulevard 29306. Phone: (864) 585-9387. www.beacondrivein.com

While you're in Spartanburg, don't pass up a chance to visit the world-famous Beacon Drive-In. It's a Southern landmark and home of the world-famous Beacon iced tea, chili cheese-a-plenty, sliced pork-a-plenty, onion rings and The Pig's Dinner. Famous for the Chili Cheese A-Plenty, a chili cheeseburger on a bun buried on a plate underneath piles of sweet onion rings and French fried potatoes and the great drive-in tea of the South – generously sweetened, laced with a touch of lemon, served over a pack of shaved ice. They sell more tea than any other single restaurant in the U.S.A.! Bring a big appetite because when they say "a-plenty" they mean lots - your meal is topped with a mound of fries and onion rings. The Beacon's been around since 1946 and is open six days a week at 6:30am-10:00pm, Sunday 11am-8pm. It serves a million customers a year, all a-plenty.

SPARTANBURG REGIONAL HISTORY MUSEUM

Spartanburg - 200 East St. John Street, Chapman Cultural Center 29306. Phone: (864) 596-3501. www.visitspartanburg.com/directory/spartanburg-regional-history-museum-112/ Hours: Tues-Sat 10am-5pm, Sunday 1-5pm. Adm: FREE

Permanent exhibits at the Museum offer a walk through time from the early days of Spanish explorers like Juan Pardo to the late 20th century. Other permanent exhibits focus on the broad military history of Spartanburg County from the fight for American Independence to the training camps located here during World Wars I & II. Camps Wadsworth and Croft and the men who trained there left an indelible mark on Spartanburg. To satisfy curious minds and active hands, Spartanburg By the Numbers and Spartanburg Firsts offer details about our history behind small doors just waiting to be opened. There is also plenty to see in the Where People Meet exhibit, where you can glimpse the leisure activities of Spartans for the last 100 years or so.

SPARTANBURG SCIENCE CENTER

Spartanburg - 200 East St. John Street, Cultural Center 29306. Phone: (864) 583 2777. www.spartanburgsciencecenter.org. Hours: Thursday-Saturday 10:00am-5:00pm. Sunday 1-5pm. Admission: $5.00 (age 5+).

The Science Center's permanent collections include exhibits and resource material on many science topics such as rocks and minerals, fossils, electricity, astronomy, insects, live reptiles, health resources, animals, and the human body. You can even hold a baby snake.

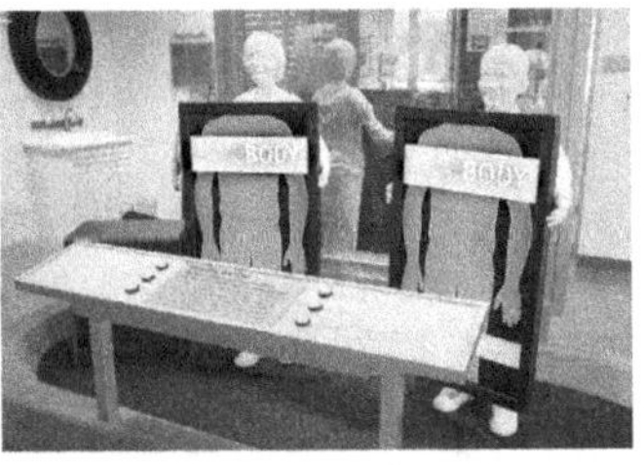

CAROLINA PANTHERS TRAINING CAMP

Spartanburg - 429 N Church Street, Wofford College, Richardson Physical Activities Building & Gibbs Stadium (I-85 exit 72). Phone: (800) 374-8326. www.panthers.com/schedule/training-camp.html.

The Carolina Panthers training camp home is Wofford College in Spartanburg, SC, where the team has prepared for the upcoming season each summer since its inaugural campaign in 1995. Special events planned each year in conjunction with the arrival of camp. All training camp practices are free and open to the public with each practice session lasting between 90 minutes and two hours. (late July - mid August)

RIDGE PEACH FESTIVAL

Trenton - 106 Church Street (I-20 exit 5 north). Smack in the middle of South Carolina peach country, this family festival includes arts and crafts, antiques, homemade peach desserts and preserves, peach ice cream, live music all day, children's areas, food vendors, a street dance and live music. www.ridgepeachfestival.com. FREE (third Saturday in June)

ROSE HILL PLANTATION HISTORIC SITE

Union - 2677 Sardis Road (I-26 exit 44 onto Hwy 49 toward Union. 29379. Phone: (864) 427-5966. www.southcarolinaparks.com/park-finder/state-park/540.aspx. Hours: Grounds open daily from 9:00am-6:00pm. Admission: Grounds are FREE. Tours: and Programs Information: Historic house museum tours focus on plantation life from 1828-1960. Held daily at 1:00pm, 2:00pm and 3:00pm. House tours are $5.00-$10.00 per person (age 6+).

In the days following the election of President Abraham Lincoln, South Carolina Gov. William H. Gist was characteristically blunt: "The only alternative left, in my judgment, is the secession of South Carolina from the Federal Union." Today, Rose Hill Plantation State Historic Site interprets the life and legacy of the man history has come to know as the "Secession Governor." The Nature Trail runs through the park extending to the Tyger River.

CHRISTMAS AT ROSE HILL

Union - Rose Hill Plantation State Historic Site. Come and view Rose Hill Plantation as it might have been in the Antebellum era. Interpreters in period walk visitors through the mansion, and explain a real Antebellum Christmas. The Mansion is decorated for the holidays throughout the month of December. Admission.

OCONEE STATION STATE HISTORIC SITE

Walhalla - 500 Oconee Station Road (I-85 north exit 1 - just off SC 11 - Cherokee Foothills Nat'l Scenic Hwy) 29691. www.southcarolinaparks.com/oconee Phone: (864) 638-0079. Hours: Grounds open daily 9:00am-6:00pm except weekends only in winter. Admission: FREE. Tours: The Station House and Richards House are open for tours on Saturday & Sunday from 1:00pm-5:00pm. Note: Nearby in Mountain Rest is OCONEE STATE PARK & CABINS for a mountain retreat.

In the late 18th and early 19th century, a small plot of land along South Carolina's western frontier served as a military compound against attack from the Cherokees and later a trading post. Oconee Station is a stone blockhouse used as an outpost by the U.S. military from about 1792 to 1799, and the William Richards House, named for the Irish immigrant who built it, was a trading post in 1805. What was it like to fear the Cherokee attack? Beyond the park's historic significance, there's a fishing pond and 1.5-mile nature trail, the latter connecting to a half-mile trail that leads into Sumter National Forest and ends at Station Cove Falls, a 60-foot waterfall that's considered one of the prettiest in the state.

- OCONEE HERITAGE CENTER: 123 Brown Square Drive. Visitors explore the history of Native Americans, Immigration, Railroads, New Deal Programs, Textile Mills, Agriculture as it relates to Oconee County. The museum offers a self-guided tour through time. Popular exhibits include the Dugout Canoes, a walk-in Stump House Tunnel exhibit and a Depression Era Tenant Farmer's House. www.oconeeheritagecenter.org. Open Tuesday, Thursday, Friday Noon-5pm and Saturday 10am-3pm.

HOLLYWILD ANIMAL PARK

Wellford - 2325 Hampton Road 29385. www.hollywild.com. Phone: (864) 472-2038. Hours: Daily 10:00am-5:00pm (April-September). Weekends only (October-March). Admission: $8.00- $12.00 per person (age 2+).

Take an Outback Safari Ride through 70+ acres of free roaming animals. Try to spot the hidden babies in the woods while being surrounded by dozens of animals, many which will eat right out of your hand. These animals include: Fallow, Sika and White Tail Deer, Zebras, Bison, Watusi Cattle, Scottish Highlanders, Donkeys, Emus... and more. Don't forget your camera. While on

Safari, be sure to look for "Tank" Hollywild's famous Rhino… you'll recognize him from the ZICAM commercials. Because this is a "feeding" zoo, the animals eat and waste almost anywhere so wear old clothes and come prepared to have some animals become greedy. Use your feed sparingly or you'll run out quickly.

HOLIDAY LIGHTS SAFARI

Wellford - Hollywild Animal Park. Drive through nearly 100 acres, magically decorated with hundreds of thousands of twinkling lights, dazzling holiday themes, light sculptures, tunnels of lights, plus herds of live animals. A visit to the Enchanted Deer Forest is included in the admission. Coupon for animal food is available on the website. Admission.

SOUTH CAROLINA APPLE FESTIVAL

Westminster - Along historic Old Main Street. No trip to the mountains is complete without a stop at a roadside stand for a bag to take home (plus a few extra to carry along on a hike or eat on the ride home). Featuring all-things-apples (including an apple baking contest), along with crafts, music, a parade and a championship rodeo. www.scapplefestival.com (begins the week after Labor Day in September)

SOUTH CAROLINA RAILROAD MUSEUM

Winnsboro - 110 Industrial Park Road (I-26 exit 74. corner of SC Hwy 34 and Industrial Park Rd-where US 321 meets) 29180. www.scrm.org. Phone: (803) 635-9893. Tours: vary by regular and special event. Generally weekends. Advanced reservations recommended.

A popular museum established 28 years ago that offers visitors rides on the Rockton & Rion Railway. There is a small museum on the property. 10 mile round trip.

TRAIN RIDE WITH SANTA

Winnsboro - South Carolina Railroad Museum. Ride the train with Santa! The train ride is a 10 mile round trip on the Museum's railroad lasting about 1 hour and 15 minutes.

APPLE HARVEST FESTIVAL

York - Windy Hill Orchard, 1860 Black Highway. In rural York County, apple lovers delight in this seasonal South Carolina festival. Patrons partake in apple picking, hay rides, cider making, pumpkin picking, apple peeling contests, Johnny Appleseed stories and delicious baked apple goods. www.windyhillorchard.com. (mid-October Saturday)

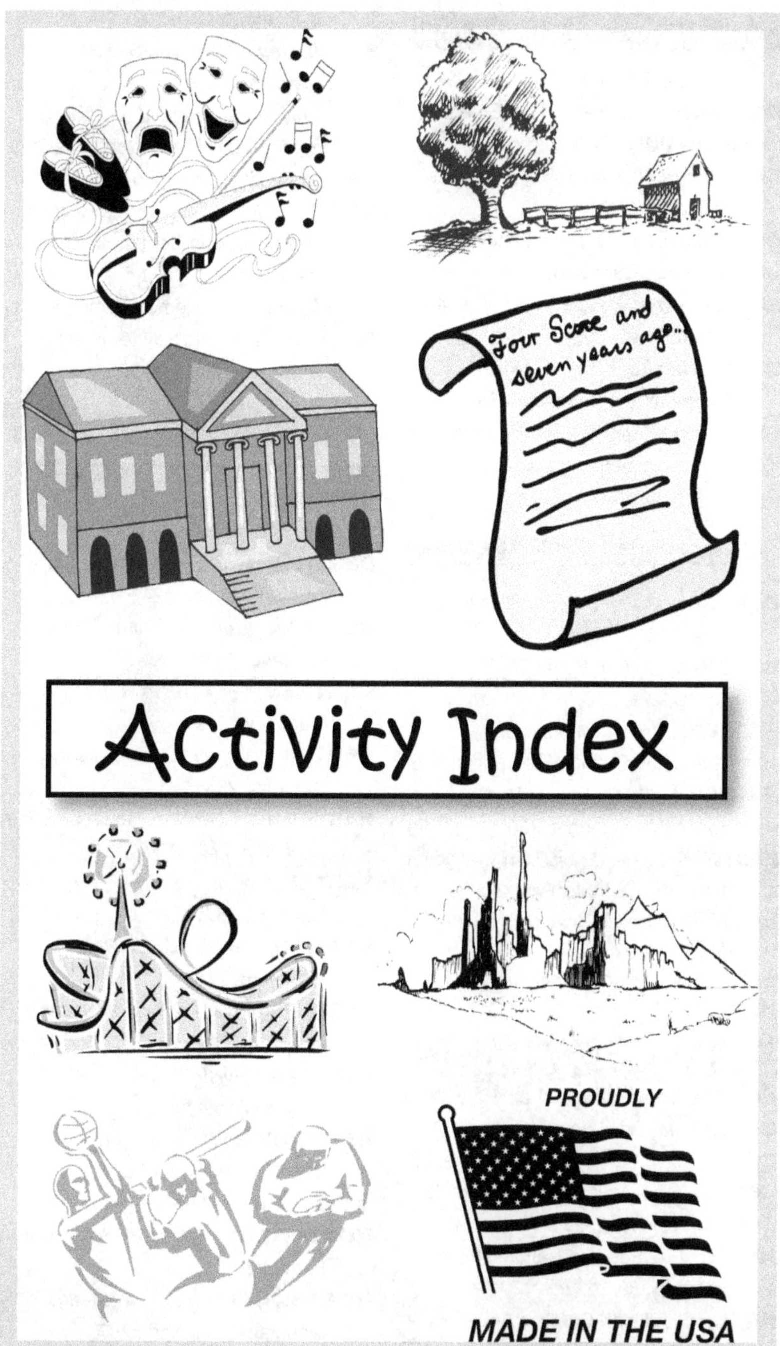
Four Score and
seven years ago...
Activity Index
PROUDLY
MADE IN THE USA

Amusements - North Carolina

Amusements - South Carolina

Animals & Farms - North Carolina

Animals & Farms - South Carolina

Animals & Farms - South Carolina (cont.)

Arts & Entertainment – North Carolina

Arts & Entertainment – South Carolina

History - North Carolina

History – North Carolina (cont.)

History – North Carolina (cont.)

History - South Carolina

History - South Carolina (cont.)

Museums - North Carolina

Museums - South Carolina

Outdoor Exploring – North Carolina

Outdoor Exploring – North Carolina (cont.)

Outdoor Exploring – South Carolina

Seasonal & Special Events – North Carolina

Seasonal & Special Events – North Carolina (cont.)

SE *Cherry Point*, MCAS Cherry Point Air Show, 139

SE *Kure Beach*, Island Of Lights New Years Eve Countdown, 145

SE *Morehead City*, Carolina Chocolate Festival, 145

SE *Morehead City (waterfront)*, NC Seafood Festival, 145

SE *Ocean Isle Beach*, North Carolina Oyster Festival, 148

SE *Southport*, North Carolina Fourth Of July Festival, 149

SE *Wilmington*, Colonial Christmas At Burgwin-Wright House, 158

SE *Wilmington*, July 4th Celebration, 158

SE *Wilmington*, North Carolina Azalea Festival, 158

SE *Wilmington*, Riverfest, 158

SE *Wrightsville Beach*, Cape Fear Kite Festival, 159

SE *Wrightsville Beach*, North Carolina Holiday Flotilla, 159

W *Asheville*, Goombay! Festival, 171

W *Asheville*, National Gingerbread House Competition, 171

W *Cullowhee*, Mountain Heritage Day, 182

W *Fletcher*, NC Mountain State Fair, 182

W *Hendersonville*, North Carolina Apple Festival, 186

W *Pisgah Forest*, Blue Ridge Corn Maze, 196

W *Valdese*, From This Day Forward Outdoor Drama, 200

W *Waynesville*, A Night Before Christmas, 200

W *Waynesville*, Apple Harvest Festival, 200

Seasonal & Special Events – South Carolina

CENTRAL *Aiken*, Battle Of Aiken, 211

CENTRAL *Columbia*, Holiday Lights On The River, 220

CENTRAL *Columbia*, South Carolina State Fair, 219

CENTRAL *Columbia (Irmo)*, Okra Strut, 220

CENTRAL *Gilbert*, Lexington County Peach Festival, 226

CENTRAL *Hartsville (McBee)*, McLeod Farms, 226

CENTRAL *Pelion*, Peanut Party, 230

EASTERN *Atlantic Beach*, Gullah/ Geechee Festival, 242

EASTERN *Charleston*, Holiday Festival Of Lights, 252

EASTERN *Charleston (Mt. Pleasant)*, Boone Hall Pumpkin Patch, 254

EASTERN *Coward*, Old Plantation Syrup Making, 256

EASTERN *Hampton*, Watermelon Festival, 258

EASTERN *Myrtle Beach*, Beach, Boogie & BBQ Festival, 275

EASTERN *Myrtle Beach*, Christmas At Myrtle Beach, 274

EASTERN *Myrtle Beach*, Sun Fun Festival, 274

EASTERN *Myrtle Beach (Murrells Inlet)*, 4th Of July Boat Parade, 275

EASTERN *St. George*, World Grits Festival, 277

NORTHWEST *Anderson*, Balloons Over Anderson, 286

NORTHWEST *Enoree*, Stewart Farms Corn Maze, 289

NORTHWEST *Greenville*, Greenville Games, 293

Science - North Carolina

Science - South Carolina

Sports - North Carolina

Sports - South Carolina

Suggested Lodging & Dining – North Carolina

Suggested Lodging & Dining – South Carolina

Tours - North Carolina

Tours - South Carolina

CPSIA information can be obtained
at www.ICGtesting.com
Printed in the USA
BVHW040948291221
625056BV00014B/491